The

Director's
V·O·I·C·E

The

Director's
V·O·I·C·E

Twenty-One Interviews

Arthur Bartow

THEATRE
COMMUNICATIONS
GROUP

The Director's Voice is published by Theatre Communications Group, Inc., the national organization for the nonprofit professional theatre, 355 Lexington Ave., New York, NY 10017.

ACKNOWLEDGMENTS

The publications and programs of Theatre Communications Group are supported by Actors' Equity Foundation, Alcoa Foundation, ARCO Foundation, AT&T Foundation, Center for Arts Criticism, Citicorp/Citibank, Consolidated Edison Company of New York, Eleanor Naylor Dana Charitable Trust, Dayton Hudson Foundation, Exxon Corporation, The William and Mary Greve Foundation, Home Box Office, Inc., Japan-U.S. Friendship Commission, The Joe and Emily Lowe Foundation, The Andrew W. Mellon Foundation, Mobil Foundation, Inc., National Broadcasting Company, National Endowment for the Arts, New York Community Trust, New York City Department of Cultural Affairs, New York Life Foundation, New York State Council on the Arts, The Pew Charitable Trusts, Philip Morris Incorporated, The Rockefeller Foundation, The Scherman Foundation, Shell Oil Company Foundation, The Shubert Foundation, The L. J. and Mary C. Skaggs Foundation, Consulate General of Spain and The Xerox Foundation.

The Director's Voice is supported in part by a grant from the Eleanor Naylor Dana Charitable Trust.

Library of Congress Cataloging-in-Publication Data
Bartow, Arthur.
The director's voice : interviews with theatre directors / by
Arthur Bartow.
p.   cm.
ISBN 0-930452-73-9 : $24.95. ISBN 0-930452-74-7 (pbk.) : $12.95
1. Theatrical producers and directors — United States — Interviews.
I. Title.
PN2285.B39   1988
792'.0233'0922 — dc19   88-4937
CIP

Design by The Sarabande Press

First Edition: July 1988

To the directors interviewed for generously sharing the details of their lifework — and to the people who have made all the difference to me: A. H. and Katherine L. Bartow, Emily Carver, Dora Hobbs Heintz, Dame Eva Turner, Carl B. Cass, Jack Lee, Judy and Joanna.

ACKNOWLEDGMENTS

A bove all, I want to thank Laura Ross for helping to focus my initial ideas for this book and for continuing her encouragement as its primary editor.

Then I thank Harold Grabau, Marsue Cumming MacNicol and John Istel for their keen eyes and helpful suggestions and Terry Nemeth for his good taste and persistent nudging.

My thanks to Penny Boyer for her dedicated assistance; for supplying valuable insights and information: George Abbott, Cynthia Babler, Rebecca Browder, Mary Bryant, Arlene Caruso, Anne Cattaneo, John Conklin, Jane Corbin, Laura Cutler, Clinton Turner Davis, Leon Denmark, Elizabeth Diamond, Mary Foster, Jane Greenwood, Linda Hunt, Robert Israel, Beverly Jacob, Tisch Jones, Sari Ketter, Gerald S. Krone, Peggy Laves, Ming Cho Lee, James Leverett, Todd London, Deborah McGee, Charles L. Mee, Jr., Grace Mizrahi, Janice Muirhead, Harry Newman, Kathy O'Callaghan, Karen Olson, Jim O'Quinn, M. Elizabeth Osborn, Richard Peaslee, Herb Scher, Marion Simon, Douglas Stein, Michelle Swanson, Ann Wareham, David Wilder, Michael Yeargan and Gilberto Zaldívar; and most particularly to Peter Zeisler and Lindy Zesch for making this book possible.

CONTENTS

Preface   xi

Introduction   xiii

JoAnne Akalaitis   1

Arvin Brown   20

René Buch   36

Martha Clarke   51

Gordon Davidson   67

Robert Falls   87

Zelda Fichandler   105

Richard Foreman   128

Adrian Hall   140

CONTENTS

John Hirsch   158

Mark Lamos   175

Marshall W. Mason   194

Des McAnuff   212

Gregory Mosher   231

Harold S. Prince   241

Lloyd Richards   255

Peter Sellars   269

Andrei Serban   286

Douglas Turner Ward   300

Robert Woodruff   309

Garland Wright   325

Directing Histories   343

PREFACE

Years ago I watched John Hirsch mesmerize an audience of theatre people as he talked about his life and directing. His passion for exploring the great issues of humankind was inseparable from his creation of theatre. At that time, very little existed in print about our nation's contemporary directors and I felt that some personal record of their work processes and achievements should be preserved as a guide for future generations of artists.

Over the following six years, I talked with directors about their work, and twenty-one of them are represented here. Alas, it was not feasible to publish a book large enough to include all the directors I originally wanted to interview. Despite these significant omissions, I believe this cross-section provides a comprehensive range of the professional directors in the United States in the latter part of the twentieth century.

Whatever their background experiences and methods of working, all of these directors have made a total commitment to live out their lives as artists. They are constantly evolving—living, changing, growing and adapting to the environment around them, reflecting a chronically chaotic world. Their statements, therefore, become signposts, snapshots, demarcation points that define their place in time and space at the moment of each conversation.

The twenty-one artists are unique. Even among those directors whose belief systems are similar, the work of each has its distinctness. Together, they serve to prove that there is no "correct" method of directing. As soon as one points to a director whose technique results in success, one can then look to another director whose method contradicts the first and whose work is also recognized as significant.

Quotes from Alan Schneider and Tyrone Guthrie introduce this book because it would be incomplete without them. The craft of directing in America owes much to these artists. Guthrie, the British Johnny Appleseed, founded two influential theatres on this continent dedicated to the classics, the Stratford Festival Theatre in Canada and The Guthrie Theater in Minneapolis. Schneider, the American-bred leader and educator, affirmed contemporary theatre as art form and proved conclusively that directors in this country can lead careers as artists, not merely as utilitarianists.

Enriched by this legacy, these twenty-one directors' voices explore the director's craft: what it is, how it is acquired, how it evolves and why it is important to those who do it—and to all of us. For wouldn't we all like to be directors? Wouldn't all of us want to spend our entire lives doing work we love and believe in?

May 1988
New York City

INTRODUCTION

T heatre's recorded history began two thousand years ago (as early as four thousand years ago if one counts existing fragments of Egyptian ritual). In early Greek theatre, the poet/playwright maintained authority over the work of the choruses. Six hundred years later the actor, in the form of Thespis, appeared and through the ensuing centuries usurped the playwright's control. By the middle of the nineteenth century, there was need for another authority who could rescue the stage from down-center, operatic, solo acting and awkward movement.

George II, German Duke of Saxe-Meiningen (1826–1914) pioneered this new role. Between 1874 and 1890, he toured his court theatrical troupe of Meiningers to thirty-eight cities in nine countries, revealing a new way of working that emphasized the collective personality of the group and inspired theatrical reforms wherever it performed. Saxe-Meiningen exercised central artistic discipline over his company, serving as producer, director and financial backer. By controlling design, he introduced historical accuracy into his productions' costumes and settings. Saxe-Meiningen anticipated the functions of the modern director, who, although arriving several millenniums late, immediately took command.

One of the critically successful visits of the Meiningers was to Moscow in 1885, where they inspired an actor/stage manager named C. S. Alexeyev, better known today as Constantin Stanislavsky (1863–1938). Stanislavsky had been working in his own private family-theatre and testing his theories about the inner interpretation of roles. By 1898, Stanislavsky and Vladimir Nemirovitch-Danchenko had opened the Moscow Art and Popular Theatre. Like Saxe-Meiningen, Stanislavsky maintained control over all phases of production and stressed ensemble acting. However, the emphasis of his work was on the actor, and the acting technique he systematized became the major influence on twentieth-century theatre in the United States.

The worldwide emergence of stage directors coincided with America's burgeoning commercial theatre and the trend toward more elaborate scenic machinery. Entrepreneurial directors were required to orchestrate the technical demands of increasingly popular stage realism and to provoke a unified response from the audience. They became technically proficient in the art of entertaining and passed along this know-how to succeeding generations. Frequently, they were also playwrights and actors, theatre people who understood their craft from the vantage point of several disciplines. These utilitarianists included such important figures as writer John Augustin Daly (1839–99), writer/actor/stage-mechanics inventor James Morrison Steele MacKaye (1842–94), writer/actor David Belasco (1853–1931) and writer/actor George Abbott (1887–   ). They perfected techniques for organizing the work process and applied them to new American plays, largely melodramas.

By the 1920s another generation of playwrights had emerged, among them Eugene O'Neill, Elmer Rice and Maxwell Anderson. They experimented with such new theatrical forms as expressionism and symbolism in noncommercial companies like the Provincetown Players. As a result, American theatre took its first tentative steps away from pure entertainment toward becoming an art form, requiring directors to broaden their knowledge and learn new techniques. Then economic depression unleashed its misery on the next generation of artists, who saw that theatre could be used as a vehicle for political and social comment.

In 1935, the Works Progress Administration appointed Hallie Flanagan to administer the Federal Theatre Project. She initiated a national program consisting of thousands of projects in thirty-one cities over a four-year lifespan, before Congress, nervous about the political content of some of the work, ended it. Nevertheless, the seeds of a national professional theatre had been scattered and began to germinate; a decade later they would spontaneously reappear across the nation as indigenous, permanent nonprofit institutions.

Another important product of the Depression years was the Group Theatre. Founders Harold Clurman, Cheryl Crawford and Lee Strasberg had earlier worked with the Provincetown Players; prominent among Group Theatre actors were Robert Lewis and Elia Kazan. Although the Group Theatre existed only from 1931 to 1941, its success with socially significant contemporary plays and its use of Stanislavsky's techniques became legend. The legend continued through Strasberg's teaching of the Method at New York's Actors Studio and through the continuing success of the actors, teachers and directors who had participated in the company.

After the depression and the war that followed, actors-become-directors Kazan and Lewis, along with Clurman, collaborated with such major writers as Tennessee Williams, Carson McCullers, William Inge and Arthur Miller. They combined theatrical realism with Method acting, creating an American directing and acting vocabulary that prevailed for forty years. Kazan became the model for countless young directors. His methods and those of the Actors Studio were emulated, and frequently misapplied, in almost every school and theatre in the country. The effects of that movement continue to resonate and doubtless will be with us in some measure into the twenty-first century.

A trickle of nonprofit theatres appeared in the late 1940s, becoming a flood of new institutions by the 1970s. They were founded on the premise of offering plays seldom produced in the commercial theatre, classics by Shakespeare, Sophocles, Brecht, Shaw and Molière. These plays made stylistic demands on American directors and actors, demands they were not always trained to meet. This resulted in an Americanized way of working that fails to benefit from European tradition and also refuses to be limited by it.

Emerging now from the avant-garde are Performance Art techniques that are finding their way into mainstream directing. Many of these techniques are counter to time-honored ideas of seamlessly unifying production elements. They mix art forms that are irreconcilable in order to explode the dreamlike quality of theatre and force thought and awareness. Today, the director is even more firmly in command and frequently becomes the initiator, using text, music and visuals as colors in the directorial palette.

With a wide range of stylistic choices before directors today, the command of technique is more and more crucial. The key to the future development of the director's craft must be, as it has been for the past one hundred years, the passing down of technique and information from senior artists to succeeding generations.

Here then, are today's artists speaking to us and to those who follow.

There are no secret shortcuts, there are no formulas, there are no rules. There's only yourself and your talent and your taste and your choices.

Alan Schneider

Directing at its best is psychic evocation and is performed almost entirely unconsciously.

Tyrone Guthrie

The

Director's
V·O·I·C·E

JOANNE AKALAITIS

O f the directors who emerged in the late 1970s and the 1980s, one of the most innovative is JoAnne Akalaitis, who developed her unique vision and method of working beginning with a long association with the brilliantly experimental Mabou Mines company. Akalaitis was a co-founder of this New York theatre collective in 1969, along with Lee Breuer, Ruth Maleczech, David Warrilow and Philip Glass.

She was born in a working-class community in Cicero, Illinois, where she says there were just Lithuanian Catholics and a couple of Italian families. In this environment theatre was not seen as an honorable or serious profession, but there were school pageants in which she frequently acted the male roles because she was the tallest. While performing in these Lithuanian "spectacles," she began to fall in love with theatre.

Planning to become a doctor, she studied at the University of Chicago. Discouraged by the predominantly male premed competition, she switched to philosophy and received a fellowship to Stanford's graduate school. There she became so involved in the theatre program that she barely made it to philosophy classes. She left graduate school and went to San Francisco to become an actress, and started as a stagehand at Jules Irving's and Herbert

Blau's Actors Workshop. There she met Maleczech, Breuer and Bill Raymond, who later became a member of Mabou Mines.

Realizing that San Francisco was not the theatre center she was seeking, Akalaitis journeyed to New York and subsequently to Paris, where she and her then husband, composer Philip Glass, were soon reunited with Breuer and Maleczech. They met David Warrilow, who was the assistant editor of *Réalité* and was being groomed to be its editor when he decided to become an actor. Along with Frederick Neumann, who was dubbing English for French films, they all began to work together.

Believing that New York was where the new theatre could happen, Akalaitis urged the others to return to America. Mabou Mines, named for a small town they once visited in Nova Scotia, was formed and almost immediately took up residence at La Mama Experimental Theatre Club. Subsequently, they spent several years in residence at the New York Shakespeare Festival, honing an experimental style based on embodying an author's metaphors and the personality of his language. They said things in more than one way, without repeating themselves, by speaking through music, design and movement in a unique acting style. The company created a body of original theatre pieces, which they called *Animations (Red Horse, B-Beaver, Shaggy Dog)*, and also set about interpreting the works of Samuel Beckett (*Play, Come & Go, The Lost Ones, Cascando*) with a fresh perspective that many feel proved to be the definitive American interpretations.

Despite achieving international recognition as one of the most innovative and literate of the avant-garde theatre companies in America, Mabou Mines's existence has always been financially precarious, and while the company continues to consider itself a collective, its members have established separate directing, writing and acting careers. As each of them has become better known nationally, their experimental work has begun to influence the country's major resident theatres.

The first play Akalaitis directed was Beckett's *Cascando* in 1975 at the Ontological-Hysteric Theater. This two-character radio play was expanded for six actors in Richard Foreman's loft theatre with an original cello score composed by Philip Glass and performed live. *Cascando* toured Europe, played for six months at the New York Shakespeare Festival's Public Theater and won for Akalaitis the first of the five Obie awards she has received for direction—more than any other director to date. (The other Obies were for *Dressed Like an Egg, Southern Exposure, Dead End Kids* and *Through the Leaves*.) Akalaitis adapted the writings of Colette for *Dressed Like an Egg* in 1977, which she also designed and performed. In 1980, she created the antinuclear piece *Dead End Kids*, a collage incorporating images from the days of medieval alchemy to the start of the cold war. Mabou Mines toured the piece, and Akalaitis later adapted it to film.

Her 1981 production of Franz Xaver Kroetz's one-woman play *Request Concert*, astonishing in its complexity, again brought her major attention as a director. Akalaitis transferred the setting from a middle-class German locale to Queens, New York. Her meticulous work with actress Joan MacIntosh on the eighty-minute, wordless solo devastatingly projected the isolation and loneliness of a single, middle-aged woman in modern society.

Akalaitis followed this in 1984 with another Kroetz play, *Through the Leaves*, and established herself as the German dramatist's foremost American interpreter. She worked with her Mabou Mines colleagues Ruth Maleczech and Frederick Neumann to bring Kroetz's stark, gritty world to life in this story of a woman butcher who, in her loneliness, allows herself to be degraded by a man who is threatened by her independence. The piece garnered Obies for each of the actors and most of the designers. Outside of Mabou Mines, her major directing projects have been at the Mark Taper Forum in Los Angeles, American Repertory Theatre in Cambridge and The Guthrie Theater in Minneapolis.

Akalaitis's directing technique is a process that frequently begins as exercises with the actors, exercises that move them beyond their preoccupations with surface values and allow them to review their own personal range of emotional colors. Then she uses those emotional colors to paint her theatrical canvas, trusting herself in rehearsal to create instinctively.

■　　■　　■

Where does the impulse for your projects begin?

I believe very strongly that ideas come from deep, subconscious events and bleed from one project to the next. Being in the creative process causes you to dream creatively. I think these events are triggered by things from the real world like a song or a picture or something from a magazine. For example, I got the idea for *Southern Exposure* from a book review in *The New York Times* of a biography of Robert Scott. *The Mormon Project*, which I worked on with Eric Overmyer, came from an article in *The New York Review of Books*. *Dressed Like an Egg* came from a photograph of Colette. She was leaning against parallel bars in her gym with such a poignant and lost and courageous look, that it really touched a lot in me. It triggered not only a work but a major piece of scenery, a Colette dress made of celastic designed by Ree Morton, which was a prop and a costume. I wore it. Ruth Maleczech and Ellen McElduff wore it, and at one point it appeared standing onstage empty.

If I don't see a picture in my mind when I read a script, I know that the play is not for me. The first images are the most important. When I first read *Leonce and Lena*, I saw a road, a colored sky, the sun, and I heard Terry Allen's music. As far as content goes, I'm interested in history and social and political issues. I feel I have a responsibility to work in these areas.

As a woman director, are those responsibilities focused differently?

I'm very conscious of being a woman director in the theatre. I constantly think about it. I cannot stop seeing myself as a feminist. Especially because society today continues to be sexist, racist, anti-Semitic, abusive of children. In 1987, I was the third woman to direct at the Guthrie in its twenty-five-year history. When I directed *Red and Blue*, one of the actors in the cast had been in the theatre for twenty-five years and I was the first woman director he had ever worked with. There's a slight improvement in that area for theatre workers and all workers. It's a lot more natural than it was several years ago.

Why haven't more women found a place for themselves as professional directors?

It is a tradition that high school drama teachers are women. In a different society, they might have been directors instead of teachers. The question really is why more women in this society haven't found a place for themselves in *all* professions. Theatre is the same as any other institution in this country, it's run by men. This is not at all the case in Mabou Mines, where any member can become anything in the company they want. It's while being on tour that we've discovered the extent of sexist behavior in this profession. In many places men stagehands and electricians have permission to make certain kinds of cynical sexist jokes with women directors. And women directors have to be better behaved than men. If a woman gets angry the same way a man might get angry, she's considered bitchy or unfeminine.

Have you been offered plays to direct that are considered to be "women-oriented"?

Yes, but I've often been disappointed in so-called women's plays, because they've sometimes been limited in their intention and parochial in content, plays about bad men and horrible mothers, abortion, miscarriage, menopause—or the psychological equivalents. I'm interested in women touching on the more mythic, tough emotive core of their femaleness. What's important is what women bring to all human situations. It's different, very positive.

What was your training as a director?

The singular most important training I had was as an actor with Grotowski during a month-long workshop in France. When I was a young actress in New York, I just picked up classes the way everyone does, and I quit them all. It wasn't that the teachers weren't interesting, I just couldn't respond to what they were teaching.

Then you worked collectively with Mabou Mines and directed your first piece there, Cascando. *You directed it with the specific image of Nova Scotia and the people from that part of Canada in mind.*

No one knew that. I set it in Nova Scotia but there was nothing said about that in the program. It was absolutely personal and had to do with how we worked together. That was *our* point of reference. The audience was just seeing this Beckett play. It took place in the littered corner of a room around a table.

That seems like an opposite direction from Beckett's usually spare stage settings.

Each Beckett play is different from the others. While I think that Beckett's work is more sacred than other contemporary writers', and I pay more attention to his pauses and indications about timing than anyone else's, when I think of his work I don't necessarily think of bare spaces. For example, Beckett says *Endgame* takes place in an empty room. We set it in a subway station with a littered subway train, water, rubble. The energy of it was vast. It had some kind of dimension in space. You have to think what it really *means* when the writer describes the set and gives stage directions. A writer is seeing something in a physical universe that should be taken as a very useful guide.

How do you begin rehearsals?

Lately, we almost always start by dancing to music that connects to the piece we're working on, but not in an obvious way. Some of the ideas in *Leon and Lena (& Lenz)* (we changed the title from *Leonce and Lena*) that I did at the Guthrie came from working with reggae music, which on the surface had nothing to do with Büchner or the play. The actors were working on character mudras in groups.

What are mudras?

The idea comes from the Kathakali theatre, which has developed a vocabulary of hand and facial gestures that are very formalized. They are abstractions or icons of character and behavior. This kind of work is basic in Asian theatre —Japanese, Chinese, Balinese. The abstract psychology it embodies is clear to the audience. It's a deeply shared language. I have been interested in trying this here, finding Western psychological mudras, which could hit the audience in a nonintellectual, almost Jungian way. Often, they're performed in slow motion.

What's the significance of slow motion?

When you slow down, your perceptions become enlarged, clarified, heady. I think your spiritual metabolism enters a different state when you are operating slowly. That allows the actor to viscerally examine herself in space and to understand relationships on a physical plane in a profound way. If you're working in slow motion, and you're being very attentive and concentrated in your work, you can actually feel the air: the air on your body and the air between your body and someone else, the air between you and the window, under your foot. This is important because when an actor then works in real time, this body research has allowed her to be in touch with the universe of the working space—to understand what are physical relationships on the stage, what props are, what constitutes a hand gesture.

The converse of this also requires imaging. When I have speed line rehearsals, I caution the actors, "It's not just saying your lines fast, you're imagining what you're doing in a compressed and intense way." It's a visualization exercise. It doesn't just happen outside, it has to be accompanied by this inside visualization.

The problem in *Leon and Lena* was how to unify the group movement without taking away the individuality. The solution was rhythmic: have everyone work with the same music, then take the music away. The actors internalized it. They sang the same song without the music. At another rehearsal, I had a wonderful surprise. I used Islamic vocal music as a warm-up and the actors' response to it gave me an idea for ending the piece as a slow-motion "goodbye dance" using simpler mudras. Terry Allen liked the Islamic music and then wrote his own version. I have to say that working with musicians and with music has enriched my work and was important from the beginning.

What images do you use when talking with composers about your ideas?

With some composers, like Philip Glass who's very organized and clear, I can say, "I need eight minutes of fast, aggressive music." The strange thing about musicians is that very simple adjectives often work amazingly well. It depends on the composer. I had been interested in Terry Allen's music for more than a year and while I was in San Francisco he drove up from Fresno to talk about

Leon and Lena. We had a strong communication at our first meeting and we built on that with an intense correspondence. Then we met in Minneapolis and spent two days talking through the play. We discussed where we thought the songs should go and what things meant. That was invaluable because when you *say* those things, it sometimes opens a door to an idea. And that was the groundwork for all the music in the play, sixteen songs. Terry is interested in emotion and meaning and it was invaluable having him in residence so that music could be developed for the people in the piece, not just technically for their voices, but psychologically. And he also played for the rehearsal. Being there in residence for so long (ten weeks) created a tremendous arena for collaboration. One of the actors in the company, Richard S. Iglewski, is a first-class sitar player. I said to Terry, "You have to hear Richard and use his playing in the piece," and he did. In so many situations you don't have time to do something like that.

You used a rock score for Through the Leaves.

The right music can come when you're not looking for it. The music in *Through the Leaves* was mainly from a German New Wave group, Trio A. My children had played it around the house for six months and it drove me crazy. But there was something in it, a mindless rhythmic pulse that really worked in *Through the Leaves*. It supported the soul of the piece. I also used Johnny Rotten's *This Is Not a Love Song* in the play. There was a time when I felt that Sid Vicious and the Sex Pistols were diabolical influences on my children. Now I think their music is remarkable. I used Sid Vicious's brilliant parody of Sinatra's *My Way* in *Green Card* at the Mark Taper Forum in 1986. The kids may know something I don't. My interest in reggae and African music comes from them. I'm even starting to like the Grateful Dead a bit more. I think the most exciting cultural phenomenon now is music coming from the Third World, Africa and Latin America.

I had wonderful discussions with Rubén Blades when he composed music for *The Balcony* at American Repertory Theatre. He has a brilliant mind, is very political and a wonderful musician. He'd say, "Tell me how many minutes. You want eight minutes, you want nine minutes?" At the same time he'd say, "Is this the song of a guy auditioning in Washington Square Park?" He is an incredible combination of a star, a businessman and a poet. I said, "This is where I hear music, and here, here and here. What do you think?" He took my guidance about that but the form of the music pretty much belonged to him. What he came up with was wonderful and unexpected because it wasn't salsa music. It was a kind of Latin poetry that I had never heard before.

It's a shame that this music is lost once the production finishes its run.

Philip Glass told me that someone is performing his overture for *Endgame* at a concert. Terry and I talked about making a record of the sixteen songs from *Leon and Lena* but that becomes a different entity. The cast album is not the same as live actors singing. It has little to do with the original event.

How do you begin text rehearsals?

One of the things I really hate as a director is to read the play through. It's so boring. I think *Endgame* is the greatest modern play, yet after the first reading, I was very depressed. It seemed long and dull. I also do not spend a long time sitting at a table talking. I start rehearsals on our feet.

So there's no investigation of the text in isolation?

Very little. I like the fact that acting is in your body. You find a lot with your body. Actors often want to sit around and talk. It's a way to avoid working, the terror of getting up and doing it. There's a deep, deep fear of acting because it's so hard.

To begin, I will say, "Let's read the scene we're going to rehearse." We read it and then I say, hopefully, "Does anyone have an idea?" Sometimes—usually not. So I say, "Okay, let's try and figure out how to do it." I try to block the play fairly early in order to know what the painting of it is, the sculpture of it, the plastic form of it.

A lot of directors delay the blocking.

I don't blame them, because it's very hard. To me the mark of a real director is blocking, where the people are in space. Someone like Richard Foreman is a master. Even among so-called "great" directors, I see a real messiness, the inability to use space. Actors block the play themselves more often than one is aware.

Once I have blocked the play, I say, "Oh, thank God. I did the hardest thing. It's over. Now I can work on it." That doesn't mean that I don't change the blocking, because I do that a lot.

You have said that a director has to be more manipulative than you like to be.

I like the process to be an open collaboration. I don't think it's helpful to manipulate a situation, to bring in a lot of negativity, to turn actors against one another, to make them feel paranoid. I try to treat actors decently. I don't scream at people or burst into tears (although I *have* yelled and I once threw a pumpkin muffin at an actor). I'm not mean to actors when they burst into tears. I say, "Would you like me to go to the dressing room with you?" I would rather have a community working together.

On the other hand, there is no such thing as a totally open collaborative situation, and at some point in the directing process you're in a position where something needs to happen that cannot happen by direct appeal. There has to be some subconscious ammunition. It's very subtle and it's not about behavior. It's about what actors need to do.

Does that mean you don't meet problems head-on?

When we're having problems, I try to be very straightforward and direct and say, "Yes, we're having problems. This may be a problem for a while, or it may go away or we may never solve it." Not all problems are solvable. In *Through the Leaves*, the problem at one point was that Ruth Maleczech and Fred Neumann deep down didn't like their characters. With Fred, I said, "You know, this is a real opportunity to play a person who is very depressed. This is a man who doesn't have fun with sex, he doesn't have fun eating. He doesn't have *fun*. He has brief moments when he gets strong. This is what this character's about. Fred, buy it!" And he did. *Through the Leaves* is the woman's play. The man's role is very difficult. What I really admired about those two actors was that they were so generous to each other. Two actors alone in a play can get very paranoid. They supported one another and weren't jealous.

Did you have to resort to manipulation during the rehearsals of **Through the Leaves?**

I don't think there was any manipulation, but there were tactics. At certain times I felt that I could not give notes. It had to do with the mood of the actors—knowing the actors very well. I think there comes a time when the director, in a sense, becomes the natural enemy. It took me a while to understand that actors have to find their own strength and, at some point, separation and independence from the director are necessary.

Through the Leaves *had so much nudity and physical intimacy. How do you break down those natural inhibitions between the actors?*

Nudity is a problem, although I don't think that requires more breaking down than any other rehearsal situation. It's all intimate. It all requires an incredible leap into the void. Ruth was fabulous. At a rehearsal, I suggested, "Let's all take off our clothes." She said, "No." She would do it in tech with the proper costumes. The costume designer was there, the dresser was there. It was very technical and easy. It was simple and very natural and in the technical rehearsal we always laughed at getting stuck at the point where they're having sex on the couch because we had to adjust the light cue or because the dog didn't bark at the right time. At that point, there was no self-consciousness. There was also nudity in *Leon and Lena* and, again, the actor took off his clothes at the first tech—never before. I felt it did not require a process of breaking down taboos or anything like that.

What other technical problems did you encounter in **Through the Leaves?**

It was a very technical piece. Kroetz's blackouts are mind-boggling. In one scene the woman is in the butcher shop and the next scene she's in an entirely different place, naked on the couch. It required an amazing amount of concentration from the actors because they had to be there mentally before they were there physically. We'd drill and drill and drill. You know—"if my left foot is before my right foot at this point, then I'm going to do this." An amazing amount of work went into that.

The problem of making transitions is a theme that comes up often with directors.

It is *the* problem. The single most important thing I have learned in the theatre, and it seems to apply to everything I direct, is Genet's maxim to the actors in *The Screens*, to perform each section of a scene as though it is a complete play. No transitions. This is very hard for actors to do. When I was working on *The Balcony* at American Repertory Theatre in 1986, the actors were trying to make transitions. Actors seek logic, they seek transitions. They seek ways to get from A to B as opposed to "I am in A. A is finished. Now I am in B." I keep using Genet's technique. I used it in *The Balcony* and in *Help Wanted*. Genet's right. It works for a certain kind of theatre. It may apply to everything. It gives a kind of jerky, "vortexy" rhythm to performance that I find is exciting. It might work for Chekhov, but it would require a tremendous commitment on the part of the actors. Actors have to be prepared in advance.

What's the nature of this preparation?

Before a run-through of *Leon and Lena*, I would ask the actors to spend a few minutes plotting the physical geography of the piece, not only the blocking, but being in space, the space between your body and another body, your body and a piece of scenery—thinking of it as a major event.

Also, we plot the *emotional* geography, i.e., where the beats are. This is a very Grotowskian notion, which I find quite dangerous, because once you engage in this journey you may make a wrong turn and never get back on the road. It takes a lot of concentration and a lot of risk because it's not about logic, it's about a series of events. It's like playing a video game and you have to make instant decisions. You know all of the signposts but they can all change in that moment when the audience is there. And that is what is so great about theatre, that it's never the same.

Some of the actors I worked with at the Guthrie came from a more traditional, classical experience. I talked a lot about geography and self-observation and I think the actors understood it. "You are always watching yourself performing." Superficially, that seems to be a kind of Brechtian axiom, but I mean it in a much deeper way. You don't necessarily have to be commenting on the scene, it doesn't have to go to that level, but you must always see what you are doing. It makes for an entirely different kind of performance. But it cannot be achieved without risk, without investigation.

What about the exercise where you ask the actors to spend one minute walking through each year of their lives?

Lee Breuer invented that exercise. The basic premise is that emotional recall is not something one can do. You cannot be five years old again. But you are in the here and now, and you can reflect and examine and respond to certain images from when you were five years old. It's a technique about a way of working, about images. Then if I say to an actor, "Find something to make this moment work," he can find some image that touched him in the exercise from when he was eight years old or twenty years old. I don't have to know what it is. It's his personal thing, and if it works, I'll see it. Instead of pushing the actor inward, it allows for a kind of presence in performing I find interesting.

In your experience, how successful have the actors been in holding on to their performances?

I went back to see the *Leon and Lena* a week after it had opened and it was not that the performances had become slick, but they had become known and studied, so that one beat was completed and there was space before the actors went on to the next beat. The geography was too "known."

Do you find that giving notes is sufficient in a case like that?

It's amazing when you give a note to an actor how it's internalized and then comes out. It's my experience that the actor either gets it right away or doesn't get it. The whole business of giving notes is so delicate and serious that it's about what the actors can take at a certain moment. If there are very serious, hard notes, can they take them? Should they get them? I've witnessed productions where the director gave more and more notes, until the company became defeated and overwhelmed by them. On the other hand, I am sympathetic to that director, because I tend to be very compulsive about detail.

But at some moment in the process, I have to say, "I've got to let this go. I've got to let these little things about timing go and hope that it's going to work out." The actors have to be able to possess the show. When I go back to see a production, I do it with foreboding and apprehension. On one level I'm afraid that they're going to be totally different, and on a much deeper level, I know I'm going to see another event happening. I'm the outsider after the show has opened, and *I should be* the outsider. One thing that's a little bit screwed up in American theatre is the business of a stage manager supervising the show after the director's departure, keeping the "director's intent." Sometimes it's successful and sometimes it's not. I think theatre institutions should make the director part of the family in a drop-in way. It's very exciting to the actors and the director as well when the director comes back.

The first Kroetz play that brought you a great deal of attention was Request Concert *in 1981 at Interart Theatre.*

Request Concert was in the works for three or four years. When I first read it, I thought that it was wonderful but that the reading of it was the event itself. I didn't see how I could ever direct it, since it was already perfect. The experience of reading it was a unit of absolute fulfillment. But I couldn't get it out of my mind. It was there for years.

Joan MacIntosh was the solo actor and it seemed to be a real collaboration.

It was intensely collaborative and just a horrible experience for both of us, in the sense that the material is just gruesome. We became good friends but it was grueling. What I found out is that Joan is a total actress, like Ruth Maleczech, Ellen McElduff and Lauren Tom. These actors investigate their roles deeply. As a result of that discovery, I felt that I had to be more responsible to Joan. *Normally*, when an actor asks me questions like "Why am I doing this?," I don't know the answer on any level. I don't ask those questions myself as an actress, so I don't know how to answer them as a director. Joan was intensely collaborative, contributing to the psychological design of the play one week and the next week needing to concentrate on being an actor and finding the character.

Since it was a play with no dialogue, the only sound during the evening came from the radio Joan listened to onstage.

That was all very carefully orchestrated. I listened to hours and hours of Muzak to pick the right music the woman would listen to. There was a point in the play when we tuned in to an actual newscast and weather report. This was intermingled with recorded sound. It was carefully timed and complicated to figure out, but it was worth it. The section with the *Paul Harvey* program was chosen as a result of listening to seven hundred hours of radio.

You've said that you never understand a play when you start. Does that mean that you spend a lot of time researching, but that you just don't try to get to the meat of it until you get into rehearsal?

I really embrace the idea of finding one's way through a piece. I don't do a lot of dramaturgy—you know, reading all the criticism of the play. Unlike a lot of directors, I do not stand in front of the cast and say, "This is what this play is about." Because I really don't know. You find out when you do it. I do know a lot about the play in advance. The kind of research I do is visual, a normal, logical kind of research like going to butcher shops prior to *Through the Leaves*. It did not involve reading criticism of Kroetz's work, and it involved very little traditional literary research. The play was there in its crystalline form and it was very strong. In preparation for *The Balcony*, I went to a lot of salsa clubs, listened to music and looked at a lot of pornography. That's the kind of research I do with the designers.

Why do you find it helpful to start rehearsals, which is really the last step in the process of the director's discovery, with such openness?

I find it's very liberating not to understand a beat. In the middle of a rehearsal, I start to inspect what the play's about. I mean, I have ideas about what I'm doing—I'm not blind. But I often do not know what we're going to do when I go into rehearsal. I know what I'm going to rehearse, but I don't know how to solve the problems and I have no detailed plan. Once you walk into a rehearsal, what you're going to do becomes clear. In the rehearsal period for *Leon and Lena* there was an almost perfect ambiance and I think it had to do with several things. For one, through careful consideration and luck and/ or some kind of amazing karma, a great company was put together. And this company of actors who were not at all alike seemed to be willing to make a contract to embark on this journey together with me. Like me, some of the actors came from outside Minneapolis. It was important that some of us were outsiders together.

Is that because the isolation forces your mind to be on the work all of the time?

I think your mind is on the piece all of the time anyway, but when you're away it's sort of living the dream—there's less distraction. I don't care if the actors' minds aren't on the piece morning, noon and night. It's when we come together to work that there's a kind of attention and focus that doesn't always happen when you're living where you're working. When I did a workshop at the Perseverance Theatre in Juneau, Alaska, about religion and the Mormons, it was very exciting to be so far away from home. And that allowed me to achieve a kind of intensity that you cannot when you have to go home and answer the phone and go to the grocery store—especially if you're a mom and have to take care of a family.

Did the long rehearsal period have a specific effect on **Leon and Lena?**

I felt as if we went through three seasons, summer, fall and winter, in Minneapolis. Having all that time allowed us to make our own world, to develop a vocabulary that was specific to the group. And it allowed us to make mistakes and not panic about them.

You said that the actors came with a variety of acting approaches. How did you bring a unity of language to the group?

I didn't spend time trying to figure out what their language was. It was my job to establish a vocabulary through exercises and talking. My language has the elements that many directors use—beats and masks, body and face vocal masks and mudras, so that when I say, "This is an exercise about the mask of a dead soul," everyone knows what a mask is and what a dead soul is. I also talk about "painting" or "sculpture"—that the actor onstage is conscious of where every other actor is, where every prop, scenic element, light and member of the audience are. So that the performance consists of constant adjustments to all these elements to make the most perfect picture or sculpture.

So you're teaching your actors to be directors as actors.

No, because directors can't do that. Only an actor can be a totally conscious performer and be aware of moving his little finger or turning his head at the right moment.

But not necessarily all actors are capable of being aware of everything that is going on about them onstage.

Indeed, and I think that is one of the core problems. Painting is purely about composition onstage, where you see the composition from outside and you constantly adjust it every millisecond to make an ever evolving and more perfect composition that changes all the time.

There is another technique called "worlds," which comes from Joe Chaikin. It's like the painting technique, only it's more psychological. The idea is that there is a world onstage and sometimes it's the world of the person who is speaking the lines in the script, but not necessarily. It could be the world of the guy standing upstage holding the coffee cup. It is the business of everyone onstage to know what the world is and to enter that world in his or her own particular, idiosyncratic, special way using body and voice.

In conventional terms, it's having the actors know where the focus of the scene should go.

Exactly, but for me this sense is very, very deep especially when actors do choral work or they have to move together. When it's not working, my comment is, "You're not in the same world. You don't know what the world is." I really believe that all it takes is this "contract" that the actor will enter whatever world is dominating the arena at any given time. It's like an act of will. I don't think that most actors know it or practice it. They're not often encouraged to see themselves in a kind of geography that is communal, emotional topography. Genet writes so brilliantly about that when he says to let your light so shine that it illuminates other actors and the stage will thereby become a place where Christian charity acts. A pretty amazing statement.

What is it the director can do to create an atmosphere to nurture the work, instead of being content to make it just another play?

We don't have to destroy ourselves and bleed to death to do it. But it's very important to create the right kind of atmosphere for working. It can seem kind of quirky of the director to say to the stage manager, "No one can smoke in the rehearsal room and no one can talk or eat." That's something I've done for several years. It's about trying to make some kind of work atmosphere. Even lighting a cigarette is distracting. The continuing effort to make this environment all about the work is very important. It has to do with several things: making certain that basic working conditions are okay, where everyone lives is okay and what they're being paid is okay; it also has to do with putting the director and the other collaborators in a situation where they can create their own world—making it all right to make a major mistake in working on the structure of a piece. We understand together that we can make mistakes. We can correct the problem but, on the other hand, we may never get out of it. The whole project may end up being a mistake. We engage in the process in good faith.

Is it possible to gauge the required amount of rehearsal time at the outset?

I think directors know. I think if you asked any director what she wanted, she wouldn't make too many mistakes about time.

Your productions are known for their strong design. George Tsypin worked with you on Leon and Lena.

That was the second time I had worked with George—he'd also designed *The Balcony. Leon and Lena* was an intensely collaborative event, the design, the acting, the music. I love the way George thinks about theatre. He's very appreciative of actors. He really looks at their work. Doug Stein, John Arnone and Jennifer Tipton do that too. They understand acting and they also understand directing. Working with strong designers is really important to my preparation for directing the play.

What constitutes a strong designer?

A strong designer is one who enters the world of the play, who gets lost in the play, who is willing to meander through a lot of mazes. I feel that good directors are designers and good designers are directors—the two occupations are really knitted occupations. Designers like Doug Stein, George Tsypin, Jennifer Tipton, John Arnone and Frances Aronson are incredible. It's never "This is what I want to do. You go design it." It's "What are *we* going to do?" These are people who are deeply involved in the soul of the theatre. Some designers don't give, nor are asked to give, a lot of input about the total production.

George stayed all though the previews of *Leon*, which he kept telling me he didn't usually do. He gave me director notes and helped me a lot. "This actor is doing such and such." It's very dangerous for a designer to do that because traditionally it's not a designer's prerogative, and it can be delicate in previews or tech rehearsals where everyone is very vulnerable or even paranoid. Sometimes designers aren't as patient as directors and don't understand when an actor is in process. They tend to be critical of a performance that is on its way to being something else. They aren't in a position to see that.

What are the benefits of having the designers stay with the director through previews even though their work is basically finished?

It's very important for the director to feel supported at that time. That affects everything. Sometimes it's quite boring for the designers, except for the lighting designer, who always has work to finish, and I have to resist the urge to entertain them by asking, "Oh, what do you feel about that cue?" The tech rehearsals should be a continuation of the community that, hopefully, was built during rehearsal. It's important that the community include the designers in a central way.

What happens when you feel you're up against the wall and that perhaps mistakes have been made?

Eight weeks into rehearsal for *Leon and Lena*, I knew I was stumped and that something was wrong, but I didn't know what to do. I was too close to see it. One of the things I've learned in theatre is that if you feel something is wrong, you have to listen to that instinct. I needed people from the outside to look at it. A friend from New York and Jennifer Tipton, the lighting designer, came in to see it. They were very brave.

What was the problem?

It had to do with a lot of things: actors' performances, timing, structure, what was being understood. We who sit in rehearsals week after week, day after day, understand the play. And when I have vague forebodings that this part is too long and we need to make cuts, and the dramaturg and the assistant have been sitting there with me and we've been laughing at the same parts, it's very hard to break away from that. We must get some kind of input at that point. That's one of the interesting things about Mabou Mines: we are so self-critical in the making of a piece that it can be very hard on the director and the writer. But that's also exciting. And it has a lot to do with what Mabou Mines is about—very technical, physicalized, precise work.

That's very like the approach you need for Shakespeare or any classical work—you need to learn the scales and internalize that technique before you can be free. With Mabou Mines, the actors never appear technical, they only seem to be in touch with some kind of subconscious area.

That's right. That's something that all the company members are in touch with, without talking about it, without learning about it, simply because of a shared history learned in a very Jungian way. That's what acting is about. Look at the Wooster Group. They're all so brilliant. The work is intense and the emotional politics of the company are utterly communicated in performance.

What is the difference between working with a designer in a conventional producing situation, and the way design is incorporated into a work for Mabou Mines?

For Mabou Mines, it is a longer process. In a regular theatre, design has to be done ahead of time. It's the difference between saying, "Maybe we should put this door onstage because somebody might walk out of it," and "Now, let's have a door here, because we need it."

Over the years, Mabou Mines has been breaking fresh ground, and in the process, winning over a lot of followers—while also frightening some people away.

We change more people than we alienate. Years ago we were in Florence, Italy, performing *B-Beaver Animation, Cascando* and *The Lost Ones.* Everyone said, "Oh God, they're going to hate it. There's Beckett, all words, all English." We were performing in an area like the Lower East Side of Manhattan, where people pee out of the windows. Everyone said, "These people are going to walk out, and talk while they're walking." So we were all freaking out. But the audience loved it. They were silent and listened. It was wonderful. And I think that was because what was communicated was something of the *spirit* or the *subconscious.*

It's been said that every great theatre piece requires a great audience.

One of the problems about being a director is that one works like a dog to make a piece that is very deep and fundamentally honest and then you go to the theatre and wonder if the audience will understand what you meant. Audiences sometimes look shockingly normal, but I find that they are amazingly capable of accepting and even embracing what can be called difficult work if that work is given in a generous spirit, if it's a real soul communication.

Why do you think Leon and Lena *worked so well in Minneapolis?*

It would work anywhere. Büchner was the first great modern writer because he was able to articulate the existential hero, saying that money, romantic love and success do not make a man happy. It is the prospect of freedom that is so terrifying and exhilarating, and seeing that personified in an attractive young actor and connecting that to the dreams of youth that are betrayed or abandoned touches something in everyone. You could say that about a lot of plays. You could say that is what *The Cherry Orchard* is about. *Leon and Lena* was successful because of the combination of script, performers and design. That was true of *Through the Leaves* and *Green Card.* These elements came together and it wasn't accidental. It was fortuitous. It doesn't happen all the time. Again, in *Through the Leaves,* although it was a more difficult working atmosphere, we created our own world.

What will allow theatre to continue to grow and become an art form in this country?

It sounds obvious, but it has to do with what theatre is to the people who do it. Theatre is too hard to do it for the wrong reasons. Many of the actors and directors I know have been talking about leaving theatre because they can't make a living doing it and because it doesn't seem to *mean* anything. I'm talking about younger people who are not saying they are thinking of going into the movies, but into something entirely different, like medical school or architecture. I say jokingly that I may leave theatre and become a caterer or go raise goats because those are two things I'm interested in doing, and they may be as interesting to me as directing plays. At the moment, directing plays is very thrilling. But I am having a problem, as other middle-aged directors are, understanding what it means to do this. Because to me it's not about going to Broadway and it's not about money—except that I would like to be able to pay my taxes and such. One of the things that impressed me about working at the Guthrie was that it was one of the few places I had worked where I met married actor couples who lived in houses like regular people. This is true at Arena Stage and American Repertory Theatre also. It engenders a kind of optimism about theatre.

When I first started directing, after each play I would say, "I will never do this again. I will never go through this process of total identification with something that's art as opposed to my children or a relationship or some political or human issue. Why should I put myself through this kind of agony?" But now, I can't wait to direct the next play. Forty years from now, I'm either going to be in the theatre or I'm going to be raising goats. If I'm in the theatre, I'm going to be doing the same thing I'm doing now—going from moment to moment. I'm not working to be an important person in the theatre. I don't have a master career or aesthetic agenda. I think that is particularly male. I am thrilled to go from one wonderful project to the next. I feel very lucky. At the same time, I sometimes find myself as excited about a new recipe for pumpkin soup as I do over a particularly striking moment on the stage. I am an artist, but underneath it all I think I'm an ordinary person.

ARVIN BROWN

A rvin Brown's talent as a director is enhanced by the confidence he places in his own innate gifts of instinct and intellect: "I basically trust my mind. It's not been true of every director I've known. So much rigidity comes from insecurity that I think some of the directors who are the most inflexible in their approach to a scene are the ones who have a deep distrust of their own perceptions."

In addition to his faith in his own perceptions, Brown is driven to fulfill them: "For me, theatre is not a craft or a simple profession. It is an art form toward which I feel a tremendous compulsion. It is totally absorbing, and, indeed, I can be overly obsessive about the work." From 1967, when he became artistic director of Long Wharf Theatre in New Haven, Connecticut, until he elected to take a three-month vacation to refresh himself in 1986, Brown was basically in pre-production or rehearsal continuously for one show after another.

Brown is known as an actor's director, and they often do their best work in the creative rehearsal atmosphere he provides. Since the very start of his directing career, major actors have been attracted to working with him.

Brown's direction has a muscular reality about it that has enlivened his productions of *All My Sons, A View From the Bridge, American Buffalo* and *Requiem for a Heavyweight*. That emotionally charged quality has infused a distinctly American vitality into his revivals of *Ah, Wilderness!* and *Watch on the Rhine*. These plays, and many others he has overseen as artistic director at Long Wharf, have found a wider audience by moving to other theatres, frequently to Broadway. Indeed, few artistic directors at resident theatres have transferred as many plays to the Broadway stage.

Brown is literally married to his art. His wife is actress Joyce Ebert, longtime veteran of the Long Wharf company. When asked about how that relationship worked, he allowed as how that was an interesting question (and a frequently asked one). Nevertheless, after offering the stock answer he has for the press (that they challenge each other in all the right ways and that they do not bring shoptalk home with them), he added that while the security of the Long Wharf home base had been healthy for his life in the theatre, that same security had resulted in sacrifices for Ebert, that her reputation might have been more widely established if she had chosen a free-lance career.

But Joyce Ebert is not Brown's only "mate" within the company. His successful "professional marriage" to executive director Edgar Rosenblum, and their firmly established mutual trust, has allowed him the freedom to spend most of his time away from his office in creative planning or directing. In this way, unlike other directors who head successful institutions, he has managed to keep his outlook fresh and avoided artistic burnout. He readily admits that he could not live his life the way he does without Rosenblum. "And yet," he says, "part of the reason our relationship has evolved is that I was willing almost from the beginning to let go of certain decision-making areas. I never had the particular kind of ego or set of impulses that made me insist that I had to be in control of all the aspects of the theatre, as I think some artistic directors have felt. When they get tired, and want to reach out to someone else, it's a terrible lesson that has to be learned in terms of shifting responsibilities. So from the beginning I wanted to have someone to share the responsibility in lots of areas. I'm basically a director of plays. That's finally what matters to me."

In recent years, Brown increasingly has turned toward directing such musicals as *Daarlin' Juno, Privates on Parade, Lost in the Stars* and the small-scale operas, *Albert Herring* and *The Tender Land*. He first became interested in their dramatic possibilities when he directed a television version of Menotti's *Amahl and the Night Visitors* with Teresa Stratas. Her work helped him to realize that musical theatre could contain the same acting values as those in drama.

Despite the vaunted reputation Brown and Rosenblum have established for Long Wharf, and the success it has engendered, they have resisted unrestrained growth. Long Wharf could support a facility twice the size of its 484-seat main stage and 199-seat second space. The number of staff members running the institution remains minimal. The emphasis of the theatre, as every actor working there knows, is to maintain Arvin Brown's focus on the work.

■   ■   ■

Did you start out to be a director?

No, I was always going to be a writer. I wrote all through my childhood and early college years, and was about to graduate from college when I got very lucky—and in a way unlucky—and got accepted into a professional writing workshop at Stanford. My two teachers for that workshop were Malcolm Cowley and Frank O'Connor. So it was a pretty phenomenal experience. I was the only student. Everyone else in the workshop was a full-time professional writer. So I was desperately trying to keep up with them and, at the same time, trying to hold my own as a full-time undergraduate student. The result was that I got disenchanted with my own writing because I was stacking it up against the work that I was seeing going on around me. It was in that class that Ken Kesey wrote *One Flew Over the Cuckoo's Nest* and Larry McMurty wrote *Horseman, Pass By*, which became *Hud*. I graduated from college questioning how good I was as a writer and whether, in fact, I wanted to go on with English and head toward teaching if I were not to be an artist. I dreaded the idea of becoming an academic. So, because I had a very high grade average and the university was promoting me for various grants and fellowships, I sort of connived with them to apply for a grant to study in England with the proviso that I would not simply do research, but would do something *alive*. I had always loved the theatre, but at that point I had no idea that there was anything I could do in it.

I said that I wanted to get a fresh slant on Shakespearean staging and was placed at the University of Bristol to study with a man named Glynne Wickham. He had staged the first American production of Pinter's *The Birthday Party* at the Actors Workshop in San Francisco, which I had seen and loved. I was thrilled with the idea of getting to know a man who had a foot in both worlds, because he was an academic and also was a terrific director in his own right. So that year I was living in Bristol and, by a fluke, their usual complement of directors for the Christmas plays just wasn't there. They came to me and asked if I would consider directing a one-act play. Because I knew nothing about directing, I was absolutely cavalier about it and said of course I would.

And I got real lucky. I went after a mysterious "dark lady" in my graduate class who I understood had had a major career in England before something had gone wrong, a breakdown or something. This woman had been with the Royal Court and the Royal Shakespeare Company, and had been an up-and-coming star. So I dove off the deep end and asked her to do Strindberg's *The Stronger*. I waved the role in front of her and she bit. She was truly a superb actress, and it was a tremendous introduction. There I was, never even having watched a director work, doing it all by some weird instinct.

Do you remember how you communicated, not having worked previously with actors?

I remember thinking the reason I wanted to do *The Stronger* was that I had seen a television version of it, and I didn't think the play meant what it seemed to me was stressed in that television production. That was my first realization that a director can alter and shape the meaning of the text. I remembered feeling very strongly, in the television production, that the stronger woman was clearly the silent woman and the talking woman was very weak and insecure. I remember thinking, knowing very little about Strindberg, that both women were weak. The relationship between the two of them was kaleidoscopic, and I thought that there was a way of doing the play which was much more ambiguous and, therefore, fascinating for such a short piece.

That was really all I had to go by. So I launched in and I remember working the actresses and finding, by instinct, places where I felt their characters were on top of the moment, places where I felt their characters were vulnerable. And I guess that the result was that there was a kind of irony in the production that was tremendously successful.

I found that the same instincts that had driven me toward writing, the sense of creating a world that was perhaps not my world, peopling it, being fascinated by human relationships, the development of character, all those still held sway in directing with the exception of the fact that the original vision was not mine. It was someone else's. I found that to be once removed from the original vision, to interpret someone else's original vision, was much more congenial for me than facing that blank sheet of paper, thinking it all had to come from here. [He touches his temple.]

It was also my encountering the collaborative aspect of theatre that made me fall in love with it. I was and have always been a collaborative animal. Even when I was writing well and proud of my work, the loneliness of it devastated me. Where with directing, I found that panicked as I might be, other people were in it with me.

So I did that one-act, and then I did another one-act with students later in the year, again in my spare time. That brought me down to earth because I discovered that not all actors were going to be as resourceful and as skillful as had been the case in the first play I directed.

Then I came back to the States and took another grant at Harvard in English mainly because that whole year in England had seemed so specialized and so unique that I wasn't really willing to make any life choices, coming out of that very small experience. So I went to Harvard and absolutely hated it. I hated the sense of escape on the part of many people. These were the prime years of the Vietnam situation and I felt that all of us were there, in one way or another, escaping—escaping the draft, escaping ourselves. And I was violently opposed to the war even then, had no compunction about not serving, but I was depressed a lot of the time by the feeling of futility that I saw around me. Harvard put a particularly unfortunate focus on English studies in that era. I don't know what it would be like now, but I really found that good, exciting teaching tended to be legislated against among the graduate students, that they were taught to try to make English as close to a science as they possibly could. Everything had to be reduced to a science in those days and there was no encouragement for the creative, exciting teacher. Actually, in retrospect, I am grateful that the Harvard experience was as extreme as it was because it helped me make some decisions that might have taken a few more years to make. I was so miserable at Harvard that year that I knew I had to be in the theatre. Shoring up my support around me at all times, I went through the qualifying exams in order to get my master's, although I had no intention of going on.

Then I enrolled in the Yale drama school, primarily because it was easy for me to get in given my academic credentials. I had no experience, and I was terrified because I knew enough about the theatre already to know what a challenging and scary and competitive world it was—particularly for a director—and here I was with these two little one-acts to my credit.

Since your background was writing, were you already familiar with the literature of the theatre?

Yes. I knew plays and I knew them well. From childhood, I had gone to every play I could possibly get into. You know, I grew up in Los Angeles, and it wasn't a rich field, but there were shows that came to town. I saw everything from the time that I was old enough to go on my own to the theatre. In retrospect, I was preparing without knowing. But, again, I knew nothing about the role of the director, and I felt right from the beginning that I was not an actor. In those days, if you weren't going to be an actor, who knew what else was available in the theatre?

The first year at Yale was particularly valuable because through Nikos Psacharopoulos, who was my real mentor, I found out that a lot of what I had done by instinct was justifiable and was somehow going to be my style, my method. The only time I found drama school life to be difficult was when people were telling me how to do something which, by instinct again, I rebelled against. That's probably what happens when you have a strong bent for something. There were certain things that I never had to be taught. I just had to be told that it was okay to do them. And, of course, the drama school offered me an opportunity to work that I wouldn't have had elsewhere.

How did you make the transition from school into the profession?

Jon Jory and Harlan Kleiman founded Long Wharf Theatre. They were watching my classroom work although I was unaware of it at the time. They already had the plan to build the theatre and they came to ask me to leave school and join up with them as a sort of staff director for the apprentice program and children's theatre. And I would be given one full-length play on the main stage in the first season. I was thrilled—I had been in school for so long. So I left Yale when the theatre was ready, at the end of my second year.

I began working on staff, and suddenly the end of the first season was approaching, and they hadn't given me my play. And there was only one play left, *Long Day's Journey Into Night*. Everyone else was too tired to do it. So the first full-length play that I ever directed was *Long Day's Journey*.

When I look back on those early times in my life I think, "How could I have had the nerve?" To make matters even more difficult, up to that point there had been no nationally known actors at Long Wharf. It had largely been a group from the Cleveland Play House. But because they all were tired and decided not to do the show, we had to cast from the field. And the first person who decided she wanted to do it was Mildred Dunnock. And then I cast Frank Langella. I suddenly found myself with a pretty high-powered cast for my first time out.

It was really very scary. I spent most of the first period trying to keep the cast from finding out that I had no experience whatsoever. In retrospect, I'm sure they knew. I made some big mistakes initially. An example was walking into my first rehearsal with the blocking carefully planned out with my little stick figures from the night before—only to have Dunnock say to me, as I described to her how wonderful it would be if she crossed the room over to the sofa, "Why?" That really threw me. No one had ever said, "Why?" And it was a pretty disastrous first morning. By lunchtime, I realized that I was in bad trouble. Again, whatever that impulse was that drove me toward this as a profession took over. I said, "I have to do some thinking, and I want you all to go to lunch and come back and we'll talk." And I pretty much leveled with them when they got back. "Look," I said, "I'm doing this far too rigidly. This is real nonsense, so I'm throwing everything out the window.

Let's start from scratch." I was so frightened. I can't tell you how scary it was to suddenly chuck all my careful notes and plans on the first day of rehearsal and wing it.

Were you able to gain their confidence after that rocky start?

They must have realized how young and inexperienced I was, but I think they also felt that I was making the right move. They were tremendously supportive, although I continued to learn valuable lessons from them. I remember once asking Milly Dunnock her advice on a certain aspect of the production and having her tell me that she couldn't think in those terms and didn't want to. She was responsible for her character and the production was my province. That was a great object lesson for me.

Another thing happened that was a tremendous kindness, one of those things that help you to survive these fraught situations. One day as Frank Langella was leaving for the commute back to New York, he handed me a note and said, "Read it after I'm gone." And I read the note. It said, "I think you're doing a wonderful job. Love, Frank." I've never forgotten that. If I had to name any one single thing that got me through that first production, it was that little note. Because I already knew that he was a tough guy in his own way, and that he wasn't going to bullshit me completely. That injection of confidence in some way carried me right to the end.

Anyway, the production was a huge success. They then offered me two shows the following season, and the second show I did was *Three Sisters*, which also went very well. It was after that second production that I was offered the theatre. And I've been there all these years.

Who are the artists during that time who have been your closest and best collaborators?

Boy, there are so many now that I've passed this twenty-year mark. Ron Wallace, the lighting designer, has been with me since the very first show. There is a real feeling that we have grown up together.

What happens in a collaboration of that duration? Does it become nonverbal?

Yes, very much so after an initial conceptual stage. Ronnie is a fine visual artist and a self-taught man of considerable culture. And over the years, as he's become more conversant with the world of painting, the world of design, interior design, architecture, I find that I can sometimes use tones of images with him in a conceptual conversation at the beginning of the rehearsal process. For example, once on a Gorky play I said, "The feeling I want here is Corot. This is a silver-light play." I've never in my life done a cue-to-cue run-through with Ron Wallace. I don't see anything like a finished result in lights until very late in the technical dress process. Ron tends to paint around me, and I find that when this system works at its best, it frees me not to think about light until there is a finished form. And then I can say in broad terms, "This is too dark. This is too light. There are holes there." Whatever. But I've never had the relationship with Ron that so many directors have with lighting designers where they really go moment by moment painting exactly what they want.

You mentioned Corot. Does your background also include experience with the visual and fine arts that helps you work from a range of images?

I have always been fascinated by painting. I took a lot of art courses, went to museums from an early age and I have traveled a great deal. I think a love of painting has formed my visual sense in terms of theatre. Travel has contributed to every fundamental aspect of my work as it has evolved. I have assimilated a great deal from a constant exposure to France, to England.

To be honest, although I'm proud of my abilities in the visual area, they didn't come naturally to me in the theatre. I always separate in my mind those things that I did practically as I breathed and things that I had to consciously learn. I had to train myself visually to a certain extent. I certainly had to train myself technically. I had no knowledge or interest in the technical aspects of the theatre. To this day I don't have much. But I've learned, thank God, from the experience of doing so many plays year in and year out. I mean, I know how to read ground plans. I'm seldom taken aback by spatial relationships or what a set looks like when I get into the theatre. I know what I'm going to see. But that's by dint of hard work. I still depend on a good stage manager, and I'm lucky to have worked with the best to help me sidestep certain problems in rehearsal that might accrue later.

Early in your process of investigating a play, do you have a strong image of how you want the play to look?

I have a strong sense of tone, and very often I approach the visual look of a play as a certain corrective for what is most immediately obvious in the text. For example, if I were to do *Long Day's Journey* (and I made this very clear the second time I did the play), I would not aim for the most claustrophobic, depressing set that I could find. I would much rather that the sense of claustrophobia build out of the characters' attitude toward their environment rather than telegraphing an environment that on its own hook makes an overly strong statement. Very often, I've tried to work against the prevailing tone of the play in the visual environment—as long as the play isn't falsified by doing that. I use "painterly" images, once in a while architectural references. Sometimes I have spatial ideas, although I try to limit those because my sense of

27

space is nowhere equivalent to that of the designers I am lucky enough to work with. And I find sometimes that to present them with too strong an idea of what I'm expecting in spatial terms limits their imaginations.

Hal Prince says the worst thing that can happen is to get back from artists exactly what you ask for.

Boy, I agree with him on every level. I agree with him in terms of designers, in terms of actors, in terms of writers. And that is the most frightening of all, the process of working on a new script with a writer. Sometimes, because I was a writer, my ideas can be very strong, very articulate. And yet it doesn't matter how articulate they are—I'm not the playwright. And sometimes I find, particularly with young writers, that they're overly anxious to please and far from being resistant or defensive about what I might suggest. They do it too fast, and it doesn't go through that organic process by which the play was originally written. That to me is an ongoing difficulty. I constantly try to find the tools of communication that will be specific and yet allusive, so that the imagination of the people you are talking to is never constrained. It's very hard to do. You're always running the risk of not being specific enough, allowing too great a freedom so that people feel adrift.

Have you tended to work repeatedly with those people who pick up on your style and who find a freedom as a result of it?

Absolutely. This goes right back to the fact that the collaborative process is central to me and I am very likely to go after artists who crave it as much as I do. So I have never been particularly interested in artists who tend to view their work in hierarchical terms. Mind you, I would like to believe that in most of the experiences of my life I have held the reins, that there has been a strong central voice. But I am very uncomfortable in situations where I feel people are dealing with me with kid gloves, are hesitant about suggestions or voicing concerns. I may not necessarily like the kind of disruptions at rehearsals that create a tense atmosphere; I might prefer they deal with me privately if things are getting difficult; but I do want them to deal with me.

Is it simply instinctive with you to provide a nurturing atmosphere at rehearsals in order for your actors to flourish, or do you consciously set it up?

First of all, there are a lot of givens for that whole process. The first is that I love actors. I think that is central for any director who works the way I do, and you can't fake that. As a matter of fact, the older I get the less faking there is. When I was young and inexperienced, as I described during my first rehearsal on *Long Day's Journey*, I pretended to a kind of freedom and a kind of ease and relaxation that I didn't always feel. I don't always feel it now, but

I come a lot closer to it than I did twenty years ago. The respect and admiration that I have for actors on almost every possible level has always been true, but the more confident I get in myself, the older I get, the less threatened by possible conflict, the more this is able to express itself. I think like all true things in human nature, it's taken for what it is. People know that I'm not kidding about it, that I'm genuinely thrilled by what they do. And my ego, which is a considerable one, is satisfied, for the most part, by creating a world in which what they do can flourish.

A director who recently observed your rehearsals said that you never leave a scene without making the actors feel good about something they have achieved. You make an observation, whether it is praise or not, that implies a feeling of progress.

I'm not sure I've had that said to me before. But in thinking about it I guess it is probably true. It's the director's version of "Don't ever allow yourself to fall asleep without resolving a fight with your wife." It would be very painful for me to leave a scene on a note of tremendous insecurity or with negative impulses, either mine or the actors'. I've often said, "We haven't got this scene yet. On the other hand, here's where we've come." I try not to kid actors. I don't like for them to leave rehearsals feeling that they absolutely have it when I feel they don't. I often make them feel that they've made strides. Sometimes, in very young or insecure actors, I find that I need to be a bit more forthcoming with specific praise. Eventually, I do that. But I'm always reluctant to do it too soon because I don't know what tomorrow will bring or the day after. And there are actors who feel as hemmed in by praise as they do by criticism.

When auditioning new, unfamiliar actors, how do you determine that you want to work with them?

One's instincts become pretty well honed after time. I do an awful lot by instinct. It's very important to me to have some sense of an actor as a human being. Even in the most awkward audition situations, I have evolved a series of exercises which I often use with young actors, sensory exercises, movement exercises, anything without making them more tense than they are when they come in, to try and break down those terrible defensive postures that so many actors bring into auditions.

And I do talk to actors. Some are made very uncomfortable by this; and I have heard it expressed that they would just as soon deal with the audition as a professional situation where they walk in and do their pieces and leave, or take suggestions from the director or whatever. I understand that feeling, without being sure of how valid it is, because it almost always telegraphs a fear of the self in a certain way. There's no result that is supposed to come out of having a conversation with an actor other than just getting some sense of contact. If I don't feel that, I often worry because the kind of acting I admire is a kind that is organic. It has to do with the human being as a human being and not necessarily a set of learned skills.

Does seeking this kind of actor also contribute to doing a particular genre of work?

Again and again I read that I'm a naturalistic director, at my best with a certain kind of realistic play. Whatever truth there may have been to that, I think my process over the last years has changed considerably. I'm going into areas of theatre that are quite different. For example, I'm fascinated with musical theatre, and I've done a lot of it over the past few years. What I hope I'm doing is taking that fascination of detailed human behavior and translating it into the larger-than-life context of musical theatre. Without having lost any of the original drives that took me into the theatre, I feel now that I'm in a place where I can expand. Emotional, behavioral truth is frequently missing in much of opera and in much of musical comedy. So I feel that I am tackling new things. I love imaginative stage forms when I feel that they accommodate a certain basic human thing that I'm trying to talk about. I'm not particularly interested in formal experimentation. However, I've directed a lot of cinematically styled theatre pieces recently and experimented with more freeflow staging than I used to.

What has stimulated that? Is it the influence of cinema or the natural evolution of working in the theatre?

It's both, but I think it comes from the influence of films. Writers today are writing in cinematic terms for the theatre. This can be a terrible drawback, and in many instances plays have suffered for it. Nevertheless, when a play works within this context, it's the director's responsibility to find a stage life for it that is truly theatrical and vibrant and exciting, and not just a matter of quick-take scenes that seem choppy and disconnected. That happens far too often in a lot of contemporary theatre.

How do you get inside a musical work? Is it through the music or the drama or some other element?

First of all, on the simplest level, I have to love the music. I then have to be excited about the music in relation to what the dramatic situation is. It may not be entirely resolved, but it has to be enough to get me thrilled about saying something in stage terms about that music. If I didn't feel that, I think I would want to hear the music in concert and not feel any impulse to put it onstage. Up until around 1987, I'd been interested in musical work that bounced off a certain kind of recognizable human behavior. Then I directed the American premiere of Busoni's *Turandot*, and it was an opera wildly outside of anything I'd done before, very commedia dell'arte. It bears almost no resemblance to the Puccini but it was written about the same time. It's sardonic and ironic and slapstick.

What is interesting is that many of the leading directors in the field are turning more and more to music theatre—you, Mark Lamos, Peter Sellars, etc.

In my own case, I think it's a matter of a certain kind of transcendence, if that isn't too pompous a word, that I feel in working with music that I couldn't get in other areas of theatre that are as highly stylized. That's not where my particular skills are. I think there are other directors who are brilliant at that. Peter Brook can achieve a certain kind of transcendence by a wildly eccentric staging concept that takes the basic text or the basic human relationships and puts them into some sort of Cuisinart. I can admire the result of that, but I can't do that. So I get the enhancement of soaring to another level with music.

I would never want to work exclusively with musical theatre, though. There is another kind of joy that one can get from the depth of characterization of great actors that isn't in opera for me—the experience I was able to have with Al Pacino in *American Buffalo*, or Richard Dreyfuss or Colleen Dewhurst or my wife on occasion. There is a richness of detail and acting experience that I don't think is comparable in opera or any kind of musical theatre. Although I was spoiled early on because my first really serious musical experience was directing the television version of *Amahl and the Night Visitors*. And there I probably directed the greatest singing actress we have, Teresa Stratas.

The actors you mentioned are all stars. Do you work differently with them than you would with other actors?

Well, I work with Al Pacino very differently from any other actor, but I don't think it has anything to do with his being a star. It has to do with the nature of his talent. He has a very deep process, a very profound process and it's a process that can easily be stopped by saying the wrong thing. That puts a big burden on the director but it is also very exciting. I had to learn how to work with Al. I had to learn a tremendous kind of direction by indirection. I had to accept him as a total collaborator. The process of *American Buffalo* was so exciting. I would often say, "Al, when you said that to Donny or to Bobby, I didn't understand what you meant." That's often all it would take to get a process going that would eventually result in another whole interlocking approach. I simply told him that whatever was going on was not registering. I

31

also found that it was possible to make positive suggestions to him that would get him very excited, but they had to be indirect. They had to be about milieu. One kind of thing you could say to Al and get wonderful results was, "Al, what do you suppose is happening out on the street while you're doing this?" That he would love, and it would immediately trigger something that perhaps was missing in a scene. Whereas, if you were to say to him, "Hey, Al, I think this scene ought to be a lot more conspiratorial," he couldn't do it. To use a word like "conspiratorial" to Al doesn't mean anything. Or it means too much. Of course, on a human level he's absolutely right. People don't think that they're being conspiratorial. People are conspiratorial because they're afraid of what's going on out on the street. It forces you into an imaginative world that's equal to his or that you try to make equal to his. That is the thrill of working with great artists. They force you onto their wavelength. I wouldn't work with anyone else, that I can think of, the way I work with Al. But I wouldn't want to. That process is part of the magic of that particular artistic relationship. The other ones have a whole other set of circumstances.

Over the years you've managed to do a considerable amount of directing outside of Long Wharf.

That's how I've been able to sustain myself. I could never have committed to one institution for such a tremendously long period of time if I hadn't been essentially free—not entirely, the burden of the theatre is always on me. That's the price I've paid, for the most part a willing price, all these years. But by and large, at least in terms of the possible careers one can have in the American theatre, I've been lucky because I do have a home base, and I have a theatre that I continue to respect and which continues to challenge me. At the same time, I'm never limited from taking on any other kinds of opportunities that come along.

Have you directed any theatre that you considered overtly political?

I went out to Los Angeles to do *The Normal Heart*, which was, for many reasons, the first deeply political play that I've ever had the desire to do. Its political implications were immediate and powerful and emotional because the play is deeply rooted in character. I had a wonderful experience with that in Los Angeles and an even more magic experience of coming back and doing it for a Long Wharf audience which had no preconceptions about the material or any understanding in particular of the world of the play.

In LA and New York it had an automatic audience, not necessarily gay but liberal, that it couldn't be expected to have in New Haven. It was a challenge and a thrill seeing how our message was going to get across. It gave me a feeling for what political theatre could be if the issues are immediate enough. My complaint with a great deal of American and English political theatre has been that it is head stuff. It is never blood and guts, never where people really live. Mind you, I don't want to see us have a horrible epidemic like this to be able to write political theatre, but the truth is that the greatest political theatre does come out of that kind of crucible.

The Normal Heart was talking about an issue that people were in the process of becoming terrified about. The primary thing that I felt about the New Haven audience was a *hunger to know*, which I would never have expected to encounter. The audience wanted to know about the epidemic and also about the gay lifestyle. The sense in the audience was that something horrible is happening to these people, to gays all over the country, suffering on so many levels, political, medical, sociological. People wrote. People came up to me in the lobby and around the city and asked about ways to learn more, told me of new understandings that they had toward gay cousins, gay children, gay relatives.

Your whole life is spent directing one play after another. What do you do to replenish your creative energies?

I've mentioned travel. And I love to read. I'm impatient with my life when I'm in rehearsal because I don't get to read enough and I tend to read things absolutely unrelated to theatre. It's only every fifth or sixth week that I can read the Arts and Leisure section of *The New York Times*, even when the articles are about good friends I care a great deal about. I have to force myself. My own attitude about that stuff is that it's all necessary. It's all part of our job, what we do. I never blame actors for sounding silly in some of those interviews or directors for sounding self-serving because it comes with the territory. But on the other hand, I don't feel that I have to read it. I read lots of history, lots of biography. I find that I read more biography and autobiography as I get older. I used to read four or five novels every week of my life but not so much as I get older. Maybe I see the craftsmanship too much even though I don't write. I see the limitations of too many young writers too clearly. Whereas sometimes biography can be limited too, the subject can transcend in a way that the fictional subject seldom transcends the skill of the writer.

Do you spend a lot of time disguising your own craft? Is that part of becoming a mature artist?

Craft is only apparent when something human has not been sufficiently explored. What I do find as I get older, and which I relish, is greater freedom. I walk into a rehearsal now and truly have no idea for the most part how the day is going to go. I prepare in a whole other way than I did ten years ago.

I prepare when I drive by letting my mind wander. I don't try to ride herd on it. I don't try to "direct" it toward the "problem" of the day. But often I start thinking about the play and whenever thoughts about the play come to me I just go with it. Sometimes I wake up in the morning an hour early with my mind going in terms of the play. I listen to that, and I get some of my sharpest understandings from that process, whereas I used to feel it necessary to force my mind into those channels because I thought I wasn't going to be ready. I would inevitably sit for an hour before every rehearsal in reading and rereading whatever I was going to rehearse that day. Now, I may do that or not because I find it might limit me. That hour that I sit alone with the script, forming judgments, might prevent me from seeing a moment of fresh discovery.

My thoughts are now much more about "Am I making it?" rather than "Is it going to be well received?" They are directed more to the work itself with a confidence that if the process is genuine it will reach out somehow. Now, it may not reach out critically. And that's something that I've had to learn to live with as everyone who is in the theatre does. The unfairness of certain aspects of criticism toward anyone who is in the public eye can really get you down. I mean, if it were a matter of being damned for what you don't do well and being praised for doing what you do well, as much as anyone hates to be criticized, one could live with it far more easily. In fact, everyone's experience in life with criticism is almost the reverse of that. Very often you're overpraised for things that you know damned well don't represent you or the other artists at their best, and you can be cruelly taken to task for things that are simply not true.

Then what is it that makes a play critically successful?

The critical thing is truly a crapshoot. Finally, it does not have anything to do with the actual product itself. There are exceptions to this, the odd occasion when a critic will somehow get in sync with what you are doing either negatively or positively. But, to tell you the truth, that's happened relatively infrequently in my life and I don't look at myself as someone who has been unfairly battered by the critics. I'm okay. I have no real cause for serious complaint overall, but, nevertheless, the experiences with criticism that have meant anything in my professional life have been with a handful of other professionals whose judgments of my own work I respect enormously. The critical wrap-ups have been virtually meaningless. We would like to believe in cause and effect, even when it's painful, because it's much more easily managed. It's very hard for us, working for some kind of informative response, to come to terms with the fact that our most public feedback may literally have little or nothing to do with our own efforts. I think there is a period in the growing life of any artist when he has to come to terms with that and try to let loose of it as much as he can. After you've worked for a certain matter of time, you know by and large no one thing is going to make or break you. You're going to survive this flop, you're going to survive this bad review, you're going to survive this inadequate performance. So there's a liberation in that.

RENÉ BUCH

R ené Buch has achieved what no other theatre director in New York, and few in the nation, has been able to do: establish a genuine repertory company with a permanent corps of actors performing a different play or musical every night and matinee in the course of a week, year-round. On top of that, his company, Repertorio Español, tours internationally, presenting its assortment of classics from the Spanish Golden Age, new plays and the popular operettas known as zarzuelas.

Born in Santiago de Cuba, Buch came to the United States specifically to study playwriting, but after three years of study, he temporarily lost his interest in theatre and turned to journalism. Beginning in 1952 as associate editor for the arts for *La Prensa's Visión* magazine, he later moved to the United Nations as editor of the Spanish edition of the UN journal, and finally to the *Reader's Digest* as condensed books editor for Latin America. His interest in theatre was reignited in the late 1960s, at the same time as the influx of exiles from Cuba and other Latin American countries suddenly made it seem that there might be a Spanish-speaking theatre audience in New York City. Together with producer Gilberto Zaldívar, Buch founded the Greenwich Mews Spanish Theatre in 1969, sharing theatre space on Thirteenth Street with the Village Presbyterian Church and the Brotherhood Synagogue. Buch and Zaldívar decided to risk producing Calderón's *La Dama Duende* (*The Phantom Lady*) in Spanish and conclusively proved that their Spanish-speaking audiences wanted to see plays performed in their native language.

Designer Robert Weber Federico joined them in 1971, and the next year the threesome moved to the Gramercy Arts Theatre on East Twenty-seventh Street, renaming the company Repertorio Español and opening with the Spanish version of *Who's Afraid of Virginia Woolf?*

In 1973, they were joined by another expatriate, Ofelia González, a leading actress from Cuba. From that point on, it was the careful building of the acting company that was the key to Repertorio's success. By the late 1970s, the news of the company's skill in performing the classics of Lorca and Calderón began to spread to the English-speaking community, and traditional theatre funding sources began to support their efforts. Today the company annually presents at least two hundred fifty performances in New York, from an active rotating repertoire of up to seventeen plays. A new production usually has at least a two-year life and some have been kept in the repertoire for seven years. Repertorio was the first Spanish-language theatre group to represent the United States in Latin America when it went on tour in 1980, and has appeared in Spain, Colombia, Costa Rica, the Dominican Republic, El Salvador, Ecuador, Guatemala, Honduras, Nicaragua, Peru, Venezuela, Puerto Rico, Mexico and Panama. The company presents approximately forty-five performances on tour each year.

Buch's productions are characterized by their physicality. His *Romeo y Julieta*, which first appeared in the 1978-79 season, displayed a passion frequently missing from many an English interpretation. The company acts with a clarity that makes it possible for non-Spanish-speaking audience members to understand the action of the play.

Popular with his audience are Buch's stagings of zarzuelas, the Spanish operettas whose source is folk music. Buch is especially qualified to work in this form, having studied music all his life. In 1983, Buch was incensed when a newspaper article stated that no important music had been written in Cuba prior to the Castro revolution. This led him to compile one of Repertorio's biggest hits, *Habana: Antologia. Habana* was comprised of Cuban music of the 1940s, island folk music, Cuban pop and country songs and music with an Afro-Cuban beat.

Repertorio's home, the 149-seat Gramercy Arts Theatre, is one of the oldest theatres in New York. Its proscenium stage is small by any repertory company's standards. And Buch's emphasis on the actor as the center of the play, in which everything that distracts from the actor is removed, in which ingenuity and physical skill are given precedence over settings, requires extraordinary flexibility from the actors and economy of vision from designer Federico. Because of Buch's spare style of staging, Repertorio is somehow able to finance a busy schedule of plays and musicals that would tax the resources of a much larger institution.

Buch's smoothly shaved head gives him the appearance of a kindly Pablo Picasso. He has an international view of theatre, and a working knowledge of many art forms. This renaissance director paints in a style he jokingly calls "tropical Cezanne," plays the piano and has a background in both dance and opera.

■ ■ ■

When you began Repertorio Español, the company performed in both Spanish and English. Why does it perform now only in Spanish?

We have great respect for both languages, but the United States is totally ignorant about Spanish literature. Everyone talks about Molière, Racine and Goethe, but no one mentions the Spanish classics, which are the richest after the Elizabethans. It's important that we keep these great works alive.

You have been working for twenty years to build a company.

Yes, and some of the actors have been playing together for eleven years. Our newest actor has been with us three years. This means that we all speak a common language and quickly relate to one another when a new play is staged.

In this latest play I'm staging, Tirso's *El Burlador de Sevilla (The Rake of Seville)*, the company is confused because it is the first time I've given them props. They seem to like it. I'm mixing realistic acting with a production setting that is nonrealistic. The set will be three black platforms and the actors will have four "Kabukis," people who will walk in and bring things like fishing poles and move props around. I've always had a feeling that theatre consists of an actor, a stage and an audience. I have fought for the spare look for my theatre. All other things can be dispensed with. When I did *The Glass Menagerie (Mundo de Cristal* in the United States and *El Zoológico de Cristal* in South America), there were three stools onstage, a gauze merry-go-round and that was it.

I remember once using a scrim in front of the set for a particular production; a woman came up to me and said, "I've been coming to your theatre for years, and I'm happy that you're doing so well that you can now afford a curtain." Even actors are not always aware of how I work. When we did *O.K.* by Isaac Chocron, we had a set with walls because the play demanded it. One of the actors walked in when it was up and said, "Oh my God, a *real* set." That frightened me because it was coming from a company member.

People like to see a set that they can applaud when the curtain goes up. That drives me up the wall because then I know that set is wrong. I don't like realism because I find it the phoniest style. It's always a fakery of what is real: I see a pipe or a faucet in a play, and they open it and water comes out—I just dread it because I know there is no natural way that water could come out of there. I saw a Calderón play at a festival in Texas. It was done with a huge set, and there was a change of scene during which a whole fountain rolled from the back. When it got to the center of the stage, a fount of water came out and the audience cheered. I was sick.

How did you come to choose the playwright Tirso de Molina's version of Don Juan?

It's a version that's almost never done. I've only seen one production of it, and that was in Polish—in Madrid! I thought, "This is ridiculous. It's one of the great plays." And I started working on it. The text came to us in a very corrupt edition. There were verses missing, the structure was topsy-turvy. So I made a new structure and switched a few scenes around. We divided the play into two sections instead of the classical three. The first half presents all of Don Juan's evil doings and the second part is the punishment.

We cannot come to this story virginally because we know too many versions of the Don Juan legend. So what I have done is to suggest subliminally the later versions—such as Molière's in which the character is a bit cynical — superimposed on the version by playwright José Zorrilla, which is a more romantic vision. I'm really doing a "movie" of the story by the superimposition of scenes. For instance, I have the King and the Comendador talking while the Catalinon, the equivalent of the Leporello character, walks between them, waiting for Don Juan to come out of Isabella's bedroom. And I intercut this scene with another, completely unrelated one. In the original *Don Juan*, the company must have lacked an actress to play Dona Ana, so you only heard her voice offstage. Inserting a new speech for her was the only way I could get that character to be seen before she's attacked.

Is this the first play you've reconstructed like this?

I adapted *La Celestina* (*The Old Bawd*), but that was taken from a dialogue novel by Fernando de Rojos in twenty-two scenes. The story is rather like "Romeo and Juliet find themselves in the middle of *The Threepenny Opera*." You couldn't do it as originally written unless you did it as a miniseries for television. One should explore plays as if they've never been done before. That's why I like classical theatre: I always approach Lope, Calderón or Shakespeare as if they wrote their plays yesterday and no one has ever done them.

How do you prepare the actors for the work?

I give them the play and ask them first to memorize their lines so that when we go into rehearsals they can act. I throw them right into the water when they are fresh. I put them into a position in which they *have* to act, and then they start building their characters themselves. I refuse to block the play beforehand. I cannot understand a director coming to a rehearsal knowing what he's going to be doing. I don't like the kind of theatre that's so well organized that it becomes a deadly routine. I don't like the rigidity that's imposed on an actor when he knows he has to do *this* or *that*. I set limits and give the actors freedom inside the limits. It's the actors who bring in things that really inspire me. That's why I need a company.

When I directed Amlin Gray's adaptation of Calderón's *A Secreto Agravio Secreta Venganza (Secret Injury, Secret Revenge)* at Milwaukee Repertory Theater in 1982, for the first two weeks the company looked at me with such hungry eyes. The cast was very talented but they expected me to solve every difficulty that the script presented. They were not familiar with Calderón and they were trying to play him like Shakespeare. That's analogous to playing the music of Verdi in the style of Mozart. You can't do it. I forbad them to think of Shakespeare, except maybe *Othello*. It wasn't that I expected them to solve every problem, but when I did give them a direction of some sort I hoped they would take it like a baton in a relay race. They treated my hints as if they were final answers.

There was a point in *Secreto* when an actor had to say, "I am who I am." That's the most normal line in any Spanish play you can name. I saw this actor going through self-hatred when he had to say that line, I think because he had subconsciously adopted Hamlet as a subtext for the role. And Hamlet never seems to know who he is, or at least he pretends that he doesn't. The actor was building a tragic dimension into this role that the character did not have. That was the only time I really raised my voice and said, "The *Spaniards* have no identity problems!"

That again speaks to a question raised about American actors, that they frequently have a difficulty in realizing the power of just saying the text in the classic plays.

This has been a problem when I've worked with American actors, and it happens the other way around when working on American plays translated into Spanish for my company. In the Spanish plays we've done, the lines reflect the character—they *are* the character. Even when a man is lying, the lines themselves communicate that he's lying. It's direct. There are no subconscious overtones. When we did *The Glass Menagerie*, Ofelia González, one of the great actresses I've worked with, played Amanda. But she had trouble understanding the character through the words. She sounded like soap opera—romanticized, sentimental mush—because she was saying the lines with the same belief that she brings to all her plays. I said, "Ofelia, you're playing her like a ninny." She wept, "But this woman is so corny." "Don't play the words," I said. "Play the feelings underneath!"

Are the characteristics of the classic Spanish plays also present in modern Hispanic plays?

Even modern plays written by Hispanics are more representational than English plays. The Hispanic playwright looks at the play from the outside and sees the characters from both the inside and outside. It's not like Mamet, for instance, who builds his plays through the interior of his characters and whose dirty words become rhythms and poetry. He's turning dirty words into metaphor. A Spanish playwright writes with a magic realism that is closer to the Latin American novel than it is to the realism of Stanislavsky. There is an "edge" to what he's trying to do. I find that particularly true of the work of Latin American playwrights though not that of current writers in Spain. I suspect that democracy has changed playwriting there. The government is the biggest producer, and subsidies are given to everybody, even the commercial theatre. In my mind, that implies that the artists are beginning to feel that they are a part of the bureaucracy that gives them money. And they have relaxed. There isn't the fear that was present during the Franco regime, when the audience understood that if you put a flower in a vase it meant that Franco must go. Their understanding of what was *not* said was clear. Now everything is said openly and there is no longer the effort to have layers of meaning and representation in the work.

Operating in rotating rep and maintaining pieces in the repertoire for years while developing new works—what kind of a rehearsal schedule allows for all of that activity?

It's sheer work. The company can do it because they are very well trained and we don't waste time. Our rehearsal periods are shorter than most of the other companies that I've seen. It's the difference between eight hours of rehearsal a day in some companies, and three or four a day at Repertorio over a period of four or five weeks. Whenever I rehearse a production at a theatre other than Repertorio, I find the rehearsal day is too long. It goes on for hours and hours and I don't think one achieves as much. We are used to working together and are very fast.

Your company is also extremely physical. They work hard.

I like that. They have to jump, run, fall, use their whole bodies. Young actors are wonderfully trained for this lately. In the 1950s, they were trained only from the neck up. Our actors respond rapidly to the stimuli that they give one another, and they're not scared. They try everything right from the beginning.

How do you make it attractive for them to take risks?

I am their safety net. They know that I will never let them look foolish. They know if they try something that doesn't work, I'm not going to keep it. But it is a problem when a guest director comes into the company, because that director has to earn their trust. Once that happens, they'll do anything for him or her.

In terms of rehearsing our long-running plays, such as Gloria González's *Café con Leche (Café au Lait)*, which has been in the repertoire for the past four years, that's more a matter of giving notes if I feel the company is getting stale. That's rare, since the actors are constantly refreshed by working on different pieces.

Normally, I don't see my plays after they open. I just forget them and want to get on to a new one. I don't go back until Gilberto says, "They're ruining it." One day I walked in on a student matinee performance of *La Celestina*. It had been in our repertoire for seven years with five casts. Ofelia was working to try and get the play to be what it is, and Mateo Gomez was trying to keep it alive. Everybody else was just bored. They didn't know I was there. Afterward, I went upstairs to the dressing room and got the whole cast together. "That was the last performance of this production," I told them. "We will keep it in repertory, but I'm changing the whole cast except for Ofelia and Mateo." So I started again with a different cast, a different concept and a different set.

What kind of a process do you go through to reconceptualize a well-known work?

All of that comes when I start working with the actors. I have an idea of the play and I know it's going to be different. A play like *La Celestina* never gets stale. It's like *Don Quixote* or *Hamlet*. I can always say, "Why didn't I see that before?" It's an enormous piece. I'm currently doing my fourth staging of it. Visiting Spain, as I was planning it, I discovered a series of studies on the original book that were very interesting. One was about the social milieu out of which *Celestina* was written, the end of the fifteenth century in Spain and the beginning of capitalism. That started something brewing in me and I decided I could best conceptualize that by using a modern focus.

How was it designed previously?

The first production was done abstractly, in a period that suggested mountebanks. The second time, I did it in the fifteenth century and the set was made of iron, the biggest we've ever had, like a town on different levels. The new production will be done in an empty space with a staircase at the back.

How many actors do you have on year-round contracts?

Thirteen, and then we employ about eighteen part-time actors and musicians as needed. Thanks to support we receive from arts agencies and foundations and corporations, it's possible for us to do large-scale classical plays. Otherwise, how could we do Lope de Vega's *Fuente Ovejuna* (name of the town), which requires twenty-one actors? It's also that Gilberto is an incredible producer.

Is there a change in acting style from a contemporary piece like Café con Leche *to Lope de Vega or Calderón?*

There is no change. There's not even a change in the style of blocking. I try to lift contemporary plays to a level that is nonrealistic. I try to see things that go beyond the "anecdote."

Does your company feel as comfortable with Shakespeare as they do with the classic Spanish repertoire?

Excuse me, but Shakespeare is more Spanish than you might imagine. He wrote before the imposition of Puritanism, before Queen Victoria came along and made it the official spirit of the country. The Spanish, Latins and Italians are more in touch with the Elizabethan spirit than the English are. It was proven when Zeffirelli directed *Romeo and Juliet*. Here were two kids who couldn't keep away from each other. The year before that, I saw a production at the Old Vic and it was all so "teaparty."

Where do the actors of Repertorio come from?

From all over: Cuba, Argentina, Dominican Republic, Puerto Rico, Spain, Mexico, Uruguay, Chile and Ecuador. What's incredible is that there's no jealousy in the company. When somebody does a great job, everybody loves it. An actor gets into my company first of all because he is talented and then because he is a good person. If I get a rotten apple, no matter how talented, I let him go. It's not worth it.

Ofelia González is the one who made the growth in our acting possible because she has the discipline, the devotion, the talent. If Ofelia spoke English, she'd be as well known as Jessica Tandy. I'm happy to tell you that she knows hardly a word of English. So they can't take her away from me. She is the spirit of the company. Everybody learns from her. At the same time, if I give her a small role in a play, she plays it. She never says, "It's too little. How many lines do I have?"—simply, "What do I do?"

You began as a playwright. That's where your ability to restructure **Don Juan** *came from.*

Yes. When I worked with Eduardo Machado, he rearranged parts of his play *Las Damas Modernas de Guanabacoa (The Modern Ladies of Guanabacoa)*, and we hit it off. I have great respect for playwrights. I think that they should have the final word about their work, but I know from having been a playwright that you can fall in love with certain things and be so close to the play that you can't see what's happening. Some years ago I wrote a play that was going to be done Off Broadway called *A Design for Shadows*. I wanted to rewrite the third act and told the director that I would work on it over the summer. Once it was the way I wanted it, he didn't understand it. So I took it back. I wanted a production, but not to the point of it not being done well. So there I was with a script I'd worked on for months. I suddenly said, "I want to see it and I'm going to do it." At the time I was working with the Brooklyn Heights Players and had some pull there, so I did a workshop production with the actors who always worked with me. It was successful, and afterward someone said, "How do you feel, seeing your own script on the stage?" I looked at him: "Just as when I was writing it. I haven't added one sentence. It's exactly the same." If another director had staged it, I would have been allowed to see things I didn't even know I had put in it.

You began your writing in Cuba.

I grew up wanting to be a composer. I thought I had found the perfect subjects for two particular operas that I wanted to write, *Salome* and *Electra*. And then I discovered that Richard Strauss had already written them. I also wanted to be a conductor. But conducting is a study that you have to devote your life to. I didn't know it at the time, but the closest thing to conducting is directing in the theatre. I started writing plays because of a new interest in Cuban theatre, which began in the late 1940s. Part of this revival of interest was caused by Louis Jouvet, the actor/manager whose company was touring in Havana when France fell in World War II. He couldn't go back to his homeland, so he continued playing until he could find bookings in other countries. I was fortunate enough to spend six months of my life seeing Jouvet every night. His company had such a sense of camaraderie, I knew that was the kind of theatre I wanted. They were doing plays by Giraudoux, Molière, Romains. He would play a lead one night and a small role the following evening. Everything I've done at Repertorio is based on that model.

Dance was very popular in Havana at that time. I saw Martha Graham, Ted Shawn at the end of his career dancing with Miriam Winslow. The Havana Philharmonic, in one season, had as guest conductors Walter, Stravinsky, Beecham, Koussevitzky. I saw the best production of *Tristan* I have ever seen—Flagstad with Clemens Krauss conducting. All that was happening in Havana.

So there I was, writing plays. And Ramón Antonio Crusellas, a director from a very wealthy family in Havana, supported a theatre. He would direct a play and open the doors to everyone else. They held a contest for new Cuban plays, and he encouraged me to participate. I submitted one very late on the final day of the deadline. About two months later I won the national prize.

What was the play?

Del Aqua de la Vida—From the Waters of Life. It was taken from a poem by San Juan de la Cruz that says, "From the waters of life my soul was insatiably thirsty." I was twenty at the time. It was about a boy who wants to leave provincial Santiago. His father doesn't understand him and his mother is all he loves. So it was produced, and suddenly that season I had two more done: *Springtime and the Sea* and *We the Dead*, which was a Cuban adaptation of *Electra*—so I finally got *that* in.

After that, I realized that I knew nothing about theatre and decided I wanted to go to Yale because a friend, Rubén Vigon, was there studying design with Donald Oenslager. My father paid the tuition and I entered Yale with a teaching fellowship in Spanish to support myself. At that time, Yale drama school students were taught Alexander Dean's *Manual of Direction*, which tells you to place one character here, one character there. And if you want attention on this one he is the center, and you don't turn this way, you turn that way—all those silly rules. I've spent my whole career trying to undo what I was taught at Yale even though it was the best training of that time —best in the sense that they taught academic theatre. You learned the basics. Then afterward, you could fight your own battles.

One of the best things Yale offered was the ability to take elective courses anywhere in the university. So instead of keeping myself within the drama school (learning theatre-theatre-theatre, show biz, blah-blah-blah), I took opera classes at the music school and audited composition under Paul Hindemith, playwriting under Robert Penn Warren and went to classes on design with

Josef Albers. I studied Latin American antiquity with George Kubler because I had suddenly realized that I knew more about Greece than I did about Mexico. I thought it was ridiculous that as Americans we didn't know what had happened in our own backyard.

I flunked my first year of directing because in my essay on Alexander Dean I made an argument for what I thought directors should do. I asked my professor why I had failed, because I thought I had written a very good exam. He said, "Well, you haven't said any of the things I taught you in class." I responded, "But I'm fighting them. And that's because I know them. In my country (and now I got quite uppity), as a student I'm not supposed to be a recording machine. I'm supposed to think for myself and bring new things to what I'm being taught." I never went back to that class. I have a theory that you learn more from a bad teacher than you do from a good teacher because you learn what to avoid, if you have the brains. Fortunately, the next year James Light was named professor for the second-string directing classes. He had been a friend of O'Neill, had directed all his early plays in Province-town. He was an older man who looked like Stravinsky and who was afflicted with many of the same health problems that O'Neill had. I adored him from the first day, when he announced that our reading would be *The Golden Bough* by Frazer and *On Laughter* by Bergson because they had nothing to do with the technique of theatre. They were works that tried to explain the mind of man and his fixation with ritual. It was comedy and tragedy as seen from a point of view that had nothing to do with a perfect triangle of three characters standing onstage. When I went to Yale I was one person and when I left I was what I am now. For that I owe them a great debt.

Following school, my father used his influence to get me a resident visa and I came to New York, where I worked first in journalism and then in advertising.

Then a friend from Yale called, asking me to suggest actors for a production of *The Crucible* being done by the Brooklyn Heights Players. I recommended someone who got the lead. I saw the actor in it and he was brilliant, so again I got bitten by the theatre bug. I joined the group and was their "intellectual" director, doing Cocteau, Lorca, Pirandello, Ionesco. Once, I resigned when a bylaw was passed stipulating that "no director could cast anybody who was not a Brooklyn resident." I told them that I refused to belong to a group that practiced discrimination. When the bylaw was rescinded, I went back.

About that time, the situation in Cuba changed. I was very *Fidelista* and my family was much involved. In 1959, when Castro succeeded, I went back to Cuba with great joy and the minister of culture said I should work to make the National Theatre the official company. I said, "I live in New York, you know. Send me a contract for two years but that's all, because I want to go back to New York." The contract never appeared. I came back to New York and didn't return until 1975, when I went to see my mother and father who by that time were old and sick.

How did you join with Gilberto Zaldívar to found Repertorio Español?

Gilberto came out of Cuba in 1960, and I knew him through Rubén Vigon. He called me when he got to New York, and I told him I was working with this theatre group and asked him to join us. He worked for a while as stage manager and did lighting. Then he went to the Greenwich Mews Theatre as an usher and ended up being a co-producer there with Stella Holt and Frances Drucker. I was asked to do a play in Spanish by a Cuban society called Las Artes that was trying to produce programs for Cubans in New York similar to those they had had in Cuba. During that experience, Gilberto and I realized that there was an audience who wanted to see plays in Spanish.

Was it basically a Cuban audience or more broadly based?

International. So we founded the Greenwich Mews Spanish Theatre. Holt and Drucker, who had been important in producing the black theatre of that period with Vinnette Carroll, Langston Hughes and Lloyd Richards, felt that the time had come for Hispanic theatre and backed us. We did about three plays a year at the beginning.

How did you survive during that period?

I was working in advertising at J. Walter Thompson eight hours a day. Gilberto worked for a credit card company. It was hell. After I left Thompson, I got on the federal CETA program and that kept me alive for two years. We survived, and now the theatre is stable.

There was a time when Hispanic audiences were extremely stratified, not caring to see plays from countries other than their own. Does that attitude still exist?

Somewhat, although less than it did. At first, we found that if we wanted to have an audience we had to do the classics, because an Argentinean owns Lope de Vega the same way that a Cuban or a Mexican does. When we did Calderón, all of them would come. Now we don't specify whether we're doing a Puerto Rican play, or a Cuban or South American play. We're working on the element that touches all of them, doing a play that interests everybody, using the one thing we have in common, our heritage and our language. The problem is also that the Spanish-speaking person sees theatre in Paris or on Broadway. And he'll say, "I won't go to a Spanish-speaking play in New York, it's probably very bad." So we've spent twenty years developing our reputation. Gilberto, our associate producer/designer Robert Weber Federico and I are always pushing one another to keep the standards that we want. Gilberto comes to me and says, "Last night did you see that dreadful thing? What can we do?" And when I feel that I've done something very good there's always Federico, who comes to me as a devil's advocate and says, "You're repeating yourself." And I've said to him, "Oh yes, I remember this set—it worked well two years ago." So he changes it.

It must be difficult to avoid some repetition when you work in a limited space.

Yes, but if Stravinsky can write twelve pieces for five notes, I better know how to do the equivalent with space.

How did you begin working with Federico?

Gilberto saw his design for *Cat on a Hot Tin Roof* done at a theatre in Clearwater, Florida, and we asked him to design *El Sí de las Niñas* (*Where a Girl Says Yes*) in 1971. During that production we discovered a shared chemistry. We three went to Spain and Italy and by the time we came back he was our oldest friend. We've been working together ever since. He's the only designer to whom I can say, "This play is about suffering," or whatever, and he understands what I mean and brings me a design. He doesn't make drawings until the rehearsals start and he can see where we're going. For *El Día Que Me Quieras* (*The Day You Love Me*) by the Venezuelan writer José I. Cabrujas, I wanted a setting that was neither indoors nor outdoors. Federico ended up using screens and projecting abstract patterns on them. You could be in, out, but if you looked for something tangible, it wasn't there. One of the things that scared me most when I directed at Milwaukee was that I had to approve a set about a month before I began rehearsals. At Repertorio, the set is not finished until the last day of rehearsal. We discuss things as we need them.

How does Federico design for a large company in a small space?

The point is, how do you design "nothingness"? This is the kind of question that is important to theatre people. How can you go beyond the limit? When we did *Romeo y Julieta*, Federico's set consisted of hollow pipes hung on the stage. The image he had in mind was the bells in Italian towns. In the fight scenes the bells crashed and banged, and in the love scenes they swayed gently. When Juliet told Romeo to be quiet, he stilled a pipe. The change in scene was noted when the pipes were washed in blue or lavender or gold light. The whole design took shape when I said to Federico, "There's not

going to be a balcony. I'm playing the whole balcony scene on the floor level."
He yelled with joy and came back with the idea of all those pipes.

Have you directed opera?

Yes, and I want to do more but it is very hard because singers frequently are
not actors. I had a wonderful singer in my company. She was splendid in
rehearsals, but the moment she got onstage she became a prima donna. I
went to her and said, "Look, it takes a diva fifty years to acquire these vices;
you can't start your career with *all* of them."

Were you able to shake them out of her?

No. She felt that drama is conveyed *this* way (he spreads his arms in a rigid
pose). She couldn't understand that everything must be connected, the acting
and the singing.

Is there another theatre company that works the way you do?

The Wooster Group's sense of company and ensemble collaboration is similar
to ours. We're just using a different theatrical language.

What kind of training should a young director pursue?

He shouldn't go to drama school. He should work. He should think, read,
be aware of philosophy, of music, of painting, all the arts, and of the world.
And he should read plays and all the rest of literature. You can't do Lope if
you don't know Cervantes. You can't do Shakespeare if you don't know the
history of the Tudors. You have to work and work and work and think and
think and think. He should learn choreography. I think you can learn more
about directing a play by watching choreographer Alwin Nikolais than you
can by going three years to drama school.

    The metaphor of theatre is so important that we must get artists into
the theatre. I mean artists who are capable of being technicians. I wish I knew
more about lighting than I do. Fortunately, I found Federico, whom I can
trust implicitly, and I didn't have to spend two years learning fencing because
I know I can always get a fencing master to work with the company. One
can't do it all, but one should know a bit of everything, the way a conductor
knows how each instrument produces sound.

*But the actors are your instruments, and you know how they produce their
"sounds."*

A director must also play with the visual, with the timing. Theatre is the only
form that joins space and time, light and dark and color, then humanity—

history and biography, being and intellect. It's the most complete art form. It uses everything. If a director has no "ear," for instance, one can see it in a production immediately. You know that the director is not aware of a certain rhythm. There are also temperamental differences. I, for one, am a "western hemispherian." When I go to Europe I die of boredom because of their timing. It takes hours for them to do what we do in minutes.

What is it that triggers creativity in a director?

For me it's when I read a play and I know I'm going to *die* if I can't do it. The excitement. For example, when I read Eduardo Machado's *Huevos Rotos* (*Broken Eggs*), the scope, the extension of the Cuban experience was all there. It showed how these Cuban exiles extended their feelings between California and Cuba. In the last scene, the girl walks in and says to her mother, "Let's dance." And the mother says, "Who, you and I?"

"Yes."

The mother answers, "They're going to throw us out of here."

"I've been thrown out of better places."

The stage directions indicate music is playing. But I cut the music and had them dance in silence. It's the total stopping of the life they have achieved in exile. They turn and look out at the audience and the lights go down. I like that ending now. In two or ten years, I'll look at it and say, "Oh, that was so bad."

What are you trying to accomplish now?

I need to keep my brain clear of fashion, from pressures that keep me from seeing "man." I'm not religious, while at the same time being very religious. There is a thing between man and the universe that only theatre and music can bridge. It's what the Greeks were seeking with their myths. We are searching for the same answers that they did, only differently.

When I was working at J. Walter Thompson, I said to myself, "I may have twenty years more of clear mind and energy. I'm not going to spend them selling trucks or airline trips or sewing machines." And that's when I gave up advertising and turned all my attention to the theatre. I am the luckiest man in the world. I'm doing exactly the work I want to do in exactly the way I want to do it, with the people I want to do it with. I think I'm going to have to pay for all this good fortune sometime, somehow.

MARTHA CLARKE

Martha Clarke's training and experience originate from the discipline of dance. She creates by carefully feeling her way into a work—a work that will blend movement, sound and visual effects and that will contain dozens of imagistic moments inseparably linked. These moments, dramatic fragments developed by her company during rehearsals over a period of six months or more, are connected or blended into simultaneous action. In rehearsal Clarke responds only to those lightning-flash exchanges that reveal the essence of an action. These fragments are woven into a final work that may last only sixty minutes.

Whether a production is based on Italian fairy tales, Kafka's writings, turn-of-the-century Vienna or Hieronymus Bosch's fifteenth-century triptych *The Garden of Earthly Delights*, all of Clarke's pieces ultimately are trappings that provide a framework within which she expresses her own subconscious. Clarke is not attempting in any sense to narrate her own story, but her emotions are used to filter what she sees—refracted through her own glass melancholy. She does not know where her journey will end as she begins rehearsals and travels from a familiar shore to an unknown destination. Her emotional life keeps feeding on impulses and her work attempts to link the points between inspiration and a volatile inner-emotional life. As she works, Clarke does not refuse to intellectualize, but she prefers to shape the material instinctively. The scenes become associational and do not rely on traditional through-line and motivation.

Ultimately, it is neither movement nor form that differentiates Clarke from other directors working in theatre today, it is content—the ability to get to the center of what men do to women, what women do to men, women to women, life and death and the sense of loss. It's all there, and audiences respond to those images in the same manner as they are created—viscerally.

Clarke's collaborators—the dancers, musicians, composers, designers and actors who most often comprise her core company—are constantly at risk. Everybody is exposed because there is no structured progression to the work during the rehearsal process except for Clarke tracing an invisible emotional maze. She likens her rehearsals to "doing macrame at Bellevue." And for Clarke it is at times an incredible burden to write a story and simultaneously direct a story that feeds off the impulses of her own life.

Clarke was born in 1944 into a privileged and musically gifted family in suburban Baltimore. Her father was a jazz musician before becoming an attorney; her mother played chamber music; her eccentric grandfather invited string quartets to play at their house every Tuesday night. Her aunt is the avant-garde filmmaker Shirley Clarke.

From the beginning, the family encouraged her creative development. At the age of six, she began the dance training that eventually led to her acceptance at the Juilliard School. She joined Anna Sokolow's dance company for three years and worked at the original Dance Theatre Workshop. An interest in painting was pursued at the Art Students League. Then she married sculptor Philip Grausman at age twenty and moved to Rome, returned a year later when Grausman was named artist-in-residence at Dartmouth College, had a son and gave up dancing.

Although she was not particularly ambitious, within a few years Clarke's appetite for stimulation impelled her to become creative again. The Pilobolus Dance Theater, a company that would become internationally known for its humorous contortionist physicality, had been founded by four men from Dartmouth. Clarke was a friend to their teacher, Alison Chase. Together, Clarke and Chase "flirted" their way into the company in 1972. The period with Pilobolus was a self-imposed apprenticeship in theatrical movement. What followed was seven and a half years of world travel and an opportunity for a youthful reveling that Clarke had forfeited with an early marriage—a marriage she abruptly ended in 1980.

During this term of six-way choreographic collaboration, Clarke realized she wanted to do her own work and left Pilobolus to form Crowsnest with the French dancer Felix Blaska. Through Crowsnest, she began the transition from pure dance to theatrically charged dance pieces—choreography that was Chekhovian in spirit, emotionally repressed and pervasively yearning. Crowsnest developed a substantial following in Paris and appeared at festivals in Spain, Italy and France.

Lyn Austin, producing director of the New York-based Music-Theatre Group, suspected that inside the exploring choreographer there was a theatre director and provided the time and money to allow Clarke to develop her own theatrical form. The result was a series of increasingly complex works: *A Metamorphosis in Miniature, The Garden of Earthly Delights, Vienna: Lusthaus* and *The Hunger Artist.*

It was her 1984 interpretation of Hieronymus Bosch's fifteenth-century triptych depicting heaven and hell, *The Garden of Earthly Delights*, that gained Clarke the widespread attention of critics and audiences. It paraded an anthology of events from the Garden of Eden to the netherworld, with an excursion into The Seven Sins, encompassed within an hour and performed by ten dancers and musicians who at times were earthbound and at other moments celestially somersaulted through the air on nearly invisible cables. The production opened at St. Clement's in the Hell's Kitchen section of New York, subsequently toured the United States and Europe and was later revived Off Broadway in 1987.

Garden was followed in 1986 by the even more complex and beautiful *Vienna: Lusthaus.* For this Freudian journey through turn-of-the-century Vienna, Clarke brought together collaborators who were willing to enter her subconscious world through their own dreams. Writer Charles L. Mee, Jr., provided the text (one hundred fifty-seven words), initially putting together fragments of dialogue that might have been overheard while walking through Vienna during the period—sensing the underbelly of that society. After immersing himself in impressions of Vienna, Mee began to have dreams about this subterranean world, ultimately compiling the text from his dreams with added material from Freud's *The Interpretation of Dreams.* Clarke then used Mee's text like songs in a musical— the action was suspended when the words were spoken.

Designer Robert Israel is a major support for Clarke. The environment he created for *Vienna* was a large white room with walls set in perspective and a scrim curtain stretched across the proscenium opening, creating its own sense of mystic memory. With lighting designer Paul Gallo's radiant illumination of this memory chamber and the physical appeal of the company, many of whom appeared in the nude, the resulting effect was one of startling beauty and eroticism.

If Clarke is awash with incertitude during the early months of rehearsal, it is her designers Israel and Gallo (who together have collaborated with her on *Vienna: Lusthaus, The Hunger Artist* and *Miracolo d'Amore*) whose visual poetry finally provides the bedrock environment in which she feels secure to unleash her craft. Once on the set, she can move with surprising speed and assurance. She ferociously hones the material in the final days before opening, her dancer-craft allowing her to quick-cut and instantly turn about. Clarke doesn't hesitate to let the blood flow as she truncates favorite passages in order to sharpen, focus them.

Almost always, Clarke suffers *director's paralysis* two thirds of her way into a project. The final meeting with Clarke (of a series held over a two-year period) was held exactly at this paralysis juncture in rehearsals for *Miracolo d'Amore*, in preparation to open at the New York Shakespeare Festival in June 1988.

Clarke has a willowy dancer's body and large luminous eyes in a face that Modigliani might have painted. There is a sense of fun about her and, occasionally, melancholy. Her speech is frequently punctuated by a deep-throated laugh.

At an observation that there are two months remaining before *Miracolo* is to open, she stops abruptly and earnestly asks, "That's not bad for where we're at . . . is it? I'm in the fallow state right now, and it's utterly frightening. Even though my company has gone through this hard process in previous projects, I feel guilty. The work is fun in the beginning, and we all think we're terrific, that we're all doing something terribly original, and suddenly the heart goes out of it and I feel as if we're wearing the Emperor's new clothes. The company gets up and does this minimal work that takes incredible emotional commitment and what we're looking for just isn't there. We have to go through this 'winter of our discontent,' to get to Robert's set with Paul's lighting and the costumes, and then we'll have our reward. Right now we're climbing up glass with our fingernails. It is a wicked period, and when I reach it I always want to run away and never do theatre again. I wake up in the middle of the night saying, 'I don't know how to connect this!' Who wants to live like that?"

■   ■   ■

The body of your work, after the years with Pilobolus and Crowsnest, draws inspiration and imagery ranging from writers Franz Kafka to Italo Calvino, and painters from Hieronymus Bosch to Egon Schiele. Is your work evolving in a particular direction?

The work is difficult to label and is not an end in itself. Each piece, in some way, becomes a draft for the next. They all have a common aesthetic and a running theme. It's a mongrel art form about contradictions and extreme emotions.

How would you analyze the form?

First and foremost, the dance signature is all over the work. In my heart of hearts I'm a person about movement and pictures. But I don't want to do pure dance pieces. *The Garden of Earthly Delights* was my final Pilobolean statement. After that came *Vienna: Lusthaus.* Its energy was different. *Garden* was an audience pleaser, a broad brush stroke. *Vienna* was more sophisticated, more detailed, more personal and very difficult for me because I was new to using language. I was nearly in Bellevue during rehearsals working with Chuck Mee's abstract and wild text.

Is that why Miracolo d'Amore, *doesn't incorporate text?*

Miracolo was inspired by Calvino's Italian folktales and was going to have text by Chuck Mee. But I started by improvising with actors without a text, and one day I realized the work was very primal and that words would perhaps lessen the impact of the physicality of it. So six weeks after starting, I decided to use singers instead of actors, and now it's all being sung in Italian. Richard Peaslee wrote the music and Teddy Jefferson found lyrics from Petrarch and Dante.

Other images that were used in conjunction with the folktales were the Tiepolo [Giovanni Battista, 1696-1770] drawings of Pulcinella, the commedia dell'arte figure. Pulcinella is classically a hunchback in a white suit with a ruff around his neck, a pointed hat, and sometimes is seen with a black conical mask. The image is very Venetian. In Tiepolo's drawings, sometimes there are three Pulcinellas on a page or twenty of them—all identical in dress— except that they're each very different personalities. They became the model for the men in the piece.

The women's costumes were based on illustrations by J. J. Grandville from a mid-nineteenth-century book, *The Court of Love*, in which each woman was portrayed as a different kind of flower.

How is it that the women are inspired by a different period from the men?

It's an imaginary collection of people in an imaginary place and time—and it feels right.

What range of singing voices are you using?

I have three countertenors, including John Kelly the performance artist, a coloratura and a mezzo-soprano. Three of the singers are also doubling as a string trio, playing cello, viola and violin. They are all wonderful singers. I've been interested in opera for a long time and it looks like this project will be a bridge to that world. There is the possibility of my directing an opera for Lyn Austin and of working with Peter Hall on a new opera.

The thing that's hard about *Miracolo* is that there isn't a story. Unlike *Lusthaus*, it can't draw on Viennese history, it doesn't have Kafka's writings or Hieronymus Bosch's triptych. I have perhaps one hundred twenty disparate fragments now and I have to intuit what goes with what. These fragments are all really about primary emotional states and are put together like music or dancing. Day by day, I find the process excruciating because I have to find something I believe in to thread this together.

Is that thread something logical?

It's an emotional and subjective logic, not an intellectual logic. In choreography you'll develop a lot of material and then assemble it through rhythm or shape, or perhaps you'll have some armature of a story line, but often not at all. Even though the original inspiration for this newest work was Italian folktales, somewhere along the path I strayed into the woods. (*Laughs*)

How do you get to the point of connecting with primary emotional states from folktales?

It made some kind of sense through using improvisations developed in the studio by my company. I sit and catch individual moments. Sometimes what the performers discover will be fine as ten-second items. Sometimes I'll want to use what they do as kernels and push further.

Do you give the company specific images around which to improvise?

Many images used to develop *Miracolo* came from Darwin's *The Expression of the Emotions in Man and Animals*. Other times I just said, "Get out there and entertain me." Watching them improvise is like going into the street, standing around for an hour and finding things that might catch my eye— people moving, having an exchange, sitting in a shop window. I don't want to see transitions or well-developed characters, and I tell my dancers that I don't want what they do to look like choreography. In rehearsal something happens that results in a fragment, and I may respond to one in ten fragments. A dancer may have some interaction with another dancer while a third has an interaction with a fourth. Suddenly, we throw all these fragments together and get something very interesting, which may or may not survive. Each segment is heightened by its juxtaposition to the next segment. I know when the moment is working because when you put two segments together, if they're wrong they *both* lose their air. You don't want two and two to make four. Two and two have to make five.

Milan Kundera's method of making novels has been freeing for me in making theatre. In his *The Unbearable Lightness of Being*, people die and suddenly they're alive again and he doesn't tell you why. Somehow he's so adept at leaving you stranded and picking you up again down the road that you don't even worry about how you got there. In his *The Art of the Novel*, Kundera writes, "Harsh juxtapositions instead of transitions, repetition instead of variation and always head straight for the heart of things. Only the note that says something essential has the right to exist." I want to go to the heart of each thing and not deal with the frames on either side, as in cutting film when one wants to get directly to the action. I don't want to see anything before or after. A great deal can be truncated in order to get from place to place. That's why it's been so hard to put *Miracolo* together. It's like mixing a rather abstract movie.

When does the major task of putting these fragments together happen?

I really can't put *Miracolo* together until I am on the set. Robert Israel's design is like a pie wedge placed on the square of the stage. The floor and walls of the wedge-shaped room are painted Venetian red. There are doors and windows on each of the walls of the wedge and through them you can see rooms with musicians and activity. There's a road going up the back, and it's also like looking into a little Italian piazza.

Your description conjures up surrealist images.

Bob and I looked at paintings at the Metropolitan, and we both responded to the deep perspective of Renaissance paintings such as those by Piero della Francesca [1420-1492]. And when I was in Vienna I rediscovered Pieter Bruegel, [1525-1569] the Flemish painter whose great works are there. One of his paintings, called *Children's Games*, shows a big square where there are a million-and-a-half things going on. That's what *Miracolo* is like. What I'm trying to do is make a live canvas and stretch it through time.

It's not surprising that you are attracted to Bruegel, since he was inspired by Bosch and used the same powers of minute observation to depict the world.

Miracolo is similar to *Garden*, except in that piece I had the progression from heaven to hell. This time the piece begins in chaos and ends in chaos. The new element for me in *Miracolo* is the singing.

Since the lyrics in essence serve as the text of the piece, an accompaniment, how do they serve to frame what the dancers are doing?

They're in juxtaposition. Certain sounds are used either to heighten a moment or to shatter it. The sound will have various levels because the dancers laugh, cry, make the sounds of dogs and birds. We may use tapes of other natural sounds such as the wind and the ocean. Richard Peaslee's music is very civilized, extremely beautiful, while the movement is primitive.

Miracolo *uses dancers and singers. Is there a different method you use when working with actors?*

When I'm working with dancers it is very primitive. It's like . . . [*She hunches over and makes a deep guttural sound.*] When you walk into a space as a dancer, you have a physical feeling as to whether you want to go to the right or to the left or turn your back on something. Dancing for me is visceral. No intellectual process goes on whatsoever.

Actors using words always have to bring their brains into play. When working with text, I'm much more tentative. I'll stop the actors and ask, "What do you *feel* about this, and what do you *need* to . . . whatever?," "Why don't you try it that way?" or "Just read it and we'll see."

Do you develop the elements of movement and text separately?

I keep segregating the elements of the work—one line for text, another for movement, with the musical voice going on independently, out of sync. The reason for this separation is that actors are dealing with something tangible and dancers are always in the realm of the abstract. They're different camps. When working solely with movement, I go into a completely abstract vein. With dancers you can work in a way that has no relation other than the impulse—for a while. One day I walked into rehearsals for *The Hunger Artist* with a cabbage and said to Polly Styron, "Put it on your head." And we just played with a cabbage on her head. Actors, on the other hand, need to be grounded in words and subtext and motivation.

How do you finally synchronize them?

Once I have a strong impulse about what I'm going to do with movement, and the actors have a sense of what they're doing, then I bring them together and we play back and forth. But if both the actors and the dancers come together before we've made any support for them to stand on, everything gets too amorphous. They both get worn down so that nothing really happens.

If you watched a rehearsal of mine, you would see that nine tenths of it is in such disarray. I flounder. If you walked in you would see absolutely nothing except me being uncertain. You would say, "These people are never going to get anything together." I'm not temperamental or a screamer or anything like that, but I'm foggy a lot of the time. And the actors and dancers have to search as much as I do. We're all children dropped on another planet at the beginning of this process and, tentatively, hand in hand, we find our way through this mire to whatever. The day-by-day process couldn't be more collaborative. It's really a workshop. Sometimes I just sit back and watch them and don't say anything all day except "I like this." Sometimes they'll be doing something facing in one direction and I'll stand behind them and say, "It's great from the back, just turn it around." The dancers make up physical material. The actors have suggestions about what they want to do with the text. Happy accidents happen all the time. Things we love get thrown out and things we don't like get better. It's just like other directors' processes in that respect. During the last tenth of the process I get very decisive. Then I want precision. All those finishing elements—lights, costumes and sets are very important to me. I'm in pain unless there's a chance to work over every cue, every button on a high button-boot.

Is that also an instinctive process?

Without understanding intellectually exactly what I'm doing, if I follow my instincts it's often right for my work. But sometimes I lose it. That's when it's scary. Or I'll become too impressionable or care too much that everybody's happy. I have always wanted to be the Nice Guy, but during *Vienna* I learned to make enemies at times and to disagree. I had to stop worrying every time somebody looked disgruntled and walked out early or threatened to quit, because there were times when some of the performers said they just couldn't stand the strain of working that way anymore.

Do you find that this particular process is more difficult for the actors than the dancers?

Yes. Brenda Currin, the actress with whom I've worked in *Vienna* and *Hunger Artist*, is wonderful, but she really goes through terror in the last week before we are scheduled to open. She'll say, "I don't know why I'm doing this." And I'll say, "Just do it and don't worry about it. We'll find that in the last days." That's hard for actors. It's not the way they were trained.

How do you find performers who can give you the commitment you require in terms of time, creativity and such disciplined movement and acting?

My company is made up of actors who want to dance and dancers who want to act. I like working with a nucleus of familiar faces who have survived at least one piece. I also like to work with new faces because that keeps me from getting in a rut and repeating myself. The people who are drawn to working with me are as confused about their identity as I am. (*Laughs*) We make happy playmates.

How do you audition to find these skills?

I often don't audition people. I get recommendations from friends and then we have to click. I have to like them. It's exciting when I meet people who represent a new color in the palette. For example, *Vienna: Lusthaus* was very much a product of the people's lives who worked with me. The individual parts were in a way tailored out of their own personalities. I'm the tailor but they are the material. I need a commitment like a love affair with my cast— a really thick-and-thin-'til-death-do-us-part for the working process. The work is very intimate, very process-oriented. It's several months before it becomes product-oriented. I really want their souls—not after five o'clock, but when they're in the studio.

Do they have to be technically extraordinary?

I'm not interested in a lot of technical facility. I want highly individual-looking people. I look for a bone structure and body type that are distinctive. I like the dancers' or the actors' life experiences to be in their work as well. They must have humor, intelligence, wit and generosity. They must have it with me and they must have it with each other. It's often been said that ninety percent of the success of a production has to do with casting. I believe that is true.

How did you make the transition from pure dance to being a creator/director in theatre?

In the late 1970s, Charles Reinhart, director of the American Dance Festival, knew I was very unhappy because I'd been with Pilobolus for seven years and was beginning to feel that I was dying creatively. Collaboration was too confusing six ways. Charlie said, "Start your own company," and gave me my first Crowsnest concert. He and his wife, Stephanie, helped me organize and apply for grants. Simultaneously, Lyn Austin at Music-Theatre Group suggested that I start directing theatre.

What was the first project you directed?

Actress Linda Hunt and I did a two-woman show in 1977 at Music-Theatre Group's Lenox Arts Center in Stockbridge, Massachusetts called *Portraits*. I put together a group of solos that were very theatrical and she performed Irene Fornes's *Dr. Kheal*. We intercut them. Few people saw it, but it was a very satisfying evening. My friendship with Linda was pivotal in my crossover from dance to theatre. She and I traveled in Europe in 1978. As we were coming home on an airplane together, and she was listening to some music by Gabrieli, she said, "I want to play Queen Elizabeth." Lyn Austin got in touch with George W. S. Trow, who wrote a piece called *Elizabeth Dead*, and that was my first directing of text. That was in 1980, and then we did *A Metamorphosis in Miniature* in 1982.

Linda, the late actor David Rounds and I worked on *Metamorphosis* for five weeks, and I was in utter terror. David was very ill, and it didn't come together until the last moment. It was thirty-five minutes long, and we were on the stage at the Cubiculo, which is only about twelve feet wide. There is something about the less is more principle.

So many of your works have been developed at Music-Theatre Group. What is the atmosphere that Lyn Austin, the producing director, creates?

Lyn creates an extraordinary opportunity for incubation and development of work. There's no pressure, there's no tampering. She doesn't get nervous if I hit a wall, which I frequently do.

Another important person in your development has been Joe Papp.

Joe is very supportive. I met him in 1977 or '78. He came backstage when Pilobolus was on Broadway and said that he had heard that I was restless and that anytime I wanted to do something in the theatre come to him. He produced Crowsnest at the Newman Theatre. I've had this incredible support system—Reinhart, Austin and Papp. That's why I think I've been so lucky in changing hats. Just when I've wanted to try something different, I've had wonderful godmothers/godfathers to say, "Here's the theatre, here's the cast, here's the money. Do it." The people who are behind certain artists really are unsung heroes.

The Garden of Earthly Delights *was an exceptionally beautiful production, but it had virtually no set. How were you able to create that beauty without a background?*

Ultimately, the stage was just a blank space. But the music had great charm and, outside of the hell section, the movement was lyrical. There was smoke and exquisite lighting that sculpted the bodies and made them luminous. You saw figures like the extraordinarily strong and gifted dancer Rob Besserer, this six-foot-four man, suspended in space circling in the air with a wind vine. and Margie Gillis playing Eve with her long hair hanging down. I have a weakness for beauty.

But you went into technical rehearsals with a setting designed by Jun Maeda.

He made this incredible set with no nails, just wooden dowels. But I was sitting there not knowing what to do with it, and a friend said, "Well, maybe your problem is in the set." And the set was out on the street at seven the next morning. It was awful to throw out all that money and that man's wonderful artistry. And it was also hard because you aren't always one hundred percent sure you've made the right decision. Because when my pieces open, they are all like little newborns. In the first few performances they're slimy and they cry and you want to send them back. None of them look good to me for a day or so.

Next came Vienna: Lusthaus. *What was its genesis?*

I saw an exhibition in Venice in 1984 about turn-of-the-century Vienna called *Dream and Reality*. That was the beginning, although I had anticipated *Vienna* ten years prior to that when I thought about doing a solo for myself based on Egon Schiele's paintings of women. I'd been an artist's model and I'd always felt a physical affinity to Schiele's ladies. I'd also loved the music of Strauss, Berg, Mahler. It's a period I wish I'd lived in—Paris, Vienna, Berlin, any of them have an attraction for me. I don't know why.

One tends to think of that period and those places as being romantic. But you seized upon their darker sides.

My work is very personal. And at that time I was barely surviving a tempestuous love affair. Vienna seemed to embody the elements of my own life. All my best work has been autobiographical.

The other part of the story was that Lyn Austin wanted Richard Peaslee and me to do a piece on Hiroshima and we had gotten a grant from the National Endowment for it, but Dick didn't want to do it. He came up to Connecticut one fine autumn afternoon. We were still at that time engrossed in *Garden of Earthly Delights*, which was about to reopen. And he said he just didn't feel like doing Hiroshima. And I very airily suggested, "Let's do Vienna at the turn of the century." And the ball was rolling. We were both excited about Vienna as having a very broad spectrum of emotional, visual and musical qualities to work within. It presented a range of lyricism, frivolity, brutality, schizophrenia. It was like a great minestrone.

The next step in the evolution came when Joe Papp introduced me to Charles Mee, who is a historian and who had written a play called *Investigation of a Murder in El Salvador*. Chuck asked what I was doing; and I told him I wanted to do a piece on Vienna. He asked "Do you have a writer?" I said, "I don't know if it'll have a script." And he said, "I'm writing it." He was terribly beguiling and I thought, "Well! All right." I assembled five dancers I had worked with previously, and I brought other performers in and out of rehearsals. I didn't know who I wanted or what I wanted because I didn't know what I was doing.

How do you usually begin your research?

I'll pick a subject and then read about it, look at a lot of art from the period. For *Vienna*, I studied the expressionists: Schiele, Klimt, Kokoschka. I had Chuck spoon-feed me historical details, and we went to the Austrian Institute and looked at documentary films. The boot scene Rob Besserer performed in *Vienna* was from a photograph by Duane Michals of a man with boots on his hands held in the air. I was taken with the image years ago.

And that image stays in some filing cabinet up there in your head?

Yes. And my work comes out of that filing cabinet.

In developing the piece, where did you begin?

The naked duet with the girls was the first thing we rehearsed because I really had a sense of what I wanted to do. Even though the dancers and I were very familiar with each other, the nudity was awkward in the beginning. Then it became nothing. In fact, a train used to go by as we were rehearsing in the studio in the country and the two women would be sitting naked on their sheet by the window waving.

Then I had a six-week creative paralysis during which I was numb. People threatened to quit. I have an easy disposition but when I run dry, I'm dry.

How long had you been rehearsing Vienna *at that point?*

We had been working from November 1983 to January 1984. Lyn gave me a lot of time for *Vienna* and maybe it meant that I could indulge in the paralysis a little longer than usual.

So you had about eleven weeks of rehearsals and then the dry spell hit. What caused that?

We had originally planned to do a historical Vienna, a Vienna with waltzes, Mayerling and Archduke Ferdinand's assassination. Dick Peaslee and I wanted to open with a gorgeous waltz, but as an ensemble the company really looked like mongrels from the pound. I had a six-foot-four guy next to a five-foot-four guy and a five-foot lady dancing next to someone five-eight. I couldn't get any kind of group look. Finally, the piece rejected waltzes, it rejected reality, it rejected historical details, and it became about dreams and the subconscious.

How did you hold the piece together?

There was no story, just impressions. We made maybe a hundred fragments. And I whittled those down to forty-four little pieces that were sewn together like an antique quilt. *Vienna* had no beginning, no middle, no end. You could start it anywhere like a loop. There was a feeling of war at the finish. I had to hear the logic of it, and there is no logic in dreams. Dick and I had some bad scenes, and he would complain, "There's no catharsis in the piece. There's no explosion." And I said, "But so often dreams don't have them." And all the conventional dialogue that Chuck had written was thrown out the window because dialogues really aren't in dreams. People said, "You're throwing out your best material." I heard that over and over. That was because the materials thrown out frequently were things I liked best, the regular dialogues. But they didn't work because they were too real. I usually throw out masses of material during the final process. I find that the only time I have any critical eye, really, is at the end.

Dick Peaslee wrote five waltzes that never made it into *Vienna*. He had the most frustrating time because I work in silence a lot and then the music gets put on afterwards—sort of like taking a naked body into a clothing store. We had these wonderful musicians and they would play two notes and I'd say, "No, this isn't right." Dick is such a gentle, wonderful man and he'd give me this look because the musicians would literally have played only two notes. In *Vienna* I didn't know why I was doing what I was doing most of the time. I'm a very instinctive person and I feel my way around like someone blindfolded in the attic. I stumble the piece into shape and often don't get a vision until late in the process. Then I take out my scissors and my paste, and in the very last moments before a first preview it falls together.

How did you break out of the paralysis in Vienna?

Time pressure. We had an opening date. It was like having a baby. The labor pains had to be gone through and then the piece was out there. The first previews of *Vienna* were an hour and twenty-five minutes long and I knew that they were boring. Without cutting anything, I compressed the show to an hour six minutes by overlapping scenes. A scene in which Lotte Goslar writes in the snow with her cane had originally ended the piece. It was just not working, so I put it together with another scene of two men marching. It was an arbitrary decision, but it pulled the piece together for a conclusion. If I ever get it into rehearsal again, I would like to make the visual counterpoint still more intricate, more multilayered. Things can go on simultaneously without upstaging or distracting. One saw the blocking of the vertical lines against the horizontal lines within a whole framework. And visually, that is what *Vienna* was about—taking in the entire frame all at once.

Technically, how were you able to take forty-four scenes and make them connect seamlessly?

I didn't think of the transitions as transitions. I thought of them as the meat of the material. There was no one thing that was more important than another thing. Obviously, I loved the nude sections, which were for me the most artistically interesting. They were beautiful and tender and distant at the same time. But the scenes all had the same value for me as did the players. There was no star; they were all stars.

Paul Gallo, my lighting designer, is instrumental in solving problems. He and I sat out front while *Vienna* was still ragged and he'd say, "Do you want to see the actors come on or not?" The walls of the set were white and you saw everything. But Paul would often say, "We're using this light here, so why don't you try using that doorway," or "Let him come in a scene earlier and just be there." So Paul helped choreograph some of the transitions. I believe theatre is truly collaborative. When it works nothing can beat it, and it's no longer a lonely act.

I'm very dependent on my designer, Robert Israel. New ideas for the work are always generated by our dialogue. The earth image in *Hunger Artist* came from a telephone conversation we had. He mentioned he had seen a movie set in a prison yard where there were a lot of shallow graves. I said, "That sounds great for our set."

How long did it take to stage Hunger Artist?

I couldn't stage *Hunger Artist* until we were in the dirt itself [the stage was a large earth-pit]. I had nothing when we went into the space three weeks before previews except about twenty-three visual ideas.

What was the audience's reaction to Hunger Artist?

People were baffled and intimidated. The show contained bits of biographical information about Kafka's life and our spin-off interpretation of his stories. The audience's reverence for the piece was odd. Early in the run, they were afraid to respond viscerally, afraid to laugh. And when the company didn't get laughs, the piece lost its lightness. It needed to be a dialogue between the actors and the audience. The cast was tense at first, but after a few weeks they began to loosen up and there were cheers, people laughed so much. Then the cast started *playing* for laughs. My nineteen-year-old son went to see it and called me in the country at eleven-thirty at night and said, "Mom, they were playing it for laughs tonight. You can't let 'em do that."

What is it you're seeking in theatre?

I want to be altered when I go to the theatre, to be changed. I want to feel something strong, and I want to create work that achieves that. I've been lucky. Had I not had the luxury to do my work with plenty of developmental time, I would have gone on to something else or just stopped. This is the way I need to work.

I still worry about everything I put onstage. I still worry about coming off as a jerk. I've got farther to fall now, there's no doubt about it.

GORDON DAVIDSON

G ordon Davidson has a nose for the kind of theatre that attracts heated debate. For more than twenty years, as artistic director of the Mark Taper Forum in Los Angeles, controversy has followed him, as time and again, he presents plays that raise deep questions about the social and political events of our time. Some of these works have surprised and shocked Los Angeles audiences, and no one has been more surprised than Davidson himself at these reactions. How could a charming young man from Brooklyn, with a vision of a theatre that could embrace and enlighten his community, earn the enmity of some of the most powerful citizens of that community?

In 1964, Davidson became the producing head of the Theatre Group sheltered on the campus of the University of California at Los Angeles. The Group had been in existence since 1959, and had been formed in response to an emerging hunger for culture in Southern California. It also answered the need for a theatre outlet for a large pool of actors, directors and technicians who had been displaced to Hollywood from New York when films began to open their doors to theatre-trained artists.

The first play Davidson directed at UCLA was the West Coast premiere of Rolf Hochhuth's *The Deputy*, a drama implicating Pope Pius XII in the murder of six million Jews by the Nazis. He treated the play as a symbolic and universal statement rather than a realistic attack on the Church or a melodramatic memorium. Davidson's production garnered a more positive reaction than the original Broadway production, and it toured nationally for twenty-six weeks.

Two years later, when the Los Angeles Music Center was seeking a resident company for its 750-seat, thrust-stage theatre, dubbed the Mark Taper Forum, Davidson and the Theatre Group were invited to take over the space, and they rechristened themselves the Center Theatre Group.

The Mark Taper Forum opened in 1967 with Davidson's production of *The Devils*, based on Aldous Huxley's book about an order of possessed nuns, *The Devils of Loudon*. The Center's wealthiest conservative Catholic contributors immediately called for his ouster, demanding the closing of both the play and the theatre. They attacked not only Davidson but the Music Center and Dorothy Chandler, who created it. The county board of supervisors considered establishing a local censorship committee. It was chaos. Chandler became Davidson's strongest supporter, and a new group of benefactors stepped in to fund the Center. The conflict ultimately opened the way for the Taper to tackle many other more controversial subjects.

And tackle them they did. Although Davidson has always produced a well-rounded repertoire of modern and classic plays, he tends personally to prefer directing contemporary works, many of which have ruffled feathers— and which also have earned him and the theatre an international reputation.

In 1967, when he was thirty-five, he premiered *In the Matter of J. Robert Oppenheimer*, Heinar Kipphardt's historical play, as translated by Ruth Speirs. The drama was an account of the Atomic Energy Commission's hearing in 1954, during Joseph McCarthy's ascendancy, which branded the physicist a security risk, "a man with fundamental defects in his character." (Nine years later, the agency would bestow on Oppenheimer its greatest honor, the $50,000 Fermi Prize for his "outstanding contributions to theoretical physics and for his scientific and administrative leadership.")

Davidson and Kipphardt came under fire from the real-life participants in the hearings, and their names were changed to fictitious but thinly-disguised ones. In London, a production of the play by the Royal Shakespeare Company was banned by the Lord Chamberlain, the British censor, though the ban was later bypassed through the device of private performances at a theatre club. In New York, Robert Whitehead decided not go forward with the play. It was Jules Irving, then the producing director at the Vivian Beaumont Theater at Lincoln Center, who opened the doors to a remounting of Davidson's production, bringing further success to the play and new life to the ailing Beaumont.

Davidson's greatly admired production of Daniel Berrigan's *The Trial of the Catonsville Nine* in 1969 stirred great opposition from factions in Los Angeles. It was after the courtroom drama had premiered at the Taper, subsequently opened for a long run in New York and was being remounted for the Taper audience that legal action was instituted by a right-wing group calling itself the Citizens Legal Defense Alliance. A suit was brought against the Music Center and the Center Theatre Group for permitting performances of *Catonsville*, which it called "vulgar, obscene, licentious, indecent, immoral, illegal, scandalous and objectionable."

Davidson weathered these and other attacks and went on to direct the premieres of such works as Mark Medoff's *Children of a Lesser God*, Christopher Hampton's *Savages* and *Tales from Hollywood,* Conor Cruise O'Brien's *Murderous Angels*, and to produce such works as the premieres of Luis Valdez's *Zoot Suit* and JoAnne Akalaitis's *Green Card*. In 1975, he directed the debut of Michael Cristofer's *The Shadow Box*, a play he subsequently staged at Long Wharf Theatre and then on Broadway. For his efforts, Davidson received a 1977 Tony award for best direction, while the play was voted best play and walked off with a Pulitzer prize as well.

Davidson is perhaps proudest of the Taper's "New Theatre for Now" series, initially headed by Edward Parone, that develops plays in a workshop atmosphere. In 1969, that program was honored by receiving a Margo Jones award. (The Taper received a second Margo Jones award in 1976.)

Despite controversy, international attention, awards and the wear and tear of twenty years of building the Mark Taper Forum, Davidson remains a transplanted Brooklynite concerned with the health of his profession, his audiences and society. He continues to introduce new experiences to his audiences and is puzzled and frustrated when they resist moving in the new directions he constantly tries to point them. He will not patronize them nor will he be swayed from his particular vision of what theatre should encompass.

■　■　■

What early experiences led you to take up theatre?

My father taught theatre at Brooklyn College so it was always in my blood. I didn't like the struggles my father had to face in order to advance through academia without a Ph.D., but I loved the excitement that he felt for the theatre. He always took me to shows, but it was many years later that I learned that actors had faces, because I only saw the tops of their heads from the second balcony. It was not until the late 1960s, when I started running the Taper, that I first sat in orchestra seats.

Actually, I played Bodo in *Watch on the Rhine* at Brooklyn College when I was eleven, and made myself thoroughly obnoxious by learning every line in the play and correcting everyone. But that was true to Bodo's character. In high school, Brooklyn Tech, I worked for the Board of Education radio station, WNYE, as a sound man—creaking doors, galloping horses. In my fantasies, I could imagine myself doing that for the rest of my life.

But then, I studied electrical engineering for three years at Cornell University and worked for General Electric on a work-study program. That helped me decide that I didn't want to be an applied scientist. I started asking myself what I thought I could do twenty-four hours a day without getting bored. The answer came out "theatre," and I knew that I was going into the theatre to direct.

When I called my father from school—that traditional phone call from college—and told him that I was switching to the theatre, rather than a long silence and a heavy sigh of despair, there was true happiness and excitement, even though he had also been proud that I had wanted to be an engineer. At the same time, he thought that I should get my advanced degrees so that I could "teach," because that was security. The irony is that I have received several honorary degrees, including an honorary doctorate from Brooklyn College. This gave me enormous pleasure because I dedicated it to him. After retiring, he wound up working as a professional actor because I got him an Equity contract playing in the Taper's production of *The Dybbuk*.

I spent a year in graduate study at Western Reserve University and got a Master of Arts, served six months in the Army reserve and then got my first professional job at the American Shakespeare Festival in Stratford, Connecticut, as an apprentice stage manager. That was how I got into theatre, from apprentice to Equity assistant stage manager, to stage manager and production stage manager. One job led to another. The surprise was being offered the job of running the Theatre Group at UCLA under the title of executive coordinator. I'd gone out to be assistant director to John Houseman and production stage manager for his *King Lear*. The job was about to end and I was preparing for a season of stock when John called, saying, "You're going to get a call from Abbott Kaplan," who was the head of University Extension at UCLA. I turned to Judi, my wife, who was in her eighth month with our first child, and told her that I was going to be offered a theatre. My instinct was to say, "No, I'm not an administrator; I'm a director." And as those words were coming out of my mouth, I thought, "Wait a minute! Someone's just offered you a *theatre*."

What helped persuade me was the idea that the job was finite. The prospects for the Theatre Group at UCLA were coming to an end because the arrangement for the use of borrowed performing space was running out. It looked like two years and then back to New York. This was 1964, and the regional theatre had scarcely begun. There was not yet a sense of a national movement. The Guthrie Theater had just opened its doors. But within that initial two-year period while I ran the Theatre Group, everything started to happen. The Music Center was in the process of completion and I didn't realize the import of it. First the Dorothy Chandler Pavilion opened, and at some point it was decided to have two other buildings, one with a proscenium theatre and the other, a round building, with an experimental theatre. So I didn't have to change people's thinking about theatre, I just had to excite them about what it could be.

My last production at UCLA was the first major revival of *Candide*. It was really *Candide* that got me the job at the Mark Taper Forum, along with whatever I had achieved through producing in those initial two years.

The name "Forum" has been very important to me. By the same token, our name—the producing organization which is called Center Theatre Group—is an outgrowth of the Theatre Group at UCLA, whose antecedents came from the feeling of community created by those directors and actors who founded the theatre at UCLA: John Houseman, Robert Ryan, Abbott Kaplan, Jeff Hayden and Lamont Johnson. (Also, the name carries the resonance of the original Group Theatre from the 1930s.) So there's a lineage, a heritage, and I don't want to break that. It's very important to me, especially in an age when everything is used up and nobody is aware of history, of what came before.

Your first production at the Forum, The Devils, ***was highly controversial.***

I didn't do it to be controversial nor did I know it was going to be. I just knew it as a play that had been done by the Royal Shakespeare Company. I didn't think that as a company we were equipped to do Shakespeare, but I wanted to open with a work that dealt with large, humanistic issues. At heart, *The Devils* is Shakespearean in scope. I did not think there was one ounce of controversy in it—it was a little risqué, maybe, but cloaked in respectability and in theatrical and historical authenticity. I didn't really know the community power structure of Los Angeles, although I was living there. Some of the conservative Catholic community leaders were on the county board of supervisors, and the Music Center is on county land. All of these forces— mostly people who had not seen or read the play—came together to attack it. They had "heard" that it was terrible. The great thing was that it unified support behind the theatre in a way that I don't think could have been created had I started less dramatically. It brought people to the defense of freedom of expression in a much better way than any manifesto or proclamation on my part might have. It implied: "Theatre *is* potentially controversial, full of ideas and images and material that may not please everybody." It rallied people, although there are wounds to this day, despite the fact that times have changed.

Over the years, the controversial areas have been politics and sexually explicit language. Although I've been criticized, I've never veered from my path. I don't do anything for the sake of shocking, although there are always people who are convinced that the reason I do these things is to rub people's noses in something.

The interesting thing is that the controversy actually started before I opened the theatre. *The Deputy* was potentially a very controversial play. It criticized Pope Pius's actions during World War II. But I was protected because it was done in a university setting. Chancellor Franklin Murphy buffered any criticism.

I've only directed plays that I've wanted to do. Each one has had its own particular challenge and meaning for me. Plays like *Hamlet* and *Henry IV, Part I* open up worlds of study—the world of Africa and the politics of the United Nations in *Murderous Angels* or the radical Catholic community in *The Trial of the Catonsville Nine*. I do these plays at the Taper in a controlled, protective, supportive, embracing atmosphere. When I've directed elsewhere, especially on Broadway, it's usually been in an atmosphere where it's a fight just to get it on. It's hard enough to do what we do without that.

Children of a Lesser God *was developed at the Taper. How long did you work on that play?*

Children came about rather quickly when we had an available slot in the season because I lost *Strider: The Story of a Horse*, which Bob Kalfin had directed at the Chelsea Theater Center in New York. He got an offer to take *Strider* to Broadway and I substituted *Children*. There have been a couple of occasions when a change made in an emergency, and the acceleration and intensity of that, paid off. In general, I prefer a long gestation time for developing a play. Mark Medoff, the playwright, thrives on pressure and likes to work fast.

At what stage of development was Children *when you discovered it?*

The script had been workshopped at New Mexico State University, but I didn't see it. I read it later. The interesting thing about that play was that my readers, who screen our plays at the Forum, rejected it. And that's one of the constant fears I have, that anyone running an organization lives with, the fear that something good will be passed over. And that's just the name of the game. I have to allow the people who read new plays their independent judgment and strong opinions, and I have to respect that judgment because

I can't read everything. But they also mustn't block me, and they must have that particular insight that permits them to say, "Gordon, you have to pay attention to this play."

How, then, did the play reach you?

I knew Mark and Gil Parker, his agent, and I knew I wanted to read it. Once I did, I felt there was something in it—not that the play was ready to go, but that what it was grappling with was worth it. Finally, that is always a personal choice. There is no way that a reader, or anybody evaluating—including a critic—can relate to that personal thing that has to happen between an artist and material. I just responded to it. Whether I could make it work was something that had to be explored. So we began our journey, working quickly.

There were a lot of technical problems imposed by the play.

Right. We had to accomplish sign language and all of that, and we had from late spring to late summer to work on it.

When you did Children of a Lesser God, *how did you overcome the difficulty of communicating with Phyllis Frelich, who could not hear you?*

You mean my not being able to speak *her* language. It is a two-way street. The interpreter was actually the lesser way of bridging the gulf, while being the most practical. The real gulf was bridged by time, by gaining confidence, by the fact that we are both very expressive people. We really understood each other by way of our passion and the expression of our faces. So what we constantly had to improve and deepen was the actual language communication, the use of sign and the sensitive use of the interpreter. When we rehearsed the play for the first time in L.A., the interpreter was a young man. When we rehearsed for Broadway, Phyllis requested that the interpreter be a woman because she felt that a woman could better convey what she wanted to say. And I liked the idea that when she was interpreted, I heard a female voice. The third time we worked together was on a play called *The Hands of Its Enemy.* By that time, she didn't care whether the interpreter was a man or a woman.

What was the process that went into rewriting Children?

We had a three-or four-month hiatus between the Taper production and re-rehearsing it for Broadway. In that time period, we created a new second act. It's always interesting to try to reconstruct a process—because the process *is* the process. My way of working, to the distraction of some writers, is to ask questions. I'm not a writer myself and I don't try to write the play. I try to provoke and prod and get the writer to respond to the questions that I have about the material, or that I think the writer should be asking himself or herself about the material. The answers can only be supplied by the writer.

What if you don't get the answers that you think you ought?

We live in an imperfect world. And as I get older, I'm realizing more and more that you're not always going to get it right in your lifetime and, to a certain extent, the work itself has some right to be imperfect.

. . . assuming there is such a thing as a "perfect" work. Most of the classic plays are "flawed."

That's the point. So the final judgment is based on how the work connects with an audience, whether it's tapping some of those mysteries that make it work for them. We premiered Lanford Wilson's *Burn This* in 1986. Dramaturgically, it's not a perfect play, but it speaks with a voice that quite mysteriously makes an audience feel wonderful about being in the theatre. Because it is a play in Lanford's style of lyric realism, it defies a certain kind of analysis, as opposed to a play like *Children* or others I've done which, because of their subject matter, are clearly going to either work or not, forgetting about dramaturgy. *Burn This* touches a chord of modern emotional sensibility about the complexity of relationships in the 1980s. But it does it in a more abstract, poetic way than, for instance, *The Catonsville Nine*, which was about the Vietnam War, conscience and what it takes finally to stand up and be counted.

That play came along in 1970, just as there began to be a perception of what our nation had gotten itself into.

It was slightly ahead of its time. I've been lucky over the years in that respect, because you can't necessarily predict when a work will be on the leading edge. At that time, there hadn't been a hundred plays written about Vietnam. One of the biggest problems about directing and producing is that there are many plays that you receive that are interesting, but you've already seen ten of them on the same subject and the latest one may not add any new insights even though it's perfectly valid material.

How did Catonsville *come to your attention?*

On a trip to New York, I was given a set of galleys to a book called *The Trial of the Catonsville Nine* by Father Daniel Berrigan, S.J. I didn't know Berrigan, and only vaguely remembered reading about the Catonsville raid in Maryland in 1964, when the Berrigan brothers protested by burning draft documents. I read Berrigan's organization of the trial transcript on the airplane. It was very poetic and formal. Each person spoke his testimony, then there was a kind of summary. And I started to cry on the airplane. As soon as the plane landed, before I got my luggage, I called Flora Roberts, the agent, and said, "I don't know what this is, Flora, but I have to find a way to do it." She was very excited, and that started the whole journey.

I met with Father Dan Berrigan and started to study what actually happened. I decided to do it in the Taper's "New Theatre for Now" series, essentially with the script that he wrote. Dan's original book was simply each person's testimony organized out of the transcript as poems. When we did it the first time, there was great power, but I could feel the audience begin to wear out. They heard the first testimony, the second, the third. Each one was very moving. Now came the fourth. I could see people thinking, "*The Trial of the Catonsville 'Nine.'* We're up to four—there are five more to go." Based on that experience, I realized that to make that play work I was going to have to reorganize the material. I found Saul Levitt, who had written *The Andersonville Trial*, and he turned out to be a perfect person to do this. He made it his job to try, without writing a single new word, to organize it into a more successful dramatic structure. I remember sitting in his studio down in the Village with pieces of the script all over the floor. We essentially reassembled what Dan had written in a new way.

This, by the way, was set against one of the most exciting production situations of a play I've ever experienced, because between the time that I first met Dan and the time we went into rehearsal, he went underground. Dan had been out on bail awaiting appeal, which was turned down. He was going to have to serve his sentence, and he decided that *not* to serve would be a further escalation of his protest. So he went underground, as did a number of other Catonsville people. Philip, his brother, was captured first, and, finally, Dan. But during the time he was underground, I made contact with him and said, "You know, Dan, usually an author is present for a rehearsal, and I wonder if there's a way for you to say something to the company?" A few days later, a tape arrived—a wonderful tape with his statement for the actors. Dan talked about darkness and light, about the actors' moral force pushing against the darkness. When I played that for the actors, it was an extraordinary experience.

There must also have been a certain element of danger at that point, with Berrigan a fugitive.

Danger?! Here's what happened. My phone was tapped. There was a nondescript repair truck curiously parked in front of my house for the entire duration of the rehearsal and the run of the play. It disappeared once the play closed. A number of the actors were hassled by the FBI, especially one who had some previous liberal and possibly Communist relationships. On the opening night, the FBI was in obvious presence in and around the theatre. I had decided to edit a portion of the tape that Dan had sent from underground, and to begin the play with it, so that when the house lights went out the first words one heard in the darkness were "Hello, this is Father Dan Berrigan speaking to you from the underground. I welcome you to this . . . " Well, everybody sat on the edge of his seat, but the FBI agents in the audience leapt forward because they couldn't take the chance that he wasn't there speaking his lines from the rafters like the Phantom of the Opera.

There have been many special plays like that: *Murderous Angels* about Dag Hammarskjöld and Patrice Lamumba, *Oppenheimer*, *Savages*, *Ghetto*, *Children of a Lesser God*. Those are the ones in which the rehearsal process becomes part of a bigger experience, the creating of a community of actors who are being put in touch with another community, the community of the world of the play, which in turn makes a larger connection to the community of people who come to see it. These plays represent the actors' entry into a world that needs to be experienced, to touch things that are not necessarily common to their everyday experience. This creating of a family and a commonality of experience has involved research, field trips, having resource people come in to talk, things that extend the rehearsal process over and above and beyond the simple reading of the text. Some plays don't require any more than bringing your psyche to bear upon a particular character in particular events—a play about a family, a mother, a father, whatever. In those cases, it may be better for the actors not to go outside the world of the play, just to find it totally within themselves. The plays that I have always been attracted to require a larger investigation.

Since at one time you felt uneasy because you did not have a trained actor's background, what is the method you use with actors?

My basic training and experience came from stage management, and from the influence of such designers as Jean Rosenthal and Henry Kurth. I'm not an actor, but I love and respect actors. It's desirable for a director to have acted, but not necessary. I do think you have to know something about the psychology of human beings and the techniques with which actors work. One of the most difficult things about directing a play is working with actors from a great variety of backgrounds. One of the problems is to try and create a single production style out of this incredible variety. I am not trained in Stanislavsky, the Method, or any one particular viewpoint, but I have an interest in them all, and I try to use those things that pertain to the play and my sensibility about the play—to weld together something that represents a single point of view. Clearly, I feel more comfortable with plays that come out of essentially real behavior and have some sense of immediacy. I have no formal training in high style, but I've learned from observation. From the earliest days, I have always tried to stretch myself by inviting people like Joe Chaikin, Peter Brook, Lee Breuer and JoAnne Akalaitis to come to the Taper to do workshops. All of these artists have experimented with forms that are now very much a part of our theatre. But my métier is related more to taking simple human truths that are inherent in an individual, marrying them to the style of material and letting the actor speak through that. My way of working with actors is to build trust and to challenge expectations—to stretch them.

How do you build that kind of trust?

It's very important to create an atmosphere for actors that is conducive to *their* doing a great deal of the work. I try to elicit from the actors, as I do from everyone else on the team, their contribution to the play. I really do believe that the work is a collaboration, that it's not a judgmental situation, that the actors absolutely have the right to experiment and fail. I feel that there's as much chance that they're going to teach me something about the event or the character as there is that I'm going to be able to teach them.

What do you seek or admire in an actor?

I like actors who try to develop and explore the play (rather than trying to please me), actors who do homework, who don't wait to be told everything, who are flexible, willing to make changes. They need to try, because I don't direct every pinkie move, every turn of the head. My agenda is the totality of the piece, and I bring a strong sense of timing and of how to get where we're going. I have a clock ticking in me that says, by now we should be here, and by now we should be at another place. While I don't try to force something, it's my responsibility to get the production and the actors up to a certain point for the first run-through, the first tech, the first audience, opening night. One of the happiest rehearsal times is the previews. Our productions have always had ten previews. Most theatres have two or three and then they open. I made up my mind that I would create a preview audience, which was unheard of when we started, and we've created one of considerable numbers. It's during previews that I shape the show. It's enough time for known plays. For new plays I would love a bit longer.

Do you come back to a production after it has opened?

Absolutely, although because I run an institution and have put everything else on hold during rehearsals, what often happens is that once we open I have to plunge into other things and don't get back as much as I want.

A play goes through a gestation cycle. I always feel that a show, once it opens, should play for a week or so without the director around, and then, in the ideal world, it should go back into rehearsal again. I don't often get to do that. There's a time about the second week of the run when growth has taken place and you can do a certain kind of work. At about six weeks, which is usually when you are coming to the end of a run, there's another good period for work. I've been fortunate in having had experience with some long runs like *Children* and *Shadow Box*. I've noticed that at the three-month period, the growth and solidity start to deteriorate a bit and you have to find a new way of getting it back on track.

How have you learned to communicate, to collaborate with designers?

When I was a young stage manager I worked for Martha Graham, and I think that I learned more about the theatre from being in her presence than I could from any directing teacher. I will never forget going to a preliminary design meeting about a new ballet that she was going to choreograph, based on the Phaedra legend. She summoned Isamu Noguchi, who was going to do the set, Jean Rosenthal, the lighting designer, and me. Now, having attended a number of design meetings in the past, I expected a certain procedure to be followed. I had my pad and I knew I would learn from what was being said where the platforms had to be, or the doors or what have you. To my surprise, delight, puzzlement and amazement, they never talked about the ballet. My memory of it is that we sat down in Martha's apartment on the East Side. She said, "I'm thinking of doing a new ballet based on the Phaedra legend." And then she reached over to the table and picked up a rock. She handed it to Noguchi. It had an interesting shape and he felt it. He gave it to Jean Rosenthal. She felt it. I looked at it and gave it back to Martha. And that was the end of the meeting! I was still sitting there waiting for this conversation. Noguchi went off and designed this extraordinary set. Jeannie lit it. It was a wonderful ballet. To this day, I still don't know how that happened, although I've occasionally experienced that level of communication among artists who have worked together over a long period of time. It's the ability to communicate very specifically about something through a certain amount of indirection.

Over the years, I've had some very important relationships with designers. The most important were with Peter Wexler, Sally Jacobs, Ralph Funicello, Ming Cho Lee and Doug Stein. The best work gets at the essence of something and defines it. Out of that emerges a design and, therefore, a concept.

How can you make that process of discovery with a designer work?

Well, you can't make it work every time. You can't make anything like that work every time. When creative people get together they don't always make it happen. I know the longer the gestation time, discussion time, the longer you have to live with it, the better. It's amazing. Sometimes you can press the right buttons and release the right ideas, and other times you don't get it.

When Doug Schmidt and I did the Benjamin Britten opera *A Midsummer Night's Dream* for the Los Angeles Opera in 1988, we needed to find the right visual language for the piece and we did that by looking at a lot of paintings. Lewis Brown joined us for costumes, and we all agreed that it was necessary to get the right visual metaphors going. The mechanical detail would follow, once we'd solved the problems of how you got from one place to another. We settled on a common visual stimulus, which in this case was a Victorian Pre-Raphaelite painter. Once we hit on that, ideas started to flow. But the production didn't really fall into place until Doug constructed the model, because it *lived* in three dimension and not in the sketches. In contemporary design, more often than not, models have become the key method of expression. In an earlier time, sketching, painting renditions were principally used because it was the period of proscenium and drops.

One of my great dreams is to be able to evolve a design *from* the work rather than conceptualizing it in advance and pouring the actors into it like so much liquid into a vessel. Actors have a way of creating a shape within an environment that is given them, if you allow enough freedom for them to do it, but it would be more interesting to shape that surround to fit what has been discovered during the rehearsal exploration.

Did you ever come close to that kind of experience?

I've tasted it. In our production of Joshua Sobol's Holocaust play, *Ghetto*, in 1986, the company tuned in on the essence of that play, possessed it, filled it out, guarded and protected it from themselves and me and others.

What do you mean when you say "protected" it?

We are sometimes our own worst enemies when we work on something. We try to polish it and make it right, give it shape and rhythm and a point of view that is sometimes pressured by an external such as opening night. It's rare when the actors, designers and stage managers have such an investment in the material that they become the guardians of it as well as the communicators. They protect it from their own and one another's bad habits, from the influence and seductiveness of an audience. When you create that spirit, you get a level of work that money can't buy. You can't get it all the time because certain plays don't demand it. And even when they are working, certain plays keep you at a distance.

Over the years, you've directed a fair amount of music theatre and opera. Is there a basic difference in the way you approach directing a musical piece as opposed to a play?

Music can be extremely stimulating and rewarding because it often transcends the problems of dramatic structure and illuminates in a more abstract and, therefore, profound way. I have tried to bring my knowledge of the theatre to opera in order to make the work have a greater dramatic sense. That's really common these days with young directors. They want to strengthen the libretto and its marriage to the music through better staging and interpretation, as opposed to just presenting the voice.

My first professional job directing an opera was in the 1950s. It was a little-known work called *The Barrier*, with text by Langston Hughes and a score by Jan Meyerowitz. It was based on Hughes's 1935 play *Mulatto*. The opera was short-lived but the original play had been a scandalous success because it was about miscegenation. Hughes was alive when we did the opera, and he told me that although black actors were performing on the stage with white actors during the play, which was presented in a time when there was still great discrimination in New York, the black actors were not invited to the opening night party—shocking things like that.

The Barrier was performed at New York University. In the first rehearsal, while we were getting to know one another, the music director, Maurice Peress, went over the score with the singers, and I realized that they had all been working on their vocal parts and didn't have a clue as to what the opera was about. So I stopped the rehearsal and said, "Before we get into the staging, I think we ought to read the libretto." They had never heard of anything like that. And it isn't easy to read a libretto. But I said, "Let's try it, even though a lot of it may not make sense or will sound like doggerel." I wanted everyone to have some common experience with the *piece*—not only with the story line and what was being stated in the arias, but what was being said in the duets, trios and quartets. This is important, because the singer tends to learn only his vocal line and doesn't know what the other people are singing. This process was an extraordinary revelation to those singers.

Subsequently, I did a whole series of simple stagings of well-known operas in Corpus Christi, Texas, again with Maurice Peress, who had become conductor of the Corpus Christi Symphony. We did a *Carmen*, a *Boheme* and a *Così fan tutte*. We had no money. I used singers from the City Center Opera company—Frank Poretta, John Reardon and the then relatively unknown Norman Treigle and Beverly Wolf—wonderful singers who had acting potential. So I began exploring opera in which the emphasis was on the story being told with clarity. It was not about production or sets.

I direct a musical or an opera every couple of years, and then I vow "never again," primarily because the system for producing opera is very frustrating. This is partly due to the lack of training of the singers, and partly to the lack of rehearsal time. Even if you have rehearsed for a suitable period, one of the great tyrannies of opera is that the technical and preparation time for presentation is truncated. In the theatre, the dress rehearsal marks the beginning of a whole new phase of work that then extends over another learning period from the dress rehearsals and the previews and so on. In opera, the dress rehearsal is really the first performance, and you can barely give notes because there is a day off and then with no further rehearsal the singers come in and it opens. Technically, you may be able to make some adjustments, but it's a ludicrous system. You get it on through sheer dint of effort, and the knowledge that somehow people will find their way. But you never get to refine anything, let alone make radical changes. Fundamentally, you have to wait until the next time you do the opera to cash in on how much you've learned. It's a serious and frustrating problem.

Have you had any experiences with opera where your input was closer to what you do in theatre?

Thea Musgrave composed and wrote the libretto for a new opera, a wonderful piece called *Harriet*, about Harriet Tubman and the underground railroad, that I staged in Virginia in 1985. I was interested in working on it because she came to me very early in the development, while she was still composing it. I was interested in the subject, but didn't know much about Tubman, so it gave me an opportunity to do research. It was very difficult to work on because there was always a gap between seeing the work on the libretto and finally hearing the music. It was part of a process that went on for a couple of years during which there were some radical changes in thinking. We went into rehearsal just as Thea completed the music. It meant I had to design it before the score was finished and I didn't really hear the full score until the first rehearsal. And no amount of study of the libretto can reveal an opera. It's revealed *through* the music, and you have to get really familiar with that score.

Are you trained to read music?

I have some knowledge, but I stopped playing the piano too early in life. So the more sophisticated the piece the more I need to have it explained. That's why I like to work closely with a music director. You don't often get to do that, because music directors are not often trained to work that way, or are too busy doing many other things. They do what they do and you do what you do and you're lucky when you meet somewhere across the orchestra pit.

I feel that of all artists working in opera, the director is the one for whom it is the hardest to complete his task, because of the way the system is structured.

At one point in the middle of rehearsals for *Harriet*, having made a real discovery about the piece, I suggested a rearrangement of the material. And there was absolute panic. Because it wasn't just rearranging material, it was staying up three nights in a row to reorchestrate every single part and to recopy. And since it wasn't a big-budget production where we could have seven copiers standing by, Thea was doing the orchestrations and the copying herself.

Harriet wasn't running in repertory, so we rehearsed it more or less like a play. However, we still had to get it on the stage quickly, and at the dress rehearsal the leading singer broke her ankle and we had to make amazing compromises in the first performance. We did the usual handful of performances, and I then wanted to go back to work on it. But there's been no opportunity.

Aside from those serious manpower problems of copying, how difficult is it to restructure a musical piece?

You can often make amazing cuts in music. It can collapse like magic. That's very exciting. You say you want to move this to "here" and that to "there." The composer looks and sees that this ends on an E flat and that begins on a such-and-such, and says he can do it. You can literally take a whole scene out and turn things around much the way you can with film. It's harder to do that in a play. The structure of music is mathematical and precise and therefore certain grafts can happen. Sometimes it's very hard to make a cut in a play because the way in which it's structured doesn't lend itself to that. The other side of it is that sometimes there are certain things in music you simply can't cut. It's similar to a piece of poetry where one moment builds upon another and you can't go in and chop out something because it would be like a rape. Many a playwright would probably say that is also true of the writer's word.

Is there a different approach to working with singers versus actors?

The problem is deep for many singers. It's a free-lance life. They go around from opera company to concert hall or what-have-you, and they're worked over by many, many music directors and conductors, let alone stage directors. The director is working to get something and doesn't understand that the reason he isn't getting it has nothing to do with motivation or understanding the role or anything like that. It's simply that the singer is protecting his or her voice. Some directors ask singers to stand on their heads, some don't pay any attention to them, and they get very mixed signals. So whom are they to trust, to rely on? I've discovered how strong the role played by their vocal coach or teacher is to their work. The coach is the one who supplies the continuity, the advice, is their semi-psychiatrist, semi-agent.

When you premiered Leonard Bernstein's Mass, was that considered to be an opera or a musical?

That was worked upon as you would a musical show, although Lenny didn't want it to be considered a show. It was subtitled "A Theatre Piece." We had a long and intense collaboration—Lenny, myself and Stephen Schwartz, who did lyrics with Lenny. There was a lot of give-and-take, although the primary force was Lenny. It was hard to shape that piece, partly because Lenny was ambivalent about whether it was a show or a liturgical concert. If there are sections in a musical show or theatrical piece that are not working, or seem to hold up the action, there is a tendency to try to cut them. You don't tend to do that in a musical composition. That was the source of tension in rehearsing *Mass*. We tried cutting a couple of sections at the first and only preview. The cuts helped and everyone got excited. Then Lenny said, "I want it back in," and we put it back in. I understood why, but I think the piece suffered dramatically as a result. This same argument is heard about films in which ten seconds are cut and the director says, "But the essence of the production is in those ten seconds!" And for them, it is.

Is the purpose of the opera director to focus the audience on the story or the music?

I saw a dress rehearsal of Giorgio Strehler's *The Abduction from the Seraglio* when he did it at La Scala. He controls the lighting in a very special way, using a lot of side and back lighting. You often don't see the faces. Every time he came to an aria, as opposed to the recitative, he would take the front light off the singers. I realized that what he was doing was forcing one to listen to the music in a different way. By not seeing the singers' faces, it made you listen to the music. The arias are definitely about the music and not about interacting. You're not going to understand an aria anyway, whether it's in your native language or not, because words in music are created with the vowels, and understanding is communicated through consonants. Therefore, the force of the aria is communicated through the music and through the interpretation of the musical line. So the idea of lowering the lights during an aria is an interesting idea. Again, like most interesting ideas, if everyone starts doing them then they're no longer interesting.

Do you think that technique could work with the texts of the classic plays?

It's conceivable that if you wanted the audience to listen to "To be or not to be" in a new way, some way other than contemplating the Dane, you might indeed use that technique. A critic called Strehler's Los Angeles production of *The Tempest* at the Olympic Arts Festival, "dim." He missed the point. There may not have been enough light to suit the critic, but it wasn't dim. The director made the choice not to use front light. The difficulty with removing lighting in spoken drama is that the way we understand the words is often through seeing. I have that problem constantly on the thrust stage with full lighting because there are moments when an actor's back is to a portion of the audience. It sometimes impedes comprehension. Lack of hearing in older people often has just as much to do with failing eyesight.

It's been said that you can't have great theatre without a great audience.

I have a sign on the wall of my office that says that. I'm not sure I totally believe it.

Do you think it's possible to develop a great audience?

I have changing views on that. Over the years I've committed myself to the building of an audience, and I like our audience; we don't talk down to them. Although I do worry that they are growing older with me, I have a sense of family. And I get the most amazing letters, some of which depress me when they say how much they hated a particular play. They talk about the plays they have seen, and it disturbs me that they don't seem to have built a vocabulary that helps them grow to another point where they should be. If they didn't have a history of seeing a lot of work then I wouldn't be angry. But I got a letter from someone who was very disturbed about the first three plays of the current season, not for any moral reasons, and then he talked about some of the plays he did like. And those were some of the worst plays we've ever done. I don't mind that he liked those plays, but I can't put it together with the criticism. It shows that there isn't a real consistency of taste or values.

Aren't you referring to objections raised about plays that are presented in a nonrealistic style, that affect audiences on a deeper level and that can sometimes make them feel uneasy?

It's really no different from a person who stands in front of a photo-realistic painting and says, "This is what I like because I understand it," as opposed to an expressionistic painting. There is an audience for that kind of abstract work. You see it at dance and new wave concerts. In theatre it has been harder to develop that audience, because the approach has not been consistent. You will find an audience for a particular artist or a company like Mabou Mines. What's hard to do is to take an audience like the Taper's, or any institution that produces a wide variety of work, and build catholicity of taste. I understand that. If I'm dealing with thirty thousand subscribers, I can't get every one of them to grow in the same way. But I am puzzled and worried about people who on some consistent level and in some consistent quantity are not able to build on their experience. I have discovered that the possibility of such growth is more theoretical than actual.

We've had a wonderful ten-year relationship with Professor Homer Swander from the University of California at Santa Barbara. It started when he brought some students to a preview. It grew as he added alumni from the area, until his group became so large that we added a matinee—the UCSB performance—or, as I call it, the Homer Swander Memorial Matinee, even though he's very much with us. In the early days, that was our best audience. They prided themselves on that, and wore T-shirts and buttons that said "We're the best audience." And they *were*, because they came before the performance and heard about the play: sometimes the talk was performance-oriented, sometimes free-associated, sometimes it dissected the text. That would give them the tools. Then they'd see the play and attend a post-performance seminar with the actors and the director, and then they'd have a picnic. The audience and the actors would meet on a new level. It was wonderful and rich, and I thought maybe this was a key to how people should go to the theatre in the future. Not everybody, because it is about as long as a marathon. What has fallen apart, and it raises some serious questions, is the post-performance discussion. All of them have become amateur critics. Rather than asking interesting and provocative questions about the work to illuminate what they saw, they say things like, "We didn't like this," or "None of the actors were any good except *you*." They say it right to the actors, and I won't tolerate that. The preview period is too delicate, and I won't subject any of the artists to that. It's not healthy.

What has caused this change in the way they view the work?

Self-satisfaction, smugness, the loss of a sense of adventure. Sometimes a little knowledge is hurtful. This has nothing to do with the intelligence of the audience, but their sense of themselves has changed. Rather than being open, they are semisophisticated. So this particular marriage we've been trying to develop between the creative people and the audience is in jeopardy. We're trying new ways of introducing new audiences at previews.

Do you think this reaction from audiences will tempt you to choose less dangerous work in the future?

I've always felt that the theatre has a function in society which goes beyond entertainment. It includes that, but should we settle for fun when we could be pushing the boundaries of man's psyche? The arts are perhaps the best media for expanding those boundaries. It's about finding a way to tell some truths. In the theatre I feel I can express something both to satisfy my own soul and to share it with my fellow citizens. That demands being more creative, going deeper and taking more chances.

ROBERT FALLS

F ollowing the lead of their New York Off-Off Broadway counterparts, in the early 1970s young people in Chicago began making theatres out of loft spaces and garages. Just as the explosion of creativity in New York in the late 1960s had become a crucible for the development of directors such as Richard Foreman, Marshall Mason and Garland Wright, so the Off Loop activity in Chicago gave rise to new Midwestern talents. Prominent among the Chicago directors was Robert Falls.

The early conflict in Falls's life was between politics and the theatre. He grew up on a farm in downstate Illinois, near a town which he describes as, ". . . the last picture show: 1100 people—and the local movie theatre had closed in 1959." When he had to make college plans, his last-minute decision was to go into the theatre program at the University of Illinois. After graduation, he soon gravitated to Chicago's Wisdom Bridge Theatre, where he was to become artistic director.

What followed for Falls was ten years of sustained directing and the building of a reputation that would land him the top spot at Chicago's venerable Goodman Theatre in 1985. The artistic directorship of the Goodman would seem to have been a natural and obvious career progression for this young Chicagoan, but many boards of directors at institutions the size of the Goodman have passed over a respected local director in favor of a more exotic choice from outside the city. Indeed, Falls was almost eliminated by the Goodman's search committee when he suggested, perhaps somewhat naively, that he'd like to interview each board member to ascertain *their* commitment to the theatre.

Assuming the Goodman reins at age thirty-three, Falls joined the ranks of a new generation of young artists directing major institutions—Des McAnuff at La Jolla Playhouse, Garland Wright at the Guthrie Theater, Mark Lamos at Hartford Stage Company, and Gregory Mosher, who left the Goodman to take over the Lincoln Center Theatre Company—almost all of whom grew up entirely within the nonprofit theatre movement.

Falls's directing style, like the city that spawned him, is full of energy and visual excitement. His interest in politics influences his choices and his creativity in working with actors has attracted Chicago's top talent, a group that has gained national visibility. Falls is equally at home directing Dario Fo's *We Won't Pay! We Won't Pay!*, Tennessee Williams's *A Streetcar Named Desire* or Bertolt Brecht's *Mother Courage and Her Children*, as well as new plays such as John Olive's *Standing on My Knees* and *Careless Love*.

Falls worked hard to maintain the aesthetic he developed at Wisdom Bridge when he moved to the Goodman. "I tried to hold on to the rough 'n' tumble Off Loop sensibility I was born out of. I was afraid it would be easy to fall into a certain institutional mediocrity. At the same time, no one really wants to offend. Wisdom Bridge was a small theatre formed out of my own personality. Starting at the Goodman, with an audience that had been built over sixty years, I had to work a little harder to be true to myself. I had to spend more time than I anticipated learning the ways around certain political issues of boards. Frankly, I didn't mind because it is a trade-off. I have no desire to be free. I don't think that I can make the same kind of happy living for myself being a free-lance director. If you want to direct the plays you choose and work with the artists you want, if you have a vision worth realizing, protecting and supporting, then you must be the frontline communicator to the board and to the community."

One of the reasons Falls has adapted well to his new environment is his ability to move easily from working in intimate theatre spaces to the large main stage at the Goodman. Indeed, within a season he may direct one or more Goodman productions that are conceptually large-scale and then move to a small Off Loop theatre as a guest director. This kind of collaborative rapport that Falls has developed with various theatres in Chicago is almost unheard of in other theatre centers.

Falls is a product of Midwest sensibilities and Chicago energy.

I was born on the prairie and the milk of its wheat, the red of its clover,
the eyes of its women, gave me a song and a slogan. . .

Chicago. . . They tell me you are wicked and I believe them, for
I have seen your painted women under the gas lamps luring the farm
boys. . .

Carl Sandburg

■   ■   ■

What is it in the work of certain directors, who appear from time to time,
that captures our attention?

The directors who stay in our memory are those who have had some ability
to capture perfectly the times they are in. It's the same for playwrights. It
has to do with somehow being true to yourself within a certain awareness of
pop culture—the melding of music and art with your ability to synthesize
what is going on currently.

The first director I was aware of was Elia Kazan. I grew up on a farm
reading about directors. In his films, one could see the legacy of his theatre
work. The second time I remember being aware of a director was while sitting
in a dentist's office as a child, looking at a *Life* magazine article about *Marat/
Sade*. Suddenly, seeing those incredible color photographs of Peter Brook's
production—the pouring of the red, white and blue blood, the heads, the
guillotine scene and the stylized make-up—I must have been all of ten years
old, but I was so struck.

It seems that Kazan was the complete director of the 1950s and Brook
the quintessential 1960s director. In the 1980s, the directors I responded to
most were my peers in the nonprofit theatre.

Coming from a small town in the Midwest where there was not much oppor-
tunity to see stage directors at work, how did you learn your craft?

I learned to direct in much the same way a painter learns to paint, which is
by imitating. To a certain extent, my learning how to direct plays was a process
of walking in the footsteps of other directors. I have been very lucky in that
I have been able to direct a lot of plays. I remember that Adrian Hall talked
about learning to direct in the summer stock system, where one might direct
a play a week. I did that with the American plays of the 1950s, Inge, Miller,
even musicals.

Where was that?

When I was at the University of Illinois in Champaign-Urbana. I ran a summer
theatre program there, and was always working in summer stock when I wasn't

learning how to direct in a formal program. The first full-length play I ever directed had been Michael Weller's *Moonchildren* when I was a sophomore. Many of the people who were in that production subsequently moved to Chicago and, when I was a senior, they asked if I would redirect it professionally there. It was 1975, and *Moonchildren* was the second play in the St. Nicholas Theater space following the world premiere of David Mamet's *American Buffalo* six months earlier. It was one of the first times in Chicago where a play that had opened in a small theatre had the ability to run for a long time.

So I graduated with a degree in playwriting and directing, without really knowing what that was going to mean. And I found my way to Chicago, where *Moonchildren* was playing. While it was running, I tried to pursue free-lance jobs but there weren't any, because at that time a number of young resident companies were springing up with their own directors: St. Nicholas, Victory Gardens, Steppenwolf, Wisdom Bridge, Body Politic. All of them had roots in the Second City, the improvisation troupe.

How did your move to Wisdom Bridge come about?

I was reading scripts for David Mamet at the St. Nicholas Theater. Wisdom Bridge was a company in which an old friend of mine was acting. Their artistic director was ill, and I was invited to direct a production. I went up to this space, which was an absolute hole in the wall. They had no money, of course, and they had this funky unit set built out of doors and bed frames. They had no lights. And I looked at it and said, "Well, the only play you can do on this set would be *Of Mice and Men*," because it looked like barns, and that play can be done in overalls and blue jeans. We produced the whole play for about fifty bucks. Bare light bulbs were hung over the stage and they became lights in the bunkhouse, or they could be elevated to become stars in the sky. It was enough of a success that I was asked if I would be artistic director. I didn't entirely know what an artistic director did. Had I known, I probably wouldn't have said yes.

What did being artistic director mean?

Very simply, in a theatre like Wisdom Bridge, if the plays weren't any good then no one was going to see them. My training was completely practical. I had to direct "hit" plays for the first four or five years. If I did not direct "hit" plays, I would not have a career. It was a little theatre that had to get a lot of attention and exist completely on box office. I think it was the late Liberace who said, "Without no show, there ain't no business." Even with a classic like *Hamlet*, one was continually searching to make the most striking choice.

When I began directing at Wisdom Bridge, I really had no idea what you did as an artistic director, other than re-create the plays you like most for a new audience. So I would redo a Sam Shepard play, a Marsha Norman play, an Arthur Kopit play. The breakthrough came for me when I realized that I had a point of view that was completely unique.

How did you become aware that you had something singular to contribute to a play?

At age twenty-three I was directing my first professional production of *The Tempest* at the Court Theatre in Chicago. I had already directed it as a student when I was eighteen. I thought I knew what the play was about and I went into rehearsal. In the course of working on it, I found that it was about something entirely different. Now a lot of this was because I was falling in love with an actress who was in the play, one of the sprites. There was a tremendous sense of love and forgiveness and learning how to get over it and move into some new areas—scary areas. Prior to that, I had never thought of a director as being an artist, but simply as another craftsperson who would sort of get the play on. Suddenly, while working on this play, I found that falling in love had opened me up. For the first time, I understood what saying "I love you" was about in a very open, completely honest, dangerous way. I found myself actually being able to stage during the day what was happening to me at night after rehearsals. I mean literally—images, ideas. From there, I decided that directing was really an act of risk, putting yourself on the line, completely testing how you feel about everything—love, marriage, race, hate, forgiveness, death, life. If you start really trying to respond to how you feel, then you can start encouraging everyone you work with to have direct responses. It becomes a very personal interpretation. I'm probably the only director of *The Tempest* to identify completely with the characters of Ferdinand and Miranda. When you look at Liviu Ciulei's and Giorgio Strehler's productions, you realize that their identification is with Prospero.

Did your breakthrough merely intensify the images you already had of the play, or did it literally change the interpretation of the work?

It changed the concept. It's always amazed me how directing is that curious blend of having a very strong concept of what the play will ultimately look like when it's in front of an audience, absolute pictures just like a film director, and then experimenting with the working out of those images that can ultimately be realized by the company. I will know what the whole play is going to look like. But within that I allow for the actor's impulse. My initial interest in theatre came from acting and I have continued to act in film and television.

What does keeping in touch with that acting impulse do for your directing?

The wonderful thing about acting is it continually puts you in touch with the actor's world from the other side of the bench. My first work experience in Chicago was with David Mamet and a group of directors who founded the St. Nicholas Theater. I can vividly remember auditioning for a radio version of *The Water Engine* that John Madden was directing. I was up for a role along with Steven Schachter, who was then director of the theatre. We auditioned with each other in the room, and after the audition we got up and Steve walked into the door—that whole thing of when an actor is concentrated and completely disoriented. As a director, it's good to remember the horrible awfulness of an audition.

Does it increase your trust to risk giving over creative freedom to an actor?

Absolutely. My one beef with a certain kind of European director, and even American avant-garde directors, is that I don't believe they understand acting. I'm interested in defining what it is to be an American actor doing Shakespeare or Brecht or Molière or Ibsen. The experiment comes in creating a conceptual structure—but when you are working on the floor of the rehearsal room, to allow for complete spontaneity and a work that can change from night to night. Part of me is out there to help the actor respond in an absolutely improvisational way. After I come back and see a play five weeks later—that awful five weeks later when a play is sort of set into certain patterns—I go back into rehearsal and completely change motivations, because it's that deadening sense of repetition that kills me when I go to the theatre.

Do you use a lot of improvisation in creating your work?

Not away from the text, but an enormous amount of improvisation using the text. Ferdinand and Miranda's love scene, for example, is entirely open to a number of interpretations. It can change from night to night. And, in fact, I think it should. It is a two-character scene that the actors should enjoy complete freedom to play however they feel it.

All right. So you are allowing the actors freedom on a moment-to-moment basis. That implies that the big picture is yours.

A lot of directing is looking after what the play is about on a larger metaphorical level, in a larger visual or physical sense. Then what happens is like drawing a map dot to dot. I know where all the dots are, and an actor can zigzag getting to the next dot or he can take a straight line. The very best actors are the ones who grab the freedom and run with it. It's not to say that there aren't many moments in the course of a production where I want something exactly the same way each time.

In your experience, have American actors been capable of taking the freedom, or does it terrify them?

They are certainly capable of experimenting in an emotional improvisational sense. But there's no denying that the ability to stand on stage, plant your two feet and trust in just letting the verse come out is difficult.

Where have today's Chicago actors trained? What has influenced them?

This city that I grew up in has produced some extraordinary actors and it has produced a certain style. I had an acting teacher named Edward Kaye-Martin who was the major influence on me as an actor. He's the one who taught me about improvisation and actors having freedom onstage. I learned from him about courage and using your fear in your work and always striving. He had a saying, "Go for the gold," which means always make the richest choice.

Not the most obvious choice.

No, the scariest choice, the juiciest choice. There were two great and simultaneous influences on American theatre and American acting in the 1950s. One was the Actors Studio in New York, which is the one everybody knows about, and the other was the Second City in Chicago. If we look at contemporary theatre today, television or film, a lot of it is influenced by writers, actors and directors who got their start at Second City. It's performance-oriented and improvisational. It's not of "the Method." It's very real and may seem naturalistic, but actually it isn't. It's heightened, exploded, aware of the audience. It's known as rock 'n' roll theatre. The production maintains the same awareness of an audience that a rock 'n' roll band has.

Then a theatre's or an actor's approach to the work really is influenced by the community, and there's not necessarily the same style sensibility nationwide.

That's exactly right. There definitely is a Chicago way of doing things. There's an honesty and an immediacy to the work.

Who are some of the artists outside of Chicago who have influenced you?

The avant-garde has been highly influential on my work, choreographers like Merce Cunningham, Laura Dean and David Gordon. From the beginning there was Stuart Sherman and Richard Foreman and the whole body of work of the Wooster Group and Mabou Mines. In Chicago there is really no avant-garde in the worlds of music, dance or art. No matter how interesting it may be to Chicagoans, they don't have much tolerance for it, and if they think the emperor has no clothes, then, by God, the emperor has no clothes. Chicago is "hog butcher to the world," and it's a real meat and potatoes, straightforward city. My sensibilities were formed, on the one hand, out of that, and on the other hand out of an appreciation and understanding of the avant-garde. The strength of Chicago is that it's a completely unpretentious, direct kind of town. You have to grab people's attention, you have to be entertaining. There is an undeniable energy and life force to the best of the work. What I'm interested in doing is harnessing that energy, testing that energy against great classic plays.

One of the classics you tackled with some success in 1984 was Hamlet.

Hamlet is truly the great barometer of its time. For me, wanting to do that play grew out of a real fascination with young people. My brother, at the time, was twenty-one. We are only separated in age by a decade, so I tended to assume that everyone who was twenty-one was exactly like I was. It sank in that I had little to do with the people of that age. Their complete lack of political sense and the whole obsession with style and with what was emptiest about society was quite fascinating. I asked my brother and some of his friends about this. What emerged was a sense of, "Why do anything? We're all gonna be killed by the bomb anyway." They hadn't thought much about politics, beyond, "Why bother?" Why bother to consider changing a world that can't be changed? It was cynical, nihilistic. "So party down. It's all corruption."

Suddenly, when I reread *Hamlet*, every line in that play talked about a younger generation and its disbelief in the older generation. For me, Hamlet instantly became a young man out of college dressed in the newest fashions who had spent his entire life with drugs, rock and roll, women, college. Rather than being "the sensitive youth," he was a man who wouldn't grow up and didn't see any necessity in politics. Suddenly he was confronted by the ghost of his father, and with making a political act.

How did you start to develop the production?

Wisdom Bridge used to run various workshops. I had seen Aidan Quinn do Shakespeare in a class. I finished reading *Hamlet* with him in mind. We got together and spent about a year and a half developing it.

What was your point of departure in thinking about the play?

It suddenly came to me, in the middle of the night—what if one imagined that John F. Kennedy had been murdered by Lyndon Johnson who had then married Jackie to reunite the country, on that plane coming back from Dallas? What if John-John, who is twenty years old, came back from Harvard to the ranch in Texas for a barbecue, surrounded by the new Administration? The thought was just a little modern exercise.

But it pointed you in a direction.

And you don't have to look too far to see a White House corrupted by intrigue and politics. The production started to come together in very immediate terms. Aidan was about twenty-four at the time, and very sensitive to his generation. He'd never done a Shakespearean role and was a modern man with modern responses, even though he is a rather rough and tumble west side Chicagoan. People react to him as if he is a star, and he started to come to grips with what young Hamlet is all about in terms of being a prince. One of the great difficulties in doing Shakespeare is to come to grips with what a prince and a king are. In American society, they have very little meaning.

How did you explore the play visually?

I began working with my production designer, Michael Merritt, with whom I had collaborated on a number of other projects. He was designing sets, lights and costumes. We began talking about *Hamlet* down through the ages and looking at various productions that were interesting. We discussed the times we live in—politics, religion, art—just looking for comparisons. An early image, which I think typifies the production, was after the rampart scene when Claudius says, "Though yet of Hamlet our dear brother's death the memory be green. . . " He's making a speech to the court. Well, it reminded both of us of Gerald Ford's speech on television after the resignation of Nixon, when he basically said, "Look, here we are, and we've got to get past Watergate and move forward." Claudius's speech was not that different. So it became obvious to us that it was a political speech staged for the cameras. Above and all around the audience were video cameras. The perception of King Claudius was of a contemporary politico who understood the power of the media. What the audience saw onstage was a darkened room somewhere in a hotel, prior to a victory celebration. And Hamlet came out very slowly and sat on a folding metal chair in the corner. In the next room was this victory speech by the new king, and we were seeing it on monitors at the same time as we were hearing it. It was every press conference that we had ever seen in our lives, full of those resonant images, along with a smiling Gertrude waving in the background, looking adoringly at her husband surrounded by his aides.

You know, once you arrive at an image with the designer, you start looking at other investigations of it. One was at the end of the play when we were trying to deal with the nature of tragedy and violence. I happened to turn on television while I was working on the play, and there was that massacre at a McDonald's restaurant in Southern California. And it struck me how desensitized we all are to tragedy. There is no such thing in our modern society as tragedy without television cameras on the scene either before it happens or moments after. Our entire lives have been filled with images of carnage and disaster where a camera has just arrived.

So Fortinbras entered into the room of the massacre at the end of *Hamlet* accompanied by a full barrage of cameras and newsmen. The sword fight was done realistically in a locked room. It had been quite brutal. Hamlet and Laertes started going after each other with swinging swords and swiping at each other so that numerous innocent bystanders were caught. It was controversial. Hamlet was caught in this dilemma of actually slicing the face of an innocent maid standing there. The whole moment was about the pacifist who suddenly decided the only way he could solve violence was by entering into violence, and, of course, everything went completely wrong. When Fortinbras broke into the room, there was an absolute carnage of dead people, I mean almost everyone in the room.

Shakespeare himself killed off quite a number of people in that last scene.

Yes, I'm afraid that I blew it out of proportion, as is quite often my wont. Things get heightened. So in came Fortinbras with two camera crews; and while one crew was going around recording the bodies, the other camera was recording Fortinbras, the new ruler—much like the reporter who went down to Jonestown to seize the political moment and ended up getting killed. Now, it got trickier and trickier as it went along because the final scene was played in full Elizabethan period dress as opposed to the modern dress worn in the earlier scenes. What was happening was also Pirandellian, because the camera was picking up all of these dead people lying on the floor wearing period clothes, but their images on the video screens were in modern dress. We had prefilmed the entire scene for the monitors and the camera was a dummy going around in the same direction as what was going on in the screen. It was incredibly theatrical.

How long was the production?

Four hours and twenty minutes. We did not cut the text. We did four student matinees a week and the majority of the audience was teenagers, many of whom had never been to a play before, let alone a Shakespearean play. It ran for almost six months, off and on.

They may never have been to a Shakespearean play, but there are certain famous speeches from Hamlet *that most everyone has heard. The "to be or not to be" soliloquy has become a familiar cliché. How did you get the audience to pay attention to that speech?*

Two things intrigue anyone who works on the "to be or not to be" speech. It comes right after "The play's the thing wherein I'll catch the conscience of the King," and a lot of critics have claimed it's in the wrong place, that it's really meant to be an earlier speech. There have been directors who have transferred it to an earlier point in the play. The second point is how can you possibly go out there and say, "To be or not to be"? (Not that Shakespeare could help it that this has become his most famous speech.) I think that it was originally there to demonstrate certain popular concepts of theology and psychology at Wittenberg University. As for the placement of the speech, I think he meant for it to be jarring. He literally stops the narrative.

If you can believe that it is an accurate representation of what Shakespeare wrote, then you have to believe he placed it there for a purpose.

I did. At that moment it's all plotting, plotting. And you are caught in the narrative. They set up Ophelia. Claudius and Polonius hide behind doors. I popped up the houselights, and Hamlet made his entrance through the auditorium with a can of spray paint. The audience started to giggle as he worked his way up to one of the walls onstage and wrote in spray paint, "To be or not to be." And then he looked at the audience in hushed silence and he looked at the wall and said, "That is the question." Then the houselights went down as he began, "Whether 'tis nobler. . . " Generally the audience applauded or there was an enormous laugh and release of anxiety on the actor's and audience's part. It exploded the play in this wonderful way: everybody just laughed and got over it in a perfect symbiotic relationship. And I think that they listened to the rest of that speech with completely fresh ears.

It also stayed on the wall for the rest of the play. Graffiti really is the expression of the inarticulate—in a frustrated society, the first mark of anger, frustration. So the fact that it was graffiti had real resonance. Later, when Hamlet kills Polonius mistakenly, he's probably confronted for the first time in his life with "being and not being." He's tried to avoid getting involved in anything and to stay cool through life, then he kills somebody. Well, we held for almost four minutes after he killed Polonius. Gertrude screamed and fell to the floor weeping. Hamlet realized what he'd done and pulled back against the wall, pinned under "To be or not to be." Aidan allowed real time to enter into his work onstage to deal with being and not being. And it was important.

That production ended a decade of my collaboration in the Off Loop theatre with artists and audiences at Wisdom Bridge.

How has your work changed since then?

I've found out in the past couple of years, which I think have included the best work I've done, that I need virtually a year to prepare a play. I generally do one major work a year, and one other play. That schedule has allowed these breakthroughs. Not only that, but I worked on *Hamlet* twice in a two-year period. It is unbelievable, the advantages of doing a production a second time. I was able to approach it freshly and to refine it. As much experience as you may have, there's always that moment when you look at a work and say, "I should have done. . . "

Do you come back and watch a show frequently after it's opened?

Well, if it's a two-hour play, there's usually only about fifteen minutes I love watching and the rest of it I just can't bear. I've asked other directors about this and they've had the same experience. They come back if they're forced to look at the production to give notes or whatever.

The only play that wasn't that way for me was *In the Belly of the Beast*. It was only eighty minutes long, but I was completely happy with it.

Yours was the second production of that play, after Adrian Hall's.

The version I did was Adrian's, but I had an enormous amount of freedom in terms of the text. It's an arrangement of documentary material. Probably fifteen minutes were completely my invention. Adrian provided me with the initial challenge when he said, "This is something I think you should look at." When he sent me his version and talked to me about it, Bill Petersen instantly came to mind to play that role. Bill read it and was knocked out and we began an investigation into all the aspects of the event, using as its base Adrian's original adaptation. That brought me to New York to interview the director of the halfway house on the East Side where Jack Abbott had been, the judge who presided over the trial, both attorneys and a juror. I compiled as much information in firsthand interviews as I could, and then came back and approached two other actors who had previously worked with Bill, Tim Halligan and Peter Aylward, and said, "Let's do this piece. I don't know what will become of it or what it's going to look like." I hadn't seen Adrian's production. The three-man concept was originally his.

We spent almost a month at a table debating, looking through court transcripts, watching videotapes of Abbott, listening to tape recordings that I had done of various people, editing the material, going back to the original book. I was scared of the material, thinking that there would be no audience for it. It was to open the fall 1983 season at Wisdom Bridge.

When I direct most plays, I have very strong visual images from the beginning and I go about working with the designers to get at them. In this case, I didn't have any visual ideas. I was scared. Everything about Jack Abbott scared me. He's one of those people on the street who may come up and put a knife in your back at any moment. I said, "I can't even begin to think about design, let's just get into rehearsal." So we spent about four weeks exploring the material. Then the play got staged very quickly and very easily in about ten days. By that time, it was too late to engage a set designer, so I designed the set with the help of Michael Philippi, who was designing the lights. Michael was at every rehearsal. He sat at the table unlike a lighting designer who comes in at the last moment. The lights were almost a fourth character.

Then we got in front of an audience for two weeks of previews. That's where all the work took place, because Adrian's text was about two hours long plus the material that we had added. Over the course of playing in front of an audience it became a Sophoclean experience of boiling it down, making it simple.

As it turned out, you didn't need to feel apprehensive about your audiences being interested in the subject matter. You even revived it the following season and that resulted in Peter Sellars inviting your company to present it at the Kennedy Center in Washington.

Liviu Ciulei said a wonderful thing at a conference I attended: "The quality of a community is judged by the quality of the questions its theatre asks." Over the years, that remark has had a deeper and deeper meaning because the works I have been most interested in doing are those that somehow question society the most. Three plays that have meant a great deal to me are *In the Belly of the Beast*, *Hamlet* and *Galileo*, with which I opened my first season at the Goodman. All three are about people who are completely outside of the society.

Why did you decide to open your tenure at the Goodman with Galileo?

When I was interviewed by the Goodman board and asked what I would do if I were their director, without my even thinking about it, the first play that came out of my mouth was *Galileo*. Several years before, I had read about Adrian's production, in which he made Brecht a character in the play. He was interested in the play as autobiography. I knew exactly what he was doing. Adrian and Jim Schevill did a new translation that was approved by the Brecht estate. It was their own translation, but its major contribution was that it created the character of Brecht and incorporated poems from his Hollywood and East German years.

Did you take a page out of Adrian Hall's book and add Brecht as a character?

Well, it's interesting how a page of Adrian's gets followed. For a time I really liked that idea. But then I changed my mind because to put an actor up there being Bertolt Brecht seemed a lie to me. Now, I know that the actor up there playing the role of Galileo also wasn't Galileo, but it just wasn't the same and it didn't work for me, as much as I admired the idea. Well, what happened was that we ended up turning the added material into songs. Louis Rosen took a lot of the poems and made them songs. In rehearsal I played with some of those speeches that Adrian had used, but, ultimately, none of them were left in the production. It was too literal a concept for me. Whereas Adrian had Brecht making the historical connections, much in the style of the Stage Manager in *Our Town*, I did it with the physical production.

I had already worked with Brian Dennehy at Wisdom Bridge in Ron Hutchinson's play *Rat in the Skull*, and in getting to know Brian I realized that he was an actor of the size, the sensuality, the intellectual ability and the emotional connection to play Galileo.

Where did your study of the play lead you?

As I began working on the play, what interested me most was that it was about the history of the modern world from 1938 to 1958—from the Second World War to the setting off of the atomic bomb and the cold war with the Soviet Union. The images were going to come out of that. I had a period of nine months working with Soviet designer George Tsypin, whom I had met through Peter Sellars. It was absolutely astonishing what he came up with. He's a designer who is fearless. He looks for a director, as I look for a designer, to push the other into areas where they are most afraid of going. It's taken me a long time to learn to appreciate that if there are two roads to walk down, as difficult as it may be, try to walk down the scariest.

While I was preparing *Galileo*, I went to the Soviet Union for the first time. A lot of the play deals with totalitarianism. Just being in Moscow, where you see the repression in those rooms, you start to get a sense of what the country was like under Stalin. George Tsypin, having come from a totalitarian country, understood what those images were. So he designed a production that he told me would never get on in the Soviet Union, because it would be too dangerous.

The basic metaphor for *Galileo* was simple. "The world is flat and the planets revolve around the earth." As I read the play there were a number of explosions. One brilliant moment in the play is where Galileo is waiting at the Vatican for the court astronomer to either confirm or deny his contention that the earth goes around the sun—that the earth is not the center of the universe. After a great deal of tension, the astronomer comes out and says, "He's right." I loved that, those two words, "He's right." There is an explosion of such immensity in those two words—everything.

It had been George's idea to play in Renaissance period clothes up until that moment, which is about forty-five minutes into the play. And we played the scene on a tiny forestage against a full wall with rear projections that allowed us to go swiftly from location to location in Venice. It looked like a Stratford, Canada, or Royal Shakespeare production of *Galileo*. It was all in beautiful earth colors. At the moment of "He's right," the entire stage actually exploded. The walls opened up and revealed all of the projectors and everybody started screaming. It was like the carpet had been pulled and everybody fell to the floor. Galileo, the modern man from the beginning, had thrown us completely into the twentieth century in an explosive, highly dynamic way. The whole rest of the play took place in really dark, grim, ugly surroundings. The audience, for the most part, was horrified because they had just loved the color.

Somehow we have the expectation that with enlightenment, things get prettier.

Well, the whole first part of the play is about order. Suddenly we're ripped from ordered society—that whole Renaissance image with God on one side, the devil on the other and man in the middle. It was exploded into complete chaos. The production reflected that by instantly transforming into an enormous twentieth-century black-box set. It is hard to describe because it consisted of harsh twisted metal, characters in white lab coats, and there was a variety of different suggestive images. The Church remained constant in its reds and robes.

A very clear image in the play was when Galileo recanted and took back all of his theories by force of the Church. In the text, a town crier goes across the back of the stage reading the recantation. At that moment, we had doors swing open to reveal the House Un-American Activities Committee, men in business suits in front of microphones all saying, "I, Galileo Galilei, recant everything."

There is a wonderful sequence in the play that is almost always cut because it's extraneous to the plot, where the plague sweeps through the city. . .

Another one of those extraneous or misplaced scenes great writers seem to be fond of.

. . . Well, we kept the scene, and it's very clear that it's about the Nazis. So we introduced cages of naked corpses being pulled across the stage and people being rounded up by Italian Fascists. That was followed by the scene where

101

Galileo goes to Rome. To me, that scene was a metaphor for Brecht fleeing Germany and going to Hollywood. So we played it very much as a Hollywood pool party, with butlers in 1940s outfits and music suggestive of the period. Even if the juxtaposition of the two scenes was not literally clear to an audience, there was an emotional connection.

By the end of the play, the stage turned into a Beckett-like landscape. The final scene of imprisonment was like *Endgame*. All of the scenery got stripped away and it was played against a bare white cyc, a white floor, harsh white lights, Galileo with dark glasses in a wheelchair sitting at center and Andre, his pupil, standing. After a great deal of swirling in the earlier scenes, for the last conversation of the play, which is virtually a thirty-minute debate between the two, no one moved.

These are powerful theatrical images. How does any possible conflict resolve itself when you are working with designers who want to exercise their own point of view?

Hopefully, by delighted, excited negotiation. I have very strong visual images and ideas about the way every play looks, but I don't presume to call myself a designer.

What form does that negotiation take?

What generally happens is the designers take what they like most, sometimes verbatim, and then they run with it on their own. The best thing is when they see that I'm not afraid to go "out there." That encourages them to know that what they're thinking is all right, and then it's a series of visual negotiations, of testing one another and working with one another. Nine times out of ten, what the designer has come up with is so much better than my imagination. The designers I've worked with want to collaborate too. Basically, what it's all about is, "Who's got the best idea?" The director has the impetus to do the play, and if you're dealing with a play like *Hamlet* or *Galileo*, you have a reason why you want to do that play. So I convey that reason to the actors and to the designers. Usually, why I want to do it is not just theoretical or intellectual. I see a visual reason why it's there.

What happens when the visual concept for the play is vague and doesn't easily come together?

I had a tortuous collaboration with Michael Merritt for *Mother Courage*. He would keep designing sets and we would say, "This is it. We've hit it." Two days later we would go, "It's terrible," and throw it away. To get to the set design, which was very simple, took us a year of designing. Of course, there are examples of directors and designers getting together for two design conferences and coming up with a completed idea. In this case, we kept meeting and meeting and tearing it apart and questioning, challenging, pushing, doing it over and arriving at something.

Was it so tortuous because the images of previous productions of Mother Courage *were omnipresent?*

Part of it is that you want to break all the preconceptions. I mean, Brecht had as many preconceptions about how you do Brecht as anybody.

As many as Shaw had about Shaw.

For every play that you do, there is a whole set of clichés attached. You try to understand everything about the play and then try to go through the play carefully and smartly demolishing the clichés, trying somehow to get at the metaphors and meaning of the play without being glib about them. To refer back to the "to be or not to be" scene in *Hamlet*, we arrived at the spray-painting moment not out of any sudden, "Oh, let's do that," but out of a real analysis of how historically that speech has worked in the course of that play.

With *Mother Courage*, we kept trying to go farther and farther. We didn't have a turntable or any of that stuff. The whole back wall was an enormous blackboard upon which every action that happened in the play was written in chalk. "Mother Courage does *this*." A large clock was mounted on the back wall so the audience saw in real time what was happening. It was an open stage, glossy black, with fluorescent pink, orange and yellow nylon ropes bisecting the stage. One of the strongest images of war to us was those photos of Nazi concentration camps with piles of victims' clothing. So at times the whole set was covered with clothing and Courage was pulling her wagon up mounds of coats and down mountains of shoes. At various points in the play, clothes would be thrown from the wings onstage and Courage would pull her little wagon over the mounds. Even if you didn't know what that was about, it was really scary.

The one thing about *Mother Courage* or *Hamlet* or *Galileo* is that they're really long, messy plays. Most of my training, and of all director training, is to bring order out of chaos and to make a certain beauty. And what I've learned only recently is how to let things be messy and ugly and, ultimately, honest—because our lives are sort of ugly and messy.

Do you find that audiences are distressed by that because they expect you to make it neat?

They are a little shocked by it, but I think they really do appreciate the energy and the truth of it. It's a subtle thing. Most audiences aren't aware of anything other than, "Am I seeing a good show?" And part of a good show is being

103

intellectually stimulated and emotionally involved. Is something going on? Peter Sellars is the one who says, "Being awake in the theatre is good practice for being awake in the world." I have this hunch that audiences are really thirsting to get back to an Elizabethan experience in the theatre. It's a matter of encouraging and trying to challenge all of the artists who come into the field to look at the broad canvas of political and social responsibilities of the world and to interpret it.

ZELDA FICHANDLER

Z elda (Diamond) Fichandler's parents emigrated from Russia as infants. Her maternal grandfather, an Orthodox Jew, slept on a feather bed laid over three chairs in a frame house next to a dump in suburban Boston, read learnedly from the holy scriptures and so was exempted from working in the family's small dairy business. Her father, a brilliant scientist, invented the proximity fuze, which was the detonating device for the atom bomb, and originated blind-instrument and other flying devices still used in aviation today. He took the first blind flight in an open two-man cockpit plane from Beltsville, Maryland, to Newark, New Jersey, and made aviation history. Zelda Fichandler describes her father's intelligence as "primary."

She too has made history—theatrical history—by building one of America's largest and most successful performing institutions, Washington, D.C.'s Arena Stage. Zelda Fichandler has become one of the nonprofit theatre's "primary" and most respected and eloquent spokespersons.

When she was four, her father became the head of Research and Development at the National Bureau of Standards and the family moved to Washington, D.C. Her early ambition was to become an actress, and she earned her first dollar writing an article at age eleven on that subject for the now defunct newspaper *The Washington Star*. Her teachers encouraged her to be in the theatre, but it did not seem like a serious choice and she explored other interests. Initially, deciding on a career as a journalist, she studied the Russian language and literature at Cornell University, graduating Phi Beta Kappa. Subsequently, she translated Russian for Military Intelligence and put together a handbook on the Red Army. She read Chekhov in his mother tongue before she ever read his works in English. Still not satisfied with the direction in which she was headed, she became a premed student studying to become a psychoanalyst and was the top student in a freshman chemistry class of five hundred at George Washington University. One day in the lab, she spilled hydrochloric acid down the front of her sweater, dissolving the fabric, burning herself and convincing her parents that she was going into the wrong profession. Zelda Diamond decided to take her master's degree in theatre arts, and upon graduating from George Washington University in 1950 at age twenty-five, began to look for acting jobs.

She married Thomas C. Fichandler, a statistician and economist who was knowledgeable about theatre, having spent his early years traveling around the country with his father, who was a musical director, and his mother, an opera singer. Tom Fichandler urged his wife to find a job in the theatre other than acting because he thought that as an actress she was "too intellectual," and that she watched herself too much. About that time, she was asked to direct a play called *The Public Bosom*, a satire produced by the Agricultural Players. Tom Fichandler thought the result was promising and suggested she focus her career toward directing.

In 1950, there were fewer than a handful of resident theatres in existence across the country to serve as institutional models. But along with her husband and Edward Mangum, who had been her professor at George Washington, she founded a two-hundred-forty-seven-seat arena theatre in a decrepit old movie house known as The Hippodrome. They opened with Goldsmith's *She Stoops to Conquer*, and among the cast were George Grizzard, Lester Rawlins and Pernell Roberts. The company was so impoverished that Grizzard tells the story of when the single light bulb illuminating the only dressing room (men were separated from women by a clothesline and a sheet) burned out, he was sent to purchase a new one and cautioned to buy it on 7th Street, where it was three cents cheaper than in the shops on nearby 9th Street.

Mangum left Arena in 1952 to try and establish a theatre in Hawaii, and Zelda Fichandler became the sole artistic force of Arena Stage. The company experimented with the arena style of staging for five years and fifty-five productions in the converted movie house, and further refined their work for another five when they moved to larger quarters in the ice storage area of the Christian Henrich Brewery, a Washington landmark, which was converted into a five-hundred-seat house.

In 1961, the Fichandlers opened the eight-hundred-eleven-seat Arena Stage in use today, and in 1971, they added another five-hundred-seat theatre with a fan-shaped open stage that could be used as a proscenium stage to contrast with the original arena-style theatre. They later expanded the facilities yet again, adding a cabaret space christened the Old Vat Room (in memory of their former brewery home) and a converted scene shop in which to work experimentally.

Drawing knowledge and inspiration from the experience of such theatre pioneers as Nina Vance of the Alley Theatre in Houston, Margo Jones in Dallas, Bob Porterfield at the Barter in Abingdon, Virginia and K. Elmo Lowe at the Cleveland Play House, the young Fichandler joined the resident theatre movement, built a major institution housing a year-round company of actors, and in 1984, became Chair of the Graduate Acting Program at New York University's Tisch School of the Arts, in addition to her full-time direction of Arena Stage.

Under Fichandler's direction, Arena Stage became a home base for director Alan Schneider as well as an American launching pad for such East European directors as Liviu Ciulei, Lucian Pintilie and Russian exile Yuri Lyubimov. In 1973, Arena was the first American company to tour the Soviet Union, presenting *Our Town* and *Inherit the Wind*; it was the first American theatre to participate in the Hong Kong Arts Festival, and the first regional theatre to receive a Tony award for excellence. Arena has been a home for European playwrights like Bertolt Brecht, Max Frisch, Eugène Ionesco, Slawomir Mrozek and Istvan Orkeny; has presented significant revivals of works by Albee, Miller, Williams; the classics of Shakespeare, Shaw, Molière and Ibsen. The institution has not introduced a large body of new works, but the ones that it has produced have been significant, such as *The Great White Hope, Indians, Moonchildren, Pueblo, A History of the American Film, The Madness of God, K-2* and *Women and Water*. Fichandler has directed over fifty of Arena's productions, including such works as *The Three Sisters, Death of a Salesman, Six Characters in Search of an Author* and *The Ascent of Mt. Fuji.*

Arena is one of only a few theatres in the country that maintain a resident company of actors, some of whom have been with the theatre for twenty years. Its 1967 production of *The Great White Hope* catapulted it into the national spotlight when the play moved to Broadway, giving major attention to actors James Earl Jones and Jane Alexander. This acclaim, however, was also responsible for tearing apart the extraordinary group of actors who were then assembled at Arena Stage as they moved on to Broadway and into films. Once more, Fichandler set to work rebuilding the company, the third one to be assembled since Arena's founding.

She has at various periods taken brief sabbaticals from Arena in order to find new directions in which to grow. From 1978 to 1980, she took one of these pauses and placed director David Chambers in charge of Arena in her absence. By 1984, she became more and more involved in structuring an acting program and teaching. Having previously taught direction at Boston University and lectured at the University of Texas at Austin, she began dividing her attentions between Arena and NYU and sharing responsibilities at Arena Stage with her artistic associate, Douglas Wager. In 1987, she took a one-semester leave from NYU in order to focus her full attentions on Arena and to plan for the evolution of that institution.

In the late 1970s, she and Arena executive director Thomas Fichandler separated, but they continued to operate the theatre together successfully until his retirement in 1986, at which time he was replaced by former Hartford Stage managing director William Stewart, after a carefully orchestrated period of transition.

Fichandler's directing is characterized by intensive study and preparation. She all but psychoanalyzes the characters in the particular play she is studying and physically describes the emotions of the characters onstage with utmost clarity.

■　　■　　■

What equipment does a director need?

It's so complicated. You have to be able to use other people as your instrumentality. This is an art in itself—to make your imagination proceed through the imaginations of other people. It's extraordinarily complicated. It's a lifetime job. Directing abuts all kinds of large areas—adjacent to teaching, psychoanalysis and religion.

There may be half a dozen great directors in the world today. I think there were one or two in this country who promised greatness and, for reasons I don't understand, didn't deliver it. I don't think we have world-towering directors, and one small part of it is that those things are accidental. I saw Giorgio Strehler's production of *Good Woman of Setzuan* in Paris and I really wanted to leave my profession because it was so mammoth. I heard how he rehearses. He can spend a whole day on the lifting of one prop. That's partly resources—six months of rehearsals and all the rest—but it's also personal genius, a strong point of view, high imagination, the ripening of talent. He's over sixty and has had the time and opportunity to work with one company for years.

What is the most difficult area for a director to develop?

The imagination is very hard to develop through training or teaching, because it's not about mechanics. It's about getting at imagery. What else can be imagined from what you can see? What else can be shown? Images—configurations that resonate and become more than what they seem on the surface.

The imagination *can* be exercised, however. Stanislavsky has a whole series of exercises for the imagination. But in a certain way, it is a gift. That gift or talent is best analyzed by using the example of films, in which sequences of short felt and thought passages are united to create a continuum of images in the viewer's mind, and, therefore, meaning. I don't know that there are many people who have this primary "meaning-making" gift. I don't think the flame of that gift is fanned in people. Rather, it is squelched as soon as possible. "What if I did? What if it were? What if I could?"—all of those free-floating, half-uttered combinations of thought, feelings, impulses and visual images are discouraged because they're not tidy, they're not quantifiable. And we do aim for quantifiable products. You even hear artists say, "Television is a wonderful medium because you can reach thirty million people in one night. In the theatre, you can only talk to three hundred." But it only takes the transformation of *two* people to change a whole civilization!

Moreover, I feel that directors have to have a very strong *reason* to use this image-making capacity. They should very much want to say or show something from a particular point of view. That means they have to have a strong social and political perspective. They have to want to put their imaginative ability into the service of ideas. We don't breed too much of that today. We breed a lot of nihilism, a lot of "What's it all about? What's it all for?" This kind of passivity just doesn't instigate art, because art is a very active and protesting process. It embodies an attitude toward the world. It has a point. That attitude toward art is not encouraged terribly much in our society. I think it was Camus who wrote: "If the world were clear, art would not be necessary. Art helps us to pierce the opacity of the world."

Theatre is a major tool. I'm not talking about using it for propaganda, for gaining power. I'm talking about uncovering human experience. In this country, we don't have any rational way of letting people emerge from themselves. We don't really have an art of theatre. We have a chain of theatres. In Europe, by contrast, theatre isn't detached from society. The people who work in theatre don't think that it is on one side and that society, with its social, political, moral and philosophical questions, is on the other. There, people are politicians *and* write novels. The United States is the only country whose politicians surprise us by being literate. Why should the theatre be some kind of adjacent island, when it has the capacity to touch our subconscious, which is our well of content and from which all things derive? When the subconscious becomes conscious, it has a deliberate, rational ability to change the universe.

The theatre director must also have a deep reservoir of patience and allow time for subconscious thought and feelings to arise in the bodies and minds of his/her collaborative artists. In this way, the work becomes dense and deeply revelatory, truly a collective statement about the world of the play.

Did you begin Arena in order to change the world?

I started wanting to have a theatre to fulfill my directing impulse. I also had a very strong social feeling about the need to have theatre be a part of people's lives outside of New York. There is so much money attached to Broadway. In the period before the sixties, before the idea of regional theatre caught on, men controlled the money and they hired people who could protect the money, which mostly meant other men. It's an aspect of the, "Well you were a success last time with a farce, so you'll be a success this time with a farce." Finally, the stereotypical presumptions are dissolving that say that women are too emotional in rehearsals, too intuitive, can't bring in the show on time, don't organize as well, etc.

The whole notion of an institution is the continuing dialogue with the audience. In an institution, you can't just have a series of dots. You have to connect them. It's a relationship in the most profound way between the body of the theatre and the body of the audience. And that relationship has its moons and can't be described by any single moment in time. It's a long locus. Like any relationship, it has its ups and downs and the potential for change within it.

Does that change reflect the vision of the director or does it come from the audience?

The world shifts, and as a director you have to be in touch with it. A person who runs a theatre has to be in tune with what people are thinking about even though they can't name it. We have to address the subconscious or the preconscious of our audience. We have to be *of* them, but we have to be ahead of them in the perception of the world around us and the world that is inside of them. They can't do our fieldwork for us. In 1973, we brought back the interest in Thornton Wilder's *Our Town* as a contemporary play. It was a period when a lot of people were living a life of experimentation with sexuality and marital arrangements totally different from those expressed in the play. I reread *Our Town* on a Saturday morning, still in my bathrobe at home, and wept and thought, "This is it. This is what people are really thinking while they're changing beds." And that play was gigantically successful. That's just an instance of intuiting where people's feeling systems are going while at the same time they're acting out something very different.

How can you be sure within yourself of the value of doing certain plays, sense the audience's reaction in advance?

I think you feel change and trends in yourself, and then you verify them by sharing yourself with other people and hearing what they have to say in response. If you can tune in to your own convictions, then it's easy to have the courage of those convictions because that courage is coming from a real place; it feels right to you. That's a very primitive example of what I mean about change, and how you can schedule repertory creatively. You can't go out and say, "Are you satisfied with the way you're leading your sex life?" Or, "Do you feel that your subconscious value system is different from the one you're acting out?" You can't put that on an opinion poll. If you asked an audience, "Would you like to see Thornton Wilder's *Our Town?*" they'd say, "No! That old play? Every high school does that." All workers in the theatre, all of us, need to be aware of the purposes of our work, why and for whom it is being done and what emotional, political and social reverberations are in the air that can release that awareness.

Once you have made the choice of material, what's your process for getting to the core of it?

I always do about six months of advance research because knowledge releases my imagination. Imagination is what is there after you know everything; without knowledge, one's imagination may be too thin—lacking in strength and too fragile to build on. I need to know exactly how the characters in the play live their daily lives. It doesn't matter how abstractly, in terms of form, the information is used; I have to know what their habits of thought are, what they eat, their education, what they sit on, listen to, read, believe in. I may never use it, but it gives me a sense of reality. That's the basis of my process. Along with that, I have to know what it is I want to find out, and then I go from that known to the unknown and then back again to the known, for then, what was unknown is now more known. Information just comes. The riches come up because you've pierced the skin with your questions, your search. The words on the page are only clues to the life boiling underneath them. Thought is a process, emotion is a process, embodiment in actions and images is a process.

When working with a specific scene, you might ask, "What do you think he wants from her at this moment?" He wants her to pay attention to him. Well, you work from that point of view for a moment, and you find that he really wants her to pay attention because he feels totally inadequate. So that

111

his bizarre, attention-getting behavior is caused by his not thinking he deserves the attention. At the root of the scene is his desire to feel better about himself. But if you start the process with too much discussion and inhibit the process of discovery, you don't have as dense and contradictory a moment. It's the same process a scientist uses to discover something new, or a baby uses to grow. It's the human process. A psychoanalyst might say, "What are you feeling right now?" And you might say, "Oh, I'm not feeling much of anything. I'm just . . . well, I'm hot and I don't have a lot of time, you know. They need me at the office. Damn, they always need me at the office! Every time I sit down somebody needs . . ." And you've suddenly tripped into an area where you feel totally exploited, angry—and you started out by saying you feel nothing. So it's the human process. Everybody functions this way.

All styles can come through working this way?

Well, you don't have to do *Three Men on a Horse* exactly this way, although residues of the discovery process are there. Circus performers don't have to use this method totally—but on the other hand, if they get too hung up in conscious process, if they think too much, they're going to miss their partner when they swing through the air. We can't codify all of our knowledge. Some of it has to be *bodily* incorporated. It becomes constricting and noncreative when one clutches at every single thing acquisitively, as if one can swallow and control every reflex and impulse. It's not within our ability to do that. We're not made that way. That becomes noncreative. The psychological well drys up.

You mentioned Strehler having six months to rehearse. Is there an ideal length of rehearsal time?

It's not the number of hours. Rather than rehearse twelve hours a day in one week, it's better to do it four hours a day over three weeks. That has to do with the material getting into the muscle and nervous system from the subconscious. One needs enough time to acquire instinctive knowledge and to embody that knowledge in a series of creative images. Of course, the more complex the work, the more time one needs. Directors from Europe who have been used to three to six months of rehearsal manage in the American system to make do with two months. I can be fairly comfortable with six or seven weeks for a Chekhov production, given the fact that I've never known an alternative, if I've already done a lot of preparation and am working with people I know or even with people I may not know but who work more or less the way that I do.

I remember asking Yuri Lyubimov, when he was directing *Crime and Punishment* here at Arena, how many of those stunning images he had ready when he went into rehearsal for the original production in Moscow. And he said about eighty percent of them. And then he would start from day one with the lighting designer, the scene designer, all the costumes, all the stuff, and it would take him a year to convey the images and to find the other twenty percent.

I have only a few images when I go into rehearsal, key moments that have led to the particular design for the set. I know the climactic or most excavated moments and how they are visualized. I think the way to work in a short period of rehearsal time is to inform the actors and designers more fully so that they can fully be co-contributors. Because if everyone is improvising toward truth, you can get there faster.

In the East European theatre, as I've known it through directors like Liviu Ciulei and Lucian Pintilie, the actor is just one of the theatrical means by which to express a moment. To me the actor is the *one* means and all others exist to enrich that expressivity. I think the American theatre is more psychological than European theatre. If you have a Lyubimov or a Pintilie directing at your theatre, you know that you can't budget ahead of time because any visualization that they perceive is the one they have to have. It's almost as if the visualization of a production is its statement, is its freedom. Whereas I feel that the organic visualization is the deployment of actors meaningfully in space. And any place that makes that possible, including a bare place, is true and real.

How do you proceed after having explored the material with the cast?

Oh, I'm very rational. My work eventually looks very carefully selected, not haphazard. It's organized rhythmically, architecturally, thematically, as well as psychologically. But early on, I try to create a dialectic between form and feeling that keeps going through the rehearsals. And every rehearsal, therefore, becomes different. With this approach, you never repeat anything because new stuff keeps coming up. The actors keep bringing it up. The work has to change forever because it's alive. But the intentions and objectives of each moment are eventually set and become the score of the production, within which the overall rhythms are set. However, there must always be elasticity, room for new discovery, or the production is dead. I learned that lesson very early, specifically about humor. In the early years of Arena, I revived a comedy that I had previously directed and suddenly it was no longer funny. I had to figure out why. It was because the actors were playing the outside of it and the outside isn't funny. Only the inside needs and intentions make things funny. What one aims for, in the end, is improvisation within set form.

How can these interior needs be physicalized?

That happens through making collaborators of the actors, so that they know what is in each moment, what it is they're striving to reveal. And their desires and intentions become embodied physically, almost choreographically, without too much intervention on my part. That is, I intervene very delicately, through sharing with them what I know and through releasing their imaginations so they can share what they know. Their ideas affect my imagination, which affects their imaginations. Then the process is a living exploration. If everybody knows what the series of "doings" is, then they become connected into a through-action. A thought can release the body, or the body can release the thought, which can then release the body again. You can plug into this organic biologic system in many ways. If one way doesn't work, use another. I use whatever I need to use. I've never found anything to replace the truth of psycho-physical actions that Stanislavsky described.

How does the director unify her collaborators within a project?

The play is a locked universe and each director finds her own key to it, and then leads the other contributing artists—designers, composers, actors—to find their keys, harmonious with her own. The goal is to open up the universe further so the collaborators can make it specific in terms of their own special domains: light, sound, environment, behavior, and so on. All our resources are needed for probing the world of the play. Everyone has to come aboard in high gear. What a bonus if designers know how to analyze a text almost as well as a director! What a bonanza if a director knows how to design a set, even if it isn't her central creative mission! How helpful when a lighting designer doesn't just illuminate the stage but also the interior core of this special world. And we want actors not only as actor-instruments but also as probing, intelligent actor-human beings whose dreams, politics, observations, life experiences can be beacons in the search. We have to teach ourselves and each other the art of collaboration, "co-laboring" in order to express a collective consciousness—the fundament of the act of making theatre. In the rehearsal process, in the heat of opposing viewpoints, the right way is found. However, in the end, talking and working together is not enough. It's necessary to do more, to internalize one another's viewpoints, to think as ourselves and also as the others, to permit the perceptions and needs and priorities of the others to mingle with our own while preserving our separateness.

And central to the process is the actor?

As I view the art, the actor is at the center, because the revelation of human behavior and its meaning is what the art is about. There are only a limited number of reasons why we go to the theatre in today's world: after all, it costs more than movies, it takes more energy to go, you have to pay more attention, the images are not seven times normal size and you have to enjoy words in order to get your money's worth. But the reason it persists is that the audience gets what it can't from any other form, which is the breath of the actor, the moment in which the thought or feeling is born. That's why the theatre won't die. But if it is just about visualizing moments beautifully, there's no need for it. It hasn't any real service to render to the community.

But the audience can only receive what the actor gives. The experience will go as deeply into the audience member as it emerges from the actor. An actor can't act with just his head and expect the audience to have a visceral experience. And the visceral experience is the only one that can cause change, can affect the feeling system of the audience. That doesn't mean that a visceral experience need be non-intellectual. You know what a thought can do to you—it can give you a stomachache. Thinking is feeling, feeling is thinking. But if you just want to teach people through the head, you can use pamphlets and books. The theatre is an experiential medium and, therefore, it exists in the relationship between the actors and the audience and only in the moment that the relationship occurs.

The director has to see the whole of the stage, whereas an actor is concerned with self. As a director, how do you help an actor find that perfect relationship between himself and the space he inhabits?

I used to block everything. I started more or less the way a choreographer would, with everything evolved in my head, with "steps" that I expected and hoped would reveal the internal life. I would map out the physical form in very great detail and then sort of parcel it out to the actors. Then, as I got more courage, I stopped writing the blocking on my script, and now I may have a vague notion of the physical design of a scene when I go into rehearsals, though I try to know what the kernel of the scene is. If I have thirty people on stage I may know in general where they're going to move because otherwise time would be wasted. On the other hand, thirty people can also find their own way, can improvise. I had fifty-person crowd scenes in *Inherit the Wind* and *Enemy of the People.* You'd be surprised how bodies fall into beautiful patterns if they know just what they are doing and who they want to be near or not near, how they're relating. Nature forms snow flakes, and if you watch a crowd, it tends to find its own natural forms. Geography pulls people, needs pull them, hunger pulls them, antipathy or friendliness pulls them. The polarites in life make shapes and forms. So you can set thirty people in motion and be surprised at the beautiful and meaningful sculptures they make. However, if I have thirty people in a scene, I usually have a more detailed plan than if I have two or five people. Often I don't predict the design of the scene at all. I spend a lot of time on the design of the *space*, when the psychological pulls are related to place. I work for months in finding what I call in Russian (there is no comparable English word) *zamissel*. It means "the pervading sense." *Missel* means "thought" and *za* is an intensive prefix. It's the thought that binds together all elements or the idea. The *zamissel* accounts for the whole—explains every action, every breath, every pulse, every second of the life of the play. It's like looking at a tree. The sap is in every leaf and it's also in the roots. I can spend months looking for the exact *zamissel* or idea or super-objective that will set a play in motion, unlock its hidden conflict.

The thing that a play has that life doesn't necessarily have is perpetual and purposive motion from second to second. Even if two characters are talking in a pile of sand up to their necks, there is motion in that work of art or it wouldn't be a work of art. In life, we lose track of what we're doing and forget why. We may even cease to be interested in the why and give up on it. But in a play every breath has a meaning, has a motion, (an emotion), moves out from the body into the air or towards another body. And you have to land on a *zamissel* that will explain, account for, every motion. A person said to me recently, "When I see your work, I see the feelings—not only feel them, I *see* them." I took it as a great compliment because that's what I try to do, to make a pattern from the motion of feelings, to make feelings kinetic and perceivable.

So that is the essence of your work before rehearsals, finding the zamissel?

That's what I need to understand by the time I go into rehearsals, and that's what I need to define and understand more and more clearly as I work with the designers in the planning period. I also know, or try to know—sometimes it gets redefined in the process of rehearsal—the style of the work: that is, the angle of viewing reality. It may not be head-on. Every play has its own angle. I need to know the rules of play I want to use. I need to know the general tonality. The embodiment I more or less work out with the actors, though I'll have concrete images for certain pivotal moments.

Actors in a company have to be able to act in all possible styles. For example, they may have to foreshorten psychological adjustments, not take so long with them, as in *The Importance of Being Earnest*: the architecture of the language and the formality of that particular society demand a certain kind of readiness of adjustment, a quickness of transformation from one action/thought to another—unlike Chekhov, where you may be able to take longer to get from one breath to another.

Style comes from inside the work and it's a serious task to find the right one for any given production, and hard to achieve it. Each playwright has a special style and, within the body of work of any given playwright, each play has its own style. The temperament of the playwright, the position of the play within his or her life, the age within which the play was written, the nature of the director and the times he/she lives in, the kind of space to be played in, the composition of the audience, all affect the determination of the style of a given production.

Is that the major task then, to find the style?

The central task in the theatre is to objectify, to clarify, to lay bare the wellsprings of human behavior so that we can actually *see* our own internal feelings instead of just have the sense of them in some inchoate form fluttering around inside of us. What the theatre does is to make a shape for the interior life—objectify it in form. The more the audience is able to empathize with this life, the more they can open up places within themselves that have been closed. They come to "think feelingly" about experiences that they recognize on the stage to be their very own. Theatre is a way of describing in space, time, and motion our collective memories. I know that going to the moon was a technological miracle, but to me the greatest mystery of the world is knowing about oneself and the heart of a person sitting at a foot's distance. That distance is enormous. The theatre aims to know that heart, to cross that space.

Doing a play is like going on an anthropological dig, collecting data about a culture, whether it's today's or the Greeks'. You go on this dig, ferreting around there at the bottom of things. And these little tracks on the page called words, which look like little animal marks, are just the surface. You have to find out what kind of an animal made those marks, put all the pieces together and make a world out of it. The task of the director, actors, designers is to expose whatever is in that hunk of material—not to plaster on top of it or to exhibit it, but to blow it open. And the primary revelation, of course, is always about the very nature of the human animal—his spiritual or, if you will, psychological nature. If the audience begins to recognize that what is happening onstage is related to themselves and what their life contains and means, then the situation becomes interesting to them.

People experience their lives as a tale and the theatre is a natural place for the telling of tales. Theatre and living are inextricably linked.

Do you begin the "dig" with a reading of the play?

I start off talking about what I have come to feel is central to this experience and about the means we'll use to reveal that center. We talk about that, about the core or *zamissel*, for as long as the actors want. Then we read to discover everything we can—not the particular events of the play, because the actors already know them—but everything about the whole universe of the play and especially about the nature of the people within it and their relationships to one another.

The actors will have begun their research a month or two previous to the first rehearsal having "signed up"—either individually or in small groups—to explore particular topics that interest them. For example, if we are embarking on *The Three Sisters*, we gather information about turn-of-the-century Russia: art, architecture, music, mode of dress, food, household objects, religious beliefs, political changes, the status of women, the military, education, position of serfs, method of travel, etc. These aspects of that world will be shared, either verbally or using slides, photographs, tapes, etc. as the reading takes place. The documentation provides a depth and resonance to the text and a density and reality to the moment-to-moment life of the characters. Then I move from reading, which can go on for a week or ten days, to improvisations, and then back to reading.

What is the nature of the improvisations?

Sometimes we just improvise by expressing the text in our own words; sometimes we improvise based on the past of the characters. We pick events like the first wedding anniversary, the day the kid went to high school, the day the car came home smashed. We'll improvise scenes that build muscle memory, because each of our cells has a memory gene. This process builds density and thickness for the moments of the play; a contradictory reality. In *Inherit the Wind*, when the teacher is teaching Darwin in the school, we improvised a class in which the parents dropped in to see this awful schoolteacher. So the crowd later became very interesting because in the improvisation some of the members had the experience of being intrigued by this dangerous theory they knew they weren't supposed to believe.

What was the core you found for Inherit the Wind?

The basic premise of our *Inherit the Wind* was not faith versus reason, or free speech versus censorship, or that an idea once thought must be born. We used the notion that people gain immortality through their children and, therefore, they want their children to believe what they believe. So the ferocity of the fight in the town grew and grew because the people were fighting against their own death and for their children to believe in what they believed in. We also wanted to show the social furor that this kind of individual and group passion can cause. The Scopes trial was the first one ever broadcast on the radio, and it took place in a festival atmosphere. In my research I found out that the courtroom floor actually collapsed because there were so many people, and that one afternoon session had to be held outdoors. I enlarged on that idea and set the whole play outdoors. It was really medieval, primitive, and this conceptual basis gave it a surround that was very interesting to the Soviet Union when we took the production there in 1973. It really showed them a lot about our life and how thought can be transformed into personal action and passion.

What is the next stage of the process, following the reading?

As early as the first day of rehearsals I may leave around a box of props, some random chairs and tables and whatever eventually might be on the set. It's frightening to suddenly go into something called blocking. So the move from the reading to the so-called "blocking" is never really a distinct thing for me. It just happens. Someone will wander from the reading table and then some-one will get up with them. I remember in *Ascent of Mount Fuji*, which begins with people climbing up a mountain and having a picnic, I just had a box of stuff: picnic baskets, jars, hard-boiled eggs, cucumbers, tomatoes, bread. The actors just gathered the stuff up as if they were buying it. We didn't talk about it. We'd already shown slides and pictures of Central Asians and what they ate. So the actors made up their own business and before you knew it, the picnic looked as if it had been worked on for six months. Someone was slicing the cucumbers, someone was peeling apples and somebody else was making tea. Then we started "scoring" it for focus, what I call shifting the "ball of attention," to make sure no one was hacking the cucumber while somebody else was supposed to have focus.

What other elements come into play as the rehearsal process unwinds?

At the end, I become attentive to rhythms, the rise and fall of the play, the architecture of language. The essential process is one of digging out the buried life of the play by whatever available means. What you find in the play has to be given body. It has to be made specific and corporeal. It can't stay in your head. It can't just be verbal. It has to be able to move, walk, take its position on the stage, be spatial, be configurative, represent societal, geo-graphical poles as well as psychological ones. The director, being only one human being, is able to inhabit each of the characters only so far. Half of the character belongs to the playwright, the crucial part comes from the actor. But, as far as possible, the director has to track the interior life of each actor as she/he is evolving the character. You follow them, maybe whisper things to them, suggest avenues of exploration, suggest that they go down that alley and see what happens. Eventually, one hopes that they will go away from you, beyond you and take over from you—if you've done your job well. The work doesn't belong to you at the very end. Actors can come up with telling psychological gestures that are unique to their individual embodiments of the characters. It's good if the director can cause the actor to "ruffle up" individual moments, because reality is always self-contradictory. If you play on just one note, purely and directly, the audience intuits that the moment isn't true because each moment of real living contains its opposite possibility, and we all know this. Stage life often seems false because it's oversimplified.

After the play opens, what kind of control do you exercise over the actors' work?

By then, the actors know more than you do, hopefully. When you do come back to a production and talk to them, you have to put everything in the form of a question or a suggestion. For example, once I looked in on a performance of our 1988 production of Pirandello's *Enrico IV*, and afterward said to Stanley Anderson, who was playing Enrico, "Don't you feel that at the end of Act Two, Stanley, when you're getting ready for Enrico's last performance, that you're keeping Giovanni too long outside the door? Also, don't you want to rush to complete the preparation for the performance?" And he said, "What do you mean? Is it taking too long?" I said, "Yes, it is. Maybe it doesn't feel that it's taking too long, but I feel that the audience is losing the arc of that last moment. And maybe that's why we've lost the applause at the end of the scene, because they've lost track of what you're doing. How do you feel about what I just said?"

"Yeah, that rings a bell."

Then he incorporated that note into his own thinking process because he was on the stage and I wasn't.

And once he's aware of it, perhaps he can fill in the arc in a different manner than what you might expect.

Exactly. We did recover the applause. But I couldn't have gone to Stanley and said, "It needs to go faster," because that wouldn't mean anything. He was inhabiting the moment, living the moment. He knew more about it than I did. In order for it to make sense, I had to return to the original idea of the moment.

That was your second production of Enrico IV, *wasn't it?*

I had directed it twenty years earlier with Herbert Berghof playing Enrico. I was such a different person the second time I did it. I could tell that from what I saw in the play. I was in a different place, the world was in a different place, although the words were the same. I looked at my old script and saw that I had some good notes like "the through-line of the play is Enrico's attempt to connect with other people through the roles he is playing." The basic action of the play seemed to me to be the same. However, the earlier version seemed inadequate because it left out some of the essential ideas. So I used a whole different translation, and after I got the translation I did a lot of dramaturgical work on it. I went to the Italian, which I don't really read, but I could get the rhythms and the length of sentences and the way it was punctuated. You can tell a lot from where the dashes and the dots come and the brevity or length of the lines, the music and the degree of urgency, the breaths that are taking place in between phrases, whether it takes up a little space in the text or a lot, whether it is just an interjection, or it's actually a new thought. You can tell a lot from the shape on the page.

I also think I didn't understand the paper-thin barrier between what is called madness and what is called sanity the first time I did it. There's no absolute definition. It's always about points on a continuum. That's clear to me now.

Twenty years earlier, in the 1960s, everything was seen as much more black and white than it was later.

I know. That was before R. D. Laing wrote *The Politics of Experience* or *The Divided Self* and we began to recognize that we're all schizophrenic to a manageable degree or not. That notion of duality was not as clear in the earlier production. This gave the second production a whole other level of complexity. And I don't think that I had realized then that what was so important was what Enrico was like before he fell from the horse and went mad, fixated in time. In the third act one found out how he began to get his sensory equipment in order again, his sense of touch, smell, sight. After he came to, he just continued to pretend to be mad because in that way he could better manipulate the world. I saw in this play that there was some notion of deliberate madness, self-chosen madness: the mad person finds something in that private reality, however painful it is, that he/she isn't getting in this so-called objective world. I had a psychiatrist as a consultant in preparation of the play. We discussed the nature of paranoia. It was interesting, but I found out, quite surprisingly, that you can get to the same place just dealing with the script.

At the end of the play, you find out, and Enrico finds out, that after all there is an objectively real world: his hair has really turned gray and Belcredi is really as dead as a doornail, and Enrico has to face the consquences or go mad in earnest. There is an objective social truth, a reference point within the ways that we relate to one another. In the end, you get Pirandello's definite observation that there's a world you have to behave within and believe in. It's a sad, sad play about the loss of youth and the inability to retrieve time and recapture love and the loneliness of everybody.

121

And yet, it seems that Enrico IV *was a play right for both periods in which you did it.*

It wasn't the same play that it was twenty years earlier and I wasn't the same person. That's what's so interesting about being a director. I've done *The Crucible* three times. Each time I swear that I understand that play perfectly, and each time it's different. This triangle among the play, the director and the age in which it is done is fascinating to me. In *The Crucible*, we see a man, John Proctor, who is nonheroic, who stumbles unbeknownst to himself upon his inability to conform. And this is a great tragedy for him that he has to isolate himself and stand for what he has to stand for, will he or not. It's a play that speaks today to ethical evolution as part of biology, that somewhere we know what is right, even if it sets us aside from the community, and that private individual acts can transform social structure. Now, I would never have thought that I was going to find that in the play. And I never even looked to find it. I just heard it somehow when I was reading it. And then I brought in a few of the actors from the company for some investigations, not really readings. And I began to hear that John Proctor didn't mean to be noble at all. I hadn't heard that before. I had heard other things. So that gave John and his wife, Elizabeth, an opportunity to learn something during the course of the play and, therefore, to have a new relationship by the end of the play. And it gave to the end a sense of a beginning; something new that might come of all this horror.

Doug Stein designed both Enrico IV *and* The Crucible. *Why did you choose him for these two projects?*

I saw his production of JoAnne Akalaitis's *Through the Leaves*, and I was so arrested by the detail of that set with a butcher shop on one side of the stage and a bourgeois living room on the other side, which comprised the metaphor of the play. I thought to myself, "I have to pursue this designer." Doug's the most investigative designer I've ever worked with. He's filled with curiosity and willing to go to the far edges of thought and imagination to find the design. And he's very patient, willing to take the journey with the director into the subconscious, into improvisation, into the very core of the play in order to evolve the design, leaving things totally unresolved and unconcluded until they resolve and conclude themselves. He does the work of resolving the design somewhere else, not with me. In the case of both *The Crucible* and *Enrico IV*, the first design was exactly right because it was postponed until he felt it right to put pencil to paper.

What was the visual metaphor you found for The Crucible?

Windows. They were very large and they were on the floor for the first scene so that the audience in the arena saw the first act through windows and, therefore, sometimes couldn't see much of anything. That was the first time we had dared to do that in the arena. We did the whole bedroom scene from behind windows and then in the next scene the windows flew up and we suddenly blended that world with the audience's because they could see clearly into it. That came out of all sorts of long talks about the regimented world of the Puritans, that community that gave each person license to peer into and be responsible for the world of their neighbor, this band of brothers bound by their long voyage—three thousand miles across the sea with another three thousand miles of wilderness at their back when they arrived with the conventions and righteousness of Puritanism. As we talked about the eruption of the young girl's mania, and possession and the belief in witchcraft that they brought with them from England, and as we free-associated words and themes and ideas, it became inevitable that some one image would emerge. We didn't know which one. It became windows because you can see in, because they are oppressive and because they reveal the secret life in the bedroom from outside. Also windows catch the rectangularity, the formality, the rigidity of their lives. On the outside perimeter of the stage were pews that were present all the time. In the first act, everybody made their entrance onto the stage from the pews.

The other requirement was that the production had to be able to travel. We took it to the Israel Festival in Jerusalem. The Festival built an arena for us on the stage of the opera house surrounded by bleachers.

What was the preliminary design process for Enrico IV?

For *Enrico*, we started with the idea of a film camera, which is a way I like to start the design investigation, and we went wandering around the world of that play, not limited by the restrictions of the stage. The play is contemporary, although the world-of-the-play, as constructed by Enrico's imagination, is medieval. It was written in 1922; we set it in the 1930s to distance it from us a little and still to have costumes that bore a stylistic resemblance to the clothes of today. The setting of *Enrico* was a room that has been built by an architect hired by Enrico's wealthy sister to maintain the fantasy of a man who thinks he is Enrico IV of the eleventh century. So we roamed around the imaginary villa where this room was installed and we had to imagine how it was built. We imagined the sister saying to the architect, "Now spare no expense. He thinks he's Enrico IV of Germany, so this throne room has got to support that imagined life since I want him to be comfortable and happy." We had to decide whether the architect was skilled or bad. We decided he was good. We had to ask whether this room was upstairs or down, what the access was. We put it in a corner of the villa on the top floor backed up against an outside wall.

"What does it imaginatively represent to Enrico? What are the resonances of this place?" There's a line in the script about the room being precise and balanced and orderly. So we decided that he wanted to maintain control over his universe. Looking through sketchbooks of Italian villas and books on eleventh-century medieval design, we got the feeling of the bilateral balance that the face and head have: the two eyes, the nose, the mouth; the open rafters suggested thoughts of the brain seeping out into the sky.

Then we wanted to show that the architect was putting one universe inside another, so there were inacuracies, anachronisms like covered light switches in order that Enrico's fantasy could be fanned and maintained. But we decided that Enrico also knew the switches were there. He probably used modern plumbing and got all the food he wanted flown in from Rome. He probably used an electric shaver. He had selective madness. In general, we wanted the lines of the set to be in a certain perspective in order to suck in the audience like a vacuum cleaner.

Do you use music as a design element in your productions?

I love music in the theatre, but I'm not much for underscoring in the film sense. I feel there is the text and there is the subtext, which is the feeling and thought of the actors. Underscoring either describes or contradicts. I think neither is right. I remember reading a crique of a film that said, "There was one moment of such exquisite honesty and perception that it was played without underscoring." I found that to be very funny and apt.

You have the arena space and the Kreeger, which is a modified thrust. Is there a difference in the way you stage for those two configurations?

I think I'm an arena-style director, but I feel totally at home in the Kreeger because I direct as if it's an arena. When we took *Our Town* and *Inherit the Wind* to Moscow and Leningrad, I had to put *Inherit* onto a fifty-five-foot-wide proscenium stage. I probably made four minor adjustments because in the design of the set I had already accounted for the geographic and psychological pulls.

I find that the same principles of collision and withdrawal, the forces of attraction and repulsion, apply on a proscenium as they do in an arena. As an example, when you look though a microscope at a slide, the natural motion within a cell is either to go toward or away from the nucleus depending on the magnetic field. And if you look at people at an accident, in an operating room or in a living room, their actions are derived from wanting to get near one person and away from the other, needing to get to the center of the action or to the periphery of the action. Most human action is organized in terms of forces of attraction and repulsion. So the arena lays that bare, just as though you are looking at a cell or a series of cells on a slide through a microscope. It's essentially a form that choreographs the psychology of motion; the meaning and needs become visible. These principles apply to any stage I've found.

What have you found as head of an important actor-training conservatory program?

Before I went to NYU, I didn't fully understand the influence and force of role models. It's important not only to teach, but to stand for something, to have an artistic value system that can be revealed in the work. I say to students at the beginning of the year, "When you go out of here, I want you to have a level of taste so that you can identify good work and bad work. Once you go out, you may never meet anyone who defines good acting exactly in the way that we're defining it here. Nonetheless, the existence of a level of taste is what dictates how you pick your work. There has to be some standard that you carry within you and then if you deviate from it, if you're doing a soap commercial, you know exactly what you're doing. You'll not be corrupted if you know this is a deviation from playing Nina in *The Seagull*."

The basis of good actor training is freeing the wisdom of the body. An actor needs to learn to breathe properly so that the wisdom can enter it. He needs alignment and a relaxed voice and to be free of fear. He needs a state of easy readiness in order to catch the impulse from the other person. He needs the freedom of imagining, the freedom to think that what he does is right and that what he needs will be there if he trusts that it will be. And if it isn't right, what the hell, he'll do it another way. There is power in trust of one's self and of one's environment, including the environment of the other actors. If it isn't right this time, throw it away. Fine, it was just a little exercise. In order to train in this method, you have to undo everything that society has tried to do. Up to that moment you've learned to read, "Don't walk on the grass," the instructions, a bit of information—you haven't learned that language really exists to reveal thought and feelings. Fundamentally, we are all taught too soon to be socialized animals. If you waste the identifying signals of the human body, you have wasted your greatest resource. Education means "to lead out from." And what you really lead out is what's already in there.

Technique is the shaping into desired form the released impulses of the body/mind. I believe it's Alec Guinness who wrote that technique was like blowing down a glass tube. Wonderful image, that.

What would you say to a young director striving to get into the profession?

It's very hard to get into this field. You have to make your own opportunities at the very beginning. You have to do something somewhere; get some people in a room, just to see whether *you* like it. There's too much concentration on getting other people to like your work. Young directors have to find out whether *they* really like their work, or if they want to change it before they start showing it. You have to find out whether you have a work method and whether you have something that's ready for you to feel good about. These are practical considerations. "If I show this work, will it be seen as good?" Directors can work in any city. You don't have to work in New York. Anyplace there are people, there is an audience. You simply have to start anywhere you can, under any circumstances. It becomes a matter of persisting until you find a play that reveals your work as special—defined by your personality, your insights and your personal set of images. The price of being a director is high. It's a life of enormous concentration, but of great rewards. And raising a family is creative, too.

How have you managed to do that—lead Arena Stage and take on the responsibilities of caring for a family?

It just happened naturally. My oldest son was born in January, 1952, my other son four and a half years later. Arena Stage opened in August 1950 in The Hippodrome and again in The Old Vat in November, 1956. So the children were raised along with the institution by Tom and me together. We had no rules about how that was to happen. The functions fell into a natural division. I had more to do with the psychological and physical welfare of the children, Tom with the house and yard. It all breathed together. It seemed neither a problem nor anything that had to be rationally figured out.

It's just that having a family and constructing a career in the theatre are hard things to accomplish simultaneously.

Young women ask me, "What do you do when the child is sick?" But that's no question. If the child is sick, you're with the child. You answer the loudest need at any given moment. You don't have to have that written on a sampler. It isn't that it's very hard to raise children and run a theatre. It isn't difficult to structure. What is hard is to have the energy and psychic attention for both those domains. It's hard to tune in sensitively and creatively to that many people in one day. That takes a lot out of you, and there are things you give up. Tom and I didn't have a social life for decades and we didn't have a life of objects. Something has to go. You can really strip down once you know that what matters is your work, your children, your relationships.

So much has been made of the fact that most of the early resident theatres were founded by women.

Founding a theatre is different from *going into* the theatre. It's a big deal. It's taking on a tribe. George Tabori once said to me while we were working on *Mother Courage* that he thought the impulse to found a theatre was the same impulse as founding a family. Perhaps women channeled the creative abilities that couldn't be channeled into the commercial theatre into making our own kitchens so we could cook the dishes we wanted. In the early years, we didn't know what we were doing. We didn't know what forces were going to come along. We all started our theatres whimsically, capriciously even, and they were small. It was a way to do our work, direct plays. Then it got to be very large and complex economically and our responsibilities ramified to constructing buildings and raising funds and charting courses through these very treacherous economic and social waters.

Is that why fewer women came along later to found theatres?

Maybe fewer women wanted to do it because more wanted to be individual creative artists. Who wants to run a theatre now? Not many men want to do it either, anymore. When I took a sabbatical and David Chambers ran the theatre, he couldn't get out of there fast enough when I came back. I vaguely thought and hoped that he'd get into a power struggle with me. That would have interested me, to hear that someone really wanted to run this theatre. But David really wanted to do his own work. Later, he did take on his own theatre, after resting up a bit, I think, and looking back on the great pleasure of making a personal statement through a theatre collective. And now Garland Wright has taken on the Guthrie, and I applaud that and am grateful for that.

Then what is it that continues to interest you about Arena?

I like running an institution because I can control its statement, its repertory, its interface with the world. A theatre stands for a world viewpoint, and I like to be the one who determines that viewpoint through a particular aesthetic: the choice of plays, actors, directors, designers. The stage, of course, is the center of the art. It's the diamond in the setting and it's the spot toward which all arrows point. An institution is an artwork, and building one is a work of personal creativity. But it's an artwork on a pretty large social scale, and it's a public art, not a private act of contemplation, meditation. What is tiresome, heavy at times, is the repetitiveness, the endlessness of one season after another and the increasing hazards of bigness, box office and institutionalization. I want to direct more, to write, to teach, to do my personal work that I have put into the background all of these years. Not that building an institution isn't a personal work. It is.

RICHARD FOREMAN

O ntological-Hysteric Theater—
Ontological: "The principal area of metaphysical speculation, called ontology, is the study of the ultimate nature of being."—Actual, mystical, truthful, imagistic, poetic, witty, intellectual.

Hysteric: "Freud concluded that hysterical symptoms, in which psychological conflicts are converted into bodily disturbances, were symbolic representations of a repressed unconscious event accompanied by strong emotions that could not be adequately expressed or discharged at the time. He found that cathartic reactivation of the memory could remove the hysterical symptoms."—Hidden, iconographic, hieroglyphic, subliminal, allusive, histrionic.

Theatre (of the absurd): "Apparently pointless situations and dialogue, typically expressing the existential nature of man's self-isolation, anxiety, frustration."—Hallucinatory, vaudevillian, illogical, burlesque, alien, visceral, menacing, inscrutable.

128

A deafening thud, blinding lights, an irritating buzzer, and Kate Manheim is revealed in the nude! What is an audience to think? Does anyone quite understand what Richard Foreman is doing while he baffles, amuses, shocks, bewilders and entrances audiences with a precisely choreographed directing technique that is as perversely dense and symbolic as the plays he himself writes?

Foreman's productions command our interest because they are meticulously crafted, intensely intelligent works that result in a flow of funny, erotic or frightening images that appear to have a logic that is itself imbalanced—a realism that is unreal. The challenge then is to find the meaning of the symbols, to understand the insinuation of style. But Foreman rejects such an approach, saying, "The minute man knows the message, he sleeps." Viewing, Foreman believes, is more important than understanding; yet his theatre aggressively demands an intellectual response. What a spot for an audience to be in! Those famous lights flashed in the eyes of the spectators are not just a disquieting theatrical technique—they literally put the public in the spotlight, placing the burden of effort on them to be aware, to postpone making conclusions—to keep the sleeper awake! In the best Brechtian tradition, the audience is constantly reminded of its own feelings, while Foreman uses the work to notate his own consciousness.

A major influence for much of Foreman's mystical and intellectual speculation is to be found in his interest in the ancient writings of the Jewish Kabbalah, with their teaching of the patterns of poetic interplay between literal and figurative meaning, the enigmatic joining of soul and body, the balance of and oscillation between "a state of grace" and "rigorous judgement." The title of his 1977 play *Book of Splendors; Part II (Book of Levers) Action at a Distance*, appears to be a direct reference to the Kabbalah, which is based on the belief that every word, letter, number, and even accent contains mysteries interpretable by those who know the secret. These esoteric Kabbalistic teachings are theories of trope, or turns of language, which are complex substitutions for God—like poems. God and language are one and the same. Like the Kabbalah, Foreman's writings suggest a reality that stands behind our world of appearances—neither things nor acts, but relational events, representations of the inner reality of our lives.

Foreman is a theorist/writer/director/designer. His production designs for his early works were playfully constructivist, three-dimensional mathematical creations that constantly shifted, manipulating the stage's proportions. The settings constructed in his tiny seventy-seat loft theatre in the Soho district of New York, were cabinet-like doll-houses that, with the deep perspective of the narrow loft space (the stage was fourteen feet wide and eighty feet deep), took on womb-like qualities. An architectural signature of his work has always been strings stretched across the stage defining some nonexistent area, overlaying the playing space yet strangely out of sync with it.

The actors he preferred to use in the early productions were nonprofessionals, visually interesting, "found objects" chosen for their spiritual qualities rather than their acting technique. Kate Manheim, Foreman's perennial actress-muse, has performed in more of his productions than any other actor and will forever be associated with Rhoda, the vulnerable heroine of such epics as *Rhoda in Potatoland, Sophia = (Wisdom) Part 3: The Cliffs* and *Classical Therapy or A Week Under the Influence.* (The Kabbalah manifests the God Presence as being in the shape of woman, an image of erotic mysticism.) Abundant nudity was an integral part of the early Foreman plays but has diminished as he has matured.

While Foreman's approach to theatre ultimately rejected the traditional training he received at Brown and Yale universities, the rigorous approach to literature and playwriting that he acquired in those institutions focused his talent for organization of mind and effort. Even among the extraordinary collection of American avant-garde theatre artists developing in the 1960s, he was unique. Much of the experimental work of that period was body-oriented; Foreman, meanwhile, was at work creating a new language for the stage, an amalgam of environment, sound, movement and text. This *Gesamtkunstwerk* insisted that all of these elements were vital in the attempt to evoke the source of nature and spirit, abstraction and dream.

While struggling with the notion of striving to be a mainstream playwright in the years immediately following college, Foreman came under the influence of American avant-garde filmmakers, and that experience encouraged him to write and produce his own personal, poetical visions of what theatre ought to be. In 1968 he wrote and directed the first of the Ontological-Hysteric Theater productions, *Angelface*, which passed largely unnoticed. But, with each new production, followers of the Ontological-Hysteric grew in number and avidly crowded into the second floor loft, curious and baffled, amused and challenged. However, it was not until 1972, when *Dr. Selavy's Magic Theater*, with music by Stanley Silverman, premiered at Lenox Arts Center in Massachusetts and later was presented for a respectable Off Broadway run at the Mercer-O'Casey Theater, that Foreman began to receive "uptown" attention. The collaboration with Silverman continued through a series of highly praised, cheerfully wacky musical plays.

When he began directing in 1968, Foreman's staging was relentlessly detailed. Every movement, every body position of the actors was meticulously dictated. He states, "I was never in favor of the kind of free-formed, undisciplined 'soup-theatre' of a lot of the work done in the 1960s." In his desire to control all production elements, and to be an integral part of the work at all times, Foreman is visibly present at every one of the Ontological productions, sitting at the lighting console, manipulating each light and sound cue, his bespectacled face peering impassively out at the audience, sometimes calling, "CUE!," as a part of the performance. Again, "shaking the sleeper awake!" Over time, Foreman's rigorously controlled work has become less intellectually aggressive—more outward with sweeping choreography, utilizing fewer disassociation techniques and allowing viewers to experience *emotion*. Foreman describes this mellowing of the work of his middle-years as "autumnal."

A meeting with Foreman at his Soho loft is not unlike sitting down with a middle-aged Albert Einstein, amid rows and rows of bookshelves, he in his comfortable slippers, kindly, patiently and sometimes eagerly explaining for the 739th time his theory of relativity.

■　　■　　■

At first the world thought of you primarily as a playwright. Now there is the sense that the director-side of your ego has taken control. What separates these facets of your talent?

I am driven by a desire to put something into the world that I find lacking in my life, and I try to correct for that lack by making works of art that give me the environment I would rather be living in. Originally, I became a director simply because nobody else would direct my plays. I didn't really direct any material other than my own until I did *Threepenny Opera*, at Lincoln Center in 1976.

How does a young man born on Staten Island, removed to Scarsdale, who goes to Brown and Yale in the 1950s, and then goes to New York to write Broadway comedies, become a unique revolutionary artist in the theatre?

For some reason, from the time that I was very young, I had an attraction for the strangest material. I read *The Skin of Our Teeth* for the first time at about twelve and thought, "It's like a dream, it's so weird, it's wonderful." I remember seeing Elia Kazan's production of *Camino Real*, which I dragged my Scarsdale parents to, and they said, "What's this all about?"

I have always gravitated to things that try to talk to some more spiritually oriented level, rather than realistic discussions and manipulations of the real, practical, empirical world in which we live.

Then the big revelation was discovering Brecht—and especially his saying that you could have a theatre that was not based on empathy. For some reason, even at an early age what I hated in the theatre was a kind of

131

asking for love that I saw manifested on the stage, getting a unified reaction from everybody in the audience. Brecht said it didn't have to be like that, and until I was in my middle twenties, he was the beginning, middle and end of everything for me. That only changed when I came to New York and encountered the beginnings of the underground film movement, and that reoriented me, because up to that point I had thought of America as being rather unsophisticated, naive and simplistic, as compared with the complexities and aggressiveness of European art and thought. Then in America, in the middle 1960s, I discovered people my age were making their own movies, operating on a level that was akin to poetry rather than storytelling. And I thought, "Aha! Why can't the techniques of poetry that operate in film, operate in theatre?" I came to terms with trying to make an American kind of art that exploited and put onstage everything that up till then I had wanted to reject about myself. I gravitated to theatre even though I was opened up by filmmakers.

Your plays have been examined and explained and analyzed in an effort to understand their meanings. As a director, do you feel the need to insert guidelines in your work to give it clarity?

Yes, more and more. Oftentimes, however, people find those explanations confusing. First of all, things change and we get older, and I don't know if what I do is quite as hard to understand these days as it was fifteen years ago—because other people are doing similar things. Other currents of thought are in the air.

In fact, some of my explanations are couched in terms that are rather difficult because to be true to what I'm trying to get at *is* difficult. I don't think of myself as doing anything radically new or different. I think of myself as being a meeting point for all kinds of ideas, all kinds of feelings, that are around us at hand. It seems to me that I'm dealing all the time with things that are in the air, both as a director and as a writer. I take them and I try to play with them in an exhilarating way. Part of the difficulty is that people are sitting there thinking, "Yes, but is he saying that we should be this, that or the other thing?" And I don't think that's my function as an artist. My function is to enjoy and help my audience enjoy an exhilarating kind of play with all of the elements that are present in this very heterogeneous culture, where we have hundreds of years of history—and everything that's been thought and felt in all those hundreds of years—readily available on bookshelves, TV, cassettes, records. It's all there as never before, and how do you keep your head above water? Well, you learn how to ice-skate on the crystallized surface of the pond, underneath which is the morass of hundreds and thousands of years of history.

I'm trying to be a medium, to let all of these messages come through. The task is to make some kind of harmony out of them, to eliminate part of the noise so that something is perceptible. I have never been in favor of the kind of big undisciplined soup theatre that for me a lot of the 1960s mixed-media things were. Even though many people can't perceive it, I've always been an extremely structurally oriented artist who tries to clean everything up. As a director, my one criticism of myself is that I'm too neat—I've tried to keep the event too clean, too defined, too much under control, and I wish at times that I could be a little messier as a director, as I am in my writing.

Is this cleanliness, this structure, tied to the manner in which you work with actors? You've said before that you tend to be dictatorial in terms of detail, movement, placement and timing.

This is less true today than five years ago. Unless I am totally deluded, these days the vast majority of actors I work with find it a positive experience, whereas in the early days some of them definitely felt very constrained. As I move into directing plays that are not my own, this becomes increasingly the case. I still block the play and I still ask for all kinds of specific things. I never ask an actor to do something he's uncomfortable with.

Your use of space and the scenography for your plays are also "neat" and "defined," to use your words.

There's no denying that my main interest in the theatre is compositional, that I am interested in the interplay of all the elements. I am not interested in the theatre where the audience becomes seduced by a kind of empathetic relationship to the actors.

And yet, in a sense, audiences do empathize because there's so much humor in your plays and that tends to unify an audience. We laugh, we find it amusing.

I think people should laugh more. Audiences are often afraid of laughing because a) things are going so fast that they think they might miss something, and b) I come with this reputation of being tough and intellectual and radical. I've had friends of mine sit in the theatre watching my plays laughing, and people sitting in front of them look back as if it were some sacrilege.

Your famous wires stretched across the stage in your productions suggest an alchemy, a science. It has come to the point where a designer can't put a wire across the stage without having it referred to as "a Richard Foreman wire."

Yes. But all those things of mine are slowly disappearing, at least becoming more minimal. When I did a revival of Arthur Kopit's *End of the World With*

Symposium to Follow for American Repertory Theatre, we were starting to rehearse, and Bob Brustein, the artistic director, came and sat next to me. He said, "You know, this is really going well. But tell me something, are you really committed to those strings?"

With those taut strings, are you trying to frame stage areas, to bring them into more concise focus? Visually, there's somehow a connection with those drawings in antiquity, where human figures are extended along straight lines.

It's hard for me to talk about really, but somehow there is an articulation of the space—so that it's almost as if the actors are overlaid by a kind of grid. It's almost like a musical staff. I like knowing where I am physically, somehow, and also on the spiritual and emotional level those strings define some kind of force field, some kind of reverberation box, so that whatever is going on in the play reverberates even more intensely. It's like someone sketching who starts drawing lines of force, feeling the need to work with a diagonal, and then the body grows out of that.

Almost a connection with God.

Well, it does connect with God in that it connects with what I think are the most abstract spiritual energies—the kind of nervous motor energy that wants to find a way to concretely manifest itself in the three-dimensional world. It starts out as impulse. And my technique in the theatre is to feel the impulse, not knowing yet what it means or how it wants to work, but to let the impulse lead me. Then it takes on a three-dimensional, actorly, proplike form—but I always remember to keep present for the spectator a kind of interplay between the original thrust, the place that it came from and the real three-dimensional human, physical manifestation that it takes on at this particular historical moment. This impulse leads to another impulse, which leads to another impulse. I work the same way when I'm doing Brecht or Molière or Kopit.

That method is easier to envision when you're directing your own plays than in something like Don Juan *or* Threepenny Opera. *In those cases, how does that impulse manifest itself in you as a director?*

Even though I theorize after the fact, when you're actually working on something, you don't think conceptually. At least, I don't. It's important for me to delineate the way in which the play grows. The first thing I do is make a set. These days I generally design the set even when I'm working with a designer—I basically build a model that I give to the designer. The set for me means creating a kind of space that both implies the grid of this original thrust, the energy of this original abstract thrust, as well as the specific locale of the play. Given the proper set, I then have within it different layers of being so that this impulse can realize itself.

In addition to strings, a lot of my sets use railings and sorts of specific geometric divisions of space that might suggest a courthouse, a bullring, a synagogue. Now, all of these enclosures somehow immediately give me a gridlike place within which to work. That's both the suggestion of the impulse for wanting to present things to your fellow man plus defining special sacred, private places where you are alone with your soul or whatever. At the very root, it allows me to play with more public impulses as well as more private impulses within any text. That's an oversimplification, of course, but it seems to me those are the energies that are set up.

The next thing I do is get music organized. All my plays, including the classical plays and the contemporary plays that I haven't written, have music behind the text most of the time. If I'm working with a composer, I can't conceive of going into rehearsal without having the music completed, because that's going to be my play. When I'm not working with a composer, or even when I am, sometimes I've asked for forty different kinds of music with the freedom to recombine them and do whatever I want. Working by myself, I make long or short loops, and if four or five are played at the same time, they're hardly loops anymore because they're going in and out of phase all the time. From the first day of rehearsal, I insist on having my soundman, who is busy shuffling these tracks, and it evolves organically as we're rehearsing. I spend just as much time altering my music as I do dealing with the performing and I think that all kinds of wonderful things happen that way. Again, I choose music that somehow takes a section of the text and makes a comment on it or lifts it into a slightly different plane. For instance, in Arthur Kopit's play, while a general is talking about why the United States has such and such a nuclear policy, the music has an energy that suggests the kinds of desires about how one wants to live one's life that end up producing a general who's going to work for the Pentagon, who's going to try to defend America.

Do you sometimes choose music that is in opposition to the action of the play?

Oh, sure. That's an old Brechtian technique, of course, to distance, to estrange. But I don't think about that conceptually. It's a way of working that happens almost automatically. At the moment, I don't tell myself why it's interesting. It just seems right to me. We start rehearsing from the first day with all that music.

Your major collaboration has been with composer Stanley Silverman working on some five operas including Dream Tantras for Western Massachusetts,

135

Hotel for Criminals *and* **Doctor Selavy's Magic Theater,** *all of which you directed.*

The productive thing about Stanley and me is that he understands completely what I'm doing. In that sense, he's one of the most perceptive and intelligent people I've ever worked with in the theatre. We have somewhat different tastes and I think he isn't as interested in some of the really far-out things I'm interested in. We generally have one or two meetings where I give him the words and he's interested to find out what I think is going on and what kind of music I imagine. That doesn't necessarily mean he would write it that way. We're friendly, but we've never talked that seriously about anything.

What kind of predigestion of the play takes place before rehearsal?

Before I go into rehearsal I know my stuff, but I don't sit pondering over the play. I read it once or twice and make very brief notes about staging ideas in terms of the set I've designed. But they're all tentative. Any text includes hundreds of possibilities. Until I hear the specific actors that I am using, I don't know in which direction I'm going to be logically led. I will discover certain things they are emphasizing or that seem to be true because of their personality that relate to certain possibilities in the play. Then my task is to strengthen that line of interpretation.

I have a clear idea of what I think the play is saying and the direction I want to take it. It's like being shipwrecked on a new planet. How do you live on this planet? It demands certain things. There are certain rules you have to abide by to live on this planet. But, within that, you could build a house with five rooms, a two-story house or a lean-to. Those are the decisions you make in rehearsal period. The only way I know how to work is three-dimensionally, to get up immediately on your feet with the actors and feel things in the body and make it happen that way. It's my articulation of the actors and space, vis-à-vis the text psychologically, that I'm proudest of, and I have absolute total confidence that I know how to do it.

What kind of images do you give the actors?

I remember I used to say to the actors in *Don Juan* that what we were trying to evoke was something that resembled what you would see if you pictured the seashore, the waves crashing against the rocks, and there's all this foam. I'm trying to create a theatrical event which is like the energy and activity of that foaming as the waves crash against the rocks. Out of that foam, "Oh, look! There's Don Juan!" And then he gets swept back into the foam of cosmic energy. "And there's Sganarelle!" And he goes back into the foam, and what happens in the play rises and sinks in this foam of life energy. With my music and with the particular kind of blocking I do, that's what I'm after.

Your stage movement with crowd scenes is especially skillful.

Even though I've often been called a hermetic artist—and in certain ways I am—to stage a play to me is to stage a public event. That influences the way that I use crowds. That goes further than simply saying that I'm not interested in fourth-wall theatre. I want everybody to be aware of the fact that they are watching a show.

Once I wanted to do an opera for the New York City Opera. I was very young at the time. I went to Julius Rudel, and he said to me, "What are you trying to do here, and what's your interest in theatre?" I said, "Well, the best thing that was ever said to me by a friend was, 'Richard, you know, I really enjoyed watching your play. Even more than I enjoyed watching it, I enjoyed watching myself watching it.'" Rudel looked at me and said, "That is the most disgusting comment I've ever heard. That is self-indulgent. You should want to capture the audience and make them forget about themselves." Well, we come from different worlds.

This is a major conflict for audiences and theatre artists alike.

Sure. I'm perfectly open to the fact that five years from now I may decide, "Hey, Rudel was right. What is all that junk I've been doing for the last twenty years?"

Is that ability you have to move groups of people beautifully something that can be learned?

It may be. There are various theories that any talent you have is a compensation for a lack. I am terribly physically inhibited. I have never had the guts to get up in a disco or anywhere else and dance. All of a sudden, when I was staging *Threepenny Opera* at the Vivian Beaumont in Lincoln Center in 1976, I was confronted with Raul Julia and Ellen Greene, and shy Richard had to stage musical numbers and dances. Well, I can't tell you how thrilled I was when I just got up and started doing it. I can make a fool of myself because it's a controlled environment where I'm the boss and everybody knows I'm sort of smart.

A lot of people have been overwhelmed by your intellect. Is that a requirement of your work?

It's certainly not. When it comes to making art, the last thing in the world I would ever think of doing is to try applying any of the things that I've learned from reading philosophy, psychology, aesthetic theory or science. It has to be a spontaneous process, and I never think about all of that intellectual baggage when I'm making a work of art, never. At this point, when I sit down to make a work of art, I probably don't think about it any differently than Neil Simon or Hal Prince, but it just comes out different because we're different people.

Then is it a matter of substantially differing styles? You once said, "Style attacks with truth—where man most deeply is, but where he has the least developed navigational techniques."

Believe it or not, even when I was fifteen years old and used to go to Broadway theatre every weekend, I hated all the hits but occasionally I'd see flops that I thought were wonderful. Americans just don't understand that style can be content and style has things to say. Invariably, people never understand that in art, stylistic position is a moral position, an intellectual position, and carries the real content, the real meaning. That lack of understanding is continually frustrating. But it's easy to see why it's so difficult. In order to live your life in a normal capitalistic society, you have to put blinders on so that you are not distracted from the things that you have to do to get on in this world. And the message that comes through these artists' style is, "Hey, look! There's all this distracting stuff out there that contains truth, contains life!"

To add to that conflict, your early productions shocked audiences by your use of sound and lights.

I think people still tend to find my work kind of abrasive and aggressive. I still use lights in the audience's eyes. I don't use loud buzzers anymore. But a lot of that stuff is still there because I want to wake the audience up, to stop them from being seduced by what they're watching. Lucidity, clarity, waking up. That's what I'm interested in, both in my life and in my art for myself and my audience. I've discussed this with some other modern directors like Elizabeth LeCompte at the Wooster Group. We make these things up because it makes us feel better. It's not to torture people. It's to feel good, like after you've had a workout in the gym. But, of course, by doing that you sometimes run into hostility.

I've been very lucky because I've been able to do exactly what I wanted to do in the theatre for twenty years. That quest is an attempt to bring onto the stage the operations of some other energy that is not the energy of the human—the socialized human personality. I am trying to do it, believe it or not, through rhythm, serving a kind of dialectical relationship between what you see and what you hear, which becomes a kind of rhythmic articulation —an evocation of a different level of being, a different kind of energy that one can bring into life.

Since that is far easier to control when you direct your own plays, why have you extended yourself to other works?

The reason I'm doing plays other than my own now is to see if this particular kind of rhythmic articulation is applicable to all kinds of works. One way to relate to it is through the old theory of the Jewish Kabbalah, that the world we live in is a world of broken pieces of physical material, reality, and our task as human beings is somehow to find the spark of light in these things and lift them back to God, to the wholeness that they're supposed to have. I know how pretentious that sounds, but I'm trying to take things that show the picture of our fallen physical world and to find a way in which to organize them rhythmically so that somehow that material starts to swirl and lift and some other quality comes through that restores it to its rightful place in the cosmos.

Do you find yourself limited by your own frame of reference when directing your own work?

When I am directing my own material, I have no inhibitions about treating Richard, "the author," as a joke, with contempt, making fun of him all the time, making fun of my text. And I automatically do that with all texts that I'm working on. So I have to watch my p's and q's if an Arthur Kopit is around. It doesn't mean that I don't respect his text, but to me you've got to play with this stuff, you've got to handle it like it's just stuff. It's not holy. The great relaxation of dealing with one's own script is having permission to say, "What is this garbage this guy wrote? How are we going to fix this mess?"

You worked abroad for a number of years, but then returned to this country for a committed period of work. Was that because you felt that the pendulum had swung back to where audiences were willing to hear all kinds of disturbing, less rational truths?

I'm interested in America because I had a problem most of my life in wanting to cast out all of those traits that I didn't like about myself, and one of the traits I didn't like about myself was being, to the bottom of my soles, an American. I feel that the American culture is an adolescent culture. I feel that I'm an adolescent and I idolized what I thought was the greater maturity and sophistication of Europeans. I wanted to identify with that but, finally, it ain't me. European culture is more sophisticated. But I don't think that sophistication necessarily can save us. I did at one point. I had to come back and work out of the dumb, naive openness that is a great strength of America but was very hard for me to accept.

ADRIAN HALL

A drian Hall has spent most of his artistic life circumventing the conventional and steering around taboos in the process of creating provocative theatre. Along the way, he has sometimes outraged orthodox theatregoers—but Hall has invariably managed to confront and, ultimately, overwhelm his detractors. In the process, he has developed an honored place in Providence, Rhode Island, for the theatre he founded there in 1964, Trinity Square Repertory Company. (Square was later dropped from the institution's name.)

Not entirely content to have sculpted a company from New England stone, in 1983 Adrian Hall returned to his native state of Texas to put his brand on the Dallas Theater Center. As its artistic director as well as Trinity's, Hall found himself in a unique position—helmsman of two major American theatres situated some sixteen hundred miles apart—dividing his time flying back and forth between the capital of our smallest state and the enterprising "prairiegalopolis."

Hall started Trinity Square Repertory Company during the turbulent 1960s, when nonprofit theatres were exploding into existence across America. Most of these theatres declared their intent to develop and maintain resident companies capable of performing work not frequently seen in the commercial theatre—important work, including ancient and modern classics and new plays—but ultimately, few of these theatres were able to provide for enduring companies. Costs were prohibitive, and most theatres fell back on the commercial practice of hiring a pick-up cast on a show-by-show basis.

Hall caused Trinity to be one of the exceptions. He encouraged a group of gifted young actors to move to Providence with him. Keeping them together, he decided, was priority number one. "They became the center of the experience," Hall would say later, and this core group matured over a period of years into an extraordinary ensemble. Hall remained steadfast to the company concept and has sustained the cooperation of his actors during times when many of their fellows were being lured from the theatre to more lucrative jobs in film and television.

Rhode Island was not entirely hospitable territory in which to develop such a company. Trinity began with Hall, six professional actors and a budget of $3,000. They struggled for several years playing out of a church basement, a school auditorium, an old theatre. In the Company's third season, the recently formed National Endowment for the Arts, chaired by Roger Stevens, gave the institution its first major grant, which helped it to stabilize.

Trinity's program of performances for students (Project Discovery) was a major pioneering effort to integrate theatre with the public school system curriculum and brought millions of potential future audience members into the theatre. A quarter of a century later, Trinity's subscribership continues to grow, fueled by this ongoing program.

In 1973 Hall was able to move his company into what was to be their permanent home, a renovated vaudeville-movie palace that had been known as the Majestic when it was built in 1916. By that time, Trinity employed as many as eighty-five artists and technicians for ten to twelve months a year.

Then Hall weathered a major crisis in the mid-1970s, when his board of trustees dismissed him after an especially controversial season (which included Hall's and Richard Cumming's adaptation of James Purdy's *Eustace Chisholm and the Works*, a play which offended some members of the community with its vivid depiction of an abortion and its homosexual theme). Hall was given his walking papers, his supporters argued, for artistically challenging the community a bit too much, attendant with Trinity's ongoing financial problems. But, in an unprecedented action, Hall, in turn, fired the trustees and remained head of the institution. In short order he organized a new board, one that was supportive of his goals.

Hall's Trinity productions have been recognized widely through transfers to Broadway, adaptations for television, international tours and a special 1981 Tony Award. All the same, it was a courageous move on the part of the Dallas Theater Center's board to seek out Hall as artistic director. The Center, founded in 1959, was a financially successful but hidebound institution requiring new energy to bring it into the 1980s. Hall would supply the excitement, but his history of blasting away at traditional perceptions, his penchant for inflammatory subject matter—even his often demonstrated disregard for the conventions of the design and use of theatrical space—these things made him a dangerous choice. At the same time, Hall's belief in maintaining a company of actors paralleled the founding philosophy of the Center. He was a native, having been born at Van, Texas, and his theatre education had begun under Dallas theatre pioneer Margo Jones. At her urging, he studied as an actor with Gilmor Brown at the Pasadena Playhouse and later worked with Bob Porterfield, founder of the Barter Theatre in Abingdon, Virginia, as well as with other founders of the resident theatre movement.

Notwithstanding Hall's theatrical audacity, his style seemed a perfect accompaniment for the raw boned, vigorous Dallas—a city not afraid to shout about its desire to become a major-league cultural oasis. But Hall's long, successful battle to win over Providence audiences had not prepared him for this new struggle in a once familiar environment. It was twenty years after he founded Trinity, and the theatre warrior was now fifty-five. In Dallas, he was not starting a new theatre but attempting to change the course of an already existing one. When asked why he took on the Center, fraught with problems as it was, he replied, "There's no logical reason why I came. It's like Tennessee Williams, who was always so afraid of being analyzed. He kept saying in just simple ways, 'Baby, I'm afraid if I understand it, it won't interest me anymore.'"

When he arrived at the Dallas Theater Center in 1983, Texas was booming with rising oil and land prices. Five years later the economic growth was reversed when prices precipitously fell, but Hall remained optimisic and the artistic company at the Center began to be grow. Fifteen actors were put under season contracts to form a core company in 1987, and Hall's plan is to add five additional actors in each subsequent year until the company reaches thirty-five.

In 1987 hall announced his intention to withdraw as artistic director from the stable, firmly ensconced Trinity operation within a five-year period but to continue at the helm at the Dallas Theater Center, to make it a major part of the community.

Hall's major contributions to contemporary theatre have been his innovative adaptations of novels and biographical literature. In the 1960s Hall collaborated with the late Bill Goyen on adapting his novel *House of Breath* (about the dynasty of a southern Texas family) into a play called *House of Breath Black/White*. The actors playing the family members were sometimes white and sometimes black. He worked with James Reston, Jr., on a play based on Reston's book about Jonestown called *Our Father Who Art in Hell,* and Hall's long-time co-adapter/composer-in-residence Richard (Deedee) Cumming worked with him to adapt a five-hour series of Edith Wharton works for television.

Hall's spectacular stagings of these works are executed in an eminently American style that draws from such sources as vaudeville and the circus. Key to this work has been his collaboration with designer Eugene Lee. Together, they have found ways to break down the physical barriers between the audience and the work onstage. The far-reaching influence of this evolutionary work is most evident in Lee's scenic designs for such productions as Hal Prince's *Candide* and *Sweeney Todd* on Broadway. Hall has also directed television adaptations of *Feasting With Panthers* and *Brother to Dragons* for PBS and, in films, Edith Wharton's *House of Mirth* and *Ethan Frome.*

Talking with Adrian Hall is like conversing with a Texas twister. Despite his years in New England, the soft southern Texas drawl has never left him and is spit out with a staccato delivery. His conversation is characteristic of his work—animated ideas overlapping one another, anointed with humor.

■ ■ ■

What characterizes an "Adrian Hall work," and how do you achieve it?

In a production of mine you always see the warts. You've got to see the people pissing onstage and you've got to see them belch and fart and eat. And I must say, it's more difficult for actors that way. Actors can have cliché ways of doing things that frequently come from a failure to recognize that there is a problem. Knowing how to do it sometimes is simply being able to define what the problem is, and solving it. One of my favorite expressions in directing is, "Can't you pull that closer to yourself?" My company now understands it. We need some way that the actor can continually charge the thing and then make the right connection. You know, darlin', Michelangelo was right about Adam and God *almost* touching. The right connection is terribly important.

I like to think that the one thing that you take into a rehearsal hall every day of your life—in addition to a cup of black coffee—is your ability to be a virgin all over again, your ability to be naive, to start at point zero. To find the essence of the theatre, one has to look continually at opposites. You never see white quite so clearly as when it's placed against black, and you never acknowledge laughter quite so clearly as when it breaks your heart. And so I have found that pushing together these elements is far more telling than just decorating with one color. It won't happen unless you keep pushing all the elements together in ways that result in an explosion. Most of the time it doesn't happen, and you've got to be able to pick up those pieces tomorrow and try to push them a little closer to something that comes alive. If you could just see the things that are eventually discarded during my rehearsal period! Rehearsals are fraught with discovery, fraught with boredom. You just drag yourself home at night from fatigue.

The work presented at Trinity and the Dallas Theater Center is fairly wide-ranging.

I've always done a juggling act between what I wanted to work on and what constitutes "middle of the road." I certainly try to keep throwing in Ibsen, Strindberg, Shaw, Shakespeare. But if you look back into my history, it's absolutely peppered with new work.

The unique element of your theatre work has been your adaptations of literature to the stage.

We've proved that material really can be moved from one medium to another. The first international attention we had was for a piece called *Feasting With Panthers*. We had done a play about Oscar Wilde, *Years of the Locust*, by an Englishman. The Edinburgh International Festival suddenly appeared out of the blue and asked us to come. It was the first year that Grotowski was invited, the first year for "everybody," so we went and we were a great hit. When we came back, I wanted to take the piece further, add more music. The author didn't want any of that, just to take it back to London and to Broadway and that was it. So I said to Deedee Cumming, "Hell, we can do this better ourselves." So we did and called it *Feasting With Panthers*.

That was 1973, the first year of WNET-TV's *Theater in America* series. They asked all the "respectable" people like Zelda Fichandler and Bill Ball (then the general director, American Conservatory Theatre, San Francisco) and others. They did everything from *Cyrano de Bergerac* to *King Lear*. Howard Taubman was the one who was making the selections, and he came to see *Feasting With Panthers*. He said, "They've got to have one avant-garde piece." The underwriters just bought it without even knowing what it was. I was very excited. I thought it was just swell and I had no idea that anybody was going to get upset about it. We filmed it in an old textile mill in Providence. That fall, when all the theatres around the country had their work in the can, WNET announced everything but *Feasting With Panthers*. Finally, the producer called me to say there were fifteen or sixteen points they could not agree to and it looked as if it wouldn't be shown unless I was willing to make terrible cuts and changes. The points they wouldn't agree to would be so funny today—one was men dressed as women. One of the things that offended them the most—we were doing bits of Oscar Wilde's old play *Salome*, which had been written for Sarah Bernhardt in 1910—was a place where

Salome takes the head of Jokanaan and kisses the head. Well, I had this really dynamite shot of Richard Kavanaugh as Salome (he was playing all of the Dorian Gray, male-female things) where he took this dummy head, a mannequin dummy, and kissed the blood and there was a kind of spittle caught between him and the dummy head. Well, the executives of the corporation that was underwriting the series had viewed that and said, "No." So then Jac Venza, who was head of the series, indeed, a great fan of the theatre, said, "Adrian, if you will do this one cut for them, I promise you that we'll show it if it has to be at midnight. We'll not ask you to cut or change anything else." And I said, "Okay," and took those frames out. It broke my heart, but I did it. (Those few frames were restored when WNET rebroadcast *Feasting with Panthers* in a retrospective fourteen years later in 1987.) They showed it and, of course, everybody immediately pronounced this a landmark in television. The corporation immediately asked us to do another one.

At the same time as Feasting with Panthers *appeared, you began working with Robert Penn Warren.*

I found Red Warren's poem *Brother to Dragons* through somebody at Brown University in 1972. He was up at Yale so I just called and said, "Can I come to see you?" I just adored Red Warren and he was intrigued. Well, there began just the most wonderful collaboration I've ever had. *Brother to Dragons* was a turning point in my life because I loved that poem and I really wanted to find a way to stage it. Red said, "Well, just plow ahead."

What was the key to staging that poem?

It was finding American images that were real and not borrowed from our theatrical past in any way. The piece is about Thomas Jefferson's nephew, who chopped up a slave because he felt that the slave had broken his mother's cup. The boy is obviously psychotic, so the climax of the piece is when he chops up the black man. Nobody knew how to do that. Ultimately, what I did, which really set the world on fire back in those dear dark days, was to get a chopping block from a meat market and bring out a big chunk of meat. Over on the side there was a truss, a pulley like you truss pigs with. We took Ed Hall, who was playing the slave, and hung him upside down on one side of the stage and the actor took a hatchet and chopped through the meat. That image seemed to be right at the heart of a lot of what Red Warren wrote: "Give me the meat axe, give me the meat axe." Twenty years later, I worked on his *All the King's Men*, and in that book he repeats the theme as he has Willie Stark say, "I'm gonna get him, I'm gonna kill him. Give me the meat axe, give me the meat axe." Red had said to me, while we were working on *Brother*, "Why don't you work on *All the King's Men?*"

So you'd been thinking about it all that time?

Years and years. In 1985 I said to him, "Why don't you come to Dallas and work on it?" He said, "I can't do it right now, why don't you go ahead?" I'd held out hopes that he was going to be able to come, but his health, and that of his wife Eleanor, was not good.

How critical was his presence to that kind of collaboration?

I really do like to have everybody there together, working on a project like that. Actors are necessary, but I also want the designer there. I want the composer, the dramaturg, the writer. Eugene Lee, the designer with whom I've collaborated for twenty-five years, is just wonderful. He'll sit in those rehearsals and sense solutions to problems. Once, in a *King's Men* rehearsal, we were singing a Randy Newman song from the *Good Ol' Boy* album, and I said to Deedee, "Could you just stand up and push that piano off as you're playing it?" He did and everybody thought that was great fun but there was no place for the piano to go. I didn't say anything because I didn't know what we'd do. The next morning, I came into rehearsal and Eugene had notched a hole in the bleachers big enough so that the piano could go right in.

So he's constantly reworking the stage environment.

He's constantly changing it.

You opened King's Men *in Dallas and then took it back into rehearsal before the Trinity production. How much rehearsal time did you have initially?*

Five weeks, and that was not enough. I need more time than most people. I never go into a play with less than one hundred to one hundred thirty hours. In repertory, we don't get a full eight hours per day of rehearsal. On performance days we get five hours, and on matinee days we don't get any. It's funny, the one thing institutionalized theatre disregards is the really serious problem of not having enough time to make mistakes. You have got to have the time to go with something that seems right, and then, when you get far enough down the line, totally discard that if need be, and start over. That's the only way you arrive at what the work is about.

There is almost no situation in the theatre where the right to fail is protected.

It's interesting, because in other fields, such as medicine or science, we understand that research is imperative. We think nothing of spending billions on a weapon, and then the thing explodes and that's the end of it and we have to start all over. But in this desperate race to give our institutions stability so we won't blow away in the first strong wind, we've had to standardize just about everything. If I were to get caught in a situation where I couldn't open a play on time, it would be such a disaster to these institutions. And not having the time to develop a work properly leads to slick mediocrity. There is an intolerance toward experimentation built into our system. We look at it as "self-indulgent." Of course I can do it the way everyone else does it, but that's not advancing the cause of theatre. If we are to know more about our craft, then we simply have to get out there and dig and find and stop and start and throw away. And you can't expect to show a finished work every time.

How, then, did you pull the script of King's Men *together without Warren?*

I had two dramaturgs, Oren Jacoby and Marsue Cumming, and I had the play that Red wrote from his 1946 novel, and the novel itself. I had a wonderful assistant, Kimberly Cole, who's a demon on the word processor. I had her extract every line of dialogue from the novel and cross-reference them. I made charts and graphs about what the book was about and where each event occurred, where certain images came in—three hundred pages later the image would recur. I chased the lives of everybody.

The novel was rather sprawling to be contained on the stage. What did you include in addition to the central story of Willie Stark?

Red's own stage adaptation took only one strand of the tapestry: Willie Stark (Huey Long). What I wanted to do was go back to the central character of Jack Burden and let it be his story. There is a wonderful thing he says in the book about life being a kind of spiderweb, and you can't touch it without it shattering and opening to reveal a spider. That's what Jack Burden feels about life and what he's found. I wanted that at the center of the play. Jack Burden is very contemporary, like someone right out of David Rabe's *Hurlyburly*.

There is a section in the book where the Burden character becomes a historical researcher. Some family members send him diaries and such when he's in college. He opens a diary and reads a most romantic American story about a boy who grows up in 1829 in the South, goes to visit a good friend and falls passionately, hopelessly in love with the friend's wife. The friend suddenly kills himself and, of course, the man knows that it has something to do with his love affair. Eventually, the servant, a black girl, finds the dead man's wedding ring, which he had taken off in the bed in which they had made love. The wife sells the black girl down the river as a slave and the boy feels this terrible guilt and goes off to die in the Civil War. I struggled with the decision of whether or not to keep all of that in the play, it's just so romantic and rococo."

147

Did you find specific theatrical images to surround the play as you had in **Brother to Dragons?**

Central to this nineteenth-century section is the fact that black servants *watched* their masters. The *sign of eyes* became very accusatory to the aristocrats who were having their various trysts. I found a way of using interesting masks to turn the actors into those black servants. They moved around in the shadows, watching this young couple come together in the arbor and make passionate love. Threatening and ominous banjo music played, a real country sound of Americana. That's about as far away from naturalism as you can get, and it was the most exciting thing in the play. We've seen the end of what we thought was the realism of the nineteenth century, or naturalism. We've just seen the end of it in the theatre—until television or the movies do something different.

It's difficult for film and TV to be nonrealistic or to do work that is "representational."

And our actors are influenced by that. It's tough on an actor working with me for the first time when I say, "No, I want you to say that line to the audience. You know, as audience I'm a participant in this event. If you get too slick and perfect, then it becomes the whole thing by itself. You don't need me." The audience is a real and live thing.

Another major influence your work with Eugene Lee has had on the theatre has been through creating stage environments that literally put the audience into the work by eliminating the physical barriers between them and the stage. An example was your production of **The Visit** *in Providence in 1986.*

We did it in the beautiful nineteenth-century Union Station in downtown Providence, which has been abandoned for a new station several miles away. The historical society has the good sense to light it at night, and one day when Eugene Lee and I were talking about how to find the core of *The Visit*, we looked at the train station sitting up there and Eugene said, "I'll tell you one thing, if we put a banner up on that train station, it would cause such a stir." And then it gradually moved to, "Why don't we do the thing in the train station?" Then immediately there were political ramifications with the city council and the mayor and all that. In Providence, because it's a city-state, you can pick up the phone and get to anybody, the governor or the mayor, and that's something you can't do in Dallas. Well, the historical society was excited about our idea, the city council was excited about it. You see, the train station had been so central to the life of every man, woman and child in the state of Rhode Island. Everybody was terribly nostalgic. The play directed itself. It just moved into that space. It was the most natural environment for a play that I have ever found.

What did you do to adapt the space?

Absolutely nothing. We put up two bleachers on each side of it. And the great marble columns at the entrance acted as one end of the space and the marble information booth that was at the other end acted as a counterweight. The actors just ran out between the columns and went up on levels. The actors and the audience shared the same space. When the audience entered it was literally on the stage. There were five hundred nonreserved seats and every night people lined up for them. Financially, it was the most successful production Trinity has ever done.

You made the theatre connect with people's lives.

Right. It's impossible to come into that old train station, for whatever experience, in a negative frame of mind. People just walk in and say, "Isn't this wonderful!"

What are the problems of moving into a nontheatre space?

You don't know exactly how big the environment will be until you get the project started. The mundane problems with the train station were the fact that there were no toilets for the actors when we first arrived, and the electricity hadn't been turned on and so forth. I tried to rehearse the play in the theatre rehearsal hall for a couple of days, but I realized that I was never going to bring it off that way. So we started building the bleachers at night and letting the actors work in the station by day. That meant bringing in portable johns, just like on a movie set. Because I insist on what is needed in order to do the job, I'm considered "difficult" and that is why management constantly feels that I'm a "wild man."

You had five hundred seats in the train station, but obviously with that space you could easily have put in a thousand.

If you arbitrarily decide to put a thousand seats in a space, you had better count on giving up certain kinds of intimate two-people scenes.

Did the play have to be updated in any way?

I had the German script that Dürrenmatt had originally written. It had been altered for this country by the Lunts. Miss Fontanne did not want the play to be called by its original title, *The Visit of the Old Lady*, so it simply became *The Visit*. The old lady in the piece is quite grotesque, but she's a survivor and that's the joy of it. She has an artificial leg and hand. I went back to the grotesquerie in the German script. For instance, she'd had two men castrated who had testified against her forty-five years before. I found two actors who were really quite fat and we shaved their heads and they spoke in rather high voices. They had been blinded too. It was the most startling image to see those two asexual little men dressed with dapper bow ties, shaved, no hair at all on their faces, with the tapping of their canes on that marble floor of the old train station. If we had carpeted the place to reduce the sound bounce, it would have resulted in the loss of an extraordinary image.

Eugene is really into trains, so we made a little train that actually ran around during the play, and the actors were all making the train noises themselves. Most of the time, you're not lucky enough to stumble into a natural environment like that.

At Trinity you have the 544-seat flexible space upstairs and the 297-seat thrust stage downstairs. What kind of a facility do you have at the Dallas Theater Center?

We have the Frank Lloyd Wright Theater with a capacity of four hundred sixty six, and in the basement I cleaned out a bunch of offices, creating a space that seats two hundred. When I first arrived in Dallas, one of the things that I did was to build a tin barn right down in the so-called arts district, near the museum and the symphony hall. I realized there needed to be a theatre down there that would serve the urban city. Before I agreed to come, the board said they would build this temporary kind of corrugated tin thing. It's quite extraordinary.

In the early days at Providence, your work was frequently considered controversial because of its language and subject matter. Did you have a similar reaction in Dallas?

In Providence we've done things, I guess, that were so controversial and so shocking that everybody had cardiac arrest. We had the greatest number of walkouts with a play based on James Purdy's novel *Eustace Chisholm and the Works*. There was an abortion done on the stage. People would jump up in the middle of the show and go running from the theatre. But I tell you, every person who walked out of that play is a subscriber now and has been for years. They do come back. If we had not done it on the stage back in those days, today we would look very silly. All of the taboos, as far as I'm concerned, have to do with time and the way society changes. An artist eventually gets hanged if he tries to freeze it. I get by with outlandish things in Providence because I have a permanent audience. And they will go out and say, "Wasn't it terrible? I hate that writer and I hate that. . . . " But they come again and boy, there's no lack of support. It took a long time, year in and year out. It didn't just happen overnight.

In Dallas, there is a group who really truly resent anything that in their opinion constitutes four-letter words. And there's nothing else, not even nudity, that is as important to them. And I don't know what to do about that. There was no doubt in my mind that I would outlive that element in Providence. I was young and committed and I had no place else to go. I had to survive, and I had to get into a situation where I could fulfill myself. And that was the only way: simply not to let the moralists or the religious purists, or whoever the hell they are, take it away from me. Now, in Dallas, it's something else again. It's a combination of an atmosphere that's just so crowded and loud and eager for, "Hey, look at me, Mom," on every corner, contrasted with that very strong element out there slapping your hand and saying, "Don't."

Are plays perceived in the same way by audiences in Dallas as in Providence?

Fool for Love was an enormous hit in Providence. It was still playing in New York. The actor Dick Jenkins has always been a big hit in Providence. People just adore him so you couldn't get a seat. Don't you know that when it came to Dallas, after one of the first "words," you could see those little gray heads getting right up and heading up the aisle, sometimes in pairs, sometimes singly. Dick Jenkins had the shotgun in his hands and this couple bounced right up out of their seats and started heading up the aisle. And he just swung the shotgun around to the audience. Everybody in the house, five hundred people, were suddenly aware of what was happening, and he said he didn't know what he was doing but he just kept that gun on them. And it took fifty seconds for them to get up the aisle. When they got almost to the top, this voice in the audience said, "Pull the trigger!" The house just broke up in laughter. So, in some funny way, they're aware that they're silly with this prudish, punishing kind of attitude.

I'm impatient. I want them to understand that it has nothing to do with saying "those words." Basically, theatre is practiced the way it was two thousand years ago. I've come to be irritated by their lack of respect for such an ancient craft. For heaven's sake, it's the end of the twentieth century in America!

And yet, in 1987, when you decided on a plan to eventually cut back your work load, your choice was to continue leading the Dallas Theater Center rather than Trinity.

Boards of trustees have to have their hands held. There is no way for someone as wildly independent as I am to keep everybody playing in the same ballpark.

With two institutions, it gets so complicated that you can't direct plays because you don't have time. I chose to leave Trinity because it is really a very solid operation. We employ about thirty-five full-time actors and there are over twenty thousand subscribers. It is as deeply entrenched in the community as an arts institution can be in this age. My presence is needed so much more in Dallas than in New England. I'm not doing it because it means less work, but it seems to me that if the American theatre is going to be healthy we have to work at cultivating its roots.

How did you survive your famous dismissal at Trinity and manage to continue the company?

In 1975, when I had my big fight and fired my board of directors, it all came to a head. What the board wanted was instant recognition for raising money—a plaque in memory of a wife, their names in the paper, silly things like that. I was hanging on to this huge company that I insisted was going to be important one day. But nobody wanted to pay for that. That was too far in the future. Their response was always, "Look at other theatres. They can do it for less money." Well, what other theatres were doing was simply hiring actors when they needed them and firing them when they didn't need them. It meant that everybody beat the path right back to New York to work at the mechanics of an acting career—unemployment. Well, that's not an indigenous theatre. I had been at Trinity eight or nine years when that rather notorious moment came and they said, "You're fired." Then it was a question of belief in myself. I knew that I could direct plays, and I knew that I could lead a company, and I knew that I had given of my life's blood to that particular organization. But I would never have had the courage to say, "No, I'm not fired, you're fired," if I hadn't really believed that the company would stand behind me to a man. I really believed it. And they did. They said, "No, we will never work in this theatre again if Adrian Hall is fired." That rather threw the board.

Everybody thought that I had signed my death warrant. There was speculation as to whether or not the board would allow me to go back into the theatre. Then the media gradually turned that around so that I became an underdog hero. A few people began to write in our behalf. Carolyn Clay and Kevin Kelly in Boston were wonderful, as was Theatre Communications Group. Then I'd been around the country enough so that people by the thousands came out of the woodwork to defend me and just got in there screaming—the most improbable people—the Church. You cannot imagine how they came to my defense. Everybody sent telegrams to the local press. The actors took to the streets. They sold things. They rang doorbells. That went on for months. We didn't know how we would survive. Gradually, the

152

board began to be perceived as the insensitive boors who were persecuting the artists.

Ultimately, it meant we had to have a legal split, and it looked like I had taken the company and the board had taken all the possessions. But you see, what they had really taken was the responsibility for the plant. I knew they didn't know that no real estate property outside a highly commercial area is valuable. I mean it's nothing but dead weight. Just getting that off our backs with the rental for a dollar a year was the greatest thing that ever happened.

If I had been less mature, in my twenties, I couldn't have weathered the storm. But I had invested all this time and I realized that if I were to walk away I would just give all of that to them.

Since that big eruption in 1975, there's been a kind of nice, placid, pleased-with-themselves audience. And if Trinity does something that they think is too commercial, they say, "Well, that's okay, but we like Trinity's kind of work better."

Are you still as committed to the company concept for Dallas as you were when you created the Trinity Square ensemble?

Perhaps it would be *easier* not to have a company. But life would not be nearly as full. In Providence, when I suddenly realized I'd been there for twenty years and I had a permanent company of extraordinary actors, what I really thought was, "Well, I've done the best I can, and these actors saw the light and they're committed." In Dallas, at first I was confused about why the talent pool was so fragmented and scattered. It was full of chaos because for twenty years the goals had always been to get to Broadway or to Hollywood. I really think, until I went there and began to scream and holler, that it hadn't occurred to anyone that nobody was growing anything for Dallas. See, what I've done in some really selfish, very specific way, is to create exactly what my needs are so that all of my time can be spent just doing the work. I mean I don't even have keys to the buildings, nor do I want them. The reason I don't have an office, the reason I don't have a secretary, the reason I don't have all those things is that I really wanted "a life in the theatre," and in order to do that you have to be as *unencumbered* as possible.

Isn't it inevitable that you will eventually lose your actors or at least a sizable number of them?

I'm always disappointed and hurt when an actor feels he has to go away, but when he does I just have to make myself come to terms with it. Barbara Meek was the kind of actress she was because she put in so many years with the Trinity company. When the chance came for her to go to Hollywood and make a lot of money in a TV series, I wasn't about to say, "No, I need you."

It caused a little hardship for me that particular season. Okay. She was written out of the series after two or three years. She came back to Providence. That kind of commitment comes only if you let go when the time to let go comes. You've got to, darlin'. I have a living testimonial that they do come back if you're square with them. It's not about solving an immediate casting problem, it's about creating a theatre. Richard Kneeland has been with me since the beginning. Richard wanted to go to New York and be in that silly Frankenstein play. There was no reason not to. Away he went. He was out six or eight months. Then, of course, he was very ready to come back. There's got to be a way that Richard Kneeland knows that he can hurt Adrian, but it won't end their friendship. That's very crucial to building a company. The only reason it hasn't succeeded for my peers, whom I respect and admire and who are so gifted, is they just get to that place where they feel, "I can't be hurt anymore and I'm not going to be."

How do you audition actors for the company?

A lot of people really like auditioning. They love calling the agents, running into New York to see three or four actors. I find it embarrassing and I don't do it very well. Since you work in the theater every day of your life, most of the audition scenes actors choose you've heard, so you're not stunned by the material. What you're really looking for are basic things: can they be heard, do they respond to me? I usually try to make some little out-of-the-way comment like, "Could you stand on your head?" And they respond to that. I like to use actors who are a little more "open." Lee Strasberg said he could tell in two minutes if someone had talent or not. I can't. Sometimes in a company situation you have to cast people in roles that are the wrong age, the wrong sex, the wrong color. You end up with everybody fighting to make the thing work with an extraordinary esprit de corps.

You've found a way of attracting acting talent and developing a company. But what about directors? How can the young director bridge that gap between the educational experience and the profession?

As a director, it's very hard to apprentice yourself to anything permanent. I get a lot of requests and we try to have programs with various universities. It takes more time than most of us are willing to give. For a young director to sit there for six weeks only to be allowed to speak two or three times, it's a waste. He's impatient. It's very tough. There's no room for people to direct their first play. I rarely choose a director whose work I've never seen. Your whole institution is in jeopardy when somebody jumps up to direct a play and doesn't know how. Over the years, there have been a number of times when I've had to go in and clean up a guest director's work. I just hate it.

It's hard for me to contain my anger at people who have screwed themselves, the actors and the material so badly.

You've had great success directing the plays of Sam Shepard and Harold Pinter. What is it about their writing that enables you to reach the heart of these works?

I like to think of that whole school of writing as simply "to the bone," without trim. If you are willing to work as an artist, to work to the bone and not decorate, not let the theatrical cliché come into it, if you are really willing to do that, then people like Harold Pinter and Sam Shepard are the people to do it with.

The most wonderful thing about working with Pinter (he came to Providence for the American premiere of his play *The Hothouse* in 1982) is that he is not at all precious about his words and changes them when the references are unclear for an American audience. He affirmed what I believe, that putting on foreign accents in an American company is not what creates a cultural difference. The spirit of a piece is not whether it is done with a precise Hungarian or Russian accent. The spirit is much harder to find.

I have been stunned at how close I feel to Pinter. And that closeness comes out of relating to his terrors. You know, we all have terrors. We all have fears of being boxed in, or not belonging, or somehow not being able to quite connect. Harold Pinter has somehow expressed those terrors that are very real for me. He came along in that era of the angry young man— he was a cockney Jew in England, and he's still to this day writing out of real anger at the bureaucracy that forces rigid kinds of stereotyped roles.

In some funny way, Sam Shepard is too. His is a special body of work that's not unrelated to my Texas background. It really does have to do with myths and American dreams that have failed. For instance, *Buried Child* was a play that I was very close to. I grew up on a ranch, on a farm. By the time I was grown my parents were quite old, so I really do relate to the idea of the end of a way of life. I understand that. Things will never be the same as they were on that farm in Texas at that time. Sam's observations have to do with dreams that have all gone bad. They've all exploded and there's great longing. *Buried Child* was one of the plays I purposely chose to take abroad on Trinity's tour to India and Syria.

Why did you make that choice?

I kind of sensed if we were to have any connection with something as exotic as an Arab country or a country like India—my goodness, that is just a conglomeration of everything in the world—the work that stood the best chance of connecting would have to do with land and family. They adored

Sam Shepard. We opened in Bombay to a standing ovation. That's because basically Sam is not writing plot. He's not writing what we used to think of as character revelation. He really is writing about cerebral things that have to do with his life and his dreams and observing the American thing.

Strangely enough, talking about Shepard and Pinter, the writers that I grew up with were Tennessee Williams and William Inge and Horton Foote—that American naturalistic school. One of the reasons that people think I'm very successful at directing Shepard is because my upbringing was in the naturalistic, Stanislavsky-Freud-oriented theatre. In the 1950s that's all there was. There were no interiors. Everybody said exactly what they meant and everybody heard it and responded accordingly. I couldn't have done Pinter's *Hothouse* the way that I chose without explaining things, just believing that the audience was going to know what the hell I was talking about and go with me and understand where I was. I couldn't have done it without my naturalistic background. It's just like a pianist who has to know those scales backward and forward, and my "scales" came out of naturalism. The fact that what is *said* in Shepard and Pinter may not be at all what is communicated—I couldn't have even gotten to it without those years of technique with Williams and Inge.

You moved The Hothouse *and Roland van Zandt's* Wilson in the Promised Land *from Trinity to Broadway. What did you learn from those experiences?*

Broadway theatre has moved so close to Las Vegas that it's very difficult to tell them apart. The audience bothers me more than anything. I'm very nervous about indifference, and the American public is so barraged by sights and sounds and entertainment and music that now people just stuff things in their ears to block it all out. It's very hard to say to people, "You have to sit and commit yourself for two hours. And it's not enough to just bring your body, you have to get in there and work and be willing to go with this." That's tough. The missing piece in the commercial theatre is knowing whom you are playing to. Broadway doesn't have a permanent audience. Consequently, you are very apt one night to be speaking to someone who has come to the theatre for the first time in his entire life—and you're dragging two thousand years behind you, trying to make it vital and real and pertinent. You may be encountering an audience where there is just no way.

Are there basic differences in the theatre of today as opposed to when you started Trinity?

God, to survive in American theatre today . . . Oh, tough. I despair that ours is a country where you have to become a middle-of-the-road institution before you can even think about long-range survival. Artists since the beginning of time have been on the outside and on the left and on the underbelly. One despairs. Must we all put on three-piece suits and comb our hair before we can make a living in our craft? I used to go everywhere from the state arts council to Washington, just go right in with my sweater and my hair not combed and say I need this amount of money or this is what I would like— talk to them. But that was a funny kind of period. That was just after John Kennedy's death and the initial excitement of the National Endowment. But that very quickly changed into managers and accountants and lawyers and people who write grant proposals—the time of the specialists.

What is important to you about your work?

I really wanted a life in the theatre. That's what I've wanted and that's what I've had, and you have to fight for it. You see, there are only two things when you're entering the American theatre. You can either have a career or a life in the theatre. I have always wanted the career to take care of itself. One of the things that seems to be prevalent is the idea that theatre should give you back instant rewards. I am astonished at university kids who talk about getting agents and doing commercials. I wish it wasn't so easy to pick up a job for fifteen minutes. I think that's a defeating thing. What people like us, the old dinosaurs and crocodiles that are still left, have to say is that a life in the theatre still does exist and it's a dream that's very possible to turn into a reality. But just don't expect to yield up all your pearls the first time you're onstage. It's just too complicated. It takes years of trying and figuring out, living and fighting back and being hurt. It's a wonderful life in the theatre and you have to work more than doctors have ever dreamed of, and you have to know more than any lawyer in the world knows. The craft yields its rewards. Finding a way to have a life in the theatre is hard in our country. I'm just so proud of being an American, but the European tradition in the theatre, their respect for that craft, is much greater than ours. I'm always amused at the ads in *The New York Times*. Nobody ever has a picture taken with his arms down. It's always in some state of exultation. And you think, "Well, that's not really the way I live my life." Quite often my arms are down and so is my head. It was not until I went to Providence, Rhode Island, and was indeed running a whole institution all by myself and could make the decisions that I began to reach down and touch my toes and to try in some gut way to say what I have to say.

In the next twenty years, it is just whether or not we're going to be able to turn these institutions into things that can truly be *theatres*. The question is whether young artists will take up the cudgel and know that they've really got to fight for this. If they don't, darlin', we're going to lose this stuff we have all literally staked our lives on.

JOHN HIRSCH

J ohn Hirsch is a walking anachronism—a director who has spent most of his life staging large-scale theatre works, a man rabbinically reflecting on the large issues facing mankind through the prism of a theatrical conscience. He speaks with a liquid Hungarian accent, and at any given moment can instantly tap into a vast reservoir of passion, experience and knowledge. He has described himself as "a biophiliac—in love with life." And few have clung more tenaciously to life or searched more diligently for life's meaning. He is an authority on survival—having walked out of the ashes of the Budapest ghetto at the end of the Holocaust at age fifteen, to wander alone through Europe going from consulate to consulate until a country could be found that would grant him refuge. He and his grandfather had been sent from the village of his birth to seek anonymity in Budapest when the Nazis invaded Hungary. His mother had made the decision that it would be those two who might survive—the grandfather to preserve the knowledge of the past, and the young John who represented the future. The family maid provided the conduit into the ghetto that saved him from the Nazis. His parents and eight-year-old brother were taken to Auschwitz, where they perished.

It was Canada that was to be his new home, and when shown a map and asked where in that country he would like to settle, he pointed to the middle, to Winnipeg, rationalizing that in the center of the land would be the greatest concentration of activity and the least risk of invasion.

He arrived, a gangly scarecrow of a seventeen-year-old boy, in October 1947 and was adopted by a working-class activist family, the Shacks, who bestowed great tenderness and helped him declare and develop his Jewish faith, something which had been denied to him in his native Hungary. The Shacks were prairie people who, through the model of their lives, taught him additional self-reliance. He became Canadian with a vengeance. He wanted to rebuild his life by sinking roots down so deep that he would never again have to be homeless. He enrolled in night school and five years later graduated from the University of Manitoba with the highest marks given in English that year.

But Winnipeg was not the center of activity Hirsch had expected, and it was particularly bereft of theatre. Soon he started a puppet theatre out of which grew the Touring Children's Theatre. Hirsch realized that he needed a deeper understanding of actors and their methods. He spent a winter in London observing at the Central School of Speech and Drama, afterward returning to Winnipeg to join in creating an open-air musical-comedy theatre called the Rainbow Stage.

In 1957 Hirsch cofounded Theatre Seventy-Seven, so named for its distance of seventy-seven steps from the street, the first professional theatre in Manitoba. He called upon Tyrone Guthrie, who had already founded the Stratford Shakespearean Festival, for moral support and practical advice, and by 1958 Theatre Seventy-Seven had developed into the Manitoba Theatre Centre with touring companies, a children's theatre and an acting school.

Michael Langham, then the artistic director of the Stratford Festival, invited Hirsch to direct *The Cherry Orchard* there in 1965, and to return in 1966 and '67. He became an associate artistic director in 1968 along with Jean Gascon. During the following two years at the Festival, his populist approach to the productions brought in new local audiences, in addition to the usual groups of tourists and Torontonians. He constantly fought institutional bureaucracy and proclaimed his distaste of pretentious drama. One of Hirsch's successes was the landmark *Colours in the Dark* by Canadian playwright James Reaney in 1968. Surprisingly, it was only the second Canadian play ever to be produced in the Festival's fourteen-year history and had been presented over the objections of the board and the production staff. Hirsch insisted that the art of the country be encouraged by the institution.

Hirsch's stagings are highly theatrical, filled with pageantry and intense subjectivity. In the early years he was particularly anxious to shake up the establishment—a mission he has never abandoned. His modernized *Richard*

III (1967) was controversial. But a Stratford production that especially shocked and even enraged some Canadian theatregoers was his burlesqued 1969 version of Petronius's *Satyricon*. The reaction to that production, and a growing realization that Canadian directors could not be fully accepted until they had gained a reputation outside of Canada, caused him abruptly to leave his resident position at the Festival at the end of his second season.

Hirsch had already begun directing in the United States in 1966. Jules Irving and Herbert Blau, then directors of the Lincoln Center Repertory Theater, had seen Hirsch's staging of *Mother Courage* in Winnipeg, the second production on this continent after their own at the Actors Workshop in San Francisco. They asked him to be resident director at Lincoln Center's Vivian Beaumont, where he worked for five years.

During the period from 1966 to 1971, he also directed Joseph Heller's *We Bombed in New Haven* on Broadway, Heathcote Williams's *AC/DC* Off Broadway, Verdi's *A Masked Ball* at the New York City Opera, Brecht's *A Man's a Man* and *A Midsummer Night's Dream* at the Guthrie, and *The Seagull* at the Habima National Theater in Tel Aviv. In 1974 his own adaptation of *The Dybbuk* opened at the Manitoba Theatre Centre, followed by another production the following season at the Mark Taper Forum in Los Angeles.

In 1974 he was invited to head the CBC television drama department in Toronto, a job he undertook with a twofold purpose, to shake things up and to save enough money to enable him to underwrite a continuing career in the theatre. Again, he fought the conservatism of the establishment by introducing new writers to television including French-speaking Canadian artists for the first time.

By 1980 the Stratford Festival was in serious institutional trouble. It appeared that this largest of all classical repertory theatres on the American continent might close. The Festival had become entangled in a nationalistic movement, Canadian Actors' Equity vowing to boycott the theatre unless a Canadian was chosen to head the institution following the resignation of the then artistic director, Robin Phillips. The theatre was also deeply in debt and the Stratford board had been exploring a number of alternatives for leadership, thereby delaying the selection of the new artistic director until the very last minute—establishing an almost impossible time frame in which to open a season. The Canadian government intervened in an effort to save North America's leading classical theatre.

Hirsch, who had been working as consulting artistic director of the Seattle Repertory Theatre since leaving the CBC in 1978, was called by the Stratford board to return. He had only a matter of weeks to assemble a company and mount the first four productions in repertory. This he accomplished with the assistance of producer Muriel Sherrin. But he found that his primary duty in that first season was as peacemaker. He had returned to a theatre being pelted with criticism from all sides, the press, the previous administration, the actors and the board. Hirsch likens Stratford at that time to the Budapest ghetto with the Russians bombing it by day and the Americans and British bombing it at night. Through that period (1981-86) Hirsch managed to maintain the theatrical standards of the Festival despite the political problems and the societal changes that were affecting the company's ability to raise money. He even established a number of new programs at the Festival and is proudest of his creation of a young Shakespeare training company.

In 1986, after five seasons, he left Stratford and began teaching at Yale University in New Haven and at Southern Methodist University in Dallas— passionately imploring students to make the connections between questions raised in great literature and their own lives. He says, "They must know that I do plays because there's something in the process deeply connected with me. It's like a child with a calcium deficiency licking the walls. You have to be personal or you're not doing art."

Hirsch is matter-of-fact when he describes his artistic vision. "Theatre is for me an ongoing illumination of man, his problems, his dreams, his visions, the society which lifts him, and his relationship to God. This is what theatre is about, always has been about. It is also a celebration, communally, of the values which a society holds. To be truly human has to be learned, and has to be relearned over and over again. And one of the places where we learn about being human is in the theatre."

Once, during a speech he was giving to Canadians on behalf of the theatre community, Hirsch referred to his contribution as an artist to society: "I am a natural resource. I should be cultivated like wheat." Like wheat, John Hirsch could have grown in any hospitable nation in the world. As fate willed it, the winds blew him across the sea to take root on the American continent.

■   ■   ■

Why a life in the theatre for this young man born in Siofok, Hungary, at a terrible time in history?

Every Hungarian is born, it is said, with two acts of a play in his head and spends the rest of his life working on the third. So I was born into an extraordinarily theatrical nation. We have the temperament, the ability to fantasize and the imagination to express our reality through the theatre. No doubt these have geographical, historical, political, pastoral and comical origins. Anyway, Hungarians love the theatre.

Were there memorable influences?

As a child, I was surrounded by music, theatre, all the arts. When I was three years old, I remember, I danced for Nijinsky, accompanied on the piano by a lady called Mrs. Mozart, a friend of our family. This quiet, bald man came into our house, and I danced for him to the tune of "Who's Afraid of the Big Bad Wolf?" Touring players used to come and perform next door in the ballroom of a hotel, and there I saw my first play, *John Hero*. I remember a backdrop on which the moon and stars and the sun all happily coexisted, painted on the same cloth. I thought that was magical.

My grandfather, in whose room I slept, told me a story every night before I went to sleep for four years. His stories of outlaws and fairy queens have had a lasting effect on my work. This may account for my attachment to the late comedies and romances of Shakespeare.

My maternal grandmother, who lived in Budapest, often took me to the Luna Park, where there was a marionette theatre, and to the theatre by Lilliputians, the little people. I was in love and astonished by all I saw. At home, I made my own puppet theatre.

Another very strong influence was the Catholic Church. You know, being Jewish in a small town, excluded from the religion of the majority, which was so mysterious and theatrical to me, served as a great stimulus for my imagination. Most of the ritualistic elements of my productions of Shakespeare's works are really my way of being a Catholic.

There is one more thing. During the war years, I was a young student in Budapest when leftists and Jewish artists were exiled from theatres. So they performed in union halls, parks, wherever they found a place. These were the only places where the truth could be spoken. Sometimes these performances took place with the police surrounding the hall taking pictures of people who went in. Many of the performers were dragged away because they were performing censored and forbidden material. From very early on, I realized that theatre deals with truth.

After World War II, you migrated to Winnipeg under the auspices of the Canadian-Jewish Congress. You were seventeen.

Yes. I knew what I wanted to do. In the refugee camp in Germany, I started a puppet theatre to make a living. I came to Canada after wandering around Europe for a year and a half. Shortly after the war, my grandfather died and I just headed off on my own to go to Israel. But I decided, after spending some time in Germany, that I didn't want to go to Israel immediately, that I'd stay in France awhile. That was a fortunate choice because the ship which was to have taken me to Israel was the *Exodus*, the ship that was not allowed to land. Most of my friends with whom I went through Germany to France were on that ship.

So the journey to Canada.

When I arrived in Winnipeg, I again started a puppet theatre with help from the Junior League. They gave me three hundred dollars to tour the schools and community halls around Manitoba.

Had you spoken any English before you arrived?

No, I spoke Hungarian and German and I had studied Latin in school.

Yet you mastered English and then came to be associated with directing the great classics.

I have a good ear for language, so I learned quickly. I never found language to be a barrier in the theatre. I've directed in Hebrew and French and I cannot speak either language. As for the classics, if you're going to do theatre, you should spend a lot of time doing the best! I just reveled in the opportunity to come into the company of these great works. They kept me sane and helped me to make sense of my life. If I hadn't been working on the plays of Shakespeare, Chekhov, Brecht and the other masters, I believe I would have gone crazy.

Literally?

Literally. I think I would have gone mad. Because I could not deal with my experiences of the war and the Holocaust directly. But all those experiences are at the center of those plays, whether it's the destruction and disappearance of a society as in Chekhov, or tragedy of a personal kind in Shakespeare. Doing these plays became an ongoing meditation on what had happened to me, an ongoing spiritual experience. They offered to me a way of making sense of the past and the present.

And they have done that, made sense from the chaos?

The *process* made sense—the meditation, the contemplation, the investigation of major questions. I never expected any answers to, "What is the meaning of life?" I have always been and will always be an archaeologist of my soul. The plays help in this exploration, which was and is a process of healing myself.

You've directed two productions of The Tempest, *one at the Mark Taper Forum with Anthony Hopkins as Prospero and Ming Cho Lee designing; the second at Stratford, with Len Cariou and designer Desmond Heeley. You have said it's an important play in your life.*

I was always interested in Shakespeare's plays because of my love of fairy tales. The late plays are the essence of all the other plays Shakespeare ever wrote. In the histories, he explored political questions; in the tragedies, man's fate; and in the comedies, he dealt with the nature of love. These preoccupations come together in the romances, where all the questions are dealt with in a concentrated way with superb economy and an intensity that only the language of poetry can give. For me, *The Tempest* is a compendium of all the plays Shakespeare ever wrote. It is by far his most philosophically rich play. It is deceptively simple on the surface and endlessly complex and ambiguous in its depth.

What did The Tempest *mean to you the first time you directed it?*

My identification with the character of Prospero was very strong, coming to the play as I did in middle age, when one has to confront giving things up. You have to give up your life so you rehearse your death. This is what Prospero is saying at the end of the play. I was always aware that through working on this play I could find out things about myself. It is a play for middle-aged directors or older ones. You have to have done a lot of living before the play reverberates with its full power. I've been working on this play since I was twenty.

As a study or just through living?

When I was at university, I had a professor who knew I would work in the theatre. He made me promise not to do either *Tempest* or *Lear* until I was at least fifty years old. I promised. Then I would read the plays from time to time, always discovering new things that would not have occurred to me earlier in my life.

Bergman's film of *The Magic Flute*, which is full of the same qualities as *The Tempest*, and also his *Fanny and Alexander*, which is really his *Tempest*, influenced my work on Shakespeare's play; as did a book called *The Timeless Theme* by Colin Still, a rather idiosyncratic British literary critic who took *The Tempest* and *The Magic Flute*, analyzed them both and formed a theory on the basis of his analysis. He wrote that it is a play about spiritual journeys, filled with echoes of *The Divine Comedy*, Virgil's *Aeneid* and the New Testament. And like all great works of art, its magnificence emanates from a glittering, impenetrable ambiguity at the center. I suppose that's why conductors keep on conducting those great symphonies, because they can never get it right. You get a bit of it right each time you do it, but never the whole thing.

And was there a difference in the way you approached The Tempest *the second time you directed it?*

The first production really didn't realize the full theatricality of the piece. I hadn't really thought through the importance of the wedding masque, the anti-masque of the dogs, the appearance of the monsters or the great baroque theatrical elements like the appearance of Ariel as a harpy. The various masques in *The Tempest* are absolutely integral to the heart of the matter; this is when the theatre, the place of illusion and dreams, becomes a metaphor of life. The second time, I was able to achieve a more elaborate production using the open stage at Stratford. The very theatrical, ritualistic aspects of the play took on a much larger presence. Next time I would like to do it in a church.

I had also thought more about the casting, and realized that there are no boring, throwaway parts. In so many productions you find that Ariel, Caliban and Prospero are well taken care of and the rest of the cast is fairly mediocre. This is a great mistake. A soppy Miranda is not what Shakespeare had in mind. Miranda is basically all his young heroines from Rosalind to Juliet rolled into one. Miranda is also close to Shaw's "New Woman."

Can an actress of seventeen, the age Miranda is supposed to be, really play the role?

A thirty-five-year-old Miranda shouldn't be playing opposite a forty-year-old Ferdinand. They represent youth and innocence. They are all that is optimistic and hopeful with the potential for a better, more humane future to contrast with the ever-present forces of evil and corruptibility that exist in the older characters.

A colleague of yours, Bob Falls, was very young when he first directed The Tempest. *He said he might have been one of the few directors to make his connection to the play through Miranda and Ferdinand.*

You really have to connect with all the characters, who range in age from seventeen to Gonzalo's seventy. The seven ages of man must be represented in the play. I think it's crucial to the play that Prospero is not ninety, but somewhere around forty-five. It's clear, you know, that you're dealing with a man who has had a major midlife crisis and run away. He couldn't bear the pressures and madness of the city, of living in society, of running the state —an ongoing theme in Shakespeare. You have it with *Measure for Measure* and with the Duke in *As You Like It*. Shakespeare says that if you want to regain your sanity, you have to run away from society. It's an essential for your spiritual well-being. But it's a paradoxical self-exile and flight because it is also the duty of the ruler to stick with it, and you cannot co-opt your responsibility. What is good for your soul, finally, must be of benefit to the society in which you live.

Which is what theatre or religion is all about.

Or any real work of art. We are social creatures. And although there is the Eastern attitude that a man in middle age must throw up worldly goods, give up everything and take to the road with his begging bowl, a Westerner says, "Yes, he must do all that, but then he must go home again to use what he has learned." Society needs people who have undergone some spiritual transformation. And that's the only possible way that society can improve, or hope to improve, through the acquired wisdom of the ruler. The play is so incredibly modern—postmodern. What Shakespeare's saying is that anyone in a responsible position, anyone who rules, must constantly dry-clean himself of his acquired image. This is what happened to Lear on the heath. He neglected for eighty years what he really truly was, the bottom-line human being. And this is especially important for people who are in a position of responsibility and who rule or lead other people. They require a much greater degree of self-confrontation and self-scraping, *regular* self-scraping. Everybody around you lies—that's what Shakespeare says. Nobody tells you the truth. They mislead you because they're afraid of you, because they don't want to hurt you. It is your responsibility to make sure that you remain yourself.

Did your actors have the same reaction to the play that you had?

Certainly Tony Hopkins and Len Cariou did. Neither played Prospero as an ancient, all-knowing sage at peace with himself. I also had a brilliant Stephano in the Stratford production, Nicholas Pennell, who did a parody of Prospero—a real parody of all rulers. It was an intellectually brilliant as well as entertaining interpretation; a shocking and funny contrast to Prospero and all the other politicians—Stephano, Mussolini, Hitler and Stalin all rolled into one. Also, my Gonzalo, Lewis Gordon, played the Wise Old Man of the play, in the Jungian sense, and created that archetype with great love and sympathy. He was the old man who had acquired the enlightenment that all rulers should have.

How did they find their way to doing that? Was it through an intellectual understanding?

I'm not an intellectual. I have a theatrical intelligence, and I was very clear about my ideas of who these characters are. What one got was the actors' response to these ideas during the exploration of the play. The emotional force of Prospero's breakdown was Len's contribution to the character. His interruption of the masque was marvelous; you witnessed a full-scale nervous breakdown, right then and there. Prospero went berserk because of the pressure of time under which he worked, the stress of having just given away his daughter, with whom he shared the island for fourteen years. And all these pressures came to a point where he couldn't bear it anymore. Len's breakdown was really frightening.

Is Lear *in some way a continuation of Prospero?*

Prospero is a continuation of Lear. Lear is somebody who never went away at the age of forty-five. He ought to have. And that's Lear's tragedy because, in a sense, he was too late. "I have given too little thought to these things," he says at the age of eighty. Unlike Lear, Prospero had a chance to go home and to put into effect what he learned.

Your productions of both Lear *and* As You Like It *were described as extremely "dark."*

Yes, well, *Lear* is a bone-bleak play. It's the most pessimistic play I know. It's about a wasted life. And that waste produced devastation for the country that Lear ruled. In many ways, you are dealing with Stalin when you're dealing with Lear. I bet Lear, like Stalin, killed his wife. I always thought of Stalin's daughter when I was thinking of Cordelia.

The same darkness that lives in *Lear* is in the comedies too. In the nineteenth century, *As You Like It* might have been filled with rabbits and cuckoos and Beerbohm Trees. That's how they saw the play. But I live in a different time.

When I did *As You Like It* the court was a phantasmagorical, E. T. A. Hoffmann, black, rococo court—the court of a tyrant. A German who went through the last world war upbraided me for putting Nazis on the stage in the court. There were no Nazis on the stage, there were no swastikas. But the fact of the matter is that he saw Nazis behind it, and that's exactly what I was doing. I work out of my guts, and I work out of my own past, and I see what I see. That's why I love to do these plays.

It's a tribute to the way you've led your life that you have been drawn to the romances and not the tragedies.

What is great about the late plays is that he uses everything in the theatre —vulgar comedy, masques, songs, dances, magic, the full battery of the art —in the service of sublime ideas. I don't consider these plays "holy relics" when I work on them, but when the play is onstage, in front of an audience, somehow there is the sense of the sacred there. We are witnessing, and celebrating, the mystery of living.

You use your past to serve the present. The fact that I survived was either chance or "Providence Divine." I have to believe in rebirth, in the seas which are merciful. Shakespeare didn't end up with the tragedies, but with the romances—the fairy tales, where he began. He came full circle. I often think I'll end up having a puppet theatre in my old age, which is the thing that I started with.

Another play you did more than once was Saint Joan, *at Lincoln Center in 1968 and eleven years later at Seattle Rep.*

Sometimes one doesn't pick things for personal reasons. At Lincoln Center they wanted to do a Shaw, and I don't think I'm very good at Shavian comedy even though I enjoy plays of ideas. But I always loved *Saint Joan*. Its scale is Shakespearean. It begins and ends with vaudeville, and in the middle of it there is a wonderful chronicle play with set pieces: political debates, marvelous operatic arias, a courtroom drama—a tremendous variety show! And if you catch on to that, realize the difference in styles and have the courage to play them—ah, well, you'll have a great show.

However, doing it requires, as you say, command over all those styles.

You must, as a director, be able to do *Three Men on a Horse* as well as *Three Sisters*. I don't do classical plays solely. I adore musicals. As a boy in Budapest, I spent afternoons playing hooky going to variety theatres. That's where my love for vaudeville and burlesque comes from. It's only in America, where people shove you into niches, that I am considered a "director of the classics." Perhaps that's changing now that Trevor Nunn, who did mostly Shakespeare for years, has become the most successful musical-comedy director in the English-speaking world.

Because of his ability to move large numbers of people around the stage?

Anybody who does the classics has to be a good traffic cop and must have a firm grasp of design, music, dancing and singing. I've gone back and forth between musicals and the classics with all sorts of other theatre in between. The fact is that I really do adore spectacle, circus and visual effects in the theatre. But it must be connected to the rest of the play. So many musicals today are nothing more than overamplified sound.

All those required skills make great demands on a person wanting to become a director. What are the basics that the job requires?

I think you have to be interested in human beings and passionately curious about the human condition. It all starts with having a very healthy ability to introspect and to be interested in the world around you in more than a cursory fashion. By that I mean that you have to read a lot: newspapers, magazines, novels, pornography, cereal boxes. Keep in touch. You have to be interested in visual arts; I daresay in science too, to find out what things *mean*. That's not very fashionable today in the theatre because people are more interested in what things *are*. I'm forever trying to figure out what things are *and* mean. I know that perhaps the search is futile, but it's been rewarding so far.

Another of the great playwrights encountered in your search has been Chekhov. His works frequently are elusive to directors.

These endless discussions about Chekhov. Is it a comedy or isn't it a comedy? Every time I do Chekhov I think about my mother, who had an incredible sense of humor. She was able to laugh in the middle of funerals. She would squeeze my hand white but she couldn't help laughing.

Is that the secret of Chekhov? The contrast of the tragedy next to the absurdity of life?

Exactly. My mother threw out a postcard from the cattle car that was taking her to Auschwitz. And, by some miracle, I got it. The postcard was in Hungarian but there was a line in French—a joke. Just a single line. So I understand Chekhov. I always thought of Chekhov as the person with whom I could have the most marvelous dinner if he were to drop by. One has the feeling that he is your contemporary. The generosity of his spirit comes so clearly through the plays. And I love Chekhov because I also came from a bourgeois world that disappeared. I know all those people, what they ate, their furniture, what concerned them. Those dinners in the *The Three Sisters* went on in my family's house every week. It was not the military who came to dinner but traveling salesmen, the local librarian, the priest or Dr. Pick, our family doctor. That bookcase in *The Cherry Orchard* was a bookcase in our salon—a bookcase that was locked because there were certain books that I was not supposed to read—Zola, Balzac and Krafft-Ebing. But I managed to steal the key and read them all.

Today, how can a director have an interior understanding of that world inhabited by Chekhov?

Anybody who has undergone change and loss ought to be able to do those plays. Look, our society is constantly changing, dissolving in front of our very eyes, so we should be able to understand Chekhov's worldview.

What is the best method a director can use to communicate these images to the actors?

There is no "best" method. You must share your feelings, your thoughts, your attitudes. If you want actors to be vulnerable, *you* have to be vulnerable. If you want them to understand that with this material they must use their brains, you have to show your brain being applied to the material. If you want them to be passionate, you can't be impassive. If you want the material connected to the core of their everyday existence, you have to reveal your own deepest connections to the work.

Much of your important work was done at the Stratford Shakespearean Festival, and you were associated there for two periods—the first time as associate artistic director and later as artistic director for five seasons, taking on the job when the institution was in great financial need. At the time you were hired for that position, you were quoted as saying to the board, "Do you know what you hire an artistic director to do? To go around giving speeches and have a presence in the right places, and take long walks in the park and figure out what should be done." How did being the artistic director of the largest theatre on this continent affect your own creative work?

I was like the mother of a large family serving chicken at the Sunday dinner. I always got the neck. And it was my own choice. In order to attract really good directors you had to give them the leg or the breast. Which meant that you did the bread-and-butter Shakespeare that season.

The second time around at Stratford I was greatly aware of the fragility of the institution. It nearly disappeared. I was also aware that not all the king's men could put that thing together the way it once was. The Stratford Festival had a San Andreas fault built right into it. It was a hundred-odd miles away from Toronto, the largest center of population in Ontario. When the Festival started, Toronto had no theatre to speak of. Now Toronto is a booming, bustling and culturally rich metropolis with eighty theatres. The competition for the audience is fierce. And the government subsidies it received were minuscule, yet the expectations were always great. Stratford is always spoken of in the same breath as Great Britain's National Theatre and Royal Shakespeare Company, which receive at least fifty percent of their budget a year in government subsidy. Obviously, most of my energies went into holding the institution together, struggling to survive, trying to stick to the mandate, striving for excellence under impossible circumstances.

Garland Wright, when he became the artistic director of The Guthrie Theater in 1986, said it was interesting what was beginning to happen to his outlook. He was afraid that he was becoming conservative. He was suddenly worried about the audiences, selling the tickets. His whole perspective had changed.

It has to. You're the custodian of an institution. You automatically reach for the neck.

170

At Stratford and elsewhere, you have worked with the major designers of the day. Again, what is the language of that collaboration?

One of the marvelous things that happens with people who are good is that they talk very little. That's the truth of it—one word, two words. And I have been very fortunate to have worked with some of the best in the world— Desmond Heeley, Beverly Emmons, Ming Cho Lee, Robin Wagner, Doug Schmidt, Michael Annals, Leslie Hurry, Tanya Moiseiwitsch. They get an idea very quickly, so you are on the same track from the beginning. That is the advantage of ongoing relationships. You develop a language, a shorthand, and away you go. And then there are certain people who have that language from the beginning. You have the same background, the same way of looking at things. It's also very exciting when you come in touch with a designer who doesn't come from the same background and doesn't look at things the way you do. Then you are challenged, you have to reconsider each and every value you hold.

Tanya Moiseiwitsch must have been designing at Stratford from the beginning. She and Tyrone Guthrie worked together to design the Festival theatre in 1953 and later the Guthrie Theater space in Minneapolis in 1963. Was there a particular working process you two evolved?

She is a great collaborator, always the brilliant servant of the play. Tanya doesn't make too many decisions without consulting the director. She and I went to the National Portrait Gallery in London and looked at pictures of people to decide about costumes for *Tartuffe*. I didn't want to do it in the period it was written, but wanted to find an age closer to us, when money and greed were the driving forces—a bourgeois society, a highly materialistic age. So we agreed that the period would be around 1860. She did an incredible set that looked as if it had forever been a part of the Festival theatre. After all, she had designed the permanent shape of the space. People were absolutely astonished. It didn't look like a set.

Is there something you could say all of those designers share in common?

They're all perfectionists. Nothing but the best will do. They, like God, live in detail. All of them still have the child alive in their souls. Tanya can turn into a three-year-old at the mention of an idea. She narrows her eyes, purses her mouth in pleasure. She lets go with her Eliza Doolittle "Oooh!" Ming Cho Lee can beam like a baby encountering his first ice cream cone when he is onto something marvelous. Artists, when working well, turn into the best kind of children; they have an innocence, a playfulness. They are open to endless possibilities. All this comes to the fore when they are not subjected to killing pressures.

What sort of pressures?

Lack of money, lack of time, the beast of bureaucracy, lack of good and caring craftsmen to execute designs, working atmospheres more suitable for turning out painting by numbers than theatre of the highest excellence.

Between the time of your first association at Stratford and your return as artistic director, you did a lot of directing in this country. An example was 1971, which was quite a busy year for you. In addition to directing at the Guthrie, you staged two plays at the Vivian Beaumont, Playboy *of the Western* World *and* Antigone. *But perhaps your most interesting project that year was Heathcote Williams's play* AC/DC *at the Chelsea Theater Center in the Brooklyn Academy of Music.*

Bob Kalfin brought me this play, at least three hundred pages long. And he said, "I very much want to do this play, but I can't make heads or tails of it. Nobody understands it. Could you read it and tell me if you would like to direct it?" I read it and I said, "Oh, I have a sense of what this is about. The difficulty is that I don't know anything about physics or electronics and there are a lot of words and phrases in it that I don't understand. So get me somebody who will go to the library and look up some of these terms." So Bob did that. I got a kind of index, a series of footnotes, and I read it again and I said, "This is very exciting. Let's do it."

What was AC/DC *about?*

The play deals with the effect of media, especially television, on us—the way we have become prey to it; how it eats into our brains, changes our perceptions of ourselves and the world; how substance and content disappear and surfaces become all-important, a world of color, texture, movement and sensations without a central anchorage of sense—a world suffering from Alzheimer's disease where nothing lasts. *AC/DC* was a horror play, a Grand Guignol of our electronic Bedlam of a world.

Then John Lahr, the writer, said, "I know Heathcote Williams, the guy who wrote this play. He will try to appear as a person from a working-class background, but I'm telling you that he is a highly educated chap from an aristocratic family. So don't fall for all the stuff he is going to hand you." So I said to Kalfin, "Get me together with Williams so we can shape it. It's huge and would take four hours to perform." Williams arrived from London with his lady, the most famous model in the world, Jean Shrimpton. They were like two beautiful Victorian wraiths. He was a delicate figure, a changeling with flaming red hair and very white, almost transparent skin. And he wore a big black cape. Shrimpton was stunningly beautiful, insubstantial and so pale. They both had skin like newborn mice. And I rode around with these Arthur Rackham figures in a Manhattan cab. They stayed at the Chelsea Hotel and Jean Shrimpton typed away in front of a fireplace with me in the room. Heathcote was nowhere to be seen.

The piece was full of riffs of speech, great language. It was the first time in New York that anybody used a battery of TV monitors onstage. *AC/DC* was fifteen or twenty years before its time, far out and new. It made me look at the world in a new way. All great works of art do that. They change my perception of reality. You see something you have always looked at but haven't seen before. It shocks you by its freshness.

Now, after this amazing saga, Europe, Canada, Stratford, the exploration of so many of the great plays, what currently enriches your life?

More and more, I realize that what I went through in my life, what I was, what I became and am still becoming, must be shared. To be human is something we have to learn. At the moment, I find that teaching theatre is exciting because it is one of the most humanizing of all the arts. At its center is man, the actor, speaking about the pain, joy, agony of living on this incredible planet. When our fate, the future of this planet, is in our hands, I feel that every artist (especially of my age) must share his or her knowledge with the young so that there will *be* a future. As I go on struggling to find out what a good life is, why and how to live it, teaching becomes a duty, a great pleasure and a way of furthering my own learning process.

I also go to the movies quite a bit these days because I'm seeing films which are closest to those things that I like to see in the theatre, small films that deal with human beings, that are exciting and fresh and accessible; and the great mythical films, *Aliens, Blade Runner, Legend*, the romances I can't find in the theatre. If the theatre is to be really alive, it has to deal with the reality of today and deal with it not just through images but through language. That is something that films are not doing. I wish for a theatre where once again language and ideas are at the center.

I think the imagistic theatre is absolutely fantastic. Robert Wilson is great when he does his own stuff. But I got a lot more out of Lee Breuer's *Gospel at Colonus*. It was Dionysian and political as well as spiritual. It was indigenous to this country and rich in ritualistic, religious elements. It was the most successful rethinking of a great classical play in a contemporary popular idiom I have encountered.

If your emotions, mind and spirit, as well as your senses, are not fed in the theatre, if you are not nurtured by some great vision clearly important

173

to your existence, what the hell is theatre for? I've been lucky. I've done everything from burlesque to *King Lear*—musicals, Broadway comedies, you name it. And I hope to keep doing that. I'm very fortunate to have directed plays that I loved, to have worked with artists of extraordinary ability. These are the great pleasures of being in the theatre—to spend most of your time in the company of passionate, brilliant, talented and committed people. It spoils you for life.

MARK LAMOS

M ark Lamos was a well-established actor who had taken some tentative
steps toward directing when, in 1979, he and Michael Langham went
to the California Shakespearean Festival in Visalia, California (Langham as
the director of the summer festival and Lamos as the associate). Lamos was
suddenly asked to take over the direction of the Festival when Langham
withdrew just before the season opened. It was a fateful career step for Lamos.

Following quickly on the heels of that artistically successful summer,
he was asked to become the acting artistic director for Arizona Theater Company in Tucson, where he had directed *Equus* and *The Show-Off* the previous
season.

As an actor with Minneapolis's The Guthrie Theater in the early 1970s,
he had distinguished himself in a range of parts such as the title role in *Doctor
Faustus*, Nick in *The Caretaker*, Guildenstern in *Rosencrantz and Guildenstern Are Dead*, Edgar in *King Lear*, Autolycus in *The Winter's Tale*, Lucio
in *Measure for Measure* and Backbite in *The School for Scandal*. Also, at the
Old Globe in San Diego, he played Hamlet and, at Stratford, Connecticut,
Feste to Lynn Redgrave's Viola in *Twelfth Night*.

He had made his Broadway acting debut in 1972 in Romulus Linney's

Love-Suicide at Schofield Barracks, and appeared as Christian de Neuvillette opposite Christopher Plummer in the Broadway musical *Cyrano* as well as Abel in Arthur Miller's *The Creation of the World and Other Business*.

Despite this impressive beginning, he began to question his desire to continue as an actor, realizing that, "The egocentricity required by acting was becoming a burden. Directing called more parts of me into play." Yet, the urge to perform remained, and from time to time in later years he would act in plays that he was also directing.

The year following his season with Arizona Theater Company, the board of trustees of Hartford Stage Company recruited him to replace their recently resigned artistic director, Paul Weidner. Weidner, who had spent twelve years building the institution in Hartford and guiding the development and construction of its new four hundred eighty nine-seat thrust theatre, had cited artistic burn out as the cause for his leaving and had joined the Peace Corps, teaching English for three years on the Ivory Coast of Africa.

Lamos credits Michael Langham as being the mentor who most influenced his early development as a director. Langham had kept in touch that first summer in Visalia proffering advice to its board of trustees and acting as an "extra artistic eye" for Lamos. Langham asked the "right" questions during rehearsals, questions that pointed up production weaknesses; however, he did not intrude on Lamos's creativity by substituting his own solutions to problems. These sessions were remembered in later years when Lamos was himself in the position of overseeing guest directors. "If I have any connection, it's to Michael. As an actor in the Guthrie company, I was in constant awe of him, but I had a lot of my own ideas about how things ought to be done. I think Michael sensed that, and when I began to direct Shakespeare, it was in response to Michael. Though I used what I'd learned from working with him, my work was against his way of directing a classic text. A real mentor evokes that response in his student. As a result, my work now is much freer. I often wonder what Michael would think about the 'floating rocking chair' in *Pericles*, the use of rock music and Mozart. Conceptually, I'm a lot looser now and more obviously personal in my approach. But my understanding of the rhythm of a whole play, my sense of a play's architecture—these came from Michael, who learned them from his mentor, Tyrone Guthrie."

During his first season at Hartford, Lamos began to receive national attention for such productions as *Cymbeline* and the marathon production of nine Greek dramas, *The Greeks* (co-directed by Mary B. Robinson). However, while the reputation of the theatre and Lamos continued to grow nationally, in the early years of his tenure there was some disaffection on the part of Hartford audiences, particularly toward a production of Derek Walcott's epic *The Isle Is Full of Noises* as directed by Douglas Turner Ward and performed by The Negro Ensemble Company. Lamos would say during this period, "I've learned so much from having Doug Turner Ward and The NEC in our theatre. I've learned more doing that than I have doing anything else these two years. And I've never gotten more hate mail. We've never had a lower audience attendance or gotten more vitriolic flak from the board. I've begun to realize that my audience here is not ready for work that is too obviously embryonic.

"Whenever I think of being burned out, those are the two icebergs that start to come toward the prow of the ship—subscribers and the board. If subscribers become upset, then so does the board that represents them. It's complex and maddening, and it's difficult to know personally how to take criticism and how much of it to let ride off your back. One must work constantly to provide the board with a sense of perspective. They need constantly to be kept aware of my aesthetic. I feel that my potential lies in reexamining large works: *Woyzeck, The Dybbuk, Peer Gynt, Coriolanus, Lorenzaccio.* I work best on a large, densely textured scale. It's simply the kind of artist I am. At times I find myself saying, 'You want an artist in your community? You want to support an artist? Then raise the kind of money that will allow me to do my work.' I've spent most of my institutional artistic life tightening my belt. The theatregoing public is cheated by it, the artists' potential is crippled. I'm asked to replace money with creativity and I am on a constant artistic diet."

The discussions with Lamos began at the end of his second Hartford season—a time when he was frustrated and hyperenergetic. The final session was four years later, prior to the 1986-87 season. By then, he was feeling more confident and powerful, having found a way to traverse that narrow line between producing artistic works and box office hits.

Director Peter Sellars has said, "Success or failure, it's all the same." For the director, the same amount of thinking, inspiration, ingenuity and hard work go into every project. But the appreciation of that effort can differ vastly. In the fall of 1985, Lamos directed an enormously popular production of *Twelfth Night* that both the critics and his audiences adored. He would spend more nights than was customary standing at the back of the house watching the performances. Finally, one of the staff members asked him why he was there so often. Without taking his eyes off the audience, he said, "I'm trying to figure out why they like it so much."

■　　■　　■

More than any other director of classic plays in this country, you have been credited with successfully developing an American style for the acting of Shakespeare and the staging of his plays.

American actors can do Shakespeare, in many ways more successfully than British actors, because they don't have the same basis of tradition underneath

177

the performance of Shakespeare's plays. Consequently, American actors don't bear the burden of the memory of the last twenty-five Ophelias or Romeos they saw, because they probably haven't seen more than one or two during their lifetimes! They treat centuries-old texts in very modern, almost naive ways. I used to regret this fact. Now I realize that it allows the actors and me to treat the text as a new play.

When I directed *All's Well That Ends Well*, I was thirty-six years old and I'd seen the play precisely twice before in my whole life! If I'd lived in England, I'm sure I would have seen it fifteen, twenty-five times, heard it on the radio, perhaps learned about it at university. The actors who audition for plays like *Cymbeline* or *Pericles* may never have seen them.

Then why is it that you believe American actors can be more successful doing those plays?

Whenever I see British actors doing Shakespeare, I feel a little bit left out. I don't feel they really let me know anything. I never see them eviscerated by their work. There are moments in every play, a comedy or a tragedy or a romance, when an actor simply has to unzip his being and open himself up. We wait for that. I never, never see that in British performers. I always think I'm about to see it with somebody like Paul Scofield. And I almost see it despite what he's "doing." I certainly don't see it with any of the new generation of British actors. I see almost more technique in them than I see in the older ones. But always, even in the worst American Shakespearean productions, there are moments of real passion and tenderness, even if all the spoken music is wrong and everything goes down the drain. Frankly, one goes to the theatre to see that passion. With American actors, I have to work against that emotional unzipping too early in rehearsals because everybody wants to do that on the first day. I try not to let it happen until much later. There's so much passion in Shakespeare's verse that an actor dealing with it can self-destruct if he doesn't understand how to use its power.

What is the major challenge in making Shakespeare accessible for modern-day audiences?

The problem is not to make Shakespeare "relevant" or "political"—because all of the plays deliver immediate and complex statements to the times in which they are performed. The greatest problem with producing Shakespeare today is the preconceptions that audiences bring to his plays. I look at a Shakespearean play and see something in it that means a great deal to me— and I see it in the text all the way through—and decide to do a production highlighting that aspect of the text. But audiences can come to the performance with their own preconceptions and can annihilate much of my work because they refuse to accept the text as a living, transforming organism that says different things each time it's staged.

Antony and Cleopatra, for instance, is an extremely political play. It's not only a love story; it's about chaos versus order. Antony and Cleopatra are the old order. Octavius Caesar is the new order and, as much as we dislike it, he's what's coming. We may find him a bore (and that may be one of Shakespeare's points) but he's going to make a better life for all of us. Antony and Cleopatra are on the side of romanticism that represents the decay of the humanistic spirit. They die beautifully, but the flames of their death smolder too long and char too many other aspects of what could be a meaningful political empire. They're operatic and useless. When I stressed that in my production at Hartford, I felt the audience couldn't deal with it. They *wouldn't* accept it and the production failed.

What was it that particularly contradicted their notion of the play?

John Conklin, the designer, and I chose to set it within an almost mythical design scheme based on the extravagantly colorful paintings of Tiepolo, the last of the great Venetian Baroque painters. We tried for a look of opulent unreality. In my blocking, too, I attempted to re-create those great lolling bodies you see in Baroque paintings. But my vision didn't translate; one critic thought that all the soldiers and spear-carriers looked "sloppy." Perhaps John and I were wrong to dress such a dryly political play in such an opulent way.

Can you think of a time when the audience let down its guard and accepted a Shakespearean production of yours without judging the "correctness" of the interpretation?

I think one of the reasons that the *Cymbeline* I did was such a success was because it is a play that very few people have ever seen. Consequently, it affected them spontaneously. They were able to experience it without the preconceptions they might bring to a more popular play. Without our really doing anything to the play other than telling its story as clearly and emotionally as possible, they were dazzled in a way that I assume Shakespeare's audiences were dazzled the first time they saw the play.

I wish more people would understand or at least accept Shakespeare's deliberate use of ambiguity. The characters don't wear black hats and white hats. One shouldn't be able to say, "The Capulets are right and the Montagues are wrong," or, "Prince Hal is good and his father is wrong." There is too much conflicting information in every play that shows you that all of them are making mistakes and all of them are doing the right things too. That is the greatness of it. Despite the rigor of Shakespeare's moral universe, his characters are completely human. I find Coriolanus to be one of the most moving people in all literature. He's cold and heartless, yes, but if played correctly, his inability to communicate should make people weep.

Do you closely adhere to Shakespeare's text, or do you edit?

What I adhere to is Shakespeare's thematic architecture. Each scene in a Shakespeare play is really a variation on its central theme. Each scene in *Merchant of Venice,* for instance, can be understood to comment ironically or wisely on the idea of giving and getting, generosity and hoarding. Once I understand the mandala of the play, how the spokes of the wheel fit, then I feel a freedom to edit carefully, change words that might be unclear to a modern audience and occasionally rewrite lines. Very occasionally, I'll rearrange or combine scenes.

Michael Langham showed me how daring you can be with the text if, with everything you are deleting, you are still honoring its main intentions. But sometimes incorrect cutting makes a scene seem twice as long. I have discovered this to my horror, and often put back as many as ten or fifteen lines because the scene seemed too long without the bridge of thought and rhythm which those lines provided.

Shakespeare and his actors edited his texts. What we have in the folios is really proof that these words were written to be spoken, acted, suited to particular talents, even particular audiences. The plays are living, breathing vessels of communication. Words must be changed if they are to be comprehensible for a modern audience. There is nothing as important as understanding what each moment is about. Of course, a director's first priority is to try to achieve that clarity through the staging. Audiences found our production of *Twelfth Night* so immediate that they accused me of rewriting the text. In fact, we changed no more than six or seven words.

Well, once you know what you want from a play, what is the process you use to get that clarity into the staging?

Directing is psychology. It's about how to work with other human beings. It's also the art of inducing a psychological effect on a group of people who have come into a theatre to experience that effect. In your mind you're saying to yourself, "What do I want the audience to feel?" From there it's a process of moving toward that feeling with actors, designers, etc., yet allowing yourself to discover the unexpected along the way. The process changes from play to play. As soon as you think you've got the rules of directing down, as soon as you've had a marvelous success, found new things in yourself, found new ways of communicating with people, think you've got that down, the next project will show you that another door waits to be opened. The newfound rules hardly apply. You have to find a whole new way. It's rejuvenating—exhausting.

But your audience at Hartford Stage doesn't change that drastically from production to production. Has being an artistic director and establishing a dialogue with a specific community affected your point of view?

For the first years at Hartford I felt much more like a director working at an institution. Now I feel more and more that the institution and I are inextricably linked, and so I find it increasingly difficult to talk about myself apart from Hartford Stage Company. I find that rather frightening.

Why frightening?

I guess because being responsible for an institution, I sometimes feel less free to explore certain theatrical ideas more than once.

Where does that sense of limitation come from?

The same audiences witness my growth. Because they see everything I do, I find it difficult to pursue certain themes and visual ideas more than once or twice. I'd like the luxury to explore and experiment more, to refine approaches that may not have worked the first time, but might show potential if developed.

I wouldn't have said this a few years ago, but I think theatre is about *sharing* an idea, not simply creating one. The theatre is a bourgeois art form; it cannot exist without an audience. It creates a little community inside a much larger community. It's not enough for us simply to put something onstage that *we* as artists desperately want to see. The trick in the theatre is to have the audience see what we're seeing. That takes enormous craftsmanship and technique—and, perhaps, occasional compromise. If you think a line or a piece of business is funny, it damn well better be funny to five hundred people sitting in the same room or you don't have theatre. If you think something is beautiful, you must learn how to communicate that effect. If we are going to change our audiences, we must first understand them. Molière changed minds by stubbornly working within a populist mode while his contemporaries created "new art," now forgotten.

Is there a time when it's acceptable to lead the audience into uncharted territory, when you are exploring ideas that are abstract and not yet absolutely clear to yourself?

Yes, as long as that motivation is centered in the idea of *sharing* ideas with the audience. By that I mean you can take them to a place in a specific work that is highly personal for you if they can be made to sense your excitement. Our production of *Pericles* was a case in point. John Conklin and I followed a highly personal, subconscious path into that play in conception and design. We "played." We experienced the production as an infinite game. The audience caught the dreamlike, free-association sense of surprise and discovery immediately (it certainly fit the picaresque quality of the play), and I felt that we could take them anywhere. It was a magic carpet ride, and I felt free to explore all of my personal reactions to the play and make them public.

All art is uncharted territory—whether it's a canvas by Turner, a Beethoven string quartet, a Spalding Gray monologue. If the audience can find a willingness simply to give themselves up to the childlike nature of every traveler in a foreign land, then a map begins to become clear, the charting of the journey becomes possible.

Many of our audiences in this country today are sitting there with their thumbs on their pulses saying, "Am I excited? Am I having fun?" And frequently they don't want to make a commitment one way or the other until they have been informed that it's okay by an independent source.

I'm beginning to feel that that is the natural state of audiences. We do feel our pulse. We're in a state of awareness that is partially giving ourselves up to an idea or a moment or a feeling, and at the same time noticing that we're crying, noticing that we're laughing, noticing that the people around us are bored or happy, noticing that *we're* going to commit even though the lady next to us is walking out in disgust—noticing all that stuff because watching a play *heightens our awareness!* So while on the one hand you want an audience to enter a kind of dream state to suspend their disbelief, I'm less and less convinced that an audience today ever truly loses itself in a theatre piece. And a great deal of the work that a lot of us are doing right now has to do with letting the audience be very aware that they are in an artificial situation, and be aware that despite all of the artifice involved with this situation called theatre, that there is still the possibility for dream, for many, many levels of response to the work—the possibility for a kind of reality *because* of this sense of artifice.

It's a situation that takes a lot of effort on the part of people who decide to be an audience. Going to a movie or punching a film up on the VCR takes very little effort and the work itself can be interrupted. You can go to the bathroom. You can get food. When you make the decision to walk into the theatre, you have committed part of the future of your life, two or three hours, to an unknown experience not under your control.

Why does there always seem to be a problem with the artist being understood in his own time?

The nature of any artist is to keep bounding ahead, even if he's working in a bourgeois form such as theatre. Whether you're talking about someone like Tyrone Guthrie, who revitalized the whole formation of an audience for the stage, or going even further back to other innovators, Meyerhold and others, it's always been, "I'm going to win you over to see things in another way." That's the great catalytic excitement in the theatre or any art form. It's similar to the painter saying, "I'm going to show you a woman's face. Her nose is going to be facing one way, her eyes another way, her hair is going to be different and she's going to be all in one plane. And I'm going to show you that because if I don't share it with you, I'll go mad." Sometimes, audiences subconsciously realize that artists are *always* speaking to their times. That's what really upsets them about the avant-garde—they secretly share its impulse.

Once the theatre had a role in portraying the events of the day. Now that the media has more or less taken on that role, what does the theatre artist have to discuss with his audience?

Dreams. Coherencies. The artist has a social responsibility to discover them, share them. He has an ethical responsibility to organize responses to the current world, feelings and visions through artifice—to attest to mysteries, hear oracles, present possibilities, unearth treasures. The artist must take the audience, and himself, to a place where he can see things from new perspectives. That is what happens in any human relationship.

Of course the major relationship a director has in the theatre is that loving/ business collaboration with the actors. At one time, you said that if you had a problem working with actors, it was that you tended to be too rigid. Is that still the case?

I went back into the mode of actor a few years ago and directed and acted simultaneously in Schnitzler's *Anatol*. That experience made me realize that actors really do know what they are doing and, ultimately, that theatre is in many ways an expression of the actor's power. After that experience, I became less rigid.

I'll explain what I mean. There were three of us rehearsing a scene in *Anatol* one day, all having a terrible time, all forgetting lines, having one of those awful days where everything is a mess. The assistant director was white-faced. And I looked at him from the stage area and I said, "Calm down. We're fine. We're all going to be fine. We all know what this is supposed to be. We all know what we haven't achieved yet and we'll be there. Don't we all feel good?" And the other two actors said, "Yeah, we're all right." And we took the assistant director out for a drink.

Was it difficult to direct and act at the same time?

It was a little schizophrenic, but it was terrifically rewarding, too. As an actor, I missed having a full-time director, but on the other hand it revitalized my faith in the idea that the actor is the life of the theatre. The enjoyable thing about it was that all the actors were again brought into the directorial process, they could say to me, "I feel funny if you're standing over here," or, "Don't you think that line really means more . . . " So, in effect, we all began directing one another. It was liberating. Very easy. Joyful.

It would be interesting to know how that kind of process would work in the larger classical plays. With so many American actors underexperienced in the classics, how do you rehearse them?

The Renaissance human being undoubtedly had a more visceral response to words and language than we do. That is why the best Shakespearean acting is the simplest, the most straightforward, uninflected. If I do anything as a director, in terms of actor coaching, it's to get actors to trust stillness—allow the words to work, ride them, trust them, let them come from inside you, locate them within your being. In verse, particularly, you must speak ideas *as* you think them.

Because I spent so many years as an actor and have an understanding of the actor's process, I expect more of actors sooner than another director might. I think too many directors make the mistake of waiting too long to tell actors what to strive for. Directing has a lot to do with understanding, as quickly as you can, how much of you the actor can take, how to hide what you do and how much you have to lead him toward an idea and let him think he is discovering it for the first time. Only when he discovers it for himself will it be truly his, truly new and fresh. Rehearsals must be happy situations, very safe. If I'm vulnerable, the actors will also be vulnerable. You must create an atmosphere in which everyone can fall flat on his face—you included. As a director, I do lots of things other directors would abhor. I jump onstage and act things out, give line readings, look very foolish. But each actor is different. To unlock his or her special gifts is the director's main goal during the rehearsal process. Once that happens, however, you must control everything in order to achieve your vision as best you can.

What are some of the qualities you look for in actors?

Adaptability. Self-assurance. A willingness to "play." I like actors who take responsibility, who feel free to disagree and show me their ideas. I like actors who ask me questions. I especially like actors who do their homework. Rehearsals should be concentrated, highly enjoyable and *short*. I like actors who come to rehearsal full of energy and ideas. I'm like a chef, frankly. I'm only as good as my ingredients. My work is completely instinctive. I plan as little as possible. I utilize as much of an actor's contribution (or a designer's) as I can, and edit out the rest. I am the organizer of others' impulses.

The kind of American actors I've had the most productive relationships with seem to enjoy a certain amount of discipline. I came from a musical background, and consequently understand discipline. Music has been a major influence in my work. I studied the violin for thirteen years. In fact, I got into college on a violin applied music scholarship. During rehearsals, I often describe what I want in musical terms. One of the most successful rehearsals I ever had occurred in 1978 when I was directing Shaw's *Too True to Be Good* at the Old Globe in San Diego. Shaw's writing echoes Handel, Mozart and Wagner. By dress rehearsals, the actors had come a long way, but they still hadn't achieved what I can only call the *Shavian music* of the long speeches. So one night, just before the first dress rehearsal, we all sat on the floor and listened to a Handel concerto for two orchestras, a duet from *The Magic Flute* and "Siegfried's Rhine Journey." As we listened, I suggested moments in the play that corresponded to the sounds. They understood instantly. The speaking of the lines suddenly had an immediacy and a poised clarity that I couldn't have achieved any other way. *They* made the discoveries.

Studying the music of great composers has helped me to understand the structure of large plays and even small scenes. I had a wonderful experience when I directed *Don Giovanni* with Christopher Hogwood as conductor in St. Louis, because Chris knew absolutely what the music meant dramatically. And he explained what orchestral comments Mozart was making inside an aria or during a recitative. Even though I'd had lots of music education, that was by far the most important musical knowledge I ever gained. In rehearsal he'd explain, "Because this melody is played by an oboe here, it's going to sound a little bit smarmy," and suddenly you realize that those six measures of Donna Anna's aria could be interpreted as a lie. In Mozart, the orchestra questions what someone has said, or agrees with it, or the orchestra pulls away from it, leaving the audience to judge. Mozart's works—string quartets, concertos, operas—are packed with political and social ideas. They're pure theatre. Mozart's music is about the individual responding to society and to nature. It's always a dialogue.

What about the musicality within Shakespeare's writing?

Shakespeare understands the inside of words. His speeches, when taken apart, line by line, word by word, and then syllable by syllable, have a kind of power that, even if you didn't understand the speech and just heard consonants and vowels coming at the rhythms that he gives to you, would create an emotional effect. If it's a passive moment, if it's an inward moment, if it's a moment of action, whatever it is, you can almost do it without understanding the meaning of it because it *sounds* like what it's describing. One of the things that makes his plays so alive is that he understood vowels and the visceral effect of pure sound: lines like "howl, howl, howl."

There are all sorts of places, little clues for actors to take off and do what they want to do, which are either pauses in a line that breaks its beats or a line that ends with silent beats. Those are textual gifts for actors to use. The most actable, most expressive lines in Shakespeare occasionally start with an "O," which can be an actor's cadenza. It can be short, long or an intake of breath. And those lines like, "never, never, never," have an ontological, emotional impact. Sometimes, on a first reading, certain words in a Shake-spearean text seem to be almost absurd, seem like Beckett; they drop into a scene and you think, "There's no reason for that word to be in that scene. The scene has nothing to do with that word." But the more you listen to it, the more you realize that the word is there precisely so that your mind will expand upon hearing such seeming impossibilities.

Cleopatra's, "Give me to drink mandragora," for instance. A line absolutely out of left field! But it serves as an aural overture to the actual meaning of the entire scene. The sadness and slowness and weight of that word—"mandragora"—informs everything in that scene. "Man" and "drag" and "ora"—"aura." It's a feast of a word.

Too many people think that there's *one way* to do Shakespeare. And there are just as many people who believe the text is a blank canvas for some kind of experimentation. There are certainly lots of rules that you've got to follow because, of course, it's poetry. But if you see the rules as clues, as places to take a breath or not, to take a moment and be thoughtful or to race through seven more lines before you take a breath—once you get the meaning of that technically in your head, it informs the acting of the moment. The verse is not, as many actors and directors think, inhibiting. It allows the actor to bring all of himself into the moment. Artifice at its most liberating.

The technique must become organic for you. There's a lot of technique being taught nowadays, and too often young actors have *only* that. They can spew out all the right words and make all the right sounds, but it's empty. And after ten seconds you're not listening to a thing. Poetry is a humanistic discipline and it's a literary discipline. To humble yourself to that idea first is the only step to take before making sense of a line. The plays of Shakespeare are so eclectic that certain moments in all of them give over to the most "Method" acting approach in the world. In other moments, however, if you do not follow the directions the playwright has given you, you will simply fail. By which I mean you will be misunderstood. It is like music. There is a reason why great musicians are great technicians. You can't move anybody with a Beethoven sonata unless you learn the composer's intentions first. Like playing music, half of acting Shakespeare is learning how to listen. How to listen to the music you are making.

You are now directing opera. Would you say that the complexity of bringing together the variety of disciplines required in opera is one of the things that has drawn you to it?

Yes. Directing opera uses most of my muscles. It's the ultimate collaboration. In 1985 I did the European premiere of Dominick Argento's opera *The Voyage of Edgar Allan Poe* in Sweden. I had everything at my disposal, in terms of time and a sense of adventurousness on the part of the staff and the artists, to achieve virtually anything I wanted.

So all the talk we hear about the large amount of European subsidy for the arts has not necessarily dulled their creative capabilities?

It was not the case with this particular work. It was obvious that *Poe* was the centerpiece of their season. They had spent more money than they had ever spent before in bringing over the director, designer, conductor and composer from the U.S., so I may have a slightly jaded view of it. The length of rehearsal time was nine weeks over a three-and-a-half-month period. There were breaks because of the arrangement of their repertory, and I would go back to Hartford for two or three weeks and then return to Sweden for rehearsals.

Did you find this interruption damaging to the continuity of the rehearsal process?

No. Actually, it was extremely beneficial to the rehearsal process because it gave everyone a time to *think*. Vocally, it was essential. By opening night the quality of the singing was perfectly meshed with the acting intentions so that it was hard ever to feel that anyone was just singing, that the utterance of the voice was not a completely natural occurrence of the moment. But beyond that, I was able to explore a lot of theatrical ideas that, for one reason or another, I hadn't been able to develop previously.

Argento's opera is hallucinatory, dreamlike. A number of ideas in it were foreshadowed by a project John Conklin and I did in Hartford through a National Endowment for the Arts grant to work with some artists in creating a performance piece from the stories of E. T. A. Hoffmann, who was another nineteenth-century hallucinatory fabulist. We were able to work on that project for only three weeks, and though we achieved only tiny, abortive results, a lot of the ideas came to complete fruition for John and me in *Poe*. Everything that came up for us on the Hoffmann project was able to be reinvestigated in this large-scale opera. We approached it as a series of hallucinations based on Poe's life and stories.

Does that mean that it was abstract?

I'm not sure. It was deeply personal. Instead of setting it on a ship, as the libretto suggests, we decided to set it in a kind of operating room, as if Poe's brain were being dissected, examined, judged. The production, in a sense, explored attempts to kill the artistic impulse or to trap it. It was the most personal work I'd ever done up to that time. I mean, literally whatever came to mind in terms of an action on the stage, in terms of choreography, in terms of design, costumes, what-have-you, I put into the production. And I couldn't have done *Pericles* the way I did two years later if I hadn't been able to do *Poe* first.

What actor-director-singer problems resulted by your not speaking their language?

Because I was a foreign director and couldn't communicate subtly with the singers, nor they with me, we had to work out many of their problems through an interpreter. They were intimidated just enough by the language barrier to do exactly what I asked. And that was unusual, because I had never really had that experience in a theatre. I'm constantly having endless dialogues with actors and singers. In Sweden I could only really say, "I want you to do this at this moment." I'd act it out for them and if they had a problem with it, they would shake their heads—but then they'd *do* it. The language problem freed me, too. By not having to negotiate so much, I could more freshly realize very personal visual statements. I didn't have to explain myself all the time. I sensed that they were used to working more easily with highly conceptual directors than their U.S. counterparts. As they got used to my ideas, they embraced them and began to bring more of their own into the process.

What was your collaboration like with the creative artists, the librettist and composer?

Dominick came in the last two weeks of rehearsal because the tenor had a heavy voice and the tessitura was too high. So Dominick moved a lot of notes around so that the tenor could get through the opera without straining. But that was as close as we got.

Which gets us into the subject of collaboration. Who are the people with whom you have had the most creative working relationships?

Designers John Conklin, Michael Yeargan, Dunya Ramicova, Pat Collins, composer Mel Marvin and sound designer David Budries. I see each production that I do as a collaborative effort. Maybe it's because I started out as an actor. A collaboration has to be a generous process, and it has to be a *regenerative* process. There is no collaboration if you come to the table and say, "I have this idea—and this is how you will assist me in presenting it." Collaboration is saying, "I understand certain potent feelings I have about the work, but I don't understand everything." And you listen to what the others might feel about it. Then you go away and something new begins to coalesce—and you begin to realize that there is a way into the project.

What happens during the "go away" period is a dream, a kind of limbo resting place. All of the ideas are like living creatures that have gotten into your head and work there while you're doing other things. So that when you come back to it in the collaborative process, there is more for everyone to explore. It's tapping into your subconscious, really—and being willing to give up a point of view in order to collaborate.

An example is the *Twelfth Night* we did in 1986. I originally felt that the production should explore the feminine/masculine idea, the yin/yang apparent in Viola and the masculine/feminine forces in the whole world. To that end, I began to look into my interest in Oriental philosophy and Oriental theatre, primarily Kabuki. The designer, Michael Yeargan, and I saw performances by the Grand Kabuki and began sharing books, ideas, colors, whatnot. And he came up with a set that was extremely beautiful, very Oriental in color and form. And I looked at the set and loved it. But I also felt, because I had been watching the actors in auditions as they read scenes from the play (which is also a collaborative process), that the Oriental form would be too rigid for the fluidity I sensed in the text.

So we had a problem. We all loved the Oriental idea. We all loved what the Oriental idea said about things in the play. But it didn't seem to be serving every element in the play. And after Michael and I had talked for a while, Jess Goldstein, the costume designer, walked in and looked at the model of the set and said, "Gee, it looks like a place where a party happened. It looks like a ballroom or something."

That one remark suddenly caused all of my subconscious feelings to come into focus: the end of partying, the end of youth, the beginning of responsibility. This is what *Twelfth Night* is about. This took us far away from any sort of Oriental concept and, instantly, from Jess's remark on looking at Michael's work, the whole idea of that production was there. I said, "Of course, that's it. And we'll put up a mirror ball there and an old piano. And it's about life as a party, and how things go wrong at a party, and how people fall in love at a party, and how potent cheap music is, and, and, and . . . "

It answered everything I wanted that play to say for me at that time, when I was turning forty. I remember saying to Michael, "It's a kind of cosmic Roseland. It's not a real Roseland. And it's maybe a sort of backstage area, but it's not really that." That was all. And a week later he came back with a model, and he said, "I think you're going to hate this. I don't know what it means, I don't know what it is, but here it is." He showed me the model and that was it. It was a platform on which I could play out these ideas about maturation, illusion, the end of youth.

Twelfth Night is also about the ephemeral nature of art, how it can lead you somewhere but it can't sustain you. You can use an artistic experience to move from one place to another, but then real life must take over, which was what the last image in the production was about.

The last moment was another example of collaboration. The diaphanous canopy that had been over the stage all night came down, and the clown wrapped himself in it and seemed to disappear or go to sleep or die. It began as Michael's idea. I was going to end the play with the ambiguous union of the couples. But dropping that gauzy overhead canopy down was beautiful and mysterious, far more ambiguous than any business with the couples wondering if they'd made the right decision. I didn't know what that meant at first, but I knew it was right. When we put it into the show, I wasn't particularly pleased by it, but I knew it was right for the moment. Only midway through the run did I begin to understand its web of meanings. The audience wasn't stunned simply by the beauty of the image, it was stunned by its metaphorical significance. They got it before I did. I loved that.

There is something satisfying when an experience has a symbolic ending as well as a real one.

Yes, and that happens at the end of every Shakespearean comedy. A character will generally say to you, "You're free now. Let me go. Free me. Go out into the world and keep working at it. Figure things out. I've taken you this far. I'm not really a clown. I'm just an actor. It's only a play. good luck."

Do the actors serve a similar function of bringing immediacy to the process?

They are a continuation of that process. After all, the actors are speaking the text, they become the center of the experience. Suddenly the text is being uttered, is coming out from inside a human body. So they bring their own responses to the prerehearsal work.

Of course, with Shakespeare your collaboration is with a playwright who can speak to you only through the text. But what is it like to work with living writers?

Kevin Heelen sent his play *Distant Fires* to us. I didn't fall in love with it on paper, but I admired it. I felt there was an ear for dialogue that was superb. I tried to find another director for it because I felt I would not be the right one, and I exhausted all kinds of possibilities. Directors I sent the play to weren't available., etc, etc. Finally, I had to do it. I fell in love with the playwright from the start and, consequently, that friendship aided the process enormously. I don't know what it would have been like if we hadn't been able to be so silly with one another. We did a considerable amount of re-thinking. He did a whole new draft of the second act, at my urging, which turned out to be not at all useful. We threw it out. We went back to what he had originally written, which was superb. I learned a lot from that.

What were the changes you wanted in the script? Were they structural?

Yes. I was aiming for more dramatic cohesiveness and, in fact, in aiming for the cohesiveness we lost the spontaneity of the moment. As soon as he thought about a dramatic confrontation, and I thought about it with him, it would become too theatrical and dead. We lost the easy give-and-take of the men. (The play is about black and white construction workers.) We found that to make it clear to an audience was, indeed, talking down to an audience. The great thing that happened during rehearsals was the realization that we had to "unearth" the original spontaneous utterances, to find out what had happened when Kevin was at the typewriter. It was thrilling because it was a look at the mind of a writer and how that writer works—and getting that writer to trust his own mind as well.

His next play, *Right Behind the Flag*, was in the thinking stage for six years. He sat down and wrote it in two weeks. He'd been talking about this play for years. But he hadn't written one word of it. Suddenly, it was there. That's Kevin's work style.

Constance Congdon, our playwright-in-residence, whose play *The Gilded Age* I directed, is different. She will rework a scene and rework a scene and after ten reworkings it's a nugget. And that's a completely different way of working. It has to do with how a playwright's talent moves. If you have talent, one of your duties is to figure out how it works. Especially if your talent involves working with other artists. You need to know at least the patterns of the way your mind works so that you can constantly be open to those urges. You can easily stop them, or you can get a lot of misunderstanding from people who don't understand you unless you say, "Look, this is what happens to me. I generally go in this way and I come out that end. Now, let's see if we can all hang on while I do that."

And with Connie, I might say, "The first eight scenes of this play are now superb and the next eight are a little less so but getting closer." She'll say, "Yes, because the first eight have been reworked the most." For her it's just a question of chaining herself to the word processor because she knows that the next application of her mind and her heart to that scene is going to reap rewards. The interesting thing is that the scenes that are superb keep getting better because she can't simply start in the middle. She has to start over. So there is a change of phrase, a new bit of dialogue in scenes that were perfectly fine three months ago, but which have ramifications in later scenes. Working with Connie was completely different than my experience with Kevin, but just as gratifying.

Not every play works equally well in every theatre space. Hartford has a rather cavernous thrust stage. Is there a kind of a stage that you find ideal?

I'm not a fan of thrust stages. Though I've worked on them for years, I find they don't solve as many problems as they create, simply because audiences in a thrust theatre are spectators. Audiences in a proscenium house seem to become more easily involved. A thrust theatre doesn't bring you in. And actors always have difficulty projecting in a thrust house. Most of the time, fifty percent of the actors have their backs to a good twenty-five to forty percent of the audience. It's very unnerving. Olivier made a comment to somebody when he first got on a thrust stage. He said, "Well, there are no secrets here, are there?" And there *ought* to be secrets in the theatre. I love illusion. I love magic tricks, and I love the idea that Houdini made an elephant disappear. It's much harder to use artifice or craft in a thrust theatre and, consequently, it often produces an artificial effect, because the artifice has to be created sculpturally. Whether it's The Guthrie, which is in many ways a superb playing space, or Stratford, Ontario, I just don't get involved. I watch performances or costumes or staging as if I'm watching an exhibition. The thrust stage may be fine for playing Shakespeare in a certain way, but too often that kind of space has encouraged stentorian, rhetorical playing. The *thrust* should be a way of fluidity—that was Guthrie's whole point in creating it with designer Tanya Moiseiwitsch after that famous impromptu at Elsinore with the Guthrie/Olivier *Hamlet*. Any drama written after 1609—even *The Tempest*, which was written for a sort of early proscenium—becomes ludicrous and threadbare and obviously theatrical when placed on a thrust stage. To watch Nora confronting Helmer in Ibsen's *A Doll's House*, five feet from pleasant-looking suburban housewives with their purses on their laps, is destructive to everything Ibsen and the actors are trying to do. The artists' attempts to create and control a suspension of disbelief is seriously marred.

There are two important things lacking in American theatres outside of New York City: prosceniums and proper acoustics. If an actor can't be heard whispering a line, the theatre should be razed. There's no point in it.

What has been Mark Lamos's contribution to the theatre?

Maybe letting people know that you can have an enormously fulfilling life and create a body of work entirely within the nonprofit theatre system in America. The resident theatre movement has come to that kind of maturity. I've acted in it since 1971 and directed in it since 1977, and I expect to continue expanding my horizons basically within it. If I've contributed anything, it's a certain approach to classical dramatic literature—which is a field that is depressingly rare, forgotten. I feel a need to join the sensibilities of my time to the historical-ethical continuum that preceded it—so that in this brilliant technological age we do not trample what was seeded for us—and ceded *to* us—not so very long ago.

MARSHALL W. MASON

M arshall Mason arrived in New York in 1961 to begin his life as a director just at the beginning of the Off-Off Broadway and regional theatre movements.

Off-Off Broadway was emerging as an outlet for young artists who felt cut off both from the big-budget Broadway stage and Off-Broadway theatre, which was beginning to ape its larger commercial brother. These young performers tested their talents in intimate makeshift lofts, churches, storefronts and bars. At the same time, the regional theatre movement, using the non-profit corporate model, had begun to take hold in cities around the nation, creating institutions devoted to the development of acting companies. The combination of these two creative impulses would eventually merge in New York City, to create such theatres as La Mama E.T.C., Circle Theatre Company, New York Shakespeare Festival, Playwrights Horizons, Manhattan Theatre Club, The Ridiculous Theatrical Company, American Place Theatre, WPA and scores of others.

New writers began creating contemporary audience-oriented works that were blasphemous, camp, poetical, pop and radically political, all seemingly based on a unified need to explore the sense of freedom and change that was rising in America. It was a rich assemblage of talents. Such writers as Julie Bovasso, Charles Ludlam, Robert Patrick, Sam Shepard, Adrienne Kennedy, Terrence McNally, Lanford Wilson, Leonard Melfi, Jean-Claude van Itallie, Ed Bullins, John Ford Noonan, John Guare, Israel Horovitz, Tom Eyen and Imamu Amiri Baraka were but a few of those emerging from this burgeoning movement. Among those who came to prominence as directors of these new works were Tom O'Horgan, Wilford Leach, Andrei Serban, Elizabeth Swados, Robert Kalfin, Kenneth Frankel, Christopher Martin, Robert Wilson, Andre Gregory, Richard Foreman, Meredith Monk, Richard Schechner, Elizabeth LeCompte and Vinnette Carroll.

One of the most enduring of the Off-Off Broadway writers is Lanford Wilson, and the collaboration he developed with Marshall Mason resulted not only in a treasury of honored and widely produced plays, but in the creation of an entire company devoted to an aesthetic based on the "lyric realism" found in his writing. Wilson was one of the first of the Off-Off Broadway writers to develop a mature voice, and these early productions of Wilson and his collaborator/director, Mason, were noted for the perfect melding of a writer's sensibilities with the direction of an acting ensemble capable of using language naturalistically yet with a sense of the musical rhythms embedded in the text.

Mason and Wilson produced their work at such performance spaces as Cafe La Mama, the Judson Poets' Theatre and one of the earliest established Off-Off Broadway theatres, Caffe Cino. Founder Joseph Cino functioned as the Dolly Levi of this new theatre movement, constantly putting talented people together, encouraging playwrights, directors and actors. All of this was happening under the noses of—and despite continuous harassment by—city authorities who took a dim view of performances presented in unlicensed spaces. Caffe Cino, its walls thick with memorabilia, yellowing photographs and glitter, is reported to have received 1250 citations from the police in one day. Ellen Stewart's La Mama had been closed numerous times, and she was harassed to the point that she was preparing to leave the country to accept the offer of a theatre space, along with twenty actors of her choice, from the Kammerspiele in Munich, when W. McNeil Lowry called from the Ford Foundation to offer the funding to purchase and renovate a building. She remained in New York, and when turning down the Kammerspiele recommended that they offer the space instead to two young men, playwright Martin Sperr and director Peter Stein.

Off-Off Broadway had found its voice and continued even though theatre spaces began to close. One of those closings in 1967 was the Caffe Cino, forced as a consequence of the tragedy of Joe Cino's suicide. The arc of life for the Cino had been a brief but important eight years.

By the late 1960s, Mason had formed Circle Theater Company (subsequently named Circle Repertory Company) with Lanford Wilson, Rob Thirkield and Tanya Berezin. It was composed of committed artists and inspired by the combined influence of American theatre literature of the 1950s (the work of William Inge, Tennessee Williams and others) and the aesthetic espoused by the reigning theatrical influence of the time, the Actors Studio. In addition to Wilson, other playwrights who came to prominence through Circle Rep and its ability to create works that were viewed as being "perfectly made and produced" were Mark Medoff, Edward J. Moore, Corinne Jacker, Patrick Meyers, John Bishop, Jules Feiffer, Megan Terry and William H. Hoffman.

At the same time, despite the acting and directing skill the members of Circle Rep applied to the works of contemporary American playwrights, the Company's ability to successfully realize the classics became an elusive goal. Efforts in this direction, combined with attempts to support an acting ensemble devoted to rotating rep while working in an intimate but economically limiting space with minimal seating capacity and technical resources, led to deepening financial problems. The burden of trying to maintain the theatre while nurturing a life as a director in his own institution and elsewhere began to wear Mason down. "Lanford shares with me the vision of the theatre, and certainly shares all of the artistic standards. But he has his life and his work, and the relationship between those two things is very good. He doesn't have to come into the office every day and deal with all of the problems. I'm looking forward to being able to lay down the day-to-day wear and tear on the spirit."

Mason discussed his directing technique in three conversations over five years. The first discussion came at the end of Circle Rep's highly successful 1981 season, in which his productions of Wilson's *Fifth of July* and *Talley's Folly* had transferred to Broadway theatres. He was preparing to direct Hume Cronyn and Jessica Tandy in *Foxfire* at The Guthrie Theater in Minneapolis, to be followed immediately by rehearsals for Wilson's *A Tale Told* at the Mark Taper Forum in Los Angeles. He was elated and energetic. "Time is one of the things that I get most concerned about. As Roger Kennedy (at that time, chairman of the John F. Kennedy Center for the Performing Arts) told me two years ago, 'You're going to be middle-aged any minute and you're not going to be able to keep up this pace.' I should be trying to do as much as I can."

The second conversation took place a year later. Mason had just announced a year's sabbatical away from Circle Rep; Tanya Berezin and Rodney

Marriott, Circle's dramaturg, would direct the company until he returned. "I have sixty-three actors, each of whom has great artistic integrity, each of whom has career needs and plans. Each feels that I'm the one they can come and talk to. We have about twenty playwrights, each of whom wants to read to me his latest revision of his third draft. And there are staff and fund-raising responsibilities. You can't be a miracle worker twenty-four hours a day. It's inhuman and it's ridiculous, and I'm getting middle-aged."

The third discussion was four years later, a few days prior to Mason announcing his resignation from Circle Rep. Saddened by the death of co-founder Rob Thirkield, faced with continuing financial problems following an unsuccessful season, he was anticipating that the National Endowment would withdraw the funds it had granted the ensemble. "This season, the economics of our situation dictate that we must be in our own space instead of renting additional space that can accommodate what we had planned, which was to present three plays or more in rotating rep instead of our normal series of single productions. Our own space cannot physically support that kind of rotation and the seating capacity is not enough to provide the income required to support the increased costs of repertory. We have received the NEA grant for the second year, but we may be in the position of having to turn it down because I'm not sure that I can deliver. If I can't achieve those things here, I begin to think of other things that I want to do. The 1985-86 season was less than successful for me because my relationship with the actors was not terrific—a situation caused by a number of things. Our concept was to hire twenty-five actors for twenty-five weeks and do three plays in rotating rep. This was a departure from what we'd done before. We didn't have a space to enable us to do rotating rep until the last minute, so I wasn't able to choose the plays until late. We lost Bill Hurt at the last minute because he was involved with a film that was delayed. The actors wanted to know what roles they were going to be playing and I had to promise each person a certain number of leads in order to get commitments for six months—and the only way I could do that was to double-cast. By double-casting I cut everybody's rehearsal time and they were all miserable." He pauses. "It was a growing experience."

The arc of Mason's eighteen years at the helm of Circle Rep ended in 1987. Tanya Berezin was named artistic director. Mason's collaboration with Lanford Wilson has continued.

■   ■   ■

How does a director learn a technique, a method for directing?

In the art of directing we have no method or set of principles similar to those Stanislavsky discovered for the actor. No two people do it the same way.

There is almost nothing you can say about what makes a good director without finding someone who will contradict it. I've come up with a few self-evident rules—they're not too revolutionary. Even so, it's surprising how few directors make use of them.

What kind of rules?

Being well organized is really a help to everybody: just being able to take time and divide it and fill it with the kind of exploration that's going to result in a flowering at a certain point. Theoretically, that point is the opening night, and then the work should go on growing after that.

Well, what is it the director does to stimulate this "flowering"?

A director is responsible for everything except the words and, in his dramaturgical role, responsible even for the way the text is shaped, the cuts that are made and the rewrites that go on in rehearsals. There is a real contribution that the director can make to the text. When I work with Lanford Wilson, we agree that the words are his responsibility and anything else is mine. Usually, he does not have a visual concept for the play. The characters just talk somehow in his head, and the ultimate visual design we arrive at for a production is a revelation to him.

What is the most interesting aspect of directing to you?

I'm most deeply attracted to the concept of directing as sculpture in motion. The changing physical relationships of the actors within an environment, the pattern of movement and the visual beauty of that, have become more and more important to me. It developed late in my directing because I started out from the actor's point of view and I didn't think about the externals at all.

So directing consists of creating that moving sculpture, and helping dramaturgically to shape and criticize the play. It's also our job to create an atmosphere of creativity that will stimulate the best work from the actor, to be a mirror, tell them what they are doing and what we see. Both for the playwright and for the actor, the director is the surrogate audience until the actual audience arrives.

When in the process does that critical, audience eye begin to operate for you?

When I'm in the rehearsal room with the actors I don't really want too much objectivity. The most important thing is trust. Together, we are trying to create the life of the play, and I only remain objective in so far as I'm trying to decide whether behavior is true to the circumstances or not. If it's true, then I'm with it and I want to stay with it and I don't care about being objective. Later, when we move into the theatre, just before the audience comes in, I must look at it and say, "Well, this moved me in the rehearsal room, but was it because I wasn't objective? Have I been fooling myself all this while?" Then you make adjustments based on this objectivity.

How do you use your time in the rehearsal hall?

In rehearsals most of the time I avoid talking about results. I prefer saying, "Take your time. I don't want this like a play, I want it like reality." And sometimes in reality a person will let five minutes pass without saying anything. A person can say, "Is it going to rain today?" And then you may drift off for five minutes before saying, "No, I think it's going to clear up." Of course, you would never want an audience to see that onstage. It's terribly boring. But at first in rehearsal the actors aren't ready to do it up to tempo. We spend most of the time in the rehearsal room slowing it down. When we get it over to the theatre, that's the time to start saying, "Okay, throw that away, throw that away." It's an easier transition for them to make at that point. The actor shouldn't be thinking about the audience before he has something to share. My theory is: create something first and then share it. David Mamet drove me crazy when I was rehearsing Malvolio for him in *Twelfth Night*. He kept saying, "You have to keep the paper down, we won't be able to see you." And I kept saying, "David, let me believe that I just found this letter and that I'm in this garden in Illyria. When we're in the theatre and I'm on the stage, I will know where the audience is and then I'll keep the paper out of my face." David believes in the theory that you should rehearse exactly what you're going to do onstage because he's afraid you'll develop habits.

Do you begin your rehearsals with a read-through?

I have ambivalent feelings about readings. I avoid them when they're for the purpose of letting people congratulate themselves prematurely. It's like an opening night for them. They come in and they listen to the play and, "It's going to be all right." I often do not ask the actors to read the play at all in rehearsal, but if we do, I try to encourage people to jump in and try things and not to hold back, not to play it safe. On the other hand, I often feel that first readings can be very damaging. Actors may realize, "Oh, my part isn't very large. I'm not on until the middle of the second act." It affects their interest. However, some plays really require readings. For example, *Childe Byron* was a poetic piece. The language was terribly important, therefore, to read it aloud together was the proper thing to do. When we did *Hamlet*, rather than having the actors commit themselves to trying to read all of it, I felt it would be more valuable for us to listen to Gielgud's recording of the play. With *A Tale Told*, we did read the play because we had gone through several revisions quickly and Lanford and I needed to hear it.

Do you spend much time on research?

Before I directed *Foxfire*, I went to Rabun Gap, Georgia, where the play takes place, and soaked up what I could about the area, what it looked like, how the people talked, how they moved, the rhythms of their lives. When we did Lanford's *Mound Builders*, we really learned the basics of field archaeology, and we even went on field trips with professors from New York University. When I did *Tobacco Road*, I went to Augusta and throughout the South. At Plains, Georgia, I experienced a Ku Klux Klan rally that ended in the death of a man when some guy drove into the middle of the rally with his car. I was going all through Georgia looking for the *Tobacco Road* sensibility. I was doing an updated version of the play at Academy Festival Theatre in Lake Forest, Illinois with Barnard Hughes and Barbara Bel Geddes, and I wanted to know what was happening in Georgia in 1977. It was not until we got to Augusta that we really found the Tobacco Road people. They were still there, five generations of women sitting on the front porch. All of the men had gone off to the swimming hole, drinking beer. I took pictures and interviewed them on tape.

Preparatory to rehearsal, I like to read books of the period or nonfiction works that relate to the problems dealt with by the play. I don't spend a lot of time reading the play and I don't "block" in advance.

Also, I've found great designers like John Lee Beatty, who has been working with me for over ten years, and Dennis Parichy, who has been working with me for close to thirty years, and my wonderful costume designers, Laura Crow and Jennifer von Mayrhauser. The quality of the visual elements can be so high it's like having a Stradivarius. I can really explore the visual expression of a play.

What is the nature of your collaboration with designers?

John and I have a very nonverbal relationship. I talk about what the play means to me, what I think it's about, the important physical elements I need. I remember that for *A Tale Told*, I went on about how important the doors were. I felt the play was about the night America started locking its doors. That set shared some of the same elements that I had asked for in the set for *Come Back, Little Sheba*: I wanted the actors to disappear from view as they went from room to room. There would be a scene going on in one room, and while the actors were still talking as they left the kitchen, they would disappear behind the staircase and come out in the front hall. I remember talking about it as a big shell of some kind, as if we were peering into an organism that inhabited this house.

Most of my discussions with John are about character and mood. I have the same kind of conferences with Dennis Parichy, although I have a much better background in lighting than I do in set design—I lighted my own shows for a long time. Dennis and I studied with the same teacher at Northwestern and I understand some basic elements, so we can really communicate: "This is a very sculptured play. I want high angles. I'm not concerned about great visibility in this scene." Or the converse, "The clarity is what is most important. I want it sunny, bright and funny." And sometimes I talk about percentage values of the light.

My costume designers tend to bring me magazines and say, "What do you think of this?" We communicate a lot through pointing and sharing. I try to get the designers stirred up and turned on by the emotional qualities of the play. I've been rewarded with designs that are far beyond my little imagination.

Sometimes we have problems. *Fifth of July* was a perfect example. John Lee had designed it twice—once at Circle Rep and then at the Mark Taper in California. By the time we got to the Broadway production he was running dry. I said no to about three sketches before he came up with the one we finally used at the New Apollo Theatre.

What triggers the imagination, and can you learn to summon it?

There is probably an unconscious area of creativity that an artist draws upon. Through rehearsals and other means, we focus our conscious attention on that mysterious source, whatever it is. Sometimes, as a result of that concentration things begin to develop more quickly. When you begin to rehearse a play after you've thought about it for a year, it's a whole different thing than if somebody hands you a script and says, "Here, can you start directing this next week?" In the first instance, you've read the play several times, explored it, idly thought about it and perhaps it has appeared in your dreams. There's a gestation period that's quite marvelous. I've never had a play too far in advance of rehearsals. The best work usually involves plays that you have wanted to do for a very long time. When I did *The Three Sisters*, for instance, I'd wanted to do that play for years and years. *Mary Stuart*, which I had first directed twenty years earlier, had been gestating in my imagination all that time before my second production. Still, the imagination *really* begins to accelerate when you know the play will open on such and such a date.

Stanislavsky was trying to harness the inspiration. And how do you do that? It's like a force of nature. It comes from the unconscious. And finding a conscious way into that source is related to psychoanalysis. I think the rehearsal process is very close to that psychoanalytic process. Stanislavsky was trying to find a way of performing every night whether you feel like it or not, whether you have the inspiration or not. Tying the imagination to the action is the key. And that's where the director becomes so important in helping the actor find the right physical action so that, as the character, he can rely upon doing that action every night.

Circle Rep has traditionally produced new plays. How much rehearsal time does that require?

Twenty-one rehearsals is the minimum number in which I think a full work can be realized. Generally speaking, I work six hours a day because I find that eight is more than I can do. With a lunch break, there are two different rehearsal periods. In the morning we review work that we've done before and in the afternoon we explore new territory. I divide the script into little beats of three or four pages maximum. These beats are marked by "French scenes," people coming and going, by change of mood, by change of objective—different elements cue the subdivisions of the play into these specific beats. I then make a rehearsal schedule with a character/scene-break-down chart. Everything we're going to do is planned in the order we're going to do it. A schedule for every scene is posted on the call-board. If an actor is called, he or she is going to work that day on that scene. I do not, therefore, waste people's time. The actors have the rehearsal plan from the beginning and they know how we're going to accomplish the work that must be done before opening night.

What kind of preparation do you expect from actors prior to putting a scene on its feet?

I require the actors to memorize their lines before we rehearse a scene because my principal role in the rehearsal process is to discover the physical life of the play with the actor. I believe that there is one move we can discover for this character in these circumstances at this moment, that is more true, more right than any other. In order to find that best move, I need the actors to be absolutely vulnerable and unsure of themselves as they try to believe in the circumstances of the scene. They cannot be tied to the pages of a script. The minute an actor gets a script in his hand, he is absolutely secure and I don't see any impulses. Also, their hands must be free to deal with objects and their eyes free to engage the other actors.

What do you do prior to the physicalization of the scene, in the early rehearsals?

I spend about the first twenty percent of the time, almost the first week, doing what I call improvisations. But there are a million approaches to acting and some actors really gain a lot from improvisations and some don't. I do not force my method on them. How they work, how they act is their business and not mine, and so I don't force them to do improvisations although I do make it possible if it is going to be useful. If two people who don't know each other are playing lovers, let's say, I have a little exercise called "the baby exercise" in which I ask them to be babies and explore each other's faces and bodies. It's amazing how quickly they can get past all kinds of socially proper things that these lovers will need to get past.

Mostly we do what I call research. We discuss the general milieu. We look up all kinds of relevant facts. For instance, in *Hot l Baltimore*, we had to learn how to run a hotel—so I would take Judd Hirsch, who was playing the desk clerk, on field trips. We'd talk to a desk clerk and find out how he did wake-up calls and what he did with his day. We read a lot of firsthand accounts of hookers. I think one or two of the actresses actually interviewed prostitutes. I encourage my actors to write a biography for their characters from birth up to the time of the play. I also encourage them to think about what items they've got in their pockets, because I think those things we carry with us have special value. I also encourage them to find parallel experiences from their own lives. We do this kind of research for almost a week, and then we start staging the play.

How do you organize that staging time?

I call it rehearsing in movie style, because we spend one whole afternoon, a three-hour session, exploring three pages of dialogue. We sit and run the lines until everybody feels comfortable. Then we explore the movement and by the end of the day we could bring in a camera and film the scene. I don't mean it doesn't get better in subsequent rehearsals or that it won't develop, because it will, but the physical life pretty much stays the same. Then the next morning we review that scene and in the afternoon go on to Scene Two. It's not quite as simple as I've described it, but that is the general principle. I spend a lot of time on the beginning of the play, because if you can get the thread going through the eye of the needle properly, then it's easy to pull it through. I try to get that first organic moment of the play really true, and then all the subsequent action should follow logically.

Once you have achieved the reality of the play, is there a need to go back and theatricalize it?

Sometimes it's necessary to do what we call a speed-through. After encouraging the company to, "Take your time, take your time," there comes that moment when I say, "Okay, today I want no pauses. I want you literally to do it as fast as you can possibly speak it. Don't stop. Don't think." By doing that, they find out where they cannot go fast.

Then, at some point before we open, usually after the speed-through, I sit everybody down and we just speak the play together and listen to the beauty of its music, the phrasing of it. This an important step, and it's something that most of the actors tune in to. It's a great help to them. It's like being a musician. Sound is terribly important, the rhythms, the music. For the writers I like to work with, Lanford or Tennessee Williams, much of their meaning is expressed in the beauty of their language. The rhythm is there. Although the actor seems to be absolutely free and spontaneous, he can count on the rhythm. My actors are disciplined. They're musicians. And within the rhythmic discipline, they can be terribly free and creative.

It's rather remarkable that you can put together a new play with no more time than most theatres allocate for reviving a known work.

We went to Woodstock one summer and had three months to work on a play, and I discovered something about myself. I had always thought, "Oh, there's never enough time in America and why don't we have the kind of luxury that they have in Europe?" But I found it's not for me. I'm by nature a quick person. When I stage with the actors, for instance, in three hours I can pretty much determine through them how a scene ought to be staged. I don't need six months to explore that.

Was that also true when you directed Shakespeare?

Well, that's very different. Six weeks was hardly enough time for *Hamlet*. When we did the first production of *The Three Sisters*, we were in a workshop situation, using the play as a basis for our explorations from August through April. Then I went into rehearsal for four weeks, but, my God, it made all the difference in the world to have had that preparation time. Someday I would love to have the experience of working with my sets and costumes from the beginning, as they do at the Moscow Art Theatre. In rehearsal, we mock up the set, using as many real props and costumes as possible, so that the actor doesn't just pantomime putting on a coat but has a *real* coat to put on —so there are no surprises later. I'm not really fond of surprises. And I have a second set of rehearsal lights. We run the lines under the ordinary fluorescents, but when we get ready to get up and do our work on the mocked-up set in the rehearsal room, it's magic time. We turn off the fluorescents and turn on the little stage lights so a real atmosphere is created. I don't encourage actors to "project" in the rehearsal room, just communicate with one another. We can make it louder later.

What started you on the road to being a director?

From childhood, I existed in a world that seemed to be quite apart from the common values of my fellow students in Texas. I was always acting, putting on plays. When I reached the age of nineteen and directed for the first time, I realized that I had been thinking as a director all my life. Always before, it was putting on a show so that I could act. I didn't know what a director was. I went to see the film *Pinky* when I was about eight or nine years old and I was knocked out by it. I said, "Somebody was responsible for this. There's something about this movie that's different from the other movies I've seen." I waited for the credits to come by again and it was, of course, directed by Elia Kazan. I still didn't know what a director was, but his was the last credit and I said, "He must be the one who's responsible for it." So I then went around saying to everybody, from my eight-year-old point of view, "Oh, my favorite director is Elia Kazan."

Texas seems to have spawned its fair share of directors.

I was never comfortable in Texas, never felt at home there. I always felt like a stranger. I had read that Northwestern University (in Evanston, Illinois) had the best drama school in the country, because Alvina Krause taught there. I was a poor kid and had to have a scholarship, and I got one. I became a director at Northwestern by virtue of almost leaving the theatre because I discovered I wasn't going to be John Gielgud. One of Miss Krause's assistants said, "Why don't you try directing?" I talked Miss Krause into letting me direct *Cat on a Hot Tin Roof*. It was an enormous success and after that my friends started referring to me as a director.

When I arrived in New York I felt at home. I gave myself five years to achieve something. I didn't want to be one of those people who kid themselves all their lives and really don't have any talent.

What happened at the end of those five years?

Was I successful? I wasn't a household word. I certainly wasn't making a living. But I was at that time the youngest member of the Society of Stage Directors and Choreographers; a member of the hallowed Actors Studio, which had been a lifetime goal for me; I had directed Ibsen's *Little Eyolf* Off

Broadway with some success; I had done a lot of work at the Caffe Cino; and I'd begun working with Lanford Wilson. I thought, "If I'm kidding myself, I'll kid myself a little longer."

Your mentioning the Caffe Cino brings up visions of a rather legendary time and place.

I made my definitive statement about the Caffe Cino in the teleplay of Robert Patrick's *Kennedy's Children* in 1981. It's not the whole story, but I feel in that television production I captured some of the spirit of the place. I experienced so much in those incredible, extraordinary years, the years of discovery for so many people who have shaped the American theatre. Working within Patrick's text, I wanted to show some of the spirit that I felt he had omitted.

What was that beginning of the Off-Off Broadway movement like?

I came to New York in September of 1961 at the age of twenty. My friend Jane Lowry, from Northwestern, was appearing in a play by Doric Wilson at the Caffe Cino, and I went down to see her. This was in the very earliest days of the Cino. As a matter of fact, the play was called *Now She Dances*, and it was the second original play done there. I had never seen anything like the Caffe Cino. The place was all glitter and glamour and wonderful and mysterious and magic, and truly like Alice in Wonderland. I mean, it was like falling down the rabbit hole. First of all, it was an extraordinary experience to find Cornelia Street, which is only a block long. And to find on Cornelia Street this ridiculous coffeehouse with fifteen or twenty tables, ice cream chairs, coffee and sandwiches, where they were trying to do plays on this infinitesimal stage. I was immediately hooked.

Joe Cino said, "Oh, you're a director. Why don't you direct something for me?" The following summer, I did my first play at the Cino by Claris Nelson called *The Rue Garden*. It was the first Off-Off Broadway play to be reviewed by *The Village Voice*. The first awakening of the Off-Off Broadway movement. As Robert Patrick put it, "It was the beginning of the end."

After directing several productions at the Cino, I organized a group called Northwestern Productions and became a producer. I had thirteen partners and all of us were recent graduates of Miss Krause. We did *Little Eyolf* and *Arms and the Man* at the Actor's Playhouse.

How did you meet Lanford Wilson?

In the summer of 1963, I read a review in *The Village Voice* of a play called *So Long at the Fair*, by Lanford Wilson. I saw the play and loved it. That play, Lanford's first, by the way, has subsequently been lost. No one has it. I met him when he was in the middle of his second production of *Home Free*. We didn't start off well together. Joe Cino introduced us by setting us down at a table and saying, "I think you two should talk." Lanford's first question was, "Oh, did you see *Home Free* the first time?"

"Yes, I did."

"Isn't it a lot better now?"

"No," I said, "I think you've ruined it."

Subsequently, we accidentally met one evening and he said, "Come and read my play *Balm in Gilead*." I liked it and agreed to do it at La Mama in January of 1965.

With Ellen Stewart designing and sewing the costumes.

Ellen Stewart had started her theatre absolutely in imitation of the Cino. She said, "Hey, I could do this," and she did.

So Joe Cino was responsible for sparking this long and creative partnership you've had and continue to have with Wilson.

Joe was the most original person I guess I've ever met. He was very warm and almost mischievous in his challenge to people to celebrate themselves and life. He had been a dancer and had gained too much weight, so he was a roundish, jolly sort of person, witty and sarcastic and capable of a good deal of intellectual byplay. He was a man of great courage. He could take risks and he believed in the magic and value of the spiritual things in life. He provided a chance for me to do my work the way I saw it, without compromise of any sort. If you went to Joe with any problem, he would say, "Do what you have to do." That's a very simple and very basic philosophy.

Did he mean take any measure necessary?

No. He meant, "Don't sit around complaining. Get up and just accomplish it. Don't procrastinate, don't blame it on others. Take your life into your own hands. Nobody is going to do it for you." That's a tremendous answer to anybody who has a desire.

We were playing a revival of Claris's *The Clown* when Joe killed himself. We were doing it because Joe Torry, who was Cino's lover, had died the previous January of an accident in winter stock somewhere. He was an electrician and had made some kind of mistake and was electrocuted. Torry's favorite play had been *The Clown* so Joe asked us to bring it back. We did it with an all-star cast featuring Lanford Wilson, Robert Patrick, Michael Powell, David Starkweather and me. In *Kennedy's Children*, Bob Patrick dwelled on the bloodbath that ended Caffe Cino. But knowing Joe Cino as well as I did, I feel quite certain that there was a great release and celebration in that event.

Those days are remembered as the beginnings of perhaps the most vital period of change and growth in American theatre history.

This was 1965. Off-Off Broadway was so new that Actors' Equity wasn't prepared for it, so it was not the problem it later became. Equity didn't know what was happening. The actors sometimes played under other names. It was a real testament to Off-Off Broadway that it existed for so long without Equity's interference because there was nothing to complain about. It was delightful.

We think of your work with Wilson as continuing in the tradition of Tennessee Williams and other poets of the American theatre. But you both also went through early periods of experimentation.

In January 1968 I did Lanford's *Untitled Play* at the Judson Poets' Theater with Al Carmines's music. It contained the first frontal male nudity on the New York stage. To this day, Lanford has refused to have the play published because he dreads it might fall into amateurish hands. It was about exploring the killer instinct in man, and we dug deep into our own souls to find what that truth was. Tanya Berezin will forever be an extraordinary actor in my view for her work in that piece. The play called for the cast to strip one of the actors naked and then humiliate him. They were to improvise whatever it took. I put it off until late in the rehearsal period, but we finally did it. It worked, but the question was, could we repeat it? After about the third time performing it, kicking this actor, spitting at him, calling him names, making him cry, the actors went to various corners of the theatre. Tanya went about halfway toward hers and stopped. She went back and said, "You SOB, you're faking. You're going to do this to all of us?" Of course, he had held back because he had played at being humiliated when he wasn't. It was one of the most disgusting things I've ever seen in my life. It earned a great deal of respect for Tanya from all of us, because she would do anything to make the scene work.

What impelled the creation of Circle Rep?

Balm in Gilead at La Mama had thirty people in it and it was really an ensemble event, and Lanford said at that time, "We must keep these people together, we must form a company out of this because they're extraordinary, remarkable artists." That play was the sort of event you write home about. It was the first full-length play done Off-Off Broadway, and the first that La Mama held over for two weeks. People lined up around the block. It was the first Off-Off Broadway hit.

Lanford began an active campaign to try to persuade me to hold this company of actors together. In April 1968 we took his *Home Free!* and *The Madness of Lady Bright* to London, where we had an important success. Circle Rep was founded the following year.

What has been your role in what may be the longest collaboration in modern times between a director and a playwright?

Let me talk about *Gingham Dog.* I had a lot to do with that specific one. It was a three-act play with five characters. Lanford had sent it around to everybody who was producing at that time, in the mid-1960s. Nobody was interested and he finally put it in a drawer. A couple of years passed and, for some reason, I dug it out and said, "Hey, Lance, there's a great play here. Let's work on this." I took it over and restructured it into two acts and cut out a character. Then I went over to Lanford's house and said, "Now, look at what I've done." It was as though I'd turned it into a movie. There were gaps where I said it was much too long, and I didn't know how to get from here to there, but I thought "this" ought to come in between, and we need a few lines about "this." I had penciled things in. As we worked, Lanford became excited about it again and we put together a production at New Dramatists. Not too long after that it was done in Washington, and then it became Lanford's first Broadway play. This was a very unusual kind of collaboration for us. Usually my role is much less active.

I remember when he brought me the first act of *Hot l Baltimore* and said, "What do you think?" I said, "Something had better happen in the second act because it's wonderful but there's no action so far." Then he wrote the second act and it did, indeed, come to something.

Have there been times when your suggestions caused friction?

We've really never had much of a disagreement, but he was most "disgruntled," I would think, over my insistence that he had to work more on *Talley's Folly.* When he finished the first draft, it was such a little gem that he didn't want to touch it. He felt that it was finished. But I had all kinds of problems with it. I felt there needed to be more suspense. Matt, the protagonist, knew everything right from the beginning, and there was no sense of danger from the house on the hill. Lanford didn't really want to go back to work on it, but he did.

What makes for a successful play? There are good works that don't succeed and indifferent plays that occasionally do.

I think plays that are successful reinforce in some way the audience's image of themselves or some value that they hold. It's like going to church when you are able to recognize something you know to be true about yourself and that recognition feels good. Success in the theatre is tied to popularity. When the theatre brings up problems you don't want to deal with, it's really difficult.

What is it about Lanford's writing that is unique to the theatre?

Lanford really introduced overlapping dialogue to the theatre. At least I'd never heard two different scenes going on simultaneously before Lanford Wilson. He showed that an audience could take in more than one thing at a time. It's common onstage now. With that technique came the understanding that realism does not necessarily negate the present-tense theatre experience. Now we understand that more than one reality can coexist in a theatrical experience simultaneously. *Balm in Gilead, The Sandcastle* and *Lemon Sky* are realistic plays that proceed while at the same time a character can turn out and say to the audience, "I subsequently died a couple of years later, and I want to thank the theatre for giving me eternal life." I don't recall ever having seen that double reality in theatre before. There are elements of that duality in a play that influenced Lanford, Brendan Behan's *The Hostage.* I guess if you go back to Shakespeare there were the soliloquies, but it was a technique long forgotten. Theatre was either presentational or representational, and the two weren't mixed. Also, Lanford elevated the language into a kind of symphony of reality.

What has been your major contribution to the theatre?

Quite possibly the concept (which was not new, but which I breathed new life into) of an alternate theatre centered around a permanent company—not only actors but resident writers and designers, a community of artists who worked together repeatedly over a period of time developing new plays. We didn't invent it, but I think the interaction of the artists was something that we were at the forefront of reexamining. Since then, the new play development process seems to have taken root throughout the country in the resident theatres. When Circle Rep started in 1969, the La Mama troupe and the Open Theatre had already begun, but they were very experimental and commune-like. Also, at that time American theatre had begun to move toward the nonverbal techniques of Grotowski. On Broadway, producers mainly were importing Pinter, with his abstract, ominous sort of play. The critics had turned their backs on Tennessee Williams by that time, so I think we came along at a critical point and refocused theatre on the literature of the spoken word and the well-made play.

I think we have had an influence on play development by returning to the idea that theatre as a medium operates with three-dimensional human beings in recognizable situations with which audiences can identify and through which they can have a cathartic experience. It seems to me that we just recycled the classic essentials of theatre, and gave them new life.

DES McANUFF

D es McAnuff is a director and a rocker, as passionate about the classics as he is about rock and roll. His eclectic tastes and interests—a hallmark of his generation—allow him to move comfortably from directing Chekhov's *The Seagull* to the jazz musical *Shout Up a Morning*, from the large canvas of Shakespeare's *Henry IV* to Lee Blessing's two-character play *A Walk in the Woods*.

He grew up in Canada after being born in Illinois. His Canadian father was killed in an automobile accident six months before his birth, but McAnuff's mother remained in Illinois long enough for him to be delivered by the same doctor who had tried to save his father because she felt that Des would be closest to him that way. Later, his stepfather, a musician, would surround and imbue McAnuff with a love of music.

In 1976, at age twenty-three, McAnuff moved to New York from Toronto. A total unknown, within five years he had opened and headed up two theatre companies, the Dodger Theatre (in residence at the Brooklyn Academy of Music and, subsequently, at the New York Shakespeare Festival in New York) and the La Jolla Playhouse; he had directed his first Shakespearean production, *Henry IV, Part 1*, for Joseph Papp's Shakespeare in the Park; and he had staged numerous acclaimed productions, including two of his own plays produced by the New York Shakespeare Festival.

Despite the diversity of McAnuff's work, he tends to find in each project a way to explore his interest in the themes of politics and moral responsibility. He is always looking for the connections between contemporary society and the lessons of history. Thus, when he wished to open the La Jolla Playhouse with a revival of Garson Kanin's *Born Yesterday*, but found it unavailable, he substituted Brecht's *The Visions of Simone Machard*, making a connection between the blacklisted authors despite the tremendous stylistic gulf separating those two works.

McAnuff's rock-oriented background and his deep respect for literary tradition show in work that combines a sense of history and a love of current culture, reverence for the text compounded with the flamboyant and hip, a fusing of traditional musical styles with modern experimental theatre. This results in work that is invariably exciting and immediate. His later directing efforts have resulted in a sense of delicately balanced acting, whereas his early works relied on style and were frequently controversial.

His production of his own play *Leave It to Beaver Is Dead* at the New York Shakespeare Festival in 1978 was proclaimed by some to be the most important play of the season, while others decried it as meaningless. The action took place in a psychodrama clinic that had previously been used for drug rehabilitation. Describing its effect, Elinor Fuchs, writing in *Soho News*, said, "The play seems to be a capstone on ideas of Western dramatic literature from Aristotle to Artaud. It may be one of those very few plays after which the theatre is never the same." The dialogue was a collage of sounds and images borrowed from popular culture, especially from television, with liberal doses of violence. The result might be characterized as a "Beckett sitcom." In the third act, a rock band appeared and played a twenty-minute set while the cast sang.

McAnuff's early work gravitated toward material that allowed him to paint surreal images onstage. Of his production of Wolfgang Hildesheimer's *Mary Stuart*, one critic said, "It's a mix of the Marx Brothers' stateroom scene in *A Night at the Opera* and some filthy suppressed canvas by Hieronymus Bosch." While teaching at Juilliard for five years, he conceived and created for the acting students *How It All Began*, a documentary on the life and times of Michael "The Bomber" Baumann, a West German terrorist, based on his autobiography which was banned in Germany. His play *The Death of Von Richthofen as Witnessed From Earth* was a surreal investigation into the origins of fascism at the close of World War I with music and flying. The writing was almost Shakespearean in its complexity, with eight major characters, a chorus of six chaser pilots and twenty-three musical numbers, also composed by McAnuff. *Von Richthofen* explored the connection between the warrior and the politician and how media hype aids that transformation.

It is phenomenal that McAnuff, a product of the optimism and desire for change that characterized the generation of young people growing up in the 1960s, should have become the artistic director of the La Jolla Playhouse, situated in wealthy and conservative Southern California. The La Jolla Playhouse was founded in 1947, when such Hollywood actors as Gregory Peck, Mel Ferrer, and Dorothy McGuire wanted a summer stock haunt to stretch their skills. The community was thrilled to have these personages in their midst, and when the high school auditorium they had been using was condemned and closed in 1964, it left a void in the hearts of those La Jolla board members who had been involved. Despite the presence of several theatres in the area, the dream of resurrecting the Playhouse persisted until 1983, when community leaders raised enough money to erect the 492-seat theatre in the Mandell Weiss Center for the Performing Arts, on the campus grounds donated by the University of California at San Diego. In searching for artistic leadership, board members realized that the summer stock model was no longer viable and looked to the example of the nonprofit resident theatres. In three separate searches ranging over two years, they interviewed established directors in both regional and commercial theatre. Their final choice was McAnuff, who they hoped would lead the Playhouse to national prominence.

But if the La Jolla community expected the Playhouse to present updated versions of 1940s and '50s plays, they were quickly disabused. The inaugural production of *The Visions of Simone Machard*, as directed by Peter Sellars, was a brave and bold choice; so much so that only forty-one percent of the subscribers from that first summer renewed. However, within a few seasons the number of patrons more than tripled the number of original subscribers as word got out that the Playhouse was a place for audiences seeking new and unusual work.

McAnuff's penchant for eclecticism was permanently woven into the fabric of the theatre. His method for developing the repertoire of the Playhouse has been to identify interesting directors first, and then to allow the artists to work on whatever they are most passionate about. What has resulted at La Jolla is a series of extraordinarily daring and challenging productions from such directors as Robert Woodruff, Peter Sellars, Emily Mann, Mark Lamos, and James Lapine. This has given the La Jolla Playhouse the national prominence the board sought. And in 1985 McAnuff's production of the musical *Big River* captured seven Tony awards when it transferred to Broadway.

As it is with many theatre artists, for McAnuff there is no line drawn between a life in the theatre and a private life. On January 1, 1984, he married actress Susan Berman on the La Jolla Playhouse stage under a huge portrait of George Orwell. Richard Riddell designed the lighting, Michael Roth played Stravinsky, Susan walked to the service on a red carpet and as the newly married couple kissed the sound system boomed out the music of *Justine* by David Johansen with its very wise words about a relationship.

The discussion with McAnuff about his work is held at their fourth-floor walk-up apartment near St. Mark's Place in Greenwich Village. The living room space is small (not the Hollywood image of a New York Tony Award-winning director); there are two guitars leaning against the wall, an acoustic and a Martin D-35 electronic; a rowing machine in the center of the floor; and a number of books strewn about, research for his next directing project.

■   ■   ■

The work that first brought you attention in the States was directing Stanislaw Ignacy Witkiewicz's play The Crazy Locomotive *at the Chelsea Theater Center in Brooklyn in 1977. You grew up in Canada, so what was the journey that led you to that small but highly influential theatre?*

I started working in Canada when I was eighteen. I'd been involved with writing rock and roll and various other kinds of music since I was thirteen, always with a vague interest in theatre. But *Hair*, when it came to Toronto, changed my mind about what theatre was. I'd thought of theatre as being *The Glass Menagerie* and Shakespeare, or for musicals it was *The Pajama Game*. *Hair* made me realize that the music I was playing and listening to was actually usable in the theatre. I auditioned as a performer for *Hair* at the Royal Alex in Toronto. When I didn't get in, I decided I would write my own musical. That's how I got started in the theatre, motivated by that precocious drive that young people have before they find out that theatre's difficult.

I was going into my last year of high school and I said to the theatre arts teacher (I didn't even formally study theatre arts), "I'm going to write a musical. If I do, will you consider putting it on instead of *Mame?*" And he said, "Of course," not thinking for a moment that I would complete it. So I spent the whole summer writing this thing called *Urbania*, about a doomed city of the future, and took it in to school and played the music. They got excited and did it. It was a freak occurrence, an eighteen-year-old writing a musical and directing it. There was a lot of national publicity, which convinced me that I was the next Irving Berlin.

Then I wrote another one, *The Champion*, and went back to the school after I graduated and produced it through the student council. It was during that period that I realized that I had no idea what I was doing. I think the extent of my knowledge of contemporary drama at that point was having read

215

one Harold Pinter play. So that's when I got serious and spent the next year doing nothing but reading. Because I had done these shows, I got accepted into the Ryerson Polytechnical Institute theatre school, and they allowed me to choose the study of acting or design. I chose acting because they had a brilliant acting teacher, Basya Hunter. I only lasted about a year and a half, but the first year I wrote four plays, one of which was *Leave It to Beaver Is Dead*. The faculty was very encouraging and, at the same time, the Toronto theatre scene was blossoming. My plays started getting Equity productions.

So from the time I was twenty until I was twenty-three, I wrote and then started directing. I became assistant artistic director of Toronto Free Theatre under Martin Kinch. Then I started taking directing more seriously and did *The Bacchae* and a couple of productions of *Dr. Faustus*. I also wrote the music for Michael Ondaatje's *The Collected Works of Billy the Kid*, which was done at the Free Theatre and then at the Folger Theatre in Washington. Meanwhile, I was writing for an anthology series being developed by John Hirsch, who was executive producer for drama at the Canadian Broadcasting Company.

About that time, I was getting a little bit frustrated with Toronto. It became clear that you could work up to the level of doing a production with a fifteen-thousand-dollar budget, and that was it. Most of the successful directors in Canada at that time, like Robin Phillips at Stratford, were imports. There was no way to find a path into directing at the St. Lawrence Centre or at Stratford.

A lot of Canadians have complained about that.

It's a small country and it stratifies quickly with the imports on the higher levels. I had been involved with the nationalist movement, based on the notion that Canadians should be running their own theatres. So it was difficult for me to decide to move to New York. I had committed to going for four months. In the back of my mind, I was leaving the country, but I didn't want to say that because I'd had too many friends do that and then turn around and come back six months later.

I just happened to meet John Hirsch the day I was leaving Canada at the CBC where I'd gone to pick up a script of *Kids*, which he had liked a lot, and another piece I was writing called *Pigs Might Fly, But They Are Very Unlikely Birds*. We sat down and started to talk. He seemed excited by my going to New York and said, "Oh, there's somebody you must meet at the Chelsea Theater Center." Well, of course, I hadn't even heard of the Chelsea Theater Center. Hirsch told me about it, and I knew Heathcote Williams's play *AC/DC*, but hadn't realized until that moment that John had directed the American premiere. I was blown away, because I had always thought of

John as "the head of CBC drama" or I knew of him through his productions of *The Dybbuk* and his work at Stratford and Manitoba. I knew very little about John's progressive side. So he told me I must call Bob Kalfin, artistic director at the Chelsea.

When I arrived in New York I made a bunch of phone calls and people were terrific and very accessible. I submitted *Leave It to Beaver Is Dead* to the Public Theater. They were very friendly, and I couldn't believe that people were being so open. The other thing I did was call Bob Kalfin at the Chelsea and set up a meeting with him. Hirsch had called him in the meantime and recommended me as a writer. I played some tapes of my music for Bob and he brought up this project, *The Crazy Locomotive*. He had a director in mind but asked if I'd read it to see if I'd be interested in working on it as a composer.

I'd been reading about Einstein, and I was also getting frustrated by this sort of Newtonian sense of time onstage, and was thinking, "Why are we stuck in these outdated ways of looking at time?" This was partially what *The Crazy Locomotive* was about in content, not just form and structure. So I got excited and began fantasizing a production. I went back to Bob and said, "I'd like to talk to you about the way I see this play being done." We had a real tight moment, and I told him about what I was thinking. Then he got excited and said, "You should run this by my colleagues, Burl Hash and Michael David." After that meeting, they said, "Fine, it sounds like a great idea." Now this is six weeks after I'd come to New York. They were taking an incredible risk to hire me as a director, a rather preposterous risk, because I hadn't worked with those sorts of stakes before. But that was the spirit of the Chelsea. It didn't matter that I was twenty-three. What they got excited by were the *ideas*. And, needless to say, I was fanatical about these ideas. I had decided I was going to revolutionize the theatre with this production.

I soon become Chelsea's dramaturg and managed to have a steady job so that I could stay in the U.S. Then there was a split in the Chelsea and Michael David and I, along with Ed Strong and Sherman Warner, decided to stay in Brooklyn and form the Dodger Theatre.

What was the work at the Dodger like?

The first Dodger production at the Brooklyn Academy was *Gimmie Shelter*, Barrie Keeffe's play. Barrie came over from England for it. He'd been described as this East End thug and I had no idea what to expect. He turned out to be the closest thing to a certain Elizabethan playwright I ever expect to meet. *Gimmie Shelter* was the first production where I felt like I was really working with actors. Before coming to New York I had never directed an actor beyond my own generation.

What effect did that have on your working process?

Because of the way I'd studied, I was fairly rigid. I was interested in acting principles and getting a company to work with a common system. Of course, I quickly realized that in America, if one was working with really good actors, that was very foolish. People brought their own experience and approach and habits. Some of the habits would be useful and some wouldn't.

How were you able to achieve a unity, given the fact that the actors came from varied backgrounds?

It was by finding some kind of common vocabulary, way of communicating, and trying to avoid buzzwords as much as possible. Because you quickly find out that terms like "inner action" or "motivation" are used in so many different ways that they just become meaningless. So it's always trying to find a new language, a new way of talking. And I think it also comes from learning that the really useful techniques in a rehearsal period are the ones that are invented then and there, so they are, in a sense, new to everyone. That's what's fresh and that's where most of the common ground lies. I think most other techniques are a defense against being caught in a situation where new techniques and ideas are not evolving.

Can you give me an example of what you mean by new techniques developed in the rehearsal period?

Here's a technique not necessarily new to dramatic literature, but new to me at that time. Barrie Keeffe modeled his play *A Mad World, My Masters* after Jacobean city comedies. In doing the play you can't just grab onto acting techniques that might apply to psychological realism. What you have to do is understand the characters as humors—goodness, lechery, snobbery. And so we tried to find improvisations or exercises that helped us to achieve this. For example, we did improvisations that involved establishing a pecking order, because understanding class structure was so critical to this play. For example, one might do something like apply for unemployment, and manage to burst through immediately and get a chair, if there's one in the waiting room. Who's stuck sitting on the floor? It's the junkies on the floor, and so on. And then, out of that a kind of style emerged that had something to do with the Jacobean city comedies. I wasn't around in the early seventeenth century, so it's guesswork.

At what point did this process start and how long would it last?

I did *A Mad World, My Masters* twice, for roughly five weeks rehearsal each time. Most of that work would be done in the first ten days of rehearsal, and then occasionally we would return to it if a particular scene wasn't working terribly well. We tried to find some kind of parallel that would help us to understand it better. *A Mad World* had been developed with a company of actors, so it lent itself very easily to an improvisational kind of work. That would be an example of a company developing a style and an approach to a play that was unconventional by American standards.

I also spend a lot of time, more and more, with actors around a table, analyzing text, especially if it's a classic. Sometimes ideas come out of that.

How long do you spend around the table?

From ten days up to two weeks. This is always within a rehearsal period of five weeks or more, so that is an enormous amount of time.

What does that do to the process?

There are a number of reasons for sitting around the table like that. If you're doing Shakespeare or Chekhov, really formidable playwrights, the text simply warrants that kind of analysis. In the Shakespearean plays I've done, I've known that I had to work very, very hard and read a great deal. Usually, I work with a dramaturg, an assistant, the designers and the composer. The process usually starts like this: I read as much as I possibly can and then clear away what's useful and what's not. Most scholars have some kind of critical ax to grind, so they're going to have a particular take on a play, something that's important to them, and they're going to tend to ignore other things. So I find it's really useful if you get a lot of these critical axes grinding together in order to see more and more layers of the play.

And then we go through and we make all kinds of notes. It might involve certain historical reference books. Every time something comes up in the text that there's any question about, we check it and try to look up all the dictionary meanings, all the layers of meaning in a particular word or phrase, examine the punctuation, look at the quarto if it exists, and the folio if it doesn't. We really try to do an in-depth analysis of the text as much as possible. But I find there's no way of getting a common understanding of the play or the ideas in the production by just presenting that to the actors. So what I basically do is repeat that process with the entire company, even if it's forty people all sitting around a huge table with the text. We all share the materials, read different things. It's sort of a sleuthing process—everyone puts on his Sherlock Holmes hat and takes this journey through the text.

And what are the results of that investigation?

All kinds of different things happen. You find that people have these extraordinary treasure chests of knowledge and information that immediately come out. First of all, if you're working with new people, and you almost always are in America, you find out all kinds of things about them—what they think about and what's important to them. I find the majority of people make use of this as a kind of period to consume before being asked to produce.

Do you find that this period of study ever interferes in some way with the natural impulse?

I don't think it interferes with intuition. If anything, it channels intuition. Spontaneity and emotion shouldn't be disconnected from knowledge. This idea that we're somehow more creative when we're less knowledgeable is nonsense. Two tenets that I don't put trust into are instinct and crisis. Instinct kept us in trees, and any potential creativity that comes out of a reaction to crisis isn't necessary. Frequently it is in rehearsals, where it might seem to an outsider that nothing's going on, that, in fact, everything's happening. Nobody's shouting or crying or pounding on the table or stomping out of rehearsal, but in a quiet way something is really being created that may be invisible to anyone who's not a part of it. That really applies to that "table work." If it does damage to anybody's healthy instincts or impulses, then I think the damage is minimal compared to the good that it does.

What comes out of it, if you're dealing with a difficult text—and most important texts are difficult—is a much deeper group understanding of the piece. So, even if you're playing Hotspur's servant, you have a really good understanding of the themes in the play, the metaphors, the images, and you have a much stronger grasp of where you fit in and what your role is. You're in a better position to support everyone else. It seems to me that great theatre experiences are about supporting each other. In order to do that, cast members really have to have knowledge about each other. We're so interdependent. I also believe that audiences pick up on that kind of understanding, even if it's a sixth sense. They know when people are talking off the tops of their heads and when they're really speaking from their hearts and brains and souls. It makes you listen in a different way, just like when you're involved in conversation with a person who's committed to what he's saying.

Do you go through the same research process for contemporary plays?

When we did Bill Hauptman's *Gillette* at the Playhouse we went through a similar process, even though it was set in 1981. We analyzed anything that was mentioned in the play, whether it was the oil boom, the first year of the Reagan Administration, the end of the Carter years or the hostage crisis. Nineteen eighty-one became a period, and we studied it very much the same way we would a history play. *Gillette* was about two blue-collar dreamers who go to the boomtown of Gillette, Wyoming, to seek their fortunes—an old

American tradition. Sometimes a contemporary play can be the most dangerous kind for Americans, because we assume we are knowledgeable about it. I'm most dangerous when I *think* I know something. And when you actually start talking about recent events and researching them, you realize that we only think we know, it's an illusion. We have to put as much thought into a contemporary play as we put into *The Seagull*.

Was the material in Lee Blessing's A Walk in the Woods *foreign to you?*

I knew very little about arms negotiations before I directed *A Walk in the Woods* at Yale Repertory Theatre in 1987, other than what I'd read in the paper and the odd essay, maybe listening to intelligent people from time to time who did know. So, going into that play, I knew full well I had to get down and dirty with the minds that really did know about it—of which there were probably two hundred in the entire world. *A Walk in the Woods* dealt with an important topic in a somewhat modest way: nuclear arms. It put a human face on the issues of arms negotiations, which, for the most part, seem to be beyond human comprehension. Lee has the ability to take on a really serious subject and bring great wit and humanity to it.

Were there major changes when you directed it the second time at La Jolla?

Lee and I had our act together because we'd done it before. The script changes were not as substantial as they might be when you work on a musical, but the changes we made were quite important. Structurally, the play was right from the beginning. It was astounding that the production was far more popular in La Jolla than anything we had done up to that point—the classics, the musicals *Big River* and *Merrily We Roll Along*. We jokingly referred to it as "rock 'n' roll arms control." It sold like a Rolling Stones concert.

How do you account for that popularity?

I think it has to do with our fascination with the Soviets and getting to know a Russian in the play much more intimately than normally we're allowed to, and the fact that we were invited inside a forum we hear a lot about but never really catch a personal glimpse of. It also has to do with people's fears. This humanizes these issues.

Blessing explored those complex issues through two very interesting and contrasting characters, an American and a Russian negotiator. How difficult is it to do plays that directly deal with political issues in this country? If the public sniffs agitprop, don't they turn off instantly?

I'm not critical of American audiences for responding negatively to agitprop theatre. I find myself being turned off if I feel I'm being lectured.

Then how does an artist present these issues without losing those he most wants to reach?

Over the last few years, I've come to believe that theatre is there to make people think, and sometimes the best way to do that is to express opposing ideological points of view, without necessarily trying to wrap everything up and sort it out for the audience. I think one of the problems with the world we live in is that we're dragging round these nineteenth-century ideologies and expecting them to apply to an age of technology where they just don't seem to apply very well. What's sad is that theatre artists, instead of going further and doing work which is truly political without being ideological, tend to just turn away from it altogether.

There has been a tendency for artists to try to neatly resolve issues so that audiences feel happy and satisfied that they understood and agreed with the conclusions drawn.

I don't necessarily feel that I have to walk into a topic with answers. I work best when various points of view are being represented, just as they are in one's day-to-day life. It's only when you have that real complexity onstage that larger truths can start to emerge. Anytime you get into blanket prejudices or easy answers, then you get into trouble. I often remember the teachers I really admired, and they were the people who could argue more than one side of an issue. They were the people who got me to think.

How long can you expect to hold an audience with ambiguity?

At a certain point, I guess people do turn off. This is what frustrates me. This is related to why a lot of people believe they can't understand Shakespeare, when that's not true at all. We don't understand it when it's not presented well, when the people who are doing it haven't taken the trouble to really understand the contradictions and the paradoxes themselves, all the things that make the plays rich and important.

One of the really fascinating things about Shakespeare is how often the endings of his plays seem somewhat open. For example, one of the discoveries in doing "the Scottish play"—when Malcolm has that last monologue to all the supposed victors—one of the things I began to question as I listened to this over and over was, "Would I really buy this? If I'd just watched Macbeth destroy an entire nation through these multiplying murders, if I'd watched this darkness descend on a nation, would I immediately turn to the next leader and trust him, or would I be more wary?" It puts a whole different light on the ending if everyone's listening skeptically while Malcolm is up there making the right noises. So the end of the play isn't necessarily this great cleansing, with everything neatly wrapped up now that we have this nice guy on the throne. Immediately, Malcolm talks about changing the political system, adopting certain English political ideas. He seems to be trying to say the things that he thinks people will want to hear. Whether they're on to him or not is what becomes interesting. So you aren't necessarily supposed to leave the theatre feeling good. Perhaps you're to feel that everyone's to be distrusted. Maybe that's one of the great lessons of the play.

What can be done to help clarify for an audience the themes in a Shakespearean play?

I try never to cut Shakespeare, a practice some people disagree with violently. They say, "Why keep some antiquated scene?" My belief is that the scenes that are cut frequently are the scenes that actually point you in the right direction.

I believe that *Romeo and Juliet* is about power and wealth and the mindlessness of the struggle for prestige. It's also about hatred and a lot of things other than simply the love between Romeo and Juliet. The mourning scene following the false death of Juliet is frequently cut to ribbons. It seems to me to be one of the most fascinating scenes. Here's the chance to examine people in mourning while we're emotionally removed from the scene. We know Juliet's not dead, so our tendency is not to feel a lot of sympathy for those people, to study them at a greater distance. When we listen, we realize they're all talking about themselves. No one ever really feels for her. Capulet is hysterical because he's lost his only heir. The scene becomes, therefore, somewhat comic-pathetic, and gives us an important clue as to what the play is really about. It's going to come down to two families who have each lost their last and only heirs. The families are going to end the play talking about money again, and building statues. Now, if you don't understand these scenes and so eliminate them, the chances are you're not going to get to the heart of the play. I always assume that Shakespeare knows what he's doing and then work like crazy to try to catch up to his thinking.

You find all kinds of clues, as in the musicians' scene, which immediately follows the mourning scene. Three musicians arrive, and they're supposed to play. They find out the bride is dead and stay after everybody else leaves. Now we know she's not dead, so Shakespeare can get away with this. Do they go over and say, "Oh, the poor thing?" No. (I had them actually sitting on the bed with the body.) They're thinking about the money. They're worried about not being paid. This is true-to-life stuff. There's nothing sentimental about this playwright. This is the way things are. The servant comes in and starts teasing them with a bag of gold. They haven't even removed the body. He's waving the gold around paralleling exactly what the upper echelons of

223

the household are doing. By cutting that one scene you can end up cutting some of the real meaning from the play. It can easily become this sort of gooey romantic tale.

How central are social, moral and political ideas to you in your directing?

I'm far more interested in those issues than I am in style. I respond first to subject matter and then style grows out of that and becomes the means to get it across. That is truer now than it was in my days in Toronto and perhaps when I first came to New York. The political, social and moral issues are important in my life, not just my work. I'm really interested in those things. To me it's a big part of being alive and trying to be responsible. To keep yourself thinking and questioning you've got to be interested in the world you live in. One would like to think that I would do that regardless of the theatre. What the theatre allows a person to do is to enter new pockets of the world and it places the responsibility on your shoulders to be as knowledgeable as you possibly can about that particular area. That mental and spiritual journey is really fascinating. You have to dive into these subjects that you may know precious little about and in three or four months be fairly well versed and have formed opinions. That really keeps me going. Another thing that's interesting about the theatre is that it deals with mortality and it's a constant reminder of the shortness of the breadth of life. Then when you become interested in the tradition of the theatre and you do a great play like *The Tempest*, it's constantly on your mind how generations have waded through this same text and struggled to apply it to their own times. And it gives you a wonderful sense of continuity. It allows you to plug into a larger continuum and perhaps there's even wisdom to be gained from that. I like to think there is. There is a certain amount of healthy humility that can go along with that and keep things in perspective and keep the faith. And so perhaps theatre does fulfill a certain religious need in me.

This ability you have to combine a sense of history and a love of current culture, respect for the text and tradition with the flamboyant and hip, it's been suggested that this is because you were raised in Canada where there is a closer relationship to British theatre.

While my teachers were extremely encouraging when I did show an interest in dramatic literature, it had more to do with a distant relative, an artist named Eric Aldwinckle. He had been the graphic designer for the Stratford Festival in the early years. His kind of appetite for all of the arts had a very big effect on me beginning when I was ten. Every few months, he would teach me about something different—music, color. He was a wonderful painter. He also composed music and wrote children's stories.

Did the knowledge that your father was a Spitfire pilot during World War II lead you to write The Death of Von Richthofen as Witnessed From Earth?

It was just one of those things that I stumbled on. Actually, the father who raised me, so in that sense my real father, John Boyd, was also in the Air Force. My grandfather had been in the Canadian armed forces during World War I, and I'd grown up with a lot of stories about pilots that I started to investigate. I was originally planning to do a piece about Billy Bishop, and I was going through my director-using-the-theatre-as-a-trampoline period, and had all kinds of fancy notions about an audience on a roller coaster and what not, and started to discover more and more amazing things about Richthofen. I guess I have always had an interest in fascism and anarchy as the two extreme political movements of this century. And they both came up as subjects in the course of my research. Finally, a story started to unfold that took place on the last night of Richthofen's life. Hitler's birthday was the day after Von Richthofen's death, and all those things sort of added up. I guess I really wanted to do something that spoke to the responsibility of leadership and our tendency to trust people to make our decisions for us. I worked for about five years on it, so this developed very, very slowly.

Another production of yours that explored myth was Wolfgang Hildesheimer's Mary Stuart, *which the Dodger Theatre produced at the New York Shakespeare Festival in 1981.*

I think *Mary Stuart* proved to me that history is rumor.

Hildesheimer did seem to believe that there is the tendency in all of us to accept the history book as fact.

This is his exact point. You know, in English the word "history" means both the subject and the study of the subject—as opposed to "religion" and "theology," where there's a definite separation. Hildesheimer lived as a German Jew through the rise of Nazi Germany, and watched what the Nazis did with history. He watched those terrible, destructive distortions, and he watched people buy in to them. So he took all of the so-called facts about the execution of Mary Stuart, researched them meticulously and created this totally absurd vision of her death—which is almost entirely based on accurate tidbits of information. Trying to re-create the execution in the play is like trying to understand the way a cat thinks. And with four hundred years of distance from the actual event, it becomes more and more difficult to understand. It's hard enough to understand what just happened in Washington today. We change the past constantly.

This is the subject of *Tradition and the Individual Talent*, the T. S.

Eliot essay. As he says, tradition is something that's alive, and we affect it. It's in our hands. We shape it and mold it every day. It's all well to look to history as a lesson, but what's very dangerous is, if the lessons are in the wrong hands, they tend to be used as manipulative tools for forces that are not enlightened. So I've come to the conclusion that if you're looking at any historical event, you must look at it from as many different viewpoints as possible. I sometimes envy people who believe they have all the answers in their ideology or in their particular religious beliefs. I'm just not one of those people. I wish I had the answers, but I don't, and people who claim they do really frighten me.

Mary Stuart *also had an extremely complex dramatic structure.*

All the simultaneous scenes caused an agonizing rehearsal period. Everything had to be cross-cued in the most complicated ways. I think we had four and a half weeks of rehearsal on that show. Frequently, we could only get twenty seconds into rehearsing a scene without something going off, and then we would have to go all the way back to the beginning. Even finding a place to start again was difficult, because sometimes there were four scenes happening simultaneously, all of which started at different moments.

It's like stopping a musical rehearsal. How do you cue all of the instruments to begin again at the place where the singer starts?

And with several conversations going on, it's much more difficult, because it isn't that *this* word happens when *that* word happens—although it is like orchestration. It is impossible to describe. I used to get headaches every day, it was so frustrating. But then we would finally get a ten-minute section to play, which was about as far as we got even in the first couple of previews. In fact, I remember the night a particular critic saw the show, an actor made an error and managed to cut about twelve minutes unintentionally. And, of course, there was panic because the play was all happening in real time, and all of these tasks had to be accomplished. It was chaos. We still got a very nice review.

Did the commercial success of Big River, *developed from Mark Twain's* Huckleberry Finn, *cause you to be taken less seriously as an artist than you had been earlier in your career?*

I'm sure I've had those feelings at times. If something goes to Broadway, there is a good chance that a certain amount of suspicion will be attached to it. Part of that is founded on something that is very real. Over the past couple of decades, Broadway has gradually been creeping toward becoming a tourist industry. The worst side of that is the Las Vegas kind of show. *Big River* was an important experience because it was an opportunity to take a journey through the heart of America, and the studies of that were very enlightening. Leslie Fiedler, the literary critic, was a really great help in understanding this novel and how it tied in to nineteenth-century literature and how it is the keystone novel in American literature and perhaps modern literature. Leslie's thoughts literally influenced the staging of it, and his perceptions about the novel influenced the writing of the piece for William Hauptman too.

When something like *Big River* is successful on Broadway, the perception of it seems to change. Before the Tony awards and all that, the perception that I saw in the profession was that we were doing something that was different, that we were plugging into certain traditions of book, of story theatre. When something becomes popular there is a tendency perhaps to forget that it played some kind of role in developing the form.

Having done *Big River*, what *hasn't* happened to me is that I don't have a tremendous appetite for continuing to be a part of mainstream culture. I do like reaching people. It's very important to me to think that the work I do is pertinent. But I'm more interested in the mainstream culture of to-morrow. I don't believe that it's possible for me to apply my craft toward maintaining a certain level of popularity. I'm just not interested in that. I don't think that I would tend to go back and do another *Big River*. That's why it was important to turn right around and do *The Seagull*. One of the ironies of winning the Tony for *Big River* is that the summer that we did it in La Jolla, I received the directing award there, but for *As You Like It*, not *Big River*, which was really great because it put my work into perspective.

Was there a different way of working on Broadway than when you developed **Big River** *initially at American Repertory Theatre and then La Jolla Playhouse?*

The biggest difference just had to do with efficiency. It was a tremendous advantage having done the show a couple of times prior to New York because we had a really clear idea of what we wanted to do. And because we could afford to use more complex technology we were able to make scenic pieces like the raft do things that we weren't able to do before. It was a development of the same idea with somewhat increased resources. We lost a certain amount of space because the La Jolla stage is bigger than most Broadway stages, so we had to be a lot more efficient. That caused us to change the way we did certain things. We didn't decide to change anything because "we were going to Broadway." *Big River* evolved from a play with songs into a musical during its three productions. The goal was always to nurture it and encourage com-poser Roger Miller to the point that we would really have something that was musical. The biggest changes we made between La Jolla and New York had to do with expanding the score. Roger started writing choral tunes at La Jolla, and then we added the black chorus, which became very important as a sort of Brechtian idea. We cut the Grangerford-Shepherdson section, the feud section, which had been in the production from the beginning, because it created a much better through line and stopped us from repeating ourselves. We hated to cut it, but it actually gave Huck and Jim a great scene in the second act and a song that we really needed. What we essentially did was to transfer the Grangerford-Shepherdson scene thematically to the King and the Duke. That enabled us to create more density and energy. It was part of the evolution of the piece. If we had thought of it sooner we would have done it. The whole Broadway experience was very much a natural expansion in terms of the work of the creative team. It didn't come as this sudden shock and I didn't feel much more pressured. The only additional pressure was that everything was so much more expensive. The amazing thing about *Big River* was the marriage of Roger Miller and Mark Twain—two different kinds of folk wisdom. It created a kind of common touch.

Again, your interest in bringing different genres together. Were the audiences helpful in developing Big River?

I think audiences are often informative, but they don't give you solutions. They help you to identify problems. The danger is that you'll think you know what the problem is because oftentimes you fix what you think is wrong and it turns out to be something else entirely. An audience can help tell you what's not working, they can't always tell you where the problem is. Particularly in a musical, if a previous scene has failed to set something up properly, then the scene you're looking at may not be landing, but it may not be for the reason you think.

Is there a basic difference between directing a play and a musical?

One of the things that I learned from doing *Big River* was that if there are three jobs to do, whether it's making the temperature drop, having someone fall in love and having a moment of danger, you're better off with each collaborator doing a different job. I can make it rain, the book writer can make somebody fall in love, the songwriter can perhaps create the danger. That was a valuable lesson for me because you do take on a lot more responsibility when you direct a musical just in terms of storytelling and of thematic development, and you have less time.

You have less time because you're dealing with more elements?

Exactly.

Over the years, your work has consistently been successful with the critics and public alike. How have you managed to head up two new theatre operations and simultaneously find the time to keep your own work so lively?

I think running theatres has affected my work. No one's exempt from the consequences of assuming that kind of responsibility. I haven't written anything, other than articles, for five years.

And La Jolla's summer season is short compared to most other institutions.

That's true. On the other hand, because of the insanity of the way in which we put seasons together, it also takes a lot longer to plan, because at La Jolla we do leave an awful lot up to the individual artists, and that's very, very draining. There are a lot of painful periods where you're waiting for people to decide what they are really passionate about. A lot of directors aren't used to that. They're used to assignments.

What led you to conceive of a theatre where the ideas come from the artists you want to work with, in all of their variety of viewpoints, rather than you originating all of the choices, as is frequently seen in institutional theatre?

Interestingly enough, doing Chekhov was very important to me in opening my head to work that I would never have done if I hadn't rubbed shoulders with a variety of theatre artists. One of the reasons I did *The Seagull* was that it's a microcosm for an art scene. It really is about all of these people who have grown up in different genres. Let's say you're a jazzman and I'm a punk rocker. It's like jamming us into a household together. Only in the case of *Seagull*, there's Masha, perhaps an existentialist; there's Nina, who's struggling to be a tragedian; there's Trigorin, who's clearly the popular novelist and short-story writer. And all of these people try to communicate with one another, and find it very, very difficult. Chekhov inspired me, because here's a guy who actually loved Maeterlinck, but who couldn't have written work that was more different; and had a great relationship with Tolstoy; who managed to appreciate these artists from a myriad of backgrounds.

Perhaps it had something to do with his being a doctor.

I'm sure that helped. He had that ability to appreciate all these colliding worlds and universes and artists. That's really what the Playhouse was about right from the beginning. It wasn't suddenly discovering we wanted to invite directors who would take larger chances. We started with Peter Sellars' production of Brecht's *Simone Machard*.

An extraordinarily brave opening for a summer theatre situated in a beach city.

I originally talked to Peter about doing *Galileo*, and then it got complicated and he was not able to do it because of the musical he was working on.

With that production, did you intend to send out a very strong message about the theatre's artistic intent?

Actually, when I first met Peter, I didn't know his work very well. Mutual friends put us together. We were supposed to have a short conversation in a pub down the street from where he was rehearsing *My One and Only*. We met in the early evening, after a technical rehearsal, and we ended up being there until two in the morning. I was tremendously excited by his mind and really felt that he was someone important.

We made a decision right from the beginning that we were going to focus on artists, and we weren't going to be prejudiced about genres. If we could get someone with Stephen Sondheim's genius around the theatre, we would do a musical. We would be open to whatever genre a person worked in or wished to work in. And I think this came from the belief that we lead eclectic lives in this country and our art should reflect that. We brought in leaders from various backgrounds to see what they might create together and to encourage them to work with one another. Sometimes it meant inviting a director who only wanted to work with his or her own people. But we hoped that if there was theatre that was exciting in different ways, some kind of cross-pollination would inevitably happen without too much encouragement from us. To a large extent that has happened.

What is Des McAnuff's contribution to the theatre?

If I have a mission, it's to ask as many questions as possible and to get the people I care about to ask as many questions as they can. It seems to me, asking questions is what creates movement and progression. When you find the answers, there is a tendency to stop dead in your tracks. Even science is coming to the conclusion that there's no such thing as objectivity, that the nature of experimentation means that you're involved in it in some way. It's why, as a director, I never strive to be objective. I accept that my viewpoint is totally subjective. I don't pretend it's anything else. I don't sit at the back and judge. And I change my mind all the time.

GREGORY MOSHER

I n 1974, a young Gregory Mosher journeyed from his native New York to Chicago to be the associate director of the Goodman Theatre. In the span of just a few more years, he became its artistic director and forged what is probably his most important artistic relationship: he linked up with playwright David Mamet, who was also just beginning his career, and Mosher has since directed the premieres of nearly all of Mamet's plays, including the Broadway productions of *Speed-the-Plow* and the Pulitzer Prize-winning *Glengarry Glen Ross*.

During eleven years at the Goodman, Mosher directed or produced more than eighty plays, half of which were American premieres from such writers as Edward Albee, Spalding Gray, John Guare, Wole Soyinka, Michael Weller, David Rabe, Elaine May, Richard Nelson, Emily Mann and Tennessee Williams. Then, in 1986, he was called upon to breathe new life into the then moribund theatre component of New York's Lincoln Center. It required some measure of either courage or foolhardiness for Mosher to uproot himself from what had become a successful and challenging artistic home and return to run the Lincoln Center Theater: its reputation for being a difficult space to work in, fraught with politics and overhead costs, was well known.

The mammoth task of piloting it had frustrated and defeated the likes of Elia Kazan, Robert Whitehead, Jules Irving, Herbert Blau, Joseph Papp and Richmond Crinkley, his immediate predecessor, who had simply become immobilized and kept the theatre dark for almost six years. Mosher, in tandem with veteran manager Bernard Gersten (late of the New York Shakespeare Festival), embarked on an eclectic producing schedule eschewing the institutional subscription system in favor of memberships and single-ticket sales.

Mosher is most comfortable directing in an intimate environment: in Chicago, he chose to present many major works in the Goodman's one hundred thirty-five-seat second space. At Lincoln Center, he prefers to direct at the cozy Mitzi E. Newhouse Theater, leaving the large-scale productions on the Vivian Beaumont's mainstage to such diverse directors as Jerry Zaks, Robert Woodruff and Wole Soyinka.

Mosher's premiere New York season was decidedly—and purposely—low-key. His directing debut at the Newhouse reopened the facility with two new Mamet one-acts, *Prairie du Chien* and *The Shawl*, followed by Arthur Miller's one-act plays collectively titled *Danger: Memory!* These were interesting works, it was agreed, but minor ones, albeit from major artists. But the momentum grew. By 1988, when Mosher directed Mamet's *Speed-the-Plow*, advance ticket sales were so brisk that the play opened directly on Broadway, while Jerry Zaks's long- running hit revival of the musical *Anything Goes* packed them in at the Beaumont.

Since arriving at Lincoln Center, Mosher has maintained a low profile in a city where directors are highly praised by critics one season and gleefully trounced the next. He prefers to see the plays themselves in the spotlight, plays such as the rousing revival of John Guare's *The House of Blue Leaves*, which he produced with Zaks directing; or *Woza Afrika!*, a festival of South African plays; or Soyinka's haunting *Death and the King's Horseman*; or Woodruff's wildly presentational "new vaudeville" version of *The Comedy of Errors*. After six dark years, something began to work at the Beaumont, but that something was difficult to characterize. Productions ranged from the old-fashioned Broadway show biz of *The Front Page* and *Anything Goes* to the experimental, to the utter theatrical simplicity of the works written and performed by the South African playwrights of the *Woza* festival—from pure entertainment to important and beautiful theatre. Gregory Mosher's tastes as a producer are wide-ranging. As a director, he prefers plays that hinge upon fine detail, in which tiny movements have important meanings and in which language is paramount.

Mosher's Lincoln Center office, where the discussion is held, is an airy and spacious hub of activity. From time to time the intercom announces incoming telephone calls: Jerome Robbins, who is rumored to be working on a theatre piece, and the South African Embassy, which is calling to question Mosher about what it is he does and why he wants a visa to enter their country. Following this call, he talks excitedly about the South African township theatre he has seen on previous trips and of the man who inspired much of it, Gibson Kente. He compares the spare theatricality of the township theatre to the simplicity of a work by Peter Brook, how both cut to the essence of the theatrical event.

Mosher is in his mid-thirties and balding. He has an air of casual reserve and aloofness that is softened when he makes a sly, lightly sarcastic joke. He speaks quietly, almost as though he is seeking anonymity, to be invisible and let the words speak for themselves.

■   ■   ■

Where do you think the primary focus of a director should be?

I'm one of those people who think that everyone involved in the collaborative process is there to support the intentions of the playwright.

Are playwrights always crystal clear about what their work requires?

Ah. I'm not talking about just sitting in a restaurant and saying, "What's your play about?" Although that's an important part of the process. I'm talking about study of the text. All the clues are there. Though it also helps immeasurably to know the playwrights, to see them in action, and to have heard their voices. The process is discovering the correct rhythm and orchestration. One could find those things by studying the text, but when the playwrights are present it's a wonderful kind of shortcut. John Guare speaks with exclamation points at the end of his sentences. Mamet often talks just like he writes, and Tennessee Williams talked sl-o-wl–y and laughed all the time. Tennessee would say something terribly serious and then burst out laughing.

Usually all a director gets is the text of the play. But the paradox is that the play is not about text; it's about action. Coming to terms with that paradox determines one's approach. That's why deconstruction and all of those approaches are irrelevant. Deconstructing the text onstage has no interest. It just avoids the fact that the play is an action.

How do we understand what that action is? By studying the text. And while the audience tends to be aware of the text as much as they are aware of the action, what you *direct* is the action. What you hang the blocking on is the action. You can't block the text.

A play, as good old Aristotle would have us know, is an *imitation of an action*. If *The Cherry Orchard* is a play and not a narrative, what action is it an imitation of? Ah well, that's where it begins to get interesting. For director

233

X, it's an imitation of one action; for director Y, another action. For one director, *Hamlet* is a story of a man figuring out the point of his being. For others, it might be about a man accepting death or a story about revenge.

Can it be all of the above?

NO! Not all of the above. That is my point. What you need as a director is not *five* good ideas. You need *one* good idea. That idea has to be expressed actively, vibrantly, and consistently. If you choose an action that is perfect for the play, then the other actions will resonate.

As an example, what's the perfect action for The House of Blue Leaves?

In our production, *The House of Blue Leaves* was about a group of people making an escape. And everything about that play—the set, the blocking, the inner emotional life of the play, even the poster graphic—came from the notion of making an escape.

Also, the set was a place from which one escapes. It had twenty locks on the door and bars on the windows. But it also revealed the place to where one escaped, New York. The dominant image, aside from the living room, was the surround, a painting of the Fifty-ninth Street Bridge, a bridge to something else. And one of the first things we saw in the play, after the initial image of a man escaping into his songs, was the lights on a bridge.

But how does one decide what the action should be?

Understanding the action doesn't come easily and it's very hard to hold on to. One often wants to cheat at the crucial moment of the play. You say, "Ah, I have this great staging idea—here's a big scene. It's not really about *escape*, but . . ." Those are the moments when you really have to be rigorous and say, "That idea's not about escape. It doesn't belong in this production."

How about a play that is extremely difficult to analyze? What's the action of American Buffalo?

For every play, there are as many actions as there are directors. For me, the action of *American Buffalo* has nothing to do with what the text would have us believe it is about, which is the robbery of a coin. There can't be any payoff there. For one thing, there *is* no robbery, and for another, the first and last ten minutes of the play don't have anything to do with a coin robbery. So the play gets onto the wrong track if the director's not doing his job. The audience gets to the last ten minutes of the play and finds that the material is extraneous. They think, "Oh well, a talented playwright, good ear for dialogue, but trouble with plots." Not so. The story of that play is the destruction of a relationship between a father and son. The play begins with a father and son and ends with a father and son. Something profound has happened to that relationship in the interim. A long, long time ago, I asked David, "What is the subject of the play?" He said, "Honor among thieves." And that's true. I believe that is the subject of the play, but it's not the *action* of the play.

So the director is always coming back to action. That action has to do with the plot, but it doesn't necessarily have to do with the text, as we know from the scene in *The Cherry Orchard* in which Varya and Lopakhin play out their most complicated love life. Very late in the play, they are alone on stage. The woman is dying with love for this man. The man knows that he can't marry her. This is the moment when he has to tell her that. And the conversation goes, "Cold out." "Yeah." Pause. "So, what are you up to?" Pause. "Oh, I'm off to the so-and-so's." "How far do they live from here?" "Oh, about seventy miles." Pause. "Must be pretty cold over there too." Pause. "So where were those things I was looking for? Hmnn. Can't seem to find the key. Be summer soon." "Yup." He hears his name called, and he's gone. Well, are you going to direct the text? A six-year-old can tell you it's not a scene about the weather.

Do you find that sometimes the actors can work in opposition to the action and make it work?

Occasionally, but not often. I'm always open to what they have to say. I'm absolutely open to *how* that action is accomplished, and it's often not at all the way I had originally envisioned it.

You've said that you normally don't block until the third week of rehearsal.

Yes. I've staged plays as early as the second day of rehearsal, but inevitably I've thrown it all out and restaged in the last week, because, when the moves aren't a part of a whole process, they end up being clichés. And then you spend your time trying to get it "right" rather than discovering.

The first act of Glengarry was staged in a restaurant setting. The actors were very close together, and somehow you made a statement from that positioning.

Did you notice something? All of the plates and silverware and condiment containers were gone. You think the actors and I didn't have a few discussions about *that*? You think they didn't want a little wonton to stuff in their mouths halfway through the scene? This comes back to another point that seems to be terribly important. A drama, not a kitchen-sink thing, but a drama, has to be like a dream. It can have total clarity, but it must focus on those things which are essential, and not those which are acceptable or logical in a naturalistic sense. The function of the theatre, of course, is to reveal the dream life of the culture, not the conscious life of the culture. That we can get on the front page of the newspaper and on television. That's what is on every-body's conscious mind. What is in everybody's subconscious is its art. One of the things that seems to be helpful in the effort to subconsciously and subtly allow the audience to understand that is to strip away the trappings of real life, to take away that pot of tea and that piece of uneaten, somewhat soggy whole wheat toast, and leave just enough—the cups, perhaps—to help the audience understand we're in a restaurant.

What one remembers from that scene is how the actors' faces stood out and the distance between the actors.

That distance alternated anywhere from two feet to three feet. That's all they had to work with, which is not much in an eight-hundred-seat theatre. On the other hand, when J. T. Walsh got out that cigarette, boy, you noticed. Much more important, in a scene that's about money and sales "leads," when he pulls out that fat wad of bills, peels one off, puts it down on the table and slides out of that booth—boy, eight hundred people were looking at those ten fingers and that little piece of green paper. Just purely from a craft point of view, I never had to say to J.T., "Do the ten-dollar-bill bit a little bigger." He didn't have to exaggerate it because that work had been done by stripping away things that weren't needed anyway. You can't get the audience to focus on moments that are essential to the motor action of the play if they're distracted by all of those jars and jam.

However, don't those physical properties aid the actor in varying the rhythm of the scene?

Absolutely. Any actor will confirm that it's easier to talk to another actor, to stay connected to the scene, if he's chewing a piece of gum or smoking a cigarette. It's physical. It grounds him so he doesn't fly off into Mamet-language land and stays connected to what David is really writing about. But then, if you are not careful, the play becomes naturalistic and uninteresting. Those magnificent actors in *Glengarry* will tell you, without a lot of prompting, that there were times when they thought they'd go mad. It was only two of them at a time, locked in a restaurant booth, trying to do difficult things in front of eight hundred people, trying to get a friend to commit a crime.

Was it a restaurant to those characters? No. What was important to the essence of that room? It was where they did business, and it was the place where they went to be alone. They treated it like their office. They saw that setting as a protected place, not a big public room. Before we knew the play better, the set designer and I were kicking around the idea of doing a big set with lots of tables. And it would have taken your breath away. An empty restaurant all perfectly set with red tablecloths. "Oo, oo, that director can really stage." It would have been beautiful to look at, but it would have been so wrong. Because that first act in the restaurant is about privacy.

Is that a trap for many directors, trying to make a scene take your breath away?

I have never met a director who wanted to show us how creative he can be. Every director I've ever talked to wants to get to the heart of the play, because it's just too hard to do a play in a way that doesn't feed you in return. Some directors, myself included, do overexplain. We say, "Here is where the play is going." The urge to explain takes over because theatre is a collaborative art form and you don't want the actors' work, or the playwright's or the designers' to be in vain. The temptation is to give the audience a handle because we live in a world of instant gratification.

But don't audiences demand guideposts?

I have great faith in audiences. We only create problems when we treat them as consumers instead of collaborators in an artistic process.

They frequently view themselves as consumers.

That's because we identify them as such. "Buy this and you'll get your money's worth" is what all our advertising says. What else is "See five plays for the price of three"? What is that? It's an appeal to a consumer. Well, if that vast audience of ours has been defined or pigeonholed as consumers, why are we surprised when they tend to behave like consumers? "Well, I'm not sure I like this peanut butter. Maybe I'd like another kind of peanut butter." We can let audiences down in all kinds of ways: by being dishonest with them, by betraying our own intentions and, therefore, betraying the audience's trust. All they've asked the artists to do is what the artists want to do. Audiences have said, "I want to see what you want to show me."

You originally went to the Goodman Theatre as director of its second stage.

William Woodman, who brought me to the Goodman, was the first artistic director in their fifty-year history to have living writers working at the theatre. He dramatically raised the aesthetic and administrative standards. Bill was there for five years, and for three of those five I was the director of the second stage. During the 1970s, a bunch of young theatre people in their twenties hit Chicago. Some, like Stuart Gordon and David Mamet, had grown up there and returned after college, stirred up by the energy of Paul Sills and the Second City. Chicago had on one hand a very big, ambitious Goodman Theatre, and on the other hand a healthy, small avant-garde theatre scene. And there was an interesting tension between the two. The Goodman's Stage 2 was the bridge between them. It was a place where those who would later become known as Off- Loop theatre people came to work. Above all, there was Mamet with his own company, the St. Nicholas.

Had he developed any kind of reputation prior to that?

The St. Nicholas came to Chicago in 1974. That same spring *Sexual Perversity in Chicago* was done in New York. *American Buffalo* had been written but was not produced until the fall of 1975 at the Goodman 2, where it played for twelve performances. We thought it was quite a good run, actually. The play was generally considered to be rude and not worth a whole lot. With some exceptions, the premieres of David's plays in New York and Chicago have been greeted with "So, what is this?"

During 1985, the final year you were in Chicago, you started to develop another small stage, away from the Goodman building.

The New Theatre Company was an attempt to create an institution within an institution—a theatre that would not be susceptible to the pulls of a big institution and that would take its identity from the artists who were creating the work. Hence, it had its own name, its own building, its own stationery. I hoped that those people who liked the work of the Goodman would follow the work of the New Theatre Company, and those who were not inclined to attend the Goodman might, given a fresh chance, want to come and see the work, whether it was Mamet's translation of *The Cherry Orchard* or a new John Guare play.

The space you developed, the Briar Street Theatre, had two hundred eighty seats as compared to the Goodman's six-hundred-eighty-seat mainstage.

I never found the Goodman mainstage physically conducive to the kind of work that I like to do. It isn't a theatre where you can see the actors' eyes. And with the pantomime required in that kind of larger space, it isn't very clear to the audience what's happening. The idea for the Briar Street resulted from getting our thinking straight about the theatre's responsibility to include its audience. One must think of the audience as people who are coming to the theatre for some sort of adventure of the spirit, some exercise of the imagination.

You included a number of artists as associate directors at the Goodman.

When I became Goodman's artistic director in 1978, the first thing I did was to appoint Mamet as an associate. I wanted David involved in the process of the theatre because it would have been incomplete not to recognize, celebrate that he was giving the Goodman a lot of its direction through his plays and his taste. Richard Nelson [Playwright] and Jennifer Tipton [lighting designer] were also associates and, for different reasons, absolutely essential to what happened at the Goodman between 1978 and 1985.

You have inherited the Vivian Beaumont Theater in the heart of Manhattan, and you are making theatre succeed there where some rather illustrious predecessors could not. Why has the Vivian Beaumont not succeeded until now?

When Lincoln Center was created, the Metropolitan Opera had been around for a long time, the New York Philharmonic had been around for a long time. Robert Whitehead, Elia Kazan and a group of actors and administrators were expected to create a theatre company that could stand next to those institutions, which already had solid artistic bases and organizations to support them. There was tremendous pressure on them to serve some sort of idea of a theatre that was not necessarily consistent with their professional experience. They were made to feel that if they weren't doing Jacobean tragedy, if they weren't doing repertory, they were failing the home team. Kazan was not Tyrone Guthrie. Guthrie was a great director, but if you want Guthrie, get Guthrie. If you want Kazan, get Kazan.

The sixties were a time when Broadway was collapsing. Had all those serious American writers been able to turn to Lincoln Center, had the young writers who turned to Off Broadway been supported and encouraged, the American theatre might be very different today. The trap of any institution is to try to fulfill some abstract notion of what a nonprofit theatre should be, rather than to trust utterly the impulses of the artists who are doing the work.

The first work you directed at Lincoln Center was an evening of one-acts by Arthur Miller.

During the rehearsals of *Clara*, I was able for the first time in my career to avoid staging a play. *Clara* consisted of one piece of furniture in a thrust theatre. In that kind of space you can't arrange painterly pictures anyway, so in the third week of rehearsals, when I normally start to stage, the actors said, "Do you have to? Maybe we could just push all the way through and then everything will come from our understanding of the play and the needs of the play." I agreed, and then broke down and periodically encouraged them by saying such things as "It was better when you stayed with him longer rather than leaving." So I was editing, really. It worked because of the actors' great emotional connection to the piece, their willingness to take any kind of chance, their utter lack of preoccupation with whether or not they could be seen or heard. I made sure they could. Most important was their absolute ability to *play the action*, which was about solving a mystery. It was their own blocking so they didn't have to follow it, although it was interesting to see how little they changed it over the run of the play. The movement was only there to serve them in serving the needs of the action of the play.

For me, the most interesting moment in *Clara* was not in the text, but occurred in a scene in which the father came into the room and saw the blood of his daughter on the stage. In earlier performances, the father kept stealing glances at the blood, and one night, in front of three hundred people, the actor decided to look at it more closely, but the cop blocked his way. And the look that occurred between those two men, this strange startlement, was the play to me—and I think it was for Arthur Miller, too. It was truthful and thrilling, but not at all naturalistic.

Is there a director whose work you admire?

Peter Brook. His viewpoint is direct, not layered, strict and not distanced. He can't get the audience and the actors close enough. There is no barrier between them in his theatre in Paris. There's no little platform. The seats at the Bouffes du Nord are benches. The audience is not divided even by something as commonplace as armrests. Armrests aren't taken away in order to serve some spartan ideal, or so that the theatre will be difficult to watch, but to emphasize that the essence of theatre is a bunch of people in the same room. The less they're divided the better.

Theatre is just a process, and you learn the same things over and over again, and you learn new things. But the quest is not into one's own psyche. It's always inward to the root of the drama, a route that is so simple, the spark of the drama. Our poetic evocations of the theatre, "two planks and a passion," all allude to that. As the world gets more and more complicated and it becomes easier and easier to use machines in the theatre, the difficulty is getting back to something simple.

I really like it when shifting your weight onstage is a big deal.

HAROLD S. PRINCE

H al Prince walked into George Abbott's producing office in 1948 seeking a job, any job, in the theatre, paid or unpaid. Prince was fresh out of college and impressed Abbott, who would say of him in later years, "It was just that I thought he was smart. He read plays. Later, he developed the ability to fix up road companies." Abbott, already a legend with thirty-five years of Broadway theatre experience behind him at age sixty, took Prince into the office that they have shared, in one capacity or another, for forty years. Prince found himself working side by side with one of the most practical and knowledgeable director/producer/writers in the history of Broadway theatre. Abbott's career spans almost the entire history of indigenous American theatre. It was, after all, just before the turn of the century that American playwrights began to emerge, and Abbott, who is in his 101st year at the writing of this book, made his debut as a Broadway actor working for David Belasco in 1913.

By 1953 Prince had formed a producing partnership with Abbott's veteran stage manager Bobby Griffith. Griffith and Prince immediately drafted Abbott to direct their first musical, *The Pajama Game*. The young producers, having no source of income until the show recouped investment and running

241

costs, gave themselves jobs stage-managing their own hit production. It was six months before Prince saw the first show he produced from the audience.

Prince's public image in the early years was influenced by actor Robert Morse's performance in Richard Bissell's *Say Darling* (1958), which satirized the making of a Broadway musical. Morse's character was modeled on Prince's physical mannerisms. In the musical, the Prince character was hyperactive, hail-fellow-well-met, superficial and neurotic. Prince was outraged by the portrayal, thinking it trivialized him. He wanted nothing more than to be taken seriously as a force in theatre.

The series of producing successes that followed (*Damn Yankees, New Girl in Town, West Side Story, Fiorello!*) alone would have been sufficient to assure Prince a footnote in theatre history. But in 1961 Bobby Griffith suddenly died, and Prince, facing the prospect of producing alone, decided to revive his long-stifled ambition to direct. His first assignment was to try saving an ill-fated show floundering out of town, *A Family Affair*, for producer Andrew Siff. Then, since no one else would entrust a Broadway production to an untried director, he hired *himself* to stage *She Loves Me* in 1963. It was an artistic success and ran for 303 performances. He directed two more productions—*Baker Street* and *It's A Bird . . . It's A Plane . . . It's Superman*—before his production of *Cabaret* opened in 1966 and changed the look of the American musical. *Cabaret* was followed by a series of milestone productions including *Zorba, Company, Follies, A Little Night Music, Candide, Pacific Overtures, Sweeney Todd, Evita* and *The Phantom of the Opera*.

It is an undisputed fact that these Prince productions have advanced the art of musical theatre, with their adventurous use of theatrical space and the integration of text, lyrics and music. Prince's openness to new forms were in evidence before he staged his first show. Abbott: "I remember Hal coming to me when we were doing *Fiorello!* I was trying to do it the way I had always done shows, and the way everybody did, with a scene-in-one (a scene played on the forestage in front of the curtain as a bridge between larger scenes incorporating the full stage—also referred to as a cross-over) while you changed the scenery behind it. He said, 'Forget that. Let the designers worry about that.' That was his doing." And the scene-in-one," traditional in the American musical since the *The Black Crook* was presented in 1866, disappeared from the American musical stage. It was only a hint of the innovations Prince would eventually introduce to the staging of musicals.

One of Prince's most important collaborations has been with composer-lyricist Stephen Sondheim, who has taken the art of songwriting to new levels of theatricality. Their long professional relationship began with the Griffith/Prince (in association with Roger Stevens) production of *West Side Story* in

1957, for which Sondheim furnished the lyrics to Leonard Bernstein's music. Some time later, Sondheim took a group of one-act plays by his friend George Furth to Prince for his appraisal. To his surprise, Prince suggested that they be combined and made into a musical. In 1970 Prince and Sondheim opened the results of that effort, *Company*, and eleven years of creative teamwork began.

Both Prince and Sondheim, in their work during those eleven years together, preferred didactic theatre containing a minimum of sentimentality. Their works have "layered" meanings more common to works of literary intent, and each of them has secret metaphors for the shows they create, not always necessarily in common, but perfectly complementary. Thus, Sondheim could write a work such as *Sweeney Todd* with "obsession" as his metaphor and Prince could construct the production with the effects of the industrial revolution in mind.

The techniques for unifying the elements of music, dance and drama in the American musical theatre have been handed down directly from generation to generation. From George Abbott, Prince inherited a passion for clarity, the passion Abbott had inherited from one of the great directors of his own youth, Winchell Smith (1871-1933). Prince absorbed everything he could from Abbott and then added his own bold visual and conceptual ideas. Mentor and disciple, Abbott and Prince singly and together have been responsible for the passing down of these techniques to an astonishing number of fellow directors, including such acknowledged talents as Bob Fosse, Jerome Robbins, Lee Theodore, Ronald Field, Patricia Birch, Carol Haney, Joe Layton and Michael Bennett.

Following *Sweeney Todd* in 1979, Prince virtually ceased producing in order to concentrate on directing. He explains, "I didn't find producing hindering. I just didn't want to do it anymore. In fact, producing a show you're directing sometimes makes your life much simpler than dealing with producers." In any case, by the mid-1970s, the theatrically knowledgeable producer (who in Prince's words, "had taste first and got the money later") yielded to the kind of producer who had a limited theatrical background but who could access the millions of dollars required to produce in the commercial musical arena. Largely because of this, responsibility for all of the creative elements of the musical defaulted to the director.

In recent years, opera has become a major directing interest, and Prince now tends to fill in the gaps between musical projects by directing on the world opera stages. In fact, his method of preparing for musical shows has evolved from his work in opera, where rehearsal time is at a minimum and, therefore, the preparation process extensive. His preparations for a musical, which can take up to five years, are so complete that when the show opens it is intrinsically the same as the vision he's evolved before he set foot in the rehearsal hall.

Two discussions with Prince took place over a five-year arc. His moods during the two conversations varied greatly, depending upon the status of his current projects. The first conversation in 1981 was full of energy as he spoke of *Evita* as being the biggest hit of his career, and as he prepared to leave for Houston to direct a new American opera by Carlisle Floyd, *Willie Stark*. The next meeting was in 1986, after he had directed a series of works that had not succeeded in commercial terms. Also, during those intervening years, the Broadway commercial arena had changed radically: production costs for musicals had tripled, and with the increased budgets came increased pressure to produce spectacular musicals with the broadest potential audience appeal. He was depressed about the future state of the American musical and the difficulty he was then having in finding a venue for his work. Yet, little more than twelve months later, Prince had one of the most successful years of his directing career with three productions opening on Broadway: a revival of *Cabaret*; a new musical, *Roza*, developed at Center Stage in Baltimore and at the Mark Taper Forum in Los Angeles; the American premiere of *The Phantom of the Opera* following Prince's smash opening of it in London—a show that appears to be one of the major musicals of the decade.

In the years intervening between 1981 and 1986, his interest in subject matter for musicals changed, "I'm gravitating toward material which is not quite as cold as in the past, not as misanthropic, not as critical. I'm not so much worried these days about putting messages on the stage. So I'm not planning a show about apartheid, whereas fifteen years ago I might have. I'm dealing in my private life with how I feel about that. I'm as politically involved as I ever was, and I could get very guilty if I thought I was doing it out of some kind of intimidation. But it's not a good time for political theatre. And every night I see a real-life story acted by some great actress on television. Obviously, the day when theatre was a realistic arena dealing with current social issues is on hold."

Both the hard-edged *Evita*, in 1978, and the more romantic *The Phantom of the Opera*, in 1986, were by British composer Andrew Lloyd Webber, and both received their initial productions in London. The Prince-Webber collaboration has resulted in Prince's greatest commercial successes. But he continues to search for a viable way to develop new shows in this country, even exploring the possibility of creating a new theatre at a film soundstage in Astoria, across the East River from Manhattan in Queens. But he moved away from the idea when it became clear that it would become yet another commercial operation where he would be faced with all of the same problems plaguing Broadway producers. In August of 1987 Prince and Webber announced plans to form a company to produce their own future collaborations and other plays and musicals.

■ ■ ■

What is the basic equipment required for a young director entering the profession?

There are a lot of people who think they want to be directors. They have an absolute need for self-expression. To be able to direct, there are two things that you need: that supreme arrogance or *need* to express yourself, and the right equipment. Now, that's the problem. How do you acquire the equipment, the craft? There are fewer people from whom to acquire it than there used to be. On the other hand, they still exist and you have to get close to them and to those productions. If you can't, then it's more difficult. You must learn a lot of things. Then you must make your own rules. From the first day on, you never cease to take chances, although you don't know what they are until you take them.

You started out wanting to be a writer and a director, but you were in the profession for many years before you directed your first musical. What were the major turning points that led to your directing?

In my youth, for some reason, I was obsessed with a "sink or swim" philosophy. I was either going to have the life I'm living now, or no life at all. I had an extremely privileged childhood, but at fifteen I had a traumatic six months where I was psychologically disoriented. I broke with myself. I went to college at sixteen, came out at nineteen and put the past behind me.

An important turning point was when I established my own producing office. Several years after that, I met my wife, who saw in me someone who had been brainwashed into *thinking* that I was the Bobby Morse character in *Say Darling*. My wife saw that it was defensive behavior and encouraged me away from it. Still, there has always existed a connection between the life I'm living now and the obsession I had when I was eight years old to live this life.

Frequently, people going into the theatre become aware of that desire at an early age. How were you able to control your obsession to direct for such a long time, until the conditions eventually were right?

Obsessions focus you, and they tend to make you practical. When I started working in the theatre, I didn't blow my job opportunities. I didn't alienate myself from people for whom I worked, even when I thought they were inept or less talented than myself. I kept my mouth shut and waited for opportunities. I wanted to be a director, but I settled in the early days for being a producer. Before that, I was a stage manager, something I didn't like. I was not a good stage manager because I'm much too energetic to be the controlled, paternalistic figure that a stage manager should be. Nevertheless, I behaved as though I were. If I'd had to continue my life in that capacity, I would have blown it because it took a lot of control to appear to be what I wasn't.

Your early ambitions included a talent for writing.

My potential as a writer has been helpful as a director. I'm able to articulate what it is I seek from a scene. I'm able to ad-lib a scene to help an actor, and then get the playwright to actually turn those ad libs into worthwhile words. On the other hand, I'm not good enough to sit out there as a playwright.

Your training was largely observational until you started directing on Broadway. What were the problems posed by having so little hands-on experience?

My first directing job was *She Loves Me*. The cast wouldn't listen to me because I had no credentials. They challenged every single thing I said. You see, I did not have self-esteem as a director, so I certainly did not have their esteem. Nor did I have the craft to create the desired effects that come of experience. I only knew the end results I wanted. So I was trying, any which way I could, to get those results without knowing the best ways to do it. In those years since 1966, I've been brave, been chicken, taken the easy way out, gotten frightened out of my wits and so on. But I have learned how to deal with actors and how to use the space.

I would liken directing to painting. Much of my theatre work is abstract, but I had to know how to paint realistically first. Clarity is something that I think too many directors lose sight of and have too little respect for. The work can be abstract, but it's got to be clear. If you don't know how to organize it properly, the public just sees anarchy.

She Loves Me was sentimental realism. I didn't try to abstract anything. As the years went on, I got more daring—except when I'd get frightened and do a show like *Baker Street* (1965). I had wonderful ideas when I set out to do *Superman* (1966), but I got frightened and didn't do it as audaciously as I should have. Each show that I do is the beneficiary of all of the shows I did before it. There would have been no *Evita* if it hadn't been for *Company* or *Follies*.

Evita *was acknowledged as a success largely because of the visual concept and staging you gave it. And you have said that you spend a lot of time determining the style of the show to know how to tell the story—to understand what the "motor" is going to be. Are there characteristic structures that tend to repeat from show to show?*

I get bored with similar patterns and I get bored with structure. So I'm tempted to try and shake them up a little bit. *Follies* and even *Company* were antilinear shows. There was a through line, but it was not the conventional line. The structure of *Evita* was also untraditional. The trajectory was her life from age seventeen to thirty-three. We simply showed the banner headlines in the life of Eva Perón and didn't fill in the spaces the way one is accustomed to seeing. I think our way was more exciting for audiences. What you have to do is find the material and let that material dictate what the form and style will be.

Where do you normally find your material?

Sweeney Todd was Stephen Sondheim's idea. I had a lot of trouble understanding why he wanted to do it. It was nineteenth-century Grand Guignol and that's all it was. What convinced me to do it was the notion of a factory, which grew out of conversations with designer Eugene Lee. The factory setting would not be acknowledged in the music or book by Sondheim and Hugh Wheeler, but it would enclose the whole play and give me a reason for having a chorus and the rest of the company. That reason was the incursion of the industrial age, which created rage in people. They were denied nature, and so lost their poetry, souls, their humanity—they became machines. Machines break down and so do people. It sounds glib, but the moment I knew that I could put *Sweeney Todd* in a factory, that all those people in the play would never see the sunlight except through filthy dirty glass in a factory roof, that their entire lives would be shaped within the imprisonment of the industrial age, it was very easy to direct.

How much preparation does a show take?

I have to think on my feet, so I take a long time doing a show. *Sweeney Todd* and *Evita* each took three years. I research the people, the place, the time, the events; I absorb the world in which these events took place.

When do you begin to explore your ideas for the setting?

The scenery begins to be designed at the same time as I find a visual context for the show, so there is that simultaneous motor connection between the way a show works visually, how the people can move around the set and the way the scenes are written. It all becomes one piece. I take the concept as far as I can and then I stop. I go direct an opera or give myself a vacation, and then I come back with more objectivity. And I repeat that process, and

I come back, and it keeps renewing itself. By the time I go into rehearsal, an actor can ask a very complex, taxing question about his character like, "Who was my great-grandfather and why did I . . . ?" and I've been on it for four years and know everything I need to know about these characters, so I can respond.

Do you prepare by putting anything down on paper?

I don't write much except aesthetic notes. I'll note the mood. I'll also remind myself of other things: "Make your own rules" and "It's time." I wrote this about *A Doll's Life*, which was a musical about what happened after Nora slammed the door at the end of *A Doll's House*: "A backstage by Magritte. Poetic. Filled with presences and memories. The sexes badger each other to madness because they cannot possibly comprehend what each is really thinking." Here's a banality: "A woman cannot be a man, she bears children. Nora must have said, at one time or another, 'I'm going back home.' Slaves always understand their masters. Masters never understand their slaves. Hence, women understand men." And so on.

The minute I think a play is pretentious, things are going well. I have to be embarrassed by what I'm working on, know that I'm taking myself too seriously, and then I know at least we're taking some chances.

What other preparations do you take?

I owe a lot to Jerry Robbins. For one thing: as far as I'm concerned, he invented reading a musical before rehearsals. When I was the producer, he would have me put together a group of accomplished actors to read a play aloud, because it never leaps off the page quite as well as when you read aloud. As a director, I borrowed that. I have a reading once for the book, once again for the book and music. Finally, I personally read it aloud to the authors. In the course of my reading, there are a number of things we find out, one of them is what I disagree with. So I'll read a scene the way I think it should be, and if it isn't that way on paper, we'll stumble onto the fact that the author and I are not in sync. Then we'll make some accommodation.

Sondheim has also talked about how important to the development of a show your readings are. It's something most other musical directors don't do. He credits that kind of advance work with eliminating a lot of problems before rehearsals begin, and says that it assures that the show's music doesn't inadvertently go in a different direction from the book, a situation which sometimes isn't discovered until rehearsals get under way. How does that differ from the traditional way of putting a musical together?

There is a difference between the theatre of George Abbott's time and today. First of all, tryouts aren't very safe anymore. You can't fix a play out of town and meet expenses, so one rarely goes out of town without an enormous star. And I don't do shows with enormous stars.

Two of the directors who influenced you most were Abbott and Jerry Robbins. How did they approach a show?

George Abbott and Jerry Robbins were at opposite ends of the pole. Essentially, George was able to leave a lot of production questions unanswered before he went into rehearsals. He had so much self-confidence that he would proceed with a lot of good and indifferent material and know that he could fix the indifferent material. Jerry wouldn't begin until he thought everything was perfect, and it almost never was. So it was very hard to get him into rehearsal. I'm somewhere in between, veering more toward Jerry. For example, I have a half-inch model of every show I do, and I sit and stare at it for months before I go into rehearsal. I've never seen George do that. I don't move little tin soldiers around on the model, but by the time I actually go into rehearsals, the space I'm going to work on has been ingested.

How do you begin the rehearsal process?

The first day of rehearsals for *Sweeney Todd*, I spoke for two hours about revenge, rage. I quoted from all the great philosophers and writers on the subject—and then I never talked again. We put the show on its feet. Those two hours, before we read the play, consist of my telling the company what I've been doing for four years. That's my process. Rehearsals have to feed off of excitement, off of energy. I don't have the patience for much philosophizing. That's why, when I go into rehearsals, we read the play through once and then get up on our feet and I start to direct it. The rehearsal period isn't very long. *Evita* took three and a half weeks to rehearse. There was a first night preview and nothing was changed after that.

At what point did your work begin to diverge in form and style from the traditional Broadway musical?

Interestingly enough, when I discovered that I like opera. I like working on operas because the composer and librettist have died and you have to come up with solutions without changing what they wrote. When I did *The Girl of the Golden West* for the Chicago Lyric Opera, I didn't use horses as Puccini had envisioned. I was fine until the last four bars of the opera, when he provided enough music to have two horses leave the stage but not two people on foot. I never got that exit right because I kept wishing Puccini had given me four more bars.

What are some of the underlying artistic influences in your work?

Some years ago, I discovered I have a connection with Vsevolod Meyerhold, the Russian Constructivist director. I realize that I want the same things from the theatre that he wanted. He didn't like total realism and wanted theatre to be something *more*. The highest compliment I've gotten was after *Evita* opened in London. Josh Logan [director of musicals during the 1940s-60s] wrote me a letter saying, "I was a student apprentice with Stanislavsky in Moscow at the Moscow Art Theatre at the time Meyerhold broke away. I was absolutely excited by what Meyerhold was doing, but nothing quite worked. Last night, I saw what he was doing and it all worked—and it's *Evita*." As Meyerhold did when he broke with Stanislavsky, I too want theatre to be something *more*. But I think I understand the part of Meyerhold that didn't work. If you get too political, too didactic, you tend to get in the way of your art and to lose the buoyancy that comes from just worrying about the play, not the preachment.

Other influences include directing O'Neill and Congreve when I was at the Phoenix Theatre. Some nerve doing Congreve. I'd never even seen a Congreve play. But you get something out of that, most particularly when you fail.

But if it had not been for my seeing the Taganka Theatre in Moscow and Yuri Lyubimov's production of *Ten Days That Shook the World*, I would not have had the guts to do what I wanted with *Cabaret*. I was in the midst of preparing it in my head and, suddenly, all I saw on the Taganka stage was Lyubimov, saying, "If you know how to do something, do it." In *Cabaret*, I wanted to play with linear and nonlinear components of fragmenting time. A very few years later there was *Follies*, which was totally fragmented in terms of time, and then *Pacific Overtures*, which was also nonlinear.

After I did *Cabaret*, I felt strongly that I had made a new mold, that I had designed a show in a different fashion from anything that I had ever seen. I did not know that until it was over and I could look back at it. Later, when I went to the theatre and saw all those shows that were designed exactly like it, I thought, "Well, it was influential."

You followed Cabaret *with a string of productions that were cited as redefining* musical theatre.

I'm loath to go along with all those who have called this work "ground break-ing" and "epoch-making." That's not what you work toward at all. You work out of a need to express yourself and what you're feeling at a given time. You get bored with the status quo. That's why you break ground. You don't sit in a room and say, "Now we are going to write the 'new' musical." You just simply say, "I'm tired of going to the theatre to see musicals, because I could close my eyes and tell you what is going to happen."

In Pacific Overtures, *you were stylistically merging two cultures. How did you prepare the actors for working in a style that combined American musical theatre with classic Asian theatre?*

Because many of the actors were Asian, or of Asian descent, the most important thing was to assure them that it was all right that the show was not going to be authentic Kabuki. It was to be an American production. The actors did not want to ridicule the Kabuki style, and they knew that I could not do authentic Kabuki in six weeks. No one could. It took the longest time for them to understand what it was about, but once that happened, they were terrific and delivered what I wanted.

How did you handle it stylistically? It could not be authentic and yet it had to be recognizably derived from the traditional Asian theatre.

Exactly. I went to Japan with Sondheim to see the Noh and Kabuki theatres. I studied them a lot and filtered in that which was fascinating and used it liberally. It was the actors who came up with the sounds I wanted, sort of primeval noises that came off the Kabuki stage. I couldn't do them. I could imitate the sounds and then the actors would do various ones for me. I'd demonstrate as best I could what I wanted and they'd say, "But that's not authentic. That's not the noise you make." I'd say, "Don't worry about it. Give me this noise. It's a hybrid. We're doing an American's vision of something." It was perfectly acceptable that the two cultures mixed.

You called Pacific Overtures *a documentary vaudeville.*

I think that's what it was, a vaudeville show. It was a revue about something that happened in history. It used a lot of different vaudeville techniques, revue techniques, and it was its own hybrid. People have a lot of trouble with hybrids, although they get excited because, by its very nature, a hybrid is theatrically engaging.

Do you get distressed when you are admonished for creating a hybrid as if you didn't know you'd done it?

It's only happened once in my life, but the day after *The New York Times's* review of *Pacific Overtures*, I wrote Clive Barnes saying, "You have just killed a major work. And it's on your conscience." I'd never done that before.

Did he respond?

No, but years later when it was revived Off-Off Broadway, he said that he could see things that he hadn't seen before. Critics get a second shot. We often don't. You really can't talk about criticism. Some of the things that are so well received critically just evaporate with time.

And other works that are not so well received at first have a long future life. There have been two successful revivals of Candide *since its brief run in 1957: Gordon Davidson's West Coast production in 1965 and yours in 1974 at the Chelsea Theater Center.*

It wouldn't have happened if Bob Kalfin, the artistic director at Chelsea, hadn't been such a damned nag. Bob nagged me and I said, "No, no, no," so long that I finally said yes.

Again you created a work that was unique for American musical theatre. It had the feeling of commedia dell'arte as the actors strolled among the audience. Your setting at the Chelsea and later on Broadway turned the theatre into a free-form space with the audience sitting in groups on stools and benches.

I was afraid of *Candide*. There have been two shows in which I've been paralyzed with fear, *Candide* and *Evita*. I should be paralyzed with fear more often. I would have had a nervous breakdown and gone to a lunatic asylum in order to get out of directing either one of them.

Why was that? Was the preparation so difficult?

I was trying stage techniques that I had never seen before, and it was like flying blind. Before I go into rehearsals I begin to feel tired and funny. Sometimes, I don't sleep and it makes me crazy and I always have the symptoms of hepatitis the day before rehearsal. Those are the signs. The minute rehearsals begin and the actors respond, that goes away and from then on I'm as happy as I ever am in my life. I'm gregarious and extroverted when I'm in rehearsals. When they are over, I tend to recede back into old antisocial habits. Usually, I feel that panic for the first day or two of rehearsals and then on the third day it suddenly clicks and I say, "Wait a minute, I think it's going to work!"

How did your work with actors in Candide *differ from* Pacific Overtures?

With the kids in *Candide* I was concerned that there be no phony baloney energy. I was afraid that the exuberance and youth of those kids would just turn the thing into an amateur show. So my biggest task was to make everything real, or at least the reality of our particular concept of *Candide*. We believed every word so there was never any frantic sweating for no purpose. We made it real, then energized it. Nothing we did was gratuitous, unnecessary. Everything was useful.

The settings for Pacific Overtures *and* Candide *were spectacular.*

I need to see the set clearly. If I don't, I'm going to do a bad job. That was one of the problems with *Merrily We Roll Along*. I never got the set straight in my head. Eugene Lee, with whom I had great success in *Candide* and *Sweeney Todd*, designed it. But we never did know what we wanted in *Merrily* and we never did get it right. Everything in the theatre is a subjective experience. But this was maybe a little more so because I was infatuated with kids of that age.

Did that mean that you had to spend a lot of time teaching the cast?

There was more teaching than usual; less just allowing people to create for me and then editing them. I like editing because you have only so much time. It's amazing if you have an actor the caliber of an Angela Lansbury in a show. She's collaborative and also enormously creative. So, you make a suggestion. When she interprets it, you find yourself saying, "That's better than what I had in mind."

What happens when you need to edit her?

In Angela's case, she's very easy. I made a movie with her once. I said, "Angela, did anyone ever tell you that you do a funny thing with your mouth?" She said, "Oh God, am I doing that? Tell me every time." I had wasted days wondering how I was going to tell her that when I looked at the footage there was something funny. I would have liked to approach her more elegantly, but I could not think of another way to say it.

It was your idea to make Company *a musical. You worked a long time with George Furth on the book.*

Originally, the script was just a maverick shell. George had written seven one-acts. We used four and he wrote three new ones that joined the story. In hindsight, it wasn't all that difficult. That show has not been particularly emulated except for a few settings that have borrowed from it.

Composers have certainly emulated Sondheim's style.

He's a very bad influence on a lot of composers because he is unique. There is only one person who can write that way. One of the things that bothers me is the fact that he was nurtured at a time when you could nurture artists. He was allowed to do shows that didn't succeed at the box office although they always succeeded artistically in some measure. The score to *Anyone Can Whistle* is wonderful. The point is, today if there was a new Sondheim some-place, would he get a chance to grow regularly, year after year, and then finally get his just due? Suddenly, there was only one composer-lyricist— Sondheim! What about all the years when we were doing these shows and nobody was celebrating him? It finally happened after twenty years. *Sweeney Todd* was the beginning of people saying, "This is the state of the art." Who are the new artists and how do they get through?

Do you expect any new musical forms to come out of the avant-garde?

I'm dying to see something I think is really new. I don't think any of the experimenters has come up with anything that can be made into modern popular theatre, be it with music or without music. There are stimuli all over the place—the music of Philip Glass and Steve Reich for example, but these stimuli will have to coalesce into theatrical events that reach a wider audience. I'm not necessarily interested in reaching the *widest* audience, but I'm interested in reaching more than one hundred–sixty people in a room, because I also mistrust that a little bit.

What's the future of the American musical? Is it becoming event-oriented?

Sure. *Cats* is one example. But that is not threatening in the least. It's no more threatening than when *Hair* premiered and everybody said, "This is the musical of the future." I happened to have loved *Hair*. Nevertheless, it was not the musical of anybody's future. It was a musical of that present time. And *Cats* spoke in a very conservative time for entertainments that do not challenge. But there's more than one way to skin this cat. People say they go to the theatre to be entertained. Entertainment is simply an experience to take you out of your own life. It doesn't have to be a lot of people tap-dancing on dimes. When you come out of the theatre you should know that something has been said that was arguable. You should have something to take away with you. What's the point of leaving the theatre and saying, "I had a nice time," when you've forgotten what you saw?

LLOYD RICHARDS

There are many distinguished "firsts" in Lloyd Richards's theatre history. He was the first black artist in America to direct on Broadway, the first to direct in commercial television and the first to simultaneously have both major professional and educational careers.

Richards's initial national success came in 1959, with his direction of Lorraine Hansberry's landmark play, *A Raisin in the Sun*. America was heading into a time of social change and Hansberry's family drama rang with an honest-edged humanity that captured public and critical approval and ushered in a new age for black theatre. At twenty-nine (and almost sixty years after the establishment of a native-American theatre), Hansberry was the first black woman to see her play on Broadway.

The impact of Richards's stage directing quickly attracted the attention of television producers, and he was wooed by the networks, initially directing *The Committeeman* for "General Electric Theatre" with Sylvia Sidney and Lee J. Cobb in 1960.

His success, as impressive as it was, had not come quickly or easily. Richards was born in Toronto to Jamaican parents. Later, the family moved to Detroit, where he lost his father to diphtheria when he was nine. Richards's mother struggled to provide the basics for her five children during the Depression, but was incapacitated by blindness due to a mistreated case of glaucoma when he was thirteen. Richards, along with his elder brother Allan, supported the family by shining shoes, sweeping barbershops, selling newspapers and running elevators.

Detroit in the 1940s was one of three major cities where radio shows originated, as well as being a major stop on the theatre touring circuit. Richards majored in speech at Wayne State University and found that radio provided all kinds of acting and directing opportunities that simply did not exist for blacks in the theatre.

While he worked as an elevator operator, he would carry a pad and write plays between floors. But he found that he was not patient enough for the discipline of writing—it was not to be his method of expression. Still, these playwriting experiments helped create in him a lasting passion for the process of creating new works for the theatre.

Richards's schooling was interrupted by a call to duty in the segregated Army but he returned to Wayne State following his service to complete his education. After graduation, he forged ahead with characteristic energy. A social worker for the Detroit Welfare Department during the day, Richards acted and directed in community theatre in the evening, was a disc jockey on a local radio station for an hour at night, after which he returned to the theatre to rehearse long into the morning hours. This practice of holding multiple jobs would become the norm for him throughout his career, long after the struggles of the early years had given way to success.

Soon he found he could make a living on radio, but realized that it wouldn't lead him where he was determined to go—the theatre. He went to New York and acted Off Broadway, earning seven dollars a week. He taught acting at the Paul Mann Studio and held a part-time job as an assistant chef and waiter, trades he continued to ply for five years, even as he began to get acting jobs on Broadway. It was not until *A Raisin in the Sun* that his life changed.

Following that landmark production, Richards directed commercially for the stage and for television and continued to teach at the University of Rhode Island, Boston University, as head of actor training at New York University's School of the Arts and as professor of theatre and cinema at Hunter College.

In 1968, Richards became artistic director of the National Playwrights Conference at the O'Neill Theater Center, an annual summer festival held in Waterford, Connecticut. There he set up a program of staged readings, critiques and evaluations of new plays selected specifically for development at the Conference, influencing modes of play development nationally. Such writers as Thomas Babe, John Guare, Israel Horovitz, Wendy Wasserstein, Richard Wesley, Lee Blessing, August Wilson and Albert Innaurato came to view the O'Neill as a place to experiment with the help and collaboration of leading directors and actors.

Richards was named dean of the Yale School of Drama and artistic director of Yale Repertory Theatre in 1978, succeeding Robert Brustein, who, upon being fired, went on to found The American Repertory Theatre in residence at Harvard University. Richards was appointed by Yale president A. Bartlett Giamatti, who had introduced himself to Richards in the aisle of the Shubert Theatre when he himself was a Yale sophomore, during the New Haven tryout of *Raisin* twenty-five years earlier.

As the head of this influential training institution, Richards is in a position to inspire and encourage a whole new generation of young theatre artists of all nationalities. As artistic director of Yale Rep, he has premiered the works of such writers as Lee Blessing, August Wilson and, in a unique and enduring relationship, Athol Fugard.

But it is in his discovery of playwright August Wilson that Richards has realized the richest director/playwright collaboration of his career. The sensibility that helped release the humanity in Hansberry's *A Raisin in the Sun* has similarly affected Wilson's works, the Pulitzer Prize-winning *Fences*, as well as *Ma Rainey's Black Bottom, Joe Turner's Come and Gone* and *Piano Lesson*. Richards's regard for the importance of family and his sense of the pageant of history, combined with Wilson's lyrical and powerfully realistic depiction of the procession of generations, have resulted in a rare artistic identification between the two men. Of Wilson, Richards says, "I only met August a few years ago, but I've known him all my life. I know everything he knows."

Richards has frequently been called upon to accept leadership roles in the profession. For ten years he served as president of the Society of Stage Directors and Choreographers; he was president of Theatre Development Fund (a nonprofit corporation founded to increase audiences for commercial and nonprofit performing arts events); president of the board of directors of Theatre Communications Group; co-chairman of the Theater Panel at the National Endowment for the Arts; and in 1985, was appointed by President Reagan to be the first representative from nonprofit professional theatre on the National Council for the Arts.

Richards has the demeanor of a venerable and sage patriarch. In the years since *A Raisin in the Sun*, he has evolved from a slender, clean-shaven young man to a heavyset, bearded elder statesman. Despite his extraordinarily frenetic schedule of teaching, administering and directing, he exudes a sense of tranquillity, a quiet surface—guarded, self-disciplined, masking a Lloyd Richards known only to himself and his family.

■   ■   ■

When did you know you were a director?

I don't know when I accepted that idea. The fact that I say I am one—even that has its own little element of surprise. I didn't start out to be in the arts. I went to college to study law because I thought that to be the most secure position a young black person could aspire to. At the time I was growing up, it was medicine, law, the ministry, and if all else failed, teaching or social work. Of the five, I felt compelled toward law. I acknowledged the change to theatre after my junior year when it came time to switch to the law program. It was a final acceptance of a decision that had been gestating.

I came to theatre from acting, and that is how I relate to directing. It is very useful for me in terms of understanding both the inner workings of the actor as well as the ways to lead an actor toward what I want to happen. That's an important strength. But you're in trouble if you're only able to work with the actor and don't have an overall concept for the play, visually and intellectually. Just because you get a nice scene that plays well or an actor who functions through a scene logically, that does not necessarily mean that the scene will be effective, that it will come together in a total picture or thought that can be carried away from the production.

How do you form that overall visual and intellectual concept?

The literature must spark that for me. If I am reading a play, it affects me. I begin to visualize it as I read it. It sparks many things—rhythms, tempos, images, a sense of movement. They function together—all stemming from the fact, the idea on the page.

My first responsibility is to really understand not only what the playwright is saying but the *stimulus* for his creation. So even if I diverge from the playwright's intent, I know what I'm diverging from and what I'm eliminating or illuminating. The text provokes my vision or imagination and I have great reverence for it, but I'm not a writer. As a director, I must be more like a painter—taking somebody else's thoughts and ideas and words, in black and white, and giving them color and form in a physically and emotionally moving or intellectually provocative manner.

How do you begin to delve into a work to get at what it means to you?

The first reading of the play is the only time when one encounters the work as a life experience, sees the work fresh and is impressed by it. And it is important for me to retain that experience and to understand why I was affected by it—all the while reading and reading the play, finding out about every character, projecting the life of the characters beyond that play, getting further and further into it and expanding into its totality, finding those related things that may have affected the author and that might affect me in the same way. I begin to have an understanding of other influences that were affecting the playwright, that were aspects of his time. As an example, I always knew the work of Edvard Munch (Norwegian painter and graphic artist, 1863-1944), but I looked at it very differently when I learned that he had influenced Ibsen. It's important to understand the totality of the life of the play and its inspiration. It is the best of all possible worlds when I give myself the time to understand that.

How much time is required for this study?

Usually, a long time. The plays that I become attracted to are the ones for which, in some respects, I've been preparing myself for a long time before even encountering the work. So there's a lot of self-preparation that's gone on without my ever knowing it, until I suddenly discover, "Oh, this is what that's about!" I can have a short time with the text, but have spent a long time preparing to do the work.

Is time the most important ingredient for a director?

There's another important thing involved, and that is organizational ability— simply being able to bring together varied components and to let them function together. Organization is involved in putting together any large picture that incorporates diverse elements. That's true of the playwright and it's certainly true of the director. Relative to that, one of my favorite remembrances is Picasso's painting *Guernica*. The many components of that genius reflected themselves in just where each little or big element existed in that picture—what shapes they began to take, where they appeared before they were finally in the right place, in the right color, in the right intensity and the right relationships. All of that is organization, which follows vision and concept.

How does one train to be a director?

The training of directors is a very difficult thing to prescribe. The more you talk with directors, the more you find that they have accumulated whatever they've learned from so many diverse places that it's hard to structure a directing program to duplicate that. It demands a knowledge not only of theatre and history and life and psychology and philosophy and music and rhythm and movement, but it also requires a sensitivity and a knowledge of craft. "Oh God," you tell yourself, "I haven't got all that!" But it *does* demand all of those things. And it also demands *having something to say.*

John Hirsch says that he throws up before he goes into rehearsal.

I accept fear as a fact. You're venturing into the unknown. You're going to try to make things happen, having no way of knowing if they *can* happen. But that is what makes theatre so exciting. It has a life of its own. It's going to fight back and you're going to shape that life, or those many varied lives, into your vision. That's frightening. Have you made the right choices? Are you on the right track? Have you got everything it takes to do what you want to do? Again, it's like painting. I can have a vision, but if I sit down with paint and a piece of paper, it doesn't always come out that way, and I accept that it's not going to come out that way.

You also have had more experience behind the camera, directing television, than most of your peers.

I like the media occasionally. I never started working in television out of choice. People in television, who became interested in me through my stage work, said, "Hey, why don't you come and do *this?*" And I said, "Hey, why not?" And then you start playing with the big toys, trying to do what you want through all of that maze of technology. I'm challenged by it. It fascinates me. There was a point when I could have made the decision to go into film as such—sign away two years of my life and they'd teach me the trade, and I'd make a lot of money in the process. And I'd stand around and watch great, great cameramen working. But then it always came down to "Would you give us two, four, six years of your life?" And I could never spare that. I have to do what I have to do, when I have to do it. The most important personal right, which I've always fought and lived for, is the right to say no. Somehow, it's terribly important for anyone who wants to work in this business and get satisfaction to earn the right to say no. That right always turns out to be economically influenced.

Why do you continue to direct?

I'm compelled from necessity for change, social change. And yet I must have order around me. Maybe that's what I'm trying to do as a director: put the world in order, make it meaningful. Chaos can be a part of the process, but, ultimately, that chaos has to be brought into a form that has its own point to make.

Is your work political?

I do consider myself political. Being born a black person in a white society, you are immediately political whether you want to be or not. Even the denial of that is political. Certainly, it has affected what I've chosen to do and not to do, and, in many respects, how I've chosen to do it. I don't feel that I have had to repress my political feelings, but when I express them, I'm liable to get hit for them. I've been denied work for political reasons but I have always found a way to say what I want to say.

What led you to the profession?

When I graduated from college, I was aware that several members of my class had been invited to teach. And I thought that I was as capable as they, yet I wasn't called in. Finally, I went to someone in the department and said, "What does this mean?" And he said, "Oh, I may call a couple of black colleges in the South to see if they need any teachers." I said, "Don't bother, I don't intend to teach. I want to *do*." I left school with a sense of rebellion and I decided that I would never teach except as a part of a professional experience. So I rejected teaching as a possibility and went into the profession.

It was Paul Mann who cast me in an Equity Library show in New York. He was starting a studio and said, "Why don't you come and study with me and eventually teach?" I was a broke actor living at the Y. I said, "Fine." And with that I started teaching in the professional arena. All of the teaching that I have done has been for the profession. You get so much given to you, and you have to find ways of giving back.

How did Raisin in the Sun come about?

Sidney Poitier and I were out-of-work actors together. He knew that I had directed some stock, and he said to me—it was one of those strange things that two broke people say to one another in the middle of the night—"You know, if I ever get a major show, I'd like you to direct it." You respond, "Yeah, and if I get a show I'd like you to be in it." Those kinds of things. And then I got a call from Sidney. He said that he had been offered a play and he wanted to submit me as the director. I read *A Raisin in the Sun* and fell in love with it. He set up a meeting with Philip Rose, who produced it. We hit it off and he arranged a meeting with Lorraine Hansberry. And we also hit it off. Together, we worked on the play for a year before we went into rehearsal.

Were there a lot of changes made during that year?

When the play was first written (and that was a draft that I was not involved with), by the second act the family was already in their new house and the play was about that and about Mama. It was suggested to Lorraine that the real play was in the first act, and that she should review that, which is what she did. I wasn't there, so I can't say who said what to whom. But then, the problem was that it became a play about the son, Walter. The original play had been about Mama. If you look very carefully at the first act, it still has those elements of a play about Mama. So the demands on the actor who plays Walter are tough because he gets up in the first scene, in the first five minutes, and goes out of the house. He doesn't come back until the end of the act, and then he's got to carry the play. It was a really tough struggle to bring what had been the third act of the play back into the first act. We did a lot of rewriting and reworking, took forty-five minutes out of it in rehearsal and lost one character, the woman upstairs, which was very painful. That role later reappeared in the musical version, *Raisin*. It's a wonderful character, a wonderful scene. Beah Richards, an actress for whom I have great respect, was playing it in rehearsal. One day Lorraine came in and watched while we were in the run-through stage and said, "That character should go." "Why?" I said. "The scene is great and it works." She said, "It's redundant. That character takes something away from the later scene with Lindner." She was absolutely right. The character went out, the scene went out, and there were a lot of changes made on the road. We did a lot of reworking in Chicago. Lorraine wasn't there at the time, because of a legal problem she had involving real estate interests in New York and Chicago. She was in Chicago for opening night and then she had to get out of town or they were going to serve her with all kinds of subpoenas about her properties. So the changes were all made over the phone, and I would write them down for her every night and make suggestions. She didn't see the play for seven weeks, until we got back to New York.

It had an extraordinary cast with Claudia McNeil, Ruby Dee, Diana Sands, Douglas Turner Ward, Lonne Elder 3rd and Louis Gossett in addition to Poitier. Its run of 530 performances was some kind of record for a serious play.

Raisin was a wonderful experience, a fantastic, tough experience—a play that almost never got on. Money. In 1959, who was going to invest in a play about a black family? Finally, it had more investors than any other play that had appeared on Broadway at that time. The money was raised in dribs and drabs, little $50, $100, $200 investments. Broadway is not that receptive to a serious play, but *Raisin* had a great deal of humor in it, a great deal of very warm feeling in it, familial feeling that transcended any ethnic concepts, just leaped over them.

It was almost twenty-five years later when you connected with another major American playwright, August Wilson. After collaborating with him on four plays, has your working relationship changed?

It's strange that it hasn't. In a sense, we're probably more knowledgeable about each other now, so the shortcuts are even shorter, which makes for less essential conversation. Therefore, our collaboration has grown, in some respects, smaller.

That sounds similar to how many directors describe their long-term collaboration with designers, and the resulting "shorthand" language.

We talk in shorthand all the time.

Wilson has said that he was aware of his lack of knowledge of the conventions of stagecraft when he first began writing plays. You responded that the well-made play was not as important as the fullness of expression.

Wilson, as a poet, had worked with a different kind of imagery, one without a particular sense of the use of space and the conventions of time in the theatre. And I arrived at a point where I did not want to teach him craft. I felt he should pick up whatever he would on his own, because I did not want convention to become a restraint. In *Fences* we had some monumental problems because of the sense of time. The same person who left the stage at the end of one scene would begin the next scene, though it might be two weeks or six months later. We needed to fill out the character of Lyons, played by George Brown, so we gave him a little extra scene talking to Rose, who was upstage where she couldn't be seen, doing a fast change. That's one example of extensions we needed in the play. Things like that are craft questions that an experienced playwright understands as he writes his piece. I'm not particularly convinced that August should learn that. When we have a question or a problem, then we can go out and find the answer.

Do you ever have a sense of the play that conflicts with the playwright's original vision?

Sometimes you discover how different those things are as you proceed. I remember the first day of rehearsal for *A Raisin in the Sun*, when I was talking to the cast about the play after the first read-through. I delineated a history for every character in the family and how they arrived at where they were. It was the first time I'd said it aloud. Afterward, Lorraine came to me and said, "Well, you know, that's very interesting. I hadn't thought of it that way, but it's true." We never discussed how her history of the characters differed from mine, but the consequence was that my description worked for the actors, it was a right place for us to begin the play and it encompassed the elements that we wanted to affect the characters as they moved through the play.

There are other ways in which an author's vision can grow and influence itself. August is writing about the black community of Pittsburgh that he knows and loves so well. But it's interesting that as that community has been actualized in the theatre, the "stage" Pittsburgh has become the physical perception of that community for him. In other words, it has turned back and become a part of his vision from play to play.

Now, in addition, there is the imposition of a metaphoric element onto the realism of the work. *Fences* had a classic style in the sense that the Greek plays took place in front of temple columns and that's really the same as the back porch setting for *Fences*. It was a series of platforms for the presentation of the material. That whole porch could have been turned at a different angle rather than facing straight out, but the nature of the play is classical and we had to connect with the totality of theatre history as well as the history of the people involved. Then, in August's next play, *Joe Turner's Come and Gone*, we went inside. That play was really a classical "way station." It's the inn where Christ was born, the inn that exists historically in so many cultures and places that dealt with "wanderers," the nomads, a society in motion, that reaction of the freed slave who's out searching for his life and past, for himself and for his family. What are the essential elements needed for the house in Pittsburgh, an inn, a way station? A conception of that as a set starts from its immortality. It's a place where the light shines with sustenance, a hearth with warmth and food and companionship—the nourishing things that we need in order to take the next step in the journey. It also has the table of the Last Supper, that big table that existed from the beginning where people passing through encounter one another.

In a house, you're dealing with all kinds of history, the factual and emotional history of a space and a time that no longer exist juxtaposed against people who are living in it now. It's like looking at the markings on caves, the totality of a texture of a time, present and past.

You become an archaeologist as director.

Yes, and you're creating a tapestry of a time that is more often felt than perceived.

Is it also your intent, when guiding actors, to work subconsciously?

My intent with actors is to "feed them" in such a way that they arrive at the conclusion or the performance that they ultimately feel is theirs because they discovered it. What does it matter which of us put in whatever element?

Are there occasions when their feelings take them in the wrong direction?

Oh sure, then you do something else. That's what you're doing all the time, carrying it back to square one and keeping it on the path.

Do you encounter actors who feel that the direction in which they're going is the right one—and then the path changes?

I hope so. What you want is a creative person who adds to your own vision. I don't really put the limitations of my vision on the work. The actor's creativity is encouraged to the limit. Then I discover wonderful things that I didn't expect.

All things being equal, there is a point when a playwright knows more about an individual character than anyone else. Then, all things being equal, a director comes to know more about an individual character than the others. Finally, all things being equal, an excellent actor knows more about that character than anyone else, because he's the only one of the three of us who gets the opportunity to live that life through in relation to other people living it through. The actor's contribution comes out of that fact, and it is a major and important one to be encouraged. Actors are selected because of the possibility of their making a contribution.

You've worked on a number of plays with James Earl Jones. Have you developed the same kind of shorthand language with him that you have with August Wilson?

Not necessarily a shorthand. James has his own way of working. He is a very sensitive instrument, and immediately and totally responsive to any sort of stimuli that may come. That's the wonder of him as of any great actor.

Does that mean you have to be careful as to what stimuli you throw out?

Absolutely. If he misunderstands you, he can go so far from where you intended because he's going to use what you gave him in a very full way. If that occasional stimulus or suggestion is misperceived or misstated, then you've got a big problem to deal with and you must catch it immediately. It's one of the things you have to be conscious of. And there are many different kinds of actor-instruments to deal with.

The Fences *company was especially strong as an ensemble.*

There was a repertorial aspect to *Fences* because Jimmie and I had worked together many times, Mary Alice was a student of mine many years prior at the Negro Ensemble Company, Courtenay B. Vance was a student here at Yale, Frankie Faison was a student I'd taught at New York University and I'd cast Ray Aranha previously in a number of productions. Charles Brown was the only actor in the company I'd never worked with. In the American theatre there have been many forms of repertory. A building does not a repertory make. The American national theatre is these groups of people who work from one region to another. When you see articles about theatre in America, they're usually written from the point of view of how New York is making out. Then that is misperceived as "theatre in America." It discounts totally what the burgeoned "national theatre" really is. However, in the revolution of the regional theatre, one of the things I perceive we have lost is our capacity to make or attract what are called stars. I think the regional theatre has to address that, and that's one of the things I'm trying to do as I take projects that began here at Yale around the country. I'd like to engender a *national* perception of what has been a *regional* event. We have to share and create the celebrity of our own work.

That sense of company hearkens back to the day when most actors lived in New York and frequently worked together within a fairly small geographical area, in what were essentially commercial theatres. In those days, once a production had completed its New York run, it was the stage manager who might be hired to restage the production for stock and, thereby, gain the reputation as a director. That started careers.

That's not really the way directors develop in this day and age.

Do you tend to cast your stage managers in the same way you do actors?

Yes. If I do a show away from Yale, the stage manager is the first person I cast. I look for someone who creates a healthy working environment.

Is there an emotional state created through the working environment?

Oh, absolutely. The rehearsal room environment is very important. I cannot tolerate dissonance within the area of my hearing. If there is a wrong note, it's got to go. The stage manager is in a unique position. He's not "management" and he's not "artist." He's between both and manages both. He has to keep ends from dropping and interpret the cues. Many years ago there was one stage manager I would look for whenever I did a big show because he was the person who could walk in, look at a set one way and then another and point at little things that had to do with the smooth running of the production and any points of potential conflict. I admired how he handled the actors and calls and dealt with discipline and made things smooth within the tempo. Because the rehearsal takes its tempo from the director. If the stage manager is on a different internal tempo, that doesn't exactly help create a wonderful environment. If the workplace evolves around a personality other than the director's, say the star's, it can throw the work off.

What happens when an actor must be replaced during a run and a certain space has to be filled without benefit of the original process of creating the character?

When you have worked with a company, where you have a very unified performance, the changing of any element alters it and it isn't the same. And it is not possible to go back and re-create the unity all over again. Everybody makes an adjustment.

Who are the people who have served as role models for your career?

I have a couple of heroes. If the pictures were properly on the wall here, you would see a picture of Paul Robeson and you would see a picture of Harold Clurman. And those are two pictures that will be on my wall forever. I first encountered Robeson when I was in college. Paul came to Detroit to visit when he was doing a show. We were both members of the same national fraternity. We chatted, and I saw everything he did. I also saw Canada Lee, whose work I admired a great deal. I think between the two, they gave me the courage to go ahead and do what I intended to do anyway. Harold I got to know later. I had great respect for that man.

You have been responsible for producing Athol Fugard's new work ever since the premiere of A Lesson From Aloes *in 1980. He is quoted as saying, "What a beautiful irony, what a massive affirmation it is, that my artistic leader is a black man."*

There is such a bond, such a trust between us, I feel that whatever the plays turn out to be, they are somehow extensions of *our* thought. When I initially called Athol about *A Lesson From Aloes*, I intended to direct it. But he wanted to direct it so our relationship started. He is probably the only person, other than myself, I would have hired to direct his plays. But I *feel* as if I have directed all of his plays. The collaboration has involved our connecting and saying, "Yes, that's right." His passion and his concern are extraordinary, fierce, analogous to his deepest thoughts. I think we identify on that level. Everything that surrounds him is seen through his sense of the struggle for humanity to become human. I dare to presume that I come from somewhere in that neighborhood.

PETER SELLARS

"One of the ironies is that I'm one of the best-known directors in American theatre and very few people have seen my work."

Peter Sellars wears the expression of someone who is constantly surprised and delighted. Writers have described him as "puckish" or "elfin," but the high tessitura of his irrepressible and staccato laugh is clearly Mozartean. In fact, he is a foremost scholar and innovative director of Mozart's operas, and resembles the great boy-composer not only physically, but in his capacity to create large-scale stage works and to inspire both admiration and controversy.

At 5' 4", Sellars is an amazingly short lightning rod, though he periodically attracts bolts from the blue. The first of these came in 1980, when he received national attention for his unusual staging of a college production of *King Lear*—in which Lear arrived onstage in a Lincoln Continental. (When the actor playing Lear, a black street musician called Brother Blue, got stage fright at the last minute, the twenty-three-year-old Sellars jumped into the role.) Then, to his complete surprise, in 1983 Sellars was awarded a MacArthur Foundation "genius" fellowship providing him with five years of financial freedom. And one year later, a surprise call came from Roger Stevens, chairman of the John F. Kennedy Center in Washington, D. C., inviting him to form a new company that would perform in the Center's 1100-seat Eisenhower Theater, the 500-seat Terrace Theater and an experimental space designated as the Free Theater. Sellars promptly named the fledgling company the American National Theater, a bold title virtually calculated to attract hostility for its ambitious insinuation.

Sellars's knowledge of literature and music is extensive and prodigious. His stagings are frequently reckless and impassioned. The work can be astonishing one minute, sophomoric and banal the next. The images he creates engender delight mixed with hostility, as he breaks conventions in attempting to find modern-day equivalents for his texts. Toward that ambitious end, he stages *Antony and Cleopatra* around a swimming pool; in *When We Dead Awaken* the protagonist is played by a pile of newspapers; the Mikado arrives onstage in a red Toyota in a production that incorporates Sony Walkmans and American Express cards; Maxim Gorky's *Summerfolk* is combined with George Gershwin tunes in a four-hour production called *Hang On to Me.*

The multiplicity of these references comes from a deep intellectual disclosure of the connections of history to the dramatic work. Various periods of time are thrown together when he finds it emotionally justified. He makes connections that on the surface seem absurd unless the interior parallels are made apparent. And Sellars prefers not to insert guidelines in the work. Thus, it makes sense to Sellars to combine Gershwin music with *Summerfolk* because Ira Gershwin's lyrics perfectly parallel those of the Russian Constructivist poets of the 1920s. He sees the Cubist influence in the works simultaneously emanating from both countries. He is able to link cultural influences, leapfrog time and deftly manipulate music, language and images—great strengths that sometimes get him into trouble when audiences and the critics don't understand the analogies.

Music always shares the spotlight in Sellars's plays. For a production of Brecht's *The Visions of Simone Machard* that opened the La Jolla Playhouse in 1983, he incorporated music from Sidney Bechet's *Blues in the Air*; for *Pericles*, music by Beethoven, Debussy and Elmore Jones; for *The Count of Monte Cristo*, Beethoven; for *A Seagull*, Scriabin.

In 1982 he envisioned a commercial revival of Gershwin's *Funny Face* for which Peter Stone and Timothy S. Mayer supplied a new book and renamed it *My One and Only*. His producers secured Tommy Tune to play the lead. But prior to the opening in Boston, Sellars was fired and Tune brought in Mike Nichols, Elaine May and Michael Bennett as doctors for what ultimately became a surprise Broadway success. Tune had panicked when the show was not in any kind of finished form for the opening in Boston. Sellars had reasoned that he would have the out-of-town tryout period to shape the work with an audience. He had not anticipated the pressures that commercial enterprises inexorably exert on producers.

Fast on the heels of this setback, the board of directors of the Boston Shakespeare Company, a small, financially troubled theatre, asked him to become their artistic director. Since Boston had in the past been receptive to his work, Sellars accepted the post. Financial difficulties continued to plague Boston Shakespeare, and after one season he accepted the offer from Roger Stevens and moved to the capital city.

News of the appointment astonished the Washington community because up to that point the Kennedy Center had been used primarily as a Broadway tryout stop and to showcase state theatre productions from foreign countries. It was not obvious whether Stevens had ever seen a Sellars production, and it was even less clear how the conservative Washington audience would respond to his flamboyant innovations.

When Sellars inherited the huge Center complex on the Potomac, he stated, "We can sit here and do *Masterpiece Theatre* or we can change the status of theatre in America." With an elevated mission for a "theatre of ideas," he set out to do that by immediately cutting regular ticket prices in half, offering outstanding guest productions from around the country free of charge, and directing a series of productions that tested the intellectual commitment of his audience. While Sellars was equipped to use the large-scale space of the Eisenhower Theater with conceptual brilliance, he was unwilling to compromise his vision in order to make the work more accessible, and from the outset there was resistance from critics and audiences.

Sellars's unique imagination for the theatre is unrestrained by convention: "I never went to a theatre class in my life. I had no training. I had to learn the long way round how to solve certain problems, the things that every person who had been to directors' school knew right away I learned only by doing. I've never been an assistant director. I don't know how anyone else rehearses. It's a whole area of information that I never received, and I had to substitute my own solutions to certain things just to figure out how to make them work." Those solutions make the work interesting and also infuriate traditionalists on both sides of the curtain—audiences and theatre workers.

After two years of confronting Washington audiences with images they resisted, Sellars left ANT for a "sabbatical" of undetermined length. His final major Kennedy Center production was a forceful modern version of Sophocles' *Ajax*, set on a representation of the Pentagon, in which he cast the deaf-mute actor Howie Seago as Ajax.

Finally, it is his work in opera, particularly the operas of Mozart and Handel, that has given Sellars his greatest approbation. His innovations in that discipline seem to please critics and audiences alike. The musical framework may somehow serve to discipline his intellectual refractions so that the productions are more successful in theatrical terms. Ever ready to tackle the most difficult challenges, he directed Ivan Tcherepnin's *Santur Opera* at the Festival D'Automne in Paris and he conceived the idea for the opera *Nixon in China*, with music by the minimalist composer John Adams and libretto by Sellars's Harvard contemporary Alice Goodman, for the Houston Grand Opera's opening of the Wortham Theater in October 1987 and later at the Brooklyn Academy of Music, Kennedy Center and the Royal Netherlands Opera. His most acclaimed opera productions have been those by Mozart and Handel including *Così fan Tutte*, *Don Giovanni*, *Le Nozze di Figaro*, *Saul* and *Julius Caesar*.

Sellars opened the Museum of Contemporary Art in Los Angeles in 1987 with a production of Velimir Khlebnikov's dramatic poem *Zangezi*, originally used as the text for a 1923 event featuring a construction by Khlebnikov's sculptor-friend Vladimir Tatlin. In October, 1987, Sellars was named director of the biennial Los Angeles Festival, which originated as the Olympic Arts Festival in 1984.

■   ■   ■

At age twenty-seven, at the time you founded the American National Theater at Kennedy Center, you had already been directing for seventeen years. How could you have started working professionally in theatre when you were ten?

I started with Margo Lovelace at the Lovelace marionette theatre in Pittsburgh, where I was trained to do Punch and Judy from the eighteenth-century script. It was in the spirit of that grand old commedia tradition, as handed down to Margo from her teacher, as handed down from . . . you know, the direct lineage. Every spring the Lovelace would produce adult plays that puppets could do better than people. The first plays that I saw were by deGhelderode and Panche and Cocteau.

The Lovelace company was also known for its visual elements. What were those influences?

When I was thirteen or something, Margo introduced me to *The Scenography of Josef Svoboda*. She said, "Okay, these are aniline dyes, and this is how you paint a backdrop." And I painted this backdrop that was very literal that was almost comic book art with lines around everything colored in. And she said, "No, the most important theatrical backdrops, like ones the Bolshoi uses for the glade in *Swan Lake*, are just a blue center way in the back, and then we feel more green around the edges. Then it's dyed and overdyed, and because of all those layers, you can sit there and look at it for hours and keep seeing more layers and mist, and the light changes and . . . " Fourteen years later, in *A Seagull* at Kennedy Center, we used backdrops that had those principles and were also connected to the artist Mark Rothko.

So work with that company was your earliest introduction to the profession, and comprised almost all of your "formal" training in the theatre.

I apprenticed with Margo and right away made my own puppet company with my sister and next-door neighbors. I basically designed a new stage every month to six weeks. It's the way you learn everything. With puppets you carve them, paint their faces, make the costumes, paint the backdrops, do the lighting, wire the dimmer board, put together the music, write the script. And it all had to fit in the back of a station wagon. It was great training.

All of this was prior to high school.

That was how I grew up. The Arthur Miller and Tennessee Williams stuff I didn't read until years later. All I read at first was anything published by Grove Press: Beckett, Ionesco. When I got to Andover it took too long to teach puppeteers so I began doing plays with people. It was just after the 1960s and the curriculum had totally expanded. For reading I was handed *Finnegans Wake* and Martin Buber. The second year I was introduced to Peter Handke. If I wanted to find out about Chekhov, I would direct a Chekhov. In high school I did about forty productions. At the same time I'd been invited to the Elitch Gardens Theatre in Denver, where I started a children's company, and I did five summers there in the streets, in shopping malls and off the back of pickup trucks.

After high school I lived for a year in Paris. That was thrilling because I saw a lot of Giorgio Strehler's work, and Andrei Serban's *Trilogy* came through. The Bread and Puppet Theatre brought their bicentennial show. They couldn't get any bookings in America for it that year, only in Europe. It was this four-hour mammoth production. I remember seeing that show six times. That was an incredibly powerful year for me. At the end of that year I attended the UNIMA conference for puppeteers in Russia, saw hundreds of shows and met a lot of interesting people.

Then you returned home to America.

Then I went to Harvard, and again did about forty productions. Harvard had no theatre department so I was terribly fortunate to obtain a special major in which, with one professor, I was my own department. Basically, I could take any course in the university that I wanted to. I was able to take psychoacoustics, late Cézanne watercolors, electronic music, Hitchcock and early D. W. Griffith seminars, eighteenth-century poetics, and spatial perception at

MIT. I didn't take many official courses. I was able to have a high-powered education, and then I sorted Edmund Kean playbills and was able to do wonderful theatre history research in the Harvard theatre collection. When I did Mozart's *Bastien und Bastienne*, I could just go to Weidner Library and get out the first edition of Rousseau's *Devin du Village*, which is what it is based on, and get Charles Burney's translation of it and substitute that for the corrupt text of the Mozart opera.

While at Harvard, I founded the Explosives B, a cabaret where we did a new production every two weeks. I got to do works of Mrozek, Gertrude Stein, Aeschylus, Handke and Ibsen. We kept churning out the shows. I had started working on condensed Shakespeare by doing *Macbeth* with three actors.

Why would you want to manipulate the text like that?

Because I wanted to get at another way of reading the text. I wanted to remove the received associations that we have of that play—of all of the Shakespeare plays. You see, I've never really believed in plot that firmly because a play is about content. It's not about the story. Plot is the hook on which the playwright hangs what interests him. By entirely removing the plot I wanted to treat the play line by line, literally, for "what does this mean?" In America we are totally at the mercy of the plot. Everything is the synopsis. Like listening to the abbreviated plots at the beginning of the Metropolitan Opera broadcasts. American theatre has Milton Cross on the brain. As long as you can reduce it to a plot synopsis it must be sensible.

Of all those playwrights you produced, other than Shakespeare, who had a major influence?

In my third year at Harvard I did a production of *Three Sisters* and it was a real turning point. For the first time I worked with a translator, and we translated word for word together. Now, whenever I do something by a foreign author, I commission a new translation.

Why is it so important to do a new translation when there may be a number of recent ones available?

In Shakespeare I can analyze a speech. I know the grammar. I know why the grammar is the way it is, how the grammar connects to the character, how the deep sentence structure connects to the way the character's mind is functioning. The meter in Shakespeare will tell you the important word of the sentence. And you know where the accent goes. When you are working with a translation you can't say the same thing. So, for example, it's very important to get deep inside the grammatical structure of Chekhov's sentences so you really can understand the germ of the idea. And the Chekhov I do is very literal in Russian word order because the order in which people think of things is significant.

Chekhov's sentences are in tangles but oddly enough you find that most of us speak that way. It looks strange on the page. In fact, it looks like Beckett or Gertrude Stein—a cross between that and the King James Version of the Bible. The King James Bible also has that odd word order that is, in fact, Elizabethan. (Incidentally, that's why Gertrude Stein is a wonderful sort of return to Shakespeare in our century because she breaks up those sentence patterns and inverts them the way that Shakespeare did. And the inversions are very, very dramatic.) Suddenly, the Bible intentionally inverts sentences because it forces you to think of the idea. It forces you not to assume that this word goes with this subject. Elizabethan word order was influenced by the Greek. And the point at which the Elizabethan language and the Russian language meet is that they are both formed by Greek sentence structures.

In Chekhov the speech resembles that of Beckett. That language is so meticulous. It consists of a small vocabulary of words that are repeated over and over again in odd combinations. It's frequently undramatic. The second part of the sentence loses track of the first. It's one of the most dramatic things as people struggle to master their thoughts. And it's not that they can take for granted the act of speech. It's an effort. They can't quite express themselves, so when they finally find a word it's an event. If they can't find a word for a while, then they're hemming and hawing and kvetching and then frequently Chekhov has a person land on the *wrong* word. It's not the word he meant but it's too late. A character reaches for something and misses and falls. He's said it, and the damage is done. Translators tend to smooth all of that out. They will frequently supply the right word so it reads better, but that destroys the whole dramatic moment. Again, what is smooth in drama is not interesting to me because there is no drama there.

Your having the actors speak directly to the audience in A Seagull in Washington *was considered shocking in 1986.*

The importance of *Seagull* in 1895 was that it was poised equidistant between Chekhov's vaudevilles and *The Three Sisters*, which has its own internal mechanism. Everyone treats *Seagull* as if it's one of the later Chekhov plays, which it isn't. It still had one foot in the door of the cheap vaudevilles. I don't mean, therefore, it's funny. It's that sense that the actors come to the front of the stage and talk to us. Chekhov's dramas were reviewed by the symbolists and the realists as the apogee of their work. They simultaneously fulfilled both programs and if you leave one or the other out it's not quite accurate.

And in that production you had a pianist on the stage playing Scriabin preludes.

No theatre right on through the 1920s would think of not having an orchestra in the pit and would not think of having live music playing while the actors were emoting in those scenes. A whole number of issues were determined by specifically thinking about theatre in 1895. Scriabin was twenty-three years old, Treplev's age in 1895. Those preludes really were the outpourings of a twenty-three-year-old mad Russian genius in 1895. So while I tend to put music in all of my shows, for that show it was specific to the grain of it. The music was used whenever Chekhov called for sound. That is what determined the place of the musical cues and when there was no sound called for I didn't have any music.

Was working on the translation of Three Sisters, *so that you could get a perfectly accurate text, the major impact of doing your first Chekhov?*

That *Three Sisters* production in college was seminal because it was the first time I had done one of those huge plays absolutely uncut. I did every word and I knew why every word should be there. It signaled a new direction I would then continue, particularly in the operas, which I do with the most complete text available. People, from a totally misinformed point of view, accuse me of subverting the text. They don't realize that it may well be the only time they are really hearing the text.

They might have been justified in that belief in The Count of Monte Cristo, *where you added text from other sources.*

Yes, I did dress that one up. It was the first time that I had not worked on a text by a great master. I revised and put in a lot of Dumas. But then the crucial thing I needed was Byron and the Bible, language that had real weight because the evening needed to have that spine, that backbone, that level of really great language. The ideas were completely congruent with Dumas and the melodrama but they could express the impulses of the Dumas so much more deeply.

There were a number of startling staging effects in Monte Cristo, *but near the end of the production there was a scene played in absolute darkness. What was the reason for that choice?*

That's deprivation. The problem with America is that we take everything for granted and, therefore, nothing surprises us. It's not until we're deprived of something that we begin to notice it's missing. It's a concept that American audiences can't understand. So in order to return to drama again from the surfeit that this society exists in, it's important that you remove things, deprive people of their cue cards, remove their usual crutches. It causes people to have an authentic response for the first time.

That response is not necessarily a comfortable one.

Even if they hate it, it's authentic. It's not a preprogrammed response. What is deeply hated about the work that I do is its insistence on the content. You can't escape without it. People are so used to having the content glossed over and presented in a series of more palatable forms. What I frequently do is just pull away all the decorative elements and say, "Okay, nobody leaves the room until we confront what the people are saying." The main thing that I do is move in to the real crisis zone early in the second half of the production, and we have this long arid stretch where there's nothing decorative, nothing entertaining, nothing diverting. People have to look at the subject. And you either notice the subject matter or you're bored out of your mind and you leave the theatre.

You really do have to burrow in and concentrate. It demands a lot from an audience.

Because everyone is so harried, so rushed, so pushed, in the theatre I try and allow some repose, some space. I'm very influenced by the work of Robert Wilson in this respect. His sense of slowing down time is one of the great gifts of his work. I also happen to have a personal fixation on the slow movements of Bruckner's symphonies. I love that suspended state and that an idea takes eighteen minutes to be worked out, that there's no rush, there's no pressure to get there fast. We're going to be interested in how we get there.

A more frequent response by a director is to cut those difficult portions of the play and speed it up.

The most important plays in dramatic history all have long, flawed, boring sections. Christopher Marlowe. What are you going to do with *Tamburlaine*? And yet it's one of the great, great plays ever written. What are you going to do with the long passages that are boring in Chekhov? Even for a serious scholar, there are passages in Shakespeare that are totally incomprehensible. And they're crucial. You learn early on that Mr. Beckett must know what he's doing. It's up to us to find out. Of course we don't understand it. And we just have to sit there and work at it until we do. Because Shakespeare and Handel did know what they were doing.

Modern playwrights have largely avoided those kinds of challenges to the audience.

They are things not allowed in new plays by reviewers. There is this odd notion that everything in the theatre should be complete. You cannot dare present theatre that is half-baked. As long as it's smoothly digestible it'll be fine, like a McDonald's milk shake that will not melt in the sun. In fact, flaws are the essence of theatre. From Aristotle, the main point about theatre is that the characters are flawed. And the flaw is the basic concept of theatre. Perfection is not an issue in theatre.

Then how do you cope with the problems imposed by these plays?

I've done about eight Shakespearean plays, and I'll tell you what my recipe is when I work on them. The first thing, I go through and I find the repetitions and obscure passages that a modern audience would not understand, the language that is totally impenetrable. I also find where Shakespeare has taken a detour, and it would seem much clearer if he went right to the point. So I cut that middle section so it's really much crisper and more dramatic. I isolate those repetitions, the obscure passages and the detours—and I make *those* the base of the production, because those are the things that I first resisted. Shakespeare is a perfectly lucid writer. He could be clear if he wanted to be. If he decided to be obscure for two speeches, there must have been a reason. And then if there was a detour, there must have been a reason he didn't want to go right to his point. There is only one issue in drama, and that is exactitude. Is it precise? My productions are a bit thorny but it's what I grew up thinking art was all about. Art exists to be chewy.

That's how you deal with these mysteries. Why do you seek them so avidly?

It seems to me that drama is about the search for the unknown. The cornerstone is the stone that the builders rejected. It's the thing that doesn't fit the categories. If somebody sends me a play and I understand it, I will never do it. Why spend six weeks in rehearsal? I can understand it just reading it. You need a play that you can't figure out and have to rehearse in order to discover it. I only embark on material that I feel is wide open at the end, when I don't know where the journey will end, don't know what the final production will look or feel like. Also, a lot of the work I choose is poetic, Frank O'Hara, Ezra Pound, Khlebnikov. And I find obscure stuff. I do the Handel operas that everybody says must be cut and do the only uncut performances of them, put in every aria, and they last four hours, and fine. I love doing the plays that they say are the bad ones because they don't fit the labels, that are too long, indigestible. I get used to a level of prolixity in the text. I feel at home with it. I feel insulted when I understand a text too readily, either from an actor or a writer. When I think that I'm being sold a performance, when I feel that I'm not being challenged, when I feel that something is being presented that is obvious—I can't stand it. Why am I paying money or going to the trouble of going to the theatre to see something that is obvious? I feel very insulted at things that have no sense of privacy, no dignity, things that are anxious to reveal themselves to me. Because theatre of our period is so anxious to have a friend, it will expect nothing from the other party. It says to the audience, "Oh, you don't have to do anything. Don't worry, we'll do it all for you." That's not friendship. And it's not a long-lasting relationship.

Was American theatre ever able to digest difficult plays?

Oh, yes. We had very distinguished efforts. Real plays were allowed on Broadway right up through the early 1960s. Just the notion that Eugene O'Neill could make his career on the New York professional stage is incredible. He was one of the toughest, most unpleasant, indigestible writers in the history of world literature. And in America, in democratic America, his plays were put on and received by large numbers of theatregoers. Today, most of the American public has never seen what I would characterize as a serious piece of theatre. People have no idea what the level is we're trying to achieve. Much of the work is like those orchestral records of opera without singers for people who don't like opera.

In many ways you have received greater attention for your opera work than the theatrical productions.

My opera work has been deeply satisfying because I've worked with the same people year after year. It's the closest that I've been to an ensemble company experience, where the singers, the members of the orchestra, the conductor, designers, we all know each other. We pick up where we left off before. We don't have to start from scratch and get acquainted. The vaunted joys of a company, I have tasted in the opera world. It means the work can have a tightness and a sense of devotion.

How did you begin working in opera?

One of the summers in Denver, I had done a Wagner *Ring* cycle in the streets of downtown Denver, in under four hours, with tapes and puppets and people. The following summer, before my senior year, I ran the Loeb Theatre at Harvard. It was the interim period just before Robert Brustein came in and founded the American Repertory Theatre. I ended my little season there with the *Ring* cycle. The soprano Susan Larson, from the Boston Opera, came to see it. (Since then she's been in almost every opera production I've done.)

She was singing Elvira in a production of *Don Giovanni* and she convinced the conductor to hire me as the stage director. Edward Gorey did the sets. It was the first thing I did out of college.

Avoiding the word "concept," where did you get the idea for setting your production of Così fan tutte *in a diner?*

No, no. Use "concept." That's the funny thing that misleads people the most about my work. You know, I never devote any time to that. It doesn't interest me remotely. A coffee shop was the first stage direction in the libretto. It says, "bodega de caffè." That was very straightforward, and then I saw no reason to have more scene changes. No time was spent on that. What you do spend time on is the way it works in detail and trying to be simultaneously eighteenth and twentieth century. See, updating in itself is not interesting, and also equally uninteresting is a so-called "period" staging. Each is a falsification. The fact is that *Così* was written in 1790. So you can't say it was written in 1986 because it wasn't. At the same time you can't do it as they did in 1790 because you don't know how that was. The act of theatre is this equation: Whatever you do onstage must = the public at the time you stage it. We may be able to re-create half of the equation, the production as it was done in 1790 (although I doubt it), but the other half, the public Mozart did it for, we can never re-create. For me it has to be both. Having set the opera in a coffee shop, we then proceed to violate coffee shop behavior in the staging. The important thing in theatre is the sense of anachronism—Shakespeare knew perfectly well there were no clocks in ancient Rome. The point is to deliberately leave in these little bits of roughage that don't digest, that suddenly make you stop, that don't go down easily. It's not smooth transition from scene to scene but constantly encountering friction, something that reminds you, "Wait a minute, we're in 1601, aren't we? We're not in ancient Rome."

And we have no idea of what staging was like in Shakespeare's period.

Well, we have that one drawing of an actual Shakespearean performance in progress. *Titus Andronicus*. It's printed in the Riverside edition. It's fascinating. Because there you see Titus and Aaron in Roman costumes with breastplates and Lavinia in this long flowing white thing. Many periods have had long flowing white things. And Aaron is gesturing to the guards to take her away, and the guards are two Elizabethan beefeaters. He has cops right off the street onstage standing next to Roman costumes. There is this deliberate notion that time is circular, a concept which we lost in the early nineteenth century with the invention of photography. There is now a literalness that insists that you can isolate a section of time and remove it from all the moments around it. That, of course, is not true. At no point previous to the nineteenth century was there a notion that history was separate from the world the audience lived in. We are dealing with circular space and circular time, where the world is not what it appears to be.

That was certainly demonstrated in your production of **Monte Cristo.** *What were the design inspirations for that? It is a nineteenth-century work, but the settings had many references.*

There's a situation where the design and the direction were inseparable. My directorial ideas came directly out of ideas generated by the scenic designer, George Tsypin. There was a sense of working so closely with the design team that there were no footnotes or name tags on anyone's ideas, so that it's impossible to say who thought of what.

That big black monolithic traveling unit, the dominant scenic piece—it was impossible to identify what it was, although it became background, a space-ship, the entrance to secret rooms.

The germ of these shapes were those incredible Napoleonic secretaries that had bizarre compartments in them and odd, surprising writing desks that flipped out and places where you could keep secret things. They're in the furniture room at the Metropolitan Museum. We spent so much time in the Frick museum, at the Met, poring through books, and a long time at the National Gallery.

It also could have been something out of **Star Wars.**

Exactly. We took the image and went further with it. It was all finely digested. The work is based on a certain rigor. What's shocking is that theatre is always fifty years behind the visual arts. There could not be an exhibition of contemporary American scene design in the Museum of Modern Art. We're sitting here with the Model T Ford and are busy cranking it saying, "Wait a minute, it's going to start any minute." It's primitive compared to the European level of design. We have yet to take lighting seriously in this country, even with such gifted designers as Jennifer Tipton and Tom Skelton. Even with computerization, lighting is the thing that's added afterward. If you can create something in America under these conditions, it's impressive. I have great respect for anyone who can get a show up in this country. We have certain people who are such artists they have learned to work in no time at all and to produce work that really does have its own integrity.

Then there was your modern version of Sophocles' Ajax, in which you cast a deaf-mute actor and which you set on the loading dock of the Pentagon.

I had worked with Howie Seago at the National Theatre for the Deaf and had been struck by his tremendous power when he played Gilgamesh. He's quite amazing and irrepressible. It's visceral and it cuts very deep. You feel it boil up from inside.

Since he does not have the power of clear speech, you gave his lines to other actors.

The chorus had to share his lines. Talk about that yin-yang thing, the idea that nothing is complete until it contains its opposite—the people arguing with him then had to translate his lines. So it contained that awful thing of having to acknowledge your antagonist's argument. The Greek theatre had that collective quality. It was reaffirmed in Serban's Greek productions, in the Living Theatre and in Joe Chaikin and the Performance Group's Greek productions. Again, one of the most exciting moments in the history of world theatre was the experimental theatre movement in America in the 1960s, and it's very interesting that seminal for all of them was Greek theatre.

When you directed Ruth Maleczech in Zangezi *for the 1987 opening of the American Museum of Contemporary Art in Los Angeles, she said that she thought it was very interesting that when there was an obvious surefire theatrical solution for something, it was never the thing that you thought of, that you went somewhere else. Is that a conscious choice or simply a natural tangent your mind takes?*

Nothing comes easily. Some things I do automatically. For example, people looking at one another, something I find is vastly overrated, and which I find makes a moment happen between two actors but nowhere else. It's not realistic because most people don't look at the people they're talking to. Automatically you can spot where indirection has not been allowed to play its part.

Do you have a specific process in working with actors?

I have a real problem. I'm in such awe of them. Working with great actors like Howie Seago, Ruth Maleczech, Colleen Dewhurst and David Warrilow has been one of the privileges of my life. I can't believe the artistry that I'm seeing. I always apologize to actors immediately about how obvious I'm going to be in rehearsals. Because that's really mostly what I do in rehearsals, ask obvious questions. Oddly enough, in most cases it's fair to say that the obvious questions are the ones that are never asked, and if the first couple of premises are clichés, there is nothing to build on. It's frequently terribly important to ask the obvious question. "Is Macbeth a good or a bad person?" And then you have a person like Colleen, who proceeds to take what may have been a very obvious and plain idea and brings it back with some hidden undercurrent, and it suddenly starts to bloom and is given a mystery and a quality that is truly ineffable. You have a moment when you say, "I can't put my finger on what happened there." It hits you and you cannot say what it was and that's what you want. It's truly a moment that cannot be reduced in the materialistic way. We like to say that we own everything, and we like to own it because we can categorize it, name it, recall it, and touch it.

How did Peter Sellars, at the age of twenty-seven, receive the mandate to develop a theatre company in one of the largest and most visible theatre centers in this country?

I was running the Boston Shakespeare Company, where I expected to spend ten years. I had taken it on at a time when the company was about to go out of business and I had just gotten the MacArthur award and felt an obligation to have a company to create a body of work with a group. The year at Boston Shakespeare was very exciting. We did Tim Mayer's translation of *Mother Courage* with Linda Hunt, the American premiere of Peter Maxwell Davies' opera *The Lighthouse*, and I directed *Pericles*, *A Midsummer Night's Dream* and a series of Beckett and Chekhov evenings.

In the middle of that, a call came from Roger Stevens. He said, "I may have a proposition that might interest you. If you're ever in Washington stop by my office." A month later I was in Washington, involved with an arts education meeting, and I had finished my meeting and I thought, "Oh well, why not?" So I called and Roger was in and I said, "Mind if I come by?" And he said, "Oh, sure." When I got there, he said, "Would you be interested in running this place? Here, let me show you around." He gave me a quick tour backstage and said, "Anyway, give me a call." It was shocking. But that's the way Roger is about those things.

About that time I went to Moscow. And in a week in Russia I saw seven shows at Lyubimov's theatre and they were the most important things I had ever seen. I canceled all my other engagements and went every day. It turned out to be a very emotional time because it was the week that Lyubimov was exiled and Efros took over the Taganka Theatre, so I was seeing the last performances ever of some of those productions.

Even though Lyubimov has re-created some of those works in this country, they probably have not had the same impact.

They can't. The audience doesn't have the commitment, the actors don't have the commitment and it doesn't mean the same thing. In the Soviet Union they *need* theatre. You feel the hunger in the audience, and as the performance goes on, you feel the hunger slaked in some measure. In America the same words and gestures have no value. In Russia those gestures are so dearly bought. When you make a certain gesture two miles from the Kremlin it has a certain meaning. When you make that same gesture two miles from the White House, big deal.

The combination of seeing Lyubimov's work and a meeting I had with Efremov, director of the Moscow Art Theatre, convinced me that there was a reason to have a national theatre. Like the Soviet Union, we have some of the same interesting problems to solve. Culturally, we are much closer to Russia than France and Britain are, and yet they are the countries that have established national theatres. I came away from that visit to Moscow thinking, "It is important to have a national theatre because that is the only place where a certain standard of idealism can be set, where something apart from the usual excuses offered by the profession can be put forward. It has to think big, and if we're lucky we could pull a few things together that have not been previously pulled together."

We do have this network of theatres across the country that sort of make up our version of a national theatre.

We still have nothing here comparable to all the things that were brought to the Olympic Arts Festival in Los Angeles in 1984. We have no major theatre that we can send to other countries doing productions on that same level, which is both cutting edge and well supported. It's very hard for interesting work to happen at the large institutional level. America's large institutions are rarely able artistically to be in any kind of vanguard as they are in Europe. In this country the large institution is already held in suspicion because we have no place for culture in our society. In Germany it's assumed that every town will have at least one municipal theatre. The institution is a given and, therefore, the institutions can afford to concentrate on expanding the boundaries of the work.

Then what does the future hold for theatre in America?

Theatre will probably exist in a sort of *samizdat* state. I think there will be a group of people who know how to do it and have to do it, but I think its importance as a widespread art form has virtually vanished. The language of the theatre has to be reinvented, as the people of the Wooster Group are doing. The Wooster Group is speaking the language that the theatre will speak fifteen to twenty years from now. I'm talking about the vocabulary of stage language, of what a set looks like, how lighting behaves, how sound works, how video works, how all of those things go into creating a total work of art. The notion that a piece is made of all those various elements is very important, and in the Group's work is the first time that I've seen all of those elements combined in a really sophisticated way to create this *Gesamtkunstwerk*, where the text is as important as the video image is as important as the sound, and nothing has dominance although the words are very powerful. They are inventing the only vocabulary that can deal with the material of the last twenty years once we understand its strangeness.

It's like Picasso's *Les Demoiselles d'Avignon.* The first time you see it you say, "What a horrible thing to chop up these women that way and to give them these awful faces." It's a very threatening and dangerous painting. It's now been accepted, but when you see it in the flesh you're still shocked even though you also realize that it is one of the standard-bearers of modern art. In the Wooster Group there is a level of acting where the actors can go through five different styles in a flash. In the absence of a major writer, they use collage techniques. There will be writers who will one day be able to merge into that style, I think, but they first have to realize that it is the theatre they're writing for.

Is it that vision of the future that has led you to develop such an unusual visual vocabulary?

That's why I have to build the images of a show so that three years later someone can still remember them and rethink them and say, "Well, what was that?" When you build a production that has things that keep echoing, you can build in your own immortality. What I love about theatre is, unlike any other art form, there is no object left over. It's in your mind.

A lot of what I do is trying to return theatre to what it might have been before film and TV took over because I think theatre values have been eroded a lot. What I love is that theatre is not like television, which features one thing at a time. You move in on a close-up of her face or whatever. But theatre has three or four things happening at once and you have to decide what to look at. I try and leave it open to the audience what to look at. Obviously I guide the eye in certain situations. I also leave it open so that two people sitting next to each other saw different shows because they were each looking at a different place at a given moment. Two people watching a TV show see the same thing.

Well, most stage directors are taught to control where an audience looks at any given time and how they want them to react.

The main shock is that the American people have gotten so used to predigested culture and to being told that there is one solution and one point of view for everything. We produce theatre that's based on not letting anyone disagree. The whole objective is to make everyone in the entire audience laugh or cry at the same moment. That is professional theatre in America. It is a science. The notion of a monolithic response is basically undemocratic. That "only one thing will be permitted here and it will be rigorously timed" is one of the reasons why America has forgotten what a discussion is.

By challenging your audiences, as you admittedly do, there is the danger, every time the curtain goes up, that you are foreshortening your life span in the theatre.

There's nothing else that theatre is but risk. The minute that Molière is no longer risking the king's displeasure, he becomes like all of the boulevard comedians of his era, and we can't even think of their names. The minute it's not the most daring possible thing, it ceases to be.

ANDREI SERBAN

A ndrei Serban was considered Romania's most promising young director and somewhat of a renegade when he was a student at the Theater and Film Institute in Bucharest. Like a number of directors from homelands where diversity of opinion is not tolerated, when the choice between personal expression or the stability of state support was presented, Serban decided for freedom of expression and settled in America. In the process, he discovered a whole variety of new frustrations—money, critics and a scarcity of places willing and able to support his work.

La Mama's Ellen Stewart discovered Serban when she saw a student production he directed at a theatre festival in Zagreb, Yugoslavia. It took Stewart three years to get Serban out of Romania, a feat she accomplished with the aid of a grant from the Ford Foundation's W. McNeil Lowry.

Serban arrived in New York in 1969 at age twenty-six and set to work staging two contrasting plays he had previously directed at school, the Elizabethan revenge play *Arden of Faversham* and the more extravagant *Ubu Roi*. At first he was dismayed at what he saw of the American experimental theatre, most of which he thought was sloppy and sentimental. Only work by companies such as Joe Chaikin's Open Theater and Merce Cunningham's dance ensemble seemed disciplined enough for the rigorously trained director.

He thought that he would simply repeat his Romanian staging of *Arden* and return home. But while trying to remember his blocking for the three-and-one-half-hour tragedy, he realized that it was necessary for him "to return to zero, to start from the energy that provokes theatre action." He retained the play's key words but cut it to a length of fifty minutes, using pure movement and action to get at the core of the gory melodrama. The result was galvanizing, the climax being the ritual murder of the husband by his wife and her lover in which the husband was castrated with a giant saw. Eggs, simulating the severed organs, were used to smear his face. Serban was perceived as one of the newest and most exciting of the avant-garde directors before he even knew what experimental theatre was. Director Peter Brook saw the productions of *Arden* and *Ubu* and asked the young Romanian to assist in his production of *Orghast*. Serban worked with Brook in Europe for a year.

After *Orghast*, Serban returned to La Mama and set to work on the three productions that are the standard against which he continues to be measured: *Medea* (1971), *Electra* (1972) and *The Trojan Women* (1973), which together are known as *The Fragments of a Trilogy*. The language in the *Trilogy* was made up of Greek and Latin words chosen for sounds rather than meaning, mixed with words added from African and American Indian tongues and an abundance of inarticulate sounds. These were quintessential Serban works, as important for how they looked and felt as for what they said and did. The directing style of the three plays differed greatly—*Medea* expressed almost entirely internally, *Electra* staged in patterned, formal movements, and *The Trojan Women* characterized by explosive, orgiastic theatrical effects. With the actors, Serban explored devising sounds and perfecting physical actions as a means of *creating* powerful emotions, not just *representing* them. Incorporated in the *Trilogy* were musical scores by a young woman who had just arrived in New York from Bennington College, Elizabeth Swados.

As Serban began to direct internationally, his ability to use all sorts of theatrical space was expanded. *Medea* had been presented in La Mama's basement with an audience capacity of fifty. His 1976 production of *As You Like It* was presented in a park-like forest in La Rochelle, France, staged as a Renaissance country fair incorporating streams, bridges, a three-story house, farm animals and a miniature mountain. For this production, Serban utilized his penchant for cutting text in favor of mime, pomp and circumstance. Perhaps the images for *As You Like It* as well as the *Trilogy* were drawn from his childhood experiences in Romania, where Serban remembers forever making up shows in the garden with other children: directing them, being very wild and almost cruel—once holding a playmate captive, hidden all day from his parents.

In 1977, Serban created a major production—and a major controversy—of *The Cherry Orchard* at the Vivian Beaumont Theater at Lincoln Center. He opened up the large Beaumont stage, utilizing it in a way seldom seen. His work in large European theatres had prepared him for controlling the vast (and frequently considered unworkable) Beaumont space. Instead of setting the play in a house, the stage was covered in white fabric with pieces of furniture scattered across it. Upstage there was a scrim, and revealed beyond that was a realistic orchard. From time to time during the play, all sorts of symbolic characters could be seen wandering under its branches. Serban exercised his "painter's eye" for composition and use of space to bring about a subtext for the play. He worked to make images in what Irene Worth, the Madame Ranevskaya of that production, calls "the calligraphy of space." Serban dedicated himself to exploring what bothered Chekhov about the original Stanislavsky production, that it was too serious. The movement in the production was imposing, some of the most impressive moments being wordless. Again and again, Serban is motivated out of his belief that what the audience most immediately receives from actors is nonverbal.

Serban rehearses a production by exploring all the possibilities of a text. He may start with the absolute opposite of what one might expect of a scene; if it is between two characters who traditionally are softly cooing, he may have them shouting at one another across the stage, and then he will try fifteen or twenty other ways of approaching the scene until he finds the right one. Serban has an instinctual way of working: he'll say something inexplicable to the actors, and yet it results in something happening that is extremely interesting. He belongs to the "what if?" school of theatre. All of this experimentation is an attempt to find a way that emphasizes a profundity in the material rather than just the mundane, obvious choices. This experimentation is pursued in the design as well as the acting. With Serban, the process of discovery with the actors is never treated as finished up to the opening night and beyond. Scenes continue to be rehearsed with things eliminated or added. This challenges the actors to be totally flexible. Indeed, when Serban was rehearsing the premiere of Ronald Ribman's *Sweet Table at the Richelieu* in 1987 at American Repertory Theatre, and doing the play the way he thought the playwright intended, two thirds of the way through rehearsals the company and the writer agreed that the production had become too heavy and serious. Serban went back into rehearsal and redid the whole show. The cast literally turned on a dime and played it in a different way. The next day it was funny.

Serban refuses to give in to the system. He wants to see a new idea even if there is little time and it was not originally planned. He knows he has to push against institutional bureaucracy, but this makes it difficult for his collaborators to hold to a logical, progressive way of working.

He has an overriding desire to be original. Even in his early days in Bucharest, he incurred the wrath of the local authorities when he was invited by Liviu Ciulei to direct *Julius Caesar* at the Bulandra Theater and decided to do it Kabuki style. The production was stopped because, according to the minister of culture, "The working class couldn't understand it." Fifteen years later, Ciulei would invite Serban to the Guthrie to direct a wildly modern version of *The Marriage of Figaro*.

While continuing to push against the imaginary walls surrounding sanctified classic plays, Serban has also used his imagination to bring new life to traditional operas. His opera directing debut was with Tchaikovsky's *Eugene Onegin* for the Welsh National Opera in 1979. It was a perfect marriage, the opera company used to working in a theatre-like discipline and Serban with his knowledge from childhood of the Pushkin poem that Tchaikovsky used as the basis for *Onegin*. Following on that success, his opera work has ranged from Mozart's *The Magic Flute* at the Nancy Festival in France to Puccini's *Turandot* at London's Covent Garden.

Also in 1979, in a lighter musical vein, he attempted the accommodation to the stage of *The Umbrellas of Cherbourg*, adapted by Sheldon Harnick from a French film. While the material did not find acceptance with the public, Serban's fluid staging, using movable rain-streaked painted Plexiglas panels, again demonstrated his mastery of stage pictures. He made the piece about the buying and selling of people and gave it a hardness that the original film lacked. The designer for *Cherbourg* and *Onegin*, as well as many Serban-directed plays, was Michael Yeargin. Their method of working is to view endless numbers of pictures and photographs, exploring all the possibilities. This progresses to the model of the set; then another idea may enter that causes them to start again on a new track. Like everything else in a Serban production, the design process is never finished until opening night.

He is tall with straight, boyish yellow hair. His strong features and pronounced accent suggest a Middle-European Sherlock Holmes. He can be quite intense while directing, but this is relieved by an underlying sense of humor. Now in his mid-forties, Serban has become an international director without an artistic homeland, shuttling between Europe and America. His earlier American creative homes at La Mama and the New York Shakespeare Festival have given way to Robert Brustein's American Repertory Theatre in Cambridge and The Guthrie Theater in Minneapolis as led by Liviu Ciulei and, subsequently, Garland Wright. Like other directors of the 1970s, such as Richard Foreman and Lee Breuer, Serban began working experimentally in New York garage and loft spaces and now works largely in the more adventurous institutional theatres.

■   ■   ■

Fragments of a Trilogy *was the first project that gave you major attention in this country. You then revived the work twelve years later in 1987.*

Some people feel that those three plays were, in certain ways, my highest achievement. Half of the reason for that is that Greek tragedy, Greek poetry, is potentially the best material ever written for the theatre. Although Shakespeare's poetry is the richest and most complex in the English language, I think that a Greek tragedy universally has an archetypal quality that even a Shakespearean play doesn't have. The strength is that those Greek poets of the theatre were dealing with deeply felt essential relationships and human problems. They were, more than anybody after them, closer to, and more concerned about, the origin of our existence and the basic questions of man's identity.

The ancient languages you used in the* Trilogy *gave an extraordinary power to the work.

In the very sound of the original Greek language of Sophocles and Euripides and the Latin of Seneca, there is a special karma, a special power that works like an Indian mantra. It has a secret alchemy.

How can actors of today meet the challenge of this language and summon its alchemy?

A contemporary actor must have the curiosity to meet this language on its own terms, which is a different method of approach than studying something like *The Crucible* or *The Glass Menagerie*, where everything is small realism or detailed psychology. He must approach this unknown language with his intuition. The actor has to forget about mind analysis, and even the logical understanding of language, and has to jump into a territory of the unknown with only his imagination. Only then can he find the energy of voice and of body to reach Electra's lament of injustice, for example, or Medea's rage, or the Trojan women's state of despair.

There was the great mystery and challenge of doing these plays originally, but what was challenging in the re-creation of the work?

By doing them again in 1987, I tried to find out if what Peter Brook said in *The Empty Space* was true, that "No production of a play can stay alive unchanged longer than five years." The Greek trilogy was fourteen years old!

With films, the older they get, the more valuable, just like wine. Theatre is made for this moment, for right now. It works only in the present. That's why, for me, what is called the definitive production of a play is nonsense, because it's definitive only so long as the fashion lasts.

But the plays continue.

The plays go on but the format of the plays and the whole involvement of the audience change. The audience in *The Trojan Women* moved along with the actors and participated standing most of the time. It was a device very much in use in the 1960s and '70s which is almost gone now. So I was interested to see if this format, which I considered old-fashioned avant-garde, was just an experiment of the time or if it had something of value that could surpass stylishness.

You proved, at least in the example of Fragments, *that some works can transcend time. Did you really re-create the piece or did you change some things? After all, you were a different person twelve years later.*

Well, I had a lot of new actors to train. There were very few from the original company. They were younger, and they were different. And I always work in relation to the people I've cast. This is true in plays as well as in opera. When I direct opera and have to work with a new singer in a part, I shape the part according to the specific singer. Different actors inspire different energies. So in the *Trilogy* I did a lot of detail work which audiences, who might have seen the plays twelve years earlier, may not have been aware of.

Did the musical score and text remain unchanged?

Elizabeth Swados changed some of the musical lines and polished some of the things that were originally done in a big rush.

You've collaborated with Swados on a number of unusual works. How did that get started?

Back in 1972 at La Mama, I entered the lobby and there was this shy, thin girl who had just come out of Bennington College, who introduced herself as Liz and said she wanted to write music. She asked me to audition her to see what she could do, which I didn't need to do because just by talking to her I could tell there was "something" about her.

What was the nature of your communication on a project like the Trilogy?

It was with specific images, sound images. For example, I asked, "What is the sound of dawn? How can you make the light of the day and the heat that it brings visible in sound?" Liz immediately got hooked on these images and patterns of sounds become visible.

The actress Priscilla Smith will forever be remembered in the original and revival productions. What was the source of her extraordinary performance?

She had a great sense of devotion to the project. She just threw herself completely into the work. She had the courage to inhabit the work and to leave all destructive distractions aside. That's a rare quality that not many people have.

What was her single greatest contribution to the work?

It was the discovery that she was vocally capable of making sounds that she had never produced before. Her first role in the *Trilogy* was Medea, and it was an amazing discovery for her—and for us—that she could produce all kinds of guttural sounds. In opera they tell you it is destructive to use your voice this way and never to do it. All the "baddies" were allowed in this work.

The sounds were closely akin to vocalisms in the Japanese theatre where they don't seem to be worried about any damage to the vocal instrument.

Yes, they seem to be perfectly all right afterward.

What was the original inspiration for the Trilogy?

As a young man, I had a great chance to work as an assistant to Peter Brook, and that literally changed the direction of my life. Never before that had I questioned why I was in the theatre. I was just doing it because I felt like doing it, like most of the people in the theatre. I chose to be there out of blind love. Working with Brook helped me, not necessarily to find the answers or solutions, but to ask the questions—Why am I in the theatre? What is available to the theatre? What is possible for me?

What happened that led you to ask those questions?

During the year with Brook, we went to Iran and did an experimental work, a laboratory work based on new ways of training the actor to explore the possibilities of the voice and sound and their relationship to the emotional center. In Iran we did the *Orghast at Persepolis* and I was one of the assistants. We worked with the dead languages and also explored the awareness of the actors which doesn't come through intellectual means but through more hidden means of perception.

Were there specific exercises you did?

There were many of them. For a whole year, we only did exercises. There were all kinds done standing in a circle, one with actors transmitting a very simple sound from one to another. They passed a sound around the circle and that sound was supposed to come back to the person originating it intact, with no change in pitch, intensity, volume, quality. The quality of the *intention* in the sound was not to change.

It was like ear training.

It was ear training from a technical point of view, but it was more than that. It was a kind of perception of inner listening, a perception of the meaning of what is hidden, which its sound cannot really explain.

Was it just inner awareness that the exercises explored?

The exercises were going in several directions. One was how one relates to the group, how one can truly share a sound or a movement or a rhythm with a partner. This is purely an exercise in working together and sensing the other. Another type of exercise was meant to develop one's own subtler, more refined sense of perception, that which usually isn't called upon when playing a regular role. These exercises were purely rhythmical, not connected with character development, just based on direct body, mind and emotional connections of a new nature. They were working to discover potential that they were not even aware they had as actors.

Are these exercises valuable for all kinds of work?

Not at all. Brook himself said they were just done as experiments and then should be forgotten, like the preparation one does to get to another stage. It would be nonsense if any other group used them. They just raised questions about how much or how little we know about what is available to us.

What happened after you left the year with Brook?

I came back to New York with all that immense territory of exploration and those questions in front of me, and I started to work on the Greek plays. The whole purpose was to choose a language that not even the modern Greeks would understand, and then to work like an archaeologist. Like the people who find objects in the ground, we dug through the very hard, rocky ground of this unknown language, trying to unearth deep, hidden emotions that would come through the vibration of the sound. I did not know the languages, and if I had been a professor, a specialist, I would never have been able to do it this way. By not knowing them myself, I could be exploratory and risky.

What was so significant about discovering these hidden moments of extraordinary intensity?

Every moment, every corner of a Greek tragedy is built from one climax to another. The play releases just enough to build up to the next climax. So an actor has to know that that's his challenge, to climb acting mountains, to know how to go from the valley to the next peak.

It's the same as a vocal line for a singer.

But in this case, the actors didn't have the training of opera singers. They had more of a kind of bogus Actors Studio approach, which generally is a malady, a sickness of the American stage. American actors don't have a precise Stanislavsky method nor do they have a Meyerhold, body-oriented training. There is no clear, strong method of actor preparation in America, and it creates a vacuum. Therefore, it was in a way easier to take untrained actors and discover a method of our own.

Did you go through the same process of discovery the second time around?

Well, the second time I was more secure, much less hesitant. For the actors, these plays are overwhelming because they originally communicated to more than just one level. The unmiked voice had to reach not only twenty thousand citizens of Athens, but the Olympian gods, simultaneously trying to reverberate its message to the wind and the waves of the sea and to the stars higher up.

You have continued to be daring in your work through the years with varying degrees of acceptance. Has the danger of not winning acclaim with every production caused you to modify the way in which you approach a project?

Well, I don't know any other way of working. For example, one day I would like to direct an early expressionistic O'Neill play, but it would have to be on my own terms, not in order to try to repeat the most successful American production of it that's ever been done. But I expect the critics would tear me to pieces.

In America we have a way of comparing an artist to his previous work in a way that asks him not to repeat himself, and yet we criticize him if he strikes out into unfamiliar territory.

It's sad but true. It's just like the rhythm of a Greek tragedy: after a mountaintop one has to go down to a valley and back. It works as long as one just goes about one's work, having faith in it. No hopes, just faith and practice, and more practice. The Muse doesn't show up every day.

Your work is strongly visual. The setting for **The Cherry Orchard** *production at the Vivian Beaumont used the entire huge stage, without walls for the house, just furniture and the orchard in the background. Santo Loquasto was the designer in that case but all your work is visually exciting. Where did that visual sense come from? Training?*

My father was a photographer, so maybe I got this from him. I don't know. It's just that I get caught up in images. Sound is also important. I love music, and I feel that theatre at its best is music-like. The best of a Shakespearean play is music. It's about how the rhythms in the poetry become more than spoken language. There's a difference between the kind of dirty, prosaic speaking tone of a mediocre actor and that of an Olivier or a Scofield, who can make music out of Shakespeare. In that sense, it's like singing. I'm sensitive to that. I see sounds as images. I see sounds as energies in movement. So the tone of the speaking or the singing voice is an expression of an inner posture. The tone of voice betrays something about a person deeply related to essential emotions. So I think of *sound* as being *visual*.

Were you trained as a musician?

No, not at all. I wish I had been. I call myself a musical gypsy.

How did you start directing?

Liviu Ciulei was the artistic director of the municipal theatre in Bucharest, and he gave me my first job in the theatre while I was still a student at the drama school. I was doing very well in Romania. At nineteen, I was the enfant terrible of the Romanian stage.

And how did you find your way to America?

Ellen Stewart came to an International Theatre Institute congress and saw my work when I was a student. She immediately felt that I should come to New York and work at La Mama. She has that unique nose and determination. She got a Ford Foundation grant for me, and she learned "instant Romanian" and went to Romania to the Communist authorities just to beg them to let me go out! I came for six months just to work at La Mama and see the American theatre, which I did. I really came with only three shirts and two pairs of pants, not at all thinking I was going to stay. So I came and I did productions of *Arden* and *Ubu* at La Mama, which Peter Brook happened to see, and he asked if I would come and work with him in Paris. And I said to myself, "If I go back to Romania now, I'll just blow my chance, because I'll never get a passport from a Communist country to go out a second time." After the year with Brook, it was quite clear that I could not return. What Brook did, more than anybody else, was to inspire my curiosity for theatrical journeys, for taking complicated side paths before returning to the main road and then testing what has been found. He helped me to open my eyes in the right direction, to search for what is not easily visible rather than accepting ready-made answers. I knew I could not return to Romania with this attitude since as soon as you question anything in a Communist country, you are already against the regime. The friends Brook helped me establish were in New York and that's where I had to be.

These exploratory theatrical journeys, what should they reveal?

Of all the directors living today, Brook alone can put the fragments together. The rest of us see in fragments, one aspect or another, this style or that. Brook has a harmonious vision of theatre. He alone can get to the essence, eliminating everything that is unneeded. He brings together what all the other directors know and makes something better. He's the only one who remembers that in simplicity there is the answer to everything. He is the only one who knows how to start each time from point zero.

Can you give an example of this?

Let's take *The Cherry Orchard*, a play I had always dreamed of directing, and finally did for Joe Papp at Lincoln Center. The production created an enormous controversy among the New York elite, since it was conceived upon Meyerhold's critical observations of Stanislavsky's famous 1904 production. Chekhov called the play a comedy, in places almost a farce, not a drama. The whole scandal centered on the question, "Is one allowed to contradict Stanislavsky?" In the heat of the argument, people even forgot that Chekhov wrote a comedy. The set also broke away from the heavy realism of tradition and delicately tried to suggest the frozen beauty of white cherry trees silhouetted on a white Russian sky, memories of women in white dresses, the white nursery filled with fragile toys waiting to be picked up by nobody.

I went to see Brook's *Cherry Orchard* five years later in Paris. And when I saw that production, it had no sets, no lighting changes, just an empty stage with some carpets on the floor, no furniture, not even tables or chairs to help the actors in the void! Nothing. Just the people. Yet, he embodied in them the whole history of their characters, the whole emotional geography of Russia and what Russia means without the help of set geography. And he brought to the essence of the play the heightened attention of Chekhov the doctor, the cool observer with the sensitive, emotional heart—these two opposite elements, the heat and the cold, which are in Chekhov continuously—Brook brought them out so magnificently that I thought that my *Cherry Orchard*, in relation to his, was not all that revolutionary.

When Irene Worth made her memorable exit at the end of your Cherry
Orchard, *instead of a slow Chekhovian walk she ran faster and faster in ever
widening circles around the room. Where did that idea come from?*

That came from my feeling that Madame Ranevskaya knows that death is
coming. At the end of the play everything is taken away, there is no house,
there is nothing, there is an empty stage. She will only go back to Paris, back
to the old lover, back to decay, decadence, death—all the big "Ds." So when
she comes back into the room, just before leaving the house, there is this
one moment of remembering. It's in the text. She feels like a little girl looking
for her mother. "I feel the steps of my mother. Here they are." As she says
that, she starts to walk as if trying to smell traces of where her mother would
have walked, like an animal. And by doing that she unleashes an extraordinarily positive energy for a new beginning. Although she is old and not far
from death, she walks in a way that brings back all her childhood again. So
there is this conflict between defeat and possibility, age and the fact that
although Irene Worth was an aging actress, she became like a young person
again. It was a very moving upbeat, fresh exit rather than a more traditional
defeated, melancholic end.

Was there a special way in which you worked with Irene Worth?

Well, she was very sensitive to images. For example, I kept telling her that
Meyerhold, being very upset with the way that Stanislavsky produced *Cherry
Orchard*, had said that the staging was totally wrong: the third act is a dance
of death. The people are partying. They're dancing and dancing waiting for
the news that the cherry orchard has been sold. The dance develops into a
frenzy which develops into a nightmare. The orchard has been sold! The
dance of death! So Meyerhold went on to say, "This is a ceremony. This is
something much higher than a small realistic dance in a village. It's about
apocalypse." So I told Irene Worth of an image from Meyerhold: I told her
she was like a swan, a black swan trying regally to hold her neck up but, in
fact, underneath that she was doing a tragic, violent swan dance. She immediately started the improvisation and her body just took off, lifted. It was
extraordinary.

Do you use a lot of improvisation in creating the work?

Improvisation is what makes acting healthy. I learned from Brook that one
has to improvise even in performance, even when things are fixed, when
things are frozen. What a dreadful word, "frozen." But we use it. That shows
how the technical vocabulary of the theatre becomes deadly. How often directors say, "You must freeze it now." That means take the life out. Even in

performance, even in the "frozen situation," one has to leave something free and open for what is available there and then. Otherwise, an actor is an automaton, a shameful puppet or a bureaucrat. And since we are all under obligation to join an actor's or director's union, we are all in that danger. We wish to be protected by unions, but what we gain in security, we lose in quality. And that is a sign of mediocrity and bureaucracy. I am totally against the idea of unions, though I am obliged to be part of them. "It's five o'clock. Let's stop." I was in the middle of directing *Norma*, in the middle of "Casta Diva," which is the most beautiful aria in the world. Five o'clock came. In the middle of the high C of "Casta Diva," the Kafkaesque union voice calls, "Let's stop!" This is the heart of bureaucracy.

Cannot improvisation also distance you from the play?

Well, it does for a while. But one should not only include the mind but trust the body with all its perceptions. I call these hidden energies, hidden pre-dispositions, which we all have, "talent and inspiration." Approach it from more than one way. The head is important, the heart is important, and so is the body. Connect them and wait for the Muse to bless you. For example, the actors may go into a wild range of improvised situations that are partly great fun and partly serious discovery of possibilities. Then we go back to the text, taking this random intuitive information and applying to it the discipline, the strictness and the rigor of the writing. And we say, "Well, how much out of what we improvised can really apply to the text?" Maybe nothing. Maybe all has to be thrown out. Was that a lost day? No. Because the next day, when one is in trouble with the text, one feels that there was a certain flavor derived from the improvisation.

The Marriage of Figaro. *This was another controversial production. You opened it at the Guthrie in Minneapolis in 1982 to acclaim, and subsequently produced it in New York, where it was alternately respected for its ingenuity and trashed by the critics for its lack of emphasis on the play's political content. What is that play to you?*

It's the most political play in history! It shaped the French Revolution. Now, obviously, we live in a different time. To me, today the political aspects of the play are no longer ardent. But to see the vaudeville aspects of the plot, to see how this play came out of the roots of commedia dell'arte following the plays of Gozzi and Goldoni, to see how the clown and the aristocrat, the master and the slave relate to each other in a kind of universal, archetypal way, are of great interest. I tried to present it in modern costume for the first act and in eighteenth-century costume in the second act just to create modern equivalents. The critics wanted to see the serious political statement. That didn't interest me. And they didn't see that what I did was try to find a commedia dell'arte equivalent for today.

Is commedia a major interest of yours?

I would like to do all the Gozzi plays. He wrote for his company magical scenarios of commedia dell'arte. He used language in a way that I think a playwright ought to use language, in service of the truth of theatre, not in imitation of life. That's why Meyerhold loved Gozzi. Gozzi has been completely neglected in this country, and Europe, too. He actually reinvented the theatre.

I've attempted my Greek investigation. I've attempted the major plays of Chekhov, and then I've done the commedia dell'arte, and I've tried five years of directing opera, from Covent Garden to Los Angeles. I did Ronald Ribman's new play, *Sweet Table at the Richelieu.* So I'm trying to escape the identity box, a certain perception that my repertoire is limited. I even did a musical, *The Umbrellas of Cherbourg*, to prove the impossible to myself.

I've really covered a great deal of territory in different ways, and now I'd like to bring it together and truly create a theatre of my own, concentrate on working with a group of ten to fifteen actors instead of going all over the globe as a kind of salesman director. I'm ready to develop an expression which is not superficially my own, but *truly* my own.

Do you think that is likely to happen in this country?

I had hopes that Ellen Stewart could make that possible. After all, is raising money so much more difficult than learning instant Romanian?

DOUGLAS TURNER
WARD

"Just as the intrusion of lower-middle-class and working-class voices rein-vigorated polite, effete English drama, so might the Negro, a most potential agent of vitality, infuse life into the moribund corpus of American theatre."

So wrote Douglas Turner Ward in a *New York Times* article, "American Theatre: For Whites Only?" on August 14, 1966. He went on to make a powerful plea for the support of black theatre artists, imploring that "the most immediate pressing, practical, absolutely minimally essential active first step is the development of a permanent Negro repertory company of at least Off-Broadway size and dimension. Not in the future, but now." Ward's passionate, timely article led to the founding of America's most prominent professional black theatre institution, the Negro Ensemble Company, in New York City. A few days after the piece ran, a call came from Ford Foundation vice president W. McNeil Lowry, requesting a proposal outlining the requirements for a fully autonomous black theatre. Ford subsequently provided a three-year establishment grant for the company.

300

Ward, along with actor Robert Hooks and manager Gerald S. Krone, was working at the St. Marks Playhouse in New York's Greenwich Village presenting his one-act plays *Day of Absence* and *Happy Ending*, when he was asked to write the *Times* essay. After Lowry's call, the three men met at a restaurant where they discussed a possible structure for the new institution, and outlined how it might work. Krone and Hooks developed Ward's basic idea into a functional concept, and collectively they decided that Ward would be the artistic director, Hooks the executive director and Krone the administration director. With one visionary decision, the Ford Foundation launched twenty years of intensive work by Ward with black writers and actors.

NEC emerged full-blown in 1967, producing four new plays and launching an ambitious tuition-free training program led by such educators as Lloyd Richards, Paul Mann, Kristen Linklater and Michael Schultz. The program primarily trained actors and technicians, but Ward was there to shepherd the writers. The first seasons featured such successes as *Song of the Lusitanian Bogey* by Peter Weiss, *Summer of the Seventeenth Doll* by Ray Lawler and *Ceremonies in Dark Old Men* by Lonne Elder III. Following the first three seasons, as the Ford funding diminished, NEC could no longer support the acting company on forty-two-week contracts. However, the sense of company endured as, over the years, a core group of actors continued to appear in such plays as *The Dream on Monkey Mountain* by Derek Walcott, *The Sty of the Blind Pig* by Phillip Hayes Dean, *The River Niger* by Joseph A. Walker, *The Great MacDaddy* by Paul Carter Harrison, *The First Breeze of Summer* by Leslie Lee and, ultimately, the Pulitzer Prize-winning *A Soldier's Play* by Charles Fuller. Among the actors who have been associated with NEC are Frances Foster, Michele Shay, Denzel Washington, Roscoe Lee Browne, Al Freeman, Jr., Moses Gunn, Roxie Roker, Esther Rolle, Richard Roundtree, Glynn Turman, Cleavon Little, Ron O'Neal, Charles Brown and the late actors Adolph Caesar and Godfrey Cambridge.

Hooks left the company after the first season to follow his own burgeoning acting career and to found the DC Black Repertory company in Washington (which survived only a few seasons). Krone remained at NEC for fifteen seasons, then departed to work in TV news. Ward continued for twenty years and then relinquished artistic leadership to Leon Denmark, NEC's manager.

Following its third season, NEC struggled each year with ever diminishing financial resources. Eventually, rehearsal time was cut and to ameliorate this Ward relied increasingly on his skillful dramaturgical work with playwrights, shaping their text until the plays were absolutely ready for production. There was no time during rehearsals to test rewrites. A typical rehearsal period included reading the play around the table for three days and then putting it on its feet. Blocking was completed in two and a half additional days. Actors were required to be off book by the fourth day. By 1981, the time pressure mandated that *A Soldier's Play* be rehearsed and mounted in ten days—a major American work rehearsed in less time than is often spent on a summer stock revival.

In 1987, as a follow-up to his historic 1966 *Times* article, Ward wrote about the intervening twenty years: "Despite all the obstacles, the lack of resources and the presence of more pressing priorities, black artists created their own institutions and outlets. They catalyzed and sustained activities of remarkable scope and depth. They more than justified my prediction that, if given the opportunity, they would change the complexion of and 'infuse life into the moribund corpus of American theater.' "

■　　■　　■

Why did Douglas Turner Ward become a director?

Out of necessity. I couldn't find a director for *Daddy Goodness*, which was the last play scheduled in the first NEC season. Richard Wright had adapted it from the French play *Papa Mondieu*, and had left it eighty percent finished at his death. It was an interesting combination of folk material and satire, but it had some structural problems and anachronisms. I started as a writer and still consider writing my primary profession. So I guess my writer's sensibility made it seem less daunting to make *Daddy* work. I had Wright's last uncorrected copy with all of the typos still in it. It was a wonderful piece by a very famous black writer who was not known to have written a play. It was a discovery, and I felt that it would be a wonderful addition to the first season of the Negro Ensemble Company.

How did you approach the play?

First I assessed it from a writer's point of view. It didn't lack for action and dialogue. I felt its problems could be resolved without compromising the work, just by giving it the bridges that it needed. I proceeded to try to find a director who could give it what was missing.

I had given Michael Schultz the choice between Peter Weiss's *Song of the Lusitanian Bogey*, which was a sort of epic Brechtian piece, and Wole Soyinka's *Kongi's Harvest*, which was passion set against a wedding canvas. Edmund Cambridge was a veteran director and he chose Ray Lawler's *Summer of the Seventeenth Doll*. Ultimately, I couldn't settle on anybody else so I asked Michael to direct both *Bogey* and *Harvest*. I didn't want to make it appear that that initial season belonged to any one director, but I decided that instead of four directors there would be three. I was still left with this oddity, *Daddy Goodness*. Since it was the last production and I hadn't found a director for it, I could have chosen to drop it. But I felt that it was very important for a new company to deliver the goods it had promised. Finally, I said, "I've obviously selected it because I've seen its possibilities and sub-consciously have an idea of what the results should be. I have to take the responsibility for seeing if my vision can be justified by doing it myself."

Did you feel that was particularly risky?

No. the wonderful thing about NEC in the early days was that although we were not too secure, we also had no reputations to defend. In fact, we all talk about that first year nostalgically, those of us who have made names in the profession. We all feel the first year was the most wonderful precisely because we had no reputations to protect. We weren't faking, we weren't looking over our shoulders at any past records, so we were willing to dare anything.

Of course, the Ford Foundation had given us security with that first grant, a three-year certainty of money. We didn't have to worry about our next year or the next, or being effective. We were free. Therefore my response was to the task at hand. Later I realized I had unwittingly been functioning as a director before that, because I had been involved in nurturing and workshopping plays at New Dramatists, where, for instance, I did two staged readings of Lonne Elder's *Ceremonies in Dark Old Men*. We ended up pro-ducing that one in NEC's second season. I helped Lonne shape it by acting in it and staging it for him. I had organized readings of my own plays, the same ones that eventually were a stimulus for the beginning of NEC. So I had been functioning as a director, in a way, but without ever considering myself to be one. I just considered it my function to help.

How long had you been an actor before NEC was founded?

Close to ten years. I started acting in 1957 in the Circle in the Square's production of *The Iceman Cometh*. Elements of my approach to directing stem from acting. I will communicate to actors in any way possible. I even use body language when I run out of words. I show them and say, "Look, if this doesn't make sense right now, just imitate it for a while and then make it your own." I generally start with actors being aware of the intended result. Initially, I will not illustrate what I want by giving the exact line reading.

Do you find that when you are specific with line readings, it's difficult for actors?

Yeah, there's a threat in it, but you have to cut through that. A lot of absolutes taught in certain actor-training programs are really theoretical and should not be graven in stone.

How do you cut through their resistance?

They relax because they know that I trust them as equal participants in the process. There's no hidden agenda. I always tell them, "Look, you're hired. That already tells you I like you, I want you, you're full of dazzle. You don't have to prove anything more to me, so let's see how we can realize this particular play."

I find that a problem can arise if an actor comes in the first day and is perfect in his approach. Then two or three weeks later he may suddenly do something different and I will say, "What happened? Why did you change that?" And he will say, "But since you never said anything . . ." I concentrate so much on working with those who aren't sure about what they're doing that I forget about the ones who are right from the beginning.

While I know there are certain plays that can sustain different interpretations, that are flexible, sometimes ambiguous, when I am writing, I sometimes sit for days trying to build the right rhythm, stress, intonation and inflection into the dialogue. Maybe sixty percent of it can't be changed. If it is, it doesn't make sense. Sometimes actors come in to audition cold and they give the right reading from the beginning. By the end of the process, the question is if they can make the lines organically part of themselves without losing that correct reading.

If the actor brings so much to his role initially that is dead-on right, is there a danger that he will become bored in performance at some point?

It is a function of our craft and technique to be able to repeat the same thing ad infinitum as if we were doing it for the first time. That is not easy. But the aesthetic sense of what's right, I think, is one of the things that can sustain us. I don't think that the element of instant originality, of constantly improvised change, can sustain me as a performer. It is as much a challenge to maintain the right reading. The actor must not repeat the same line reading mechanically, but he must reach a level of original involvement in the truth of what he's doing. If an actor gets too technical he has a problem, because he then has to calculate every choice correctly. He can't make a mistake because it will show. The truthful actor can make an error and it won't show because his *conviction* will make the audience believe.

What problems do you encounter when you are directing and acting simultaneously, when you can't step back and look at yourself?

My director's critical faculty allows me to extract my acting experience after a show and to remember what may have gone off. I have this camera in my mind that I can run afterward. There was a time when I was watching a performance that I would need someone with me to write notes, or I'd scrawl them myself quickly. I have almost reached the point now where after the show I can go through the script page by page and make notes from memory. Sometimes, if I'm offstage listening to a show that's already set in terms of movement, my ear tells me ninety percent of what I need to know.

Since you are a writer, how have you related to the many new playwrights NEC has produced?

Generally the plays that I have committed to have been largely finished, so I haven't had to shape, nor have I had the desire to shape, the playwright's ideas from some point of inception. The ideas are there and all the ingredients. My biggest assist to writers can come from my questions about structure. Charles Fuller submitted *Zooman and the Sign*, and it had some significant unfinished aspects to it, but what was right was so powerful that I trusted that we would get it done. We had some differences of opinion about the script and Charles organized a reading of it. As a result he rewrote the play.

Are readings a tool you frequently use to judge a play?

I'm one of those people who loathes readings because half of the time they're useless for writers. A writer doesn't need a lot of people commenting on his work, he needs people whose opinions he *respects* to tell him what they think. The idea that a public group of people can hear a play read and have anything significant to contribute about what's wrong or right is an idiotic notion. On top of that, the play is usually read badly because it sometimes takes four weeks for the actors to understand it. So the reading is not for interpretation and, therefore, the writer hears something that he thinks is off. Well, it may not be the text that's off, but the reading. So the writer goes back to his play and changes what was right in the first place. The classic comment from people at readings is "That wasn't clear to me." When I hear that, a red flag goes up. Because that's probably the best thing in the play. Audiences have a desire for literalization. Well, it wasn't clear because inherently the playwright didn't want it to be. I take a baseball bat to writers and say, "Please, you wrote with a certain amount of spontaneity and creativity from your conscious and unconscious minds working together. Now suddenly you're going to go back, literalize that which is best left suggested? If you do, you won't leave any breathing space for the actors or the audience." It's my job as director to decide and emphasize what the audience should hang on to. Audiences are expected to bring something to the experience, so writers should suggest, imply. I have yet to come across any writer whose philosophical, political or analytical faculties are great enough that they can provide *answers* for anything. *Questions*, yes.

So Charles rewrote *Zooman* along the lines I had suggested. Again, there is a danger with each succeeding draft that the writer will further close it down, reduce the breathing space and finally sink the play. Charles, being such a fine writer, did that almost spectacularly. I went away for the summer to figure out how to deal with the problem because I had committed myself to the project and my word is my bond. I spent two months studying and working with the three versions he had written up to that point. I decided not to show him my suggested revisions on paper because I knew that would scare him. So I taped the whole play, just me reading every line, every character, using the original version and some aspects of the third version's structure. Then I invited Charles up to Martha's Vineyard where I was staying to tell him that if he insisted on doing his version of the play we'd do it at NEC, but that I couldn't myself be involved. But I never got to the bottom of my Armageddon speech because when I was describing the problems I was having with the play he kept nodding his head, "Fine, I can accept that." Then I said, "Let me show you what I think will work," and I put on the tape. When it was finished two hours later, I said, "Okay, now take back the text and rewrite it yourself with whatever you think will work, and we'll go on from there." He said, "I don't want the text, give me the tape." To a writer, listening to the words is less threatening than looking at them. When he gave me his final version he had changed only about ten percent of my version.

There have been so many major plays by black authors to come out of NEC. Was there a signal work?

NEC over the years has been very eclectic. However, at one point it got stuck with the success of its domestic drama. The critics and the public embraced the more realistic plays. We did them before white theatre went back into doing them, because they were considered old-fashioned in the late 1960s. They were a minor part of our total work.

Gus Edwards's *The Offering*, which we did in 1977, was probably signal to NEC. Gus's style in that play is very often compared to Pinter's—as much of the play appears in its silences as in its dialogue. If you looked at the play line by line, you might think that there is nothing there. A director has to know what he has in hand and to be able to visualize what is between the lines.

What has enabled you to develop the imagistic skills to enable you to do that?

Economics and material strictures have forced me to develop these skills because I have not had the luxury of testing ideas through workshops or otherwise. The pressure has meant that I had to be right about the production's ability to grab its audience. Necessity has probably refined and stimulated those abilities. I intuit. Basically, since I'm dealing with new works, usually from black life and black culture, I ransack my imagination to come up with the right choices, the meaningful essences that bring the work to life. In terms of that, I use a lot of music because the material I'm inclined toward in many instances is episodic. Music can supply the motive energy, the connective tissue. NEC's stage doesn't have a turntable so I can't make rapid transitions. The connective can be music, which I sometimes use as the emotional climax of the previous scene or a comment on the next scene. In many instances, it is a statement in itself, a part of the play in its own right.

Charles Fuller's A Soldier's Play *had a certain fluidity in the direction.*

Charles's work is very deceptive because it has a sense of the documentary to it. Going back to *The Brownsville Raid* and *Zooman and the Sign* one remembers that they were stylistically nonrealistic. In *A Soldier's Play* I felt that I was able to discard elaboration and direct its essence. There was nothing there but what was needed. We didn't attempt to create realistic details. We selected only those elements that would facilitate the motion of the play and the relationship of the characters. Everything else was eliminated. For a number of years, I had been moving toward cutting out what I considered to be extraneous in plays so that audiences could zero in on their central movement. Samm-Art Williams's *Home* was like that for me. When we were planning *Soldier's Play* I remembered the boxes we had used for the setting in *Home*. The designer created new boxes, but they didn't seem right and finally I said timidly, "Could I just go and get a couple of those boxes from *Home* and have them repainted?"

The casting in Soldier's Play *was remarkably right.*

I look back in awe at the accident of some of that casting. Charles had committed the role of Sergeant Waters to a friend, and I was saddled with him. I wanted the play so badly that, for the first time in my career, I was willing to concede that to a playwright. It turned out that the actor took another job with a regional theatre and I was able to cast my first choice, Adolph Caesar. I was probably the only person who would have cast Caesar, although now it's hard to imagine it cast otherwise. On the surface, he didn't seem the type for Sergeant Waters. He was too small, not a dark man—the opposite of everything described in the play. But I knew of Caesar's Napoleonic feistiness in real life. His smallness led to his great drive, the intensity of always proving to the world that he was a big man, a force. This was perfect for Waters.

Now that you are giving over artistic decision making at NEC, in retrospect, have the sacrifices of the past twenty years been worth it?

Oh, absolutely! There was no better alternative. What I lost in material terms I don't regret. If I had allowed myself commercial possibilities, the work wouldn't have been meaningful to me. Even with all of the difficulties at NEC, I've had the gratification of testing myself in some of the best roles written for black actors during the past twenty years.

What is the position of black theatre in this country today?

My sense is that black theatre has more or less entrenched itself in American theatre consciousness. NEC has shown that there are black writers of quality. Some of them, such as Charles Fuller, Leslie Lee, Gus Edwards and Joe Walker, are major. The future of black theatre may be in danger at the point where there is no institutional continuity. NEC is struggling to survive. The works we have been doing in the past year are not typical. They are modest little works that have a modest impact. We need to do what we did in the past—go for broke with very ambitious work, big shows with big impact. Diversity can't be beat. That must be sustained.

What is the next step for Douglas Turner Ward?

During the next twenty years, if I last that long, I would like to direct only those pieces that are absolutely compelling to me. In the past, a third of what I have directed has been from pragmatic necessity. That is not to say that I didn't like the plays, but it was necessary for me to direct them because of limited financial resources. I had to service the institution and I was the only one who could take the responsibility to honor the restrictions—those restrictions frequently involving time. Sometimes we could only afford two weeks of rehearsal. You can't ask another director to put his or her career on the line with that limitation. Another third of what I've directed has been as a responsibility to writers who didn't feel comfortable being directed by other directors. And the last third were certain works that grabbed me and which I thought I knew how to do. For this next period, I want only to do works that fall into the last category, things that are so compelling that I feel motivated without any other consideration of loyalty or programming. They may be plays that artistic directors normally want to do on a second stage, the most risk-taking things with the possibility of some impact and consequence.

ROBERT WOODRUFF

R obert Woodruff was born and raised in New York City, but in the early 1970s, feeling that in his home city there was an insurmountable wall between him and the theatre, he relocated to San Francisco, where a young director could still find a basement space in which to experiment.

There, in 1972, he co-founded the Eureka Theatre Company, and in 1976, formed the Bay Area Playwright's Festival, a month-long summer forum for the development of new plays. That first summer coincided with the national bicentennial celebration, an occasion which prompted the Marines Memorial Theatre in San Francisco to solicit new American plays. Hearing that Sam Shepard's submission, *The Sad Lament of Pecos Bill*, had been rejected, Woodruff offered to produce it at the Festival sight unseen. The ensuing production launched a collaboration between Shepard and Woodruff that continued through four years and resulted in premier stagings of *Curse of the Starving Class, Suicide in B Flat, Buried Child* (Pulitzer Prize, 1979), *Tongues, Savage/Love* and *True West.*

During that period, Shepard cemented his position as a major American playwright, and Woodruff became known as the definitive interpreter of his lean, violent, metaphorical language. Woodruff's bold, theatrical style appeared to flow directly from the text, making the plays seem deceptively simple to stage. Although they've tried, few other directors of Shepard's plays have been able to emulate it successfully. Perhaps Shepard himself has matched Woodruff's power in staging his work.

Around 1983, Woodruff began to move away from reliance on language as the motor for certain plays and to find other elements that could take on equal importance, such as bold visual imagery or performance values. A production that moved him toward this new direction was Shakespeare's *The Comedy of Errors*. Gregory Mosher, then the artistic director of the Goodman Theatre in Chicago, put Woodruff together with the Flying Karamazov Brothers to see if they could find a way of rethinking Shakespeare's early revel. They did—with a vengeance. Woodruff used the Karamazovs and other "new vaudevillians" to create a no-holds-barred, free-for-all performance that was outrageous and idiosyncratic. The production opened at the Goodman, was featured at the 1984 Olympic Arts Festival in Los Angeles and then was redirected by Woodruff at New York's Lincoln Center Theatre in 1987, after Mosher became artistic director there.

The Comedy of Errors was followed at the Goodman by another Karamazov Brothers juggling vehicle, *The Three Moscowteers*. Then Woodruff directed the West Coast premiere of a very different kind of play: Adrian Hall's *In the Belly of the Beast* at the Mark Taper Forum. The extraordinary range of Woodruff's directing abilities combined to spawn a new directorial vision, which informed his staging of the 1985 production of Brecht's *A Man's a Man* at the La Jolla Playhouse. The production was the culmination of almost fifteen years of theatre experience, incorporating the sense of aggressiveness and impending violence that Woodruff had staged in Shepard's plays, and the playful madness of the Karamazov Brothers (the production even utilized the Karamazov's pit band, the Kamikaze Ground Crew), but also relied on design as a central element of the work.

While Woodruff the director had been largely invisible in the Shepard plays, he now became omnipresent in *A Man's a Man*. He felt free to use any and all theatrical techniques and to combine them in any way to convey a particular idea. Stage conventions ceased to exist as he strove to illuminate the text in a new way: combining music, scenery, lighting, actors, language —any of which could take momentary focus or fight it out for dominance. The result was assaultive, abrasive, hilarious and visceral theatre.

Woodruff further honed this approach the following season when he staged the American premiere of Odön von Horváth's 1937 play *Figaro Gets a Divorce* (again at La Jolla Playhouse), with a story about what happens to Beaumarchais's characters when they escape the revolution that is to follow his 1784 play *The Marriage of Figaro*. The setting was placed in present-day Central America.

These visually extravagant plays, *Figaro* and *A Man's a Man*, developed through a rich collaboration between Woodruff and his designers. Constant among these is scenic designer Douglas Stein. While Woodruff is rigorously disciplined dramaturgically, he moves back and forth from the text to exciting and aggressive images, and Stein has proved to be a catalyst for Woodruff's vision of the event. An example of this was Stein's fulfillment of moments in *Figaro* when settings were simply not enough, when words printed against walls created the most powerful effect. It was a sophisticated extension of the Brechtian use of words in a physical setting. Woodruff was fascinated with the idea of text and wanted to use words in a way that had the same kind of visceral energy as artist Jenny Holzer's work. He researched political slogans from all kinds of sources, such as the book *Society of the Spectacle* and the work of artist-provocateur Hans Haacke. Stein worked them into a wall where the phrases, in English and Spanish, were displayed in letters a foot high at the top decreasing in size as the lines descended from top to bottom, like an eye chart. The effect was strange and theatrically powerful.

Woodruff applied this same visual theatricality to his production of *The Tempest* at La Jolla in 1987 with less success. He and Stein designed an environment that was a steeply raked amphitheatre, wonderfully operatic and filled with all of the artifacts of civilization: boxes of gold, plutonium, banana trees—elements of a very complex storm-like setting. But the visual process that had worked so successfully for *Man* and *Figaro* "jammed" *The Tempest* so that it was difficult for the play to get through. Still, Stein and Woodruff felt that the experimentation had opened the path to their next level of artistic development. A few months later they collaborated on a successful mounting of Shepard's *A Lie of the Mind* at the Mark Taper Forum.

Woodruff has the laid-back appearance of a middle-aged hippie, with a sharp underlying sense of humor, out of sync with an era of unfriendly take-overs, still a street-smart kid from New York with hair receding in front and long enough in back to gather into a ponytail.

■　　■　　■

Where is Robert Woodruff getting his creative challenges today?

The things I now find attractive lead me toward looking at the world in macrocosm—it's unlike someone who goes inside himself and by following one small idea creates something that explodes into a huge view of the world. At this point, I'm unable to do that. That implies a kind of openness to oneself that I find amazing.

I'm not so sure that I can achieve what I want solely through *content*. I'm relying on *form* to create a new way of looking at the work. Several pieces I've done, such as von Horváth's *Figaro Gets a Divorce* and Brecht's *A Man's a Man*, ultimately were expressions of a particular obsession I have about the United States's foreign policy in Central America and Southeast Asia.

That's quite a change from your earlier work with Sam Shepard.

With Sam you work with tremendous language and a detail of behavior that is unique to his viewpoint. His vision tends to incorporate only a small number of performers and to maintain a kind of wariness about designers. He has a great love for actors, but I think Sam often feels designers may be intrusive in the theatre. This probably goes back to his roots with the Open Theater and Genesis and working with "poor theatre" techniques—actors' theatre, dominated by the text and the acting. There's a bareness about the theatrical space he defines, so he doesn't really need bulk in terms of design support. Spectacle is not a value. *Buried Child* requires a couch, a television and a staircase. *Angel City* calls for a neon rectangle, a chair and a timpani. The bareness makes these select few objects jump out in relief and resonate.

For his production in New York of *A Lie of the Mind*, Sam split the stage in two parts with an image that had a lot to do with the idea of left brain right brain. My production later at the Taper was barer. The designer, Doug Stein, and I exposed the back wall—creating automatic myth—because that back wall at the Taper has real muscle to it. It's an enormous curved plaster cyc, and it's a whole universe. It's hard to get myth when you're working in a small space.

What other way did your production of Lie *differ from Shepard's?*

I think there was a profound sadness to the piece when Sam created and directed it. For him, it seemed to be about love and loss and being torn apart. I didn't think I could touch that quality because it was so much "him." I approached it from a sense of behavior, what happens after loss, after guilt. What kind of behavior is registered then? Maybe the characters were a little less conscious of their plight than in Sam's production, where they had more time to dwell on it. The Taper production was less thoughtful and more reactive, less poetic and more athletic.

Sam always seems to be writing about some distinct war within each of us. *A Lie of the Mind* is built astonishingly in terms of the parallelism of situation and language. Things that Sam mentions in the first act come back two and a half hours later: a word, a phrase used in a whole different way. There's a lot more about romantic love, deep feelings, in this play than in any of his other pieces. In no earlier play does a character say, "I love you more than this earth. I love you more than this life." We never heard this from him in the past. With Sam, I still can't figure out how much is carefully plotted and how much is simply intuitive.

How did you approach A Lie of the Mind *structurally?*

Lie is like a series of one-act plays. You almost have to solve the play that way. Each scene has a strong beginning, middle, end and moves in a direction that's not necessarily linear. In the first act, I think the longest scene is eight minutes. Sam's got two-minute scenes, four-minute scenes, three-minute scenes. We restored two scenes that had been cut from the New York production. It's really gunshot kind of stuff. It's the form that's interesting.

So in your recent work you are moving from Shepard's text-detailed and actor-oriented theatre to one that requires larger visual images?

The process is a journey into another "studio," where you have text *and* you have visual elements—designers, musicians and maybe fifteen or sixteen actors—where the text does not have to dominate the event all the time and it allows the lighting designer or the set designer or the composer to "play" loud. Moving from what I've done in the past to what I'm doing now is analogous to moving from a four-track studio to a sixteen-track studio. And if you're doing a mix, everybody has a track, each designer, each actor has his own score. So we lay out sixteen scores, and the mix comes when we're in the theatre doing a technical rehearsal or previews and seeing all the elements at once. Everybody may be playing all the time, and you have to make some adjustment to one or more of the scores. The work becomes more assaultive because it's denser, but it's not *only* the density of language. Not everybody has to play behind the text, support one melody. Each one can play his own melody, and there doesn't always have to be agreement. There's a tonality that you look for, but it doesn't have to be harmonic. That creates an unsettling edge that contributes to live performance. It's not a closed experience, as in situations where you have a kind of roundness, a nice landscape that everyone agrees on and where the edges of it are taken away. When you have agreement, it seals things. You've taken away the possibility of a dynamic that can come from disagreement.

How can you structure that dynamic tension of opposites?

It comes from twenty-one different collaborations at once, from constant dialogue and everyone responding to what they are hearing.

But obviously the more "tracks" you have the harder it is to control the total effect.

I don't try to control, I try to *encourage*. It's like being in a sound studio and saying, "It sounds like we need more bass here." I might say to the lighting designer, "Let's be bolder here. We need more of an edge to this moment." I might also get the result I want from an actor or turn the music up two points. I have to look and then respond to what my collaborators are finding.

Which makes the initial selection of your collaborators critical.

That's the bottom line. You have to have faith in and to celebrate the people who are around you. I mean, it was glorious working with Doug Stein and [costume designer] Susan Hilferty and [composer] Paul Dresher on *Figaro Gets a Divorce*. Paul's music was a toy. He's this great gift: a minimalist with classical chops and a real rock-and-roll soul. His contribution takes everything up a notch.

There was an eight-minute scene in *Figaro*, toward the end of the first act, that had many elements that were, in and of themselves, "wrong." Actors Olek Krupa and Shizuko Hoshi brought to the scene their own rich cultural identities—but these clashed with Roger Downey's translation. The music was obviously wrong. It should have been Chekhovian violins, about yearning to go back to Moscow. But the music was full of angst, energy, a piano that was incessantly beating. Doug Stein and I had a long fight about the look of the set. It was four rooms instead of one, and it was thirty-five feet upstage. Then Steven Strawbridge put lights on it and Susan Hilferty put clothes on the actors, and the ideas of all those people fused into something special. The ideas weren't sympathetic to the text—they were their own statement, fighting the text for preeminence.

Unity is overrated. Defining a whole and making all its pieces correspond to that oneness can lead to a stifling politeness. I'd rather take each moment and make it burn, make that color very bright.

I remember trying to find an ending for *Figaro*. In the last scene, there is a great reconciliation between Figaro and Susanna, in the midst of a victory by what is left of the revolution. But then von Horváth ends with the sound of a window shattering, which, without going into detail, is a disruptive sound. We knew he wanted an edge to the end of the piece. So we had a reveal of soldiers on the border. At a moment of great joy we inserted an image of another power lurking behind. Five years earlier in my career, I might have ended the play at that point. But instead, I had Figaro and Susanna stop dancing when they saw the soldiers, and there was a moment of stillness. Then they started again dancing harder. It made the ending soar in a celebratory way, preserving the comic nature of the piece. It had both a challenge and a response in it. There were three very big mood swings in a period of thirty seconds, and the audience didn't know where it was going to end.

You brought the von Horváth play back from a trip you made to Germany.

Actually, I brought back many pieces, including some other von Horváth works which haven't been translated yet. I love *Figaro* because it is about revolution, change. It questions what real change is, what the motivations, possibilities, responsibilities are that accompany it.

It was exciting to "discover" a fifty-year-old play—although it was really new because it was written in another language, and every translation is a new play. But the next step was to make it affecting for 1986.

How faithful to the original was Roger Downey's translation?

What is meant by "a faithful translation"? Any play must be faithful to the moment when it's presented. If it's not, it has no value. Of course, in a translation one tries to retain the sensibility of the writer and what he was trying to do when he wrote the play, but in performance it must reflect these values vis-à-vis the living moment in the theatre.

Roger worked for six months on the text. He also responded to the performers. The second act is virtually an adaptation, coming as much from Downey, myself, Bart Sher [the dramaturg] and the actors as from von Horváth himself.

Why did you cast Figaro *multiracially?*

The play is about exile, and America is a land of exiles, people who left somewhere else. These performers seemed to understand that. They were able to inform the play, inform one another and teach me. Also, just the way the play sounded when Cuban, Polish, Japanese, Czech and Mexican voices delivered the text created a musical score that could not be duplicated.

Did you search for material in Germany because you couldn't find large-scale material from American playwrights?

I only read one out of every fifty-thousand plays written, so I don't know what "American playwrights" are writing. I'm often more interested in a text that can *serve* a theatrical event as opposed to a text that needs to *encompass* a theatrical event. The difference is that in the former, the writer doesn't necessarily have to carry all the burden. He can create just one element, a spine which others can flesh out.

315

That's similar to what the great commedia *writers created in their scenarios. But today, if producers find a work too sketchy, won't they pass over it?*

Then perhaps the writer has to take more responsibility for stimulating the collaborators, so he doesn't have to present his work solely on the basis of his text. I think real producing is about bringing such people together and gambling on the result.

Surely Shepard's plays also challenge through form?

The thing about Sam's text is the space *between* the text, the moments between the words. Recently I just don't allow the spaces so the work is denser. Productions are becoming a canvas on which other people can paint, can make substantial contributions, as opposed to Sam's language being the neon, the chief ingredient.

Sam is about *live* performance, ultimately. And that's one thing I've tried to preserve in my work. Okay, what makes for live performance? That throws down the gauntlet. Often in Shakespeare the text says, these two people are in love, and the actors say the words as if they're in love. But very rarely do you see lovers onstage, rarely do you see passion. So people fall back on the text. They say, "I'll use the text 'cause the text says I'm in love." It's a great cop-out. There's a difference when you *do it*—live. The Karamazov Brothers are very much about live performance. And when you see Pina Bausch's dance company, you say, "These people are live in this room and they're delivering the goods." They know why they're there and there's a joy to the work, an idea, an investment in the politics of the statement. I want that. The performers have to generate it among themselves. They have to know why they're there and they have to project that in the theatre. Whatever the investigation of a given piece might entail, the commitment to the search, the questions, problems and dead ends of that investigation must be aired in performance.

Then generally what are the basic qualities you're seeking in a performer?

I'm counting more and more on performers who can evoke ideas and thought in a theatre, not just emotional response. They've got to be able to connect those few dots I've given them—and sometimes there's a long space between the dots—so I need visceral performers who can exchange heat on a stage. And they have to keep changing it. That almost becomes the bottom line. In rehearsal, in performance, they have to keep moving.

To keep each other alive?

To keep themselves alive, to keep exhaling. The actor can serve himself as much as the production. He can wantonly, selfishly, covetously define what he's doing as long as he's expressing that onstage. Some people are uncomfortable with that.

So you create a framework in which actors can be comfortable taking risk?

Or uncomfortable sitting on ideas. I'm not too concerned with how an idea changes, as long as it keeps moving and it starts from some truth. You see, a statement and perhaps even a whole experience will change when you become interested in each of the million moments that the audience responds to. When you do that, the overall effect defines itself.

You first worked with Shepard about the time you founded the Bay Area Playwright's Festival in 1976. What was the purpose of the Festival?

I wanted to provide an opportunity for people to come together for a month to create some work on a small, friendly scale. The first three seasons were like that. Then it changed conceptually and got rather large and expensive. I didn't feel like being a producer on that level. I didn't need the financial pressure. So we turned it into more of a laboratory where we invited people, as opposed to scripts. We said, "Come and do whatever you want, and we'll try to give you some resources. It'll be summer in Marin County and we have a swimming pool."

Actually, we were linking the Off-Off Broadway of twenty years earlier with the contemporary theatre community in Northern California and people who were currently working on the East Coast. It became an interesting cross section of artists. It had a sense of tradition and movement at the same time. The most valuable experiences were the workshops where we got ten or eleven really fine young writers from across the country, and then in a scattershot way introduced them to some vital ideas of the theatre. For three days they'd work with performance artists like Christ Hardman and Laura Farabough, three days with playwrights such as Michael Weller, Sam Shepard, Len Jenkin and Maria Irene Fornes. It was an amazing and often contradictory introduction of ideas and a bombardment of thoughts about what theatre writing can be.

When Joe Chaikin did a workshop, it was a religious experience. Again, it was all about *live* performance. I saw him do *Tongues* and *Savage/Love* maybe eighty times. That role had a shamanistic quality. He played it at the New York Shakespeare Festival and then toured Europe. In that production, he was a leader, a guide. Using the most subtle manipulation of language, he decided where he would lead the audience at any given performance. Just by his phrasing, his breath, he could say to an audience, "No, tonight we don't want to laugh that much. We want a silence here to think about this." There would be give-and-take. He would consider where the audience wanted to go, but ultimately, he knew that he was in charge. Even knowing the piece so well, I was frequently shocked at the choices he made. Sometimes he would build upon what the audience was doing and top them in their responses, still leading them all the way. Other nights, he would make sharp left turns, take them down an alley toward an unknown end. With his amazing physical instrument, he could move an audience emotionally and intellectually.

What is extraordinary is that he is performing again following his almost fatal stroke. He can still control an audience.

Not only that, Joe has a whole new language. The way he uses words is its own poetry. Now we communicate more in shorthand. He'll say a word and it'll evoke ninety things and I'll know what he's talking about. We're comfortable with this and we get places faster. Joe has always taken conversation, language so seriously. Before his stroke, we'd be having a conversation and if the talk drifted off into something else or a joke, Joe would get adamant: "Are we going to discuss *this* now?" He wanted to know the purpose of the way we were using language at that moment. Discussion was not something to dabble in, but an explosion of thought.

Is Shepard similar to that?

There's a very little boy in him. There's a great excitement about what he writes. He's really tickled by his words. I remember watching the first production of *Fool for Love* in San Francisco. Sam and I were sitting together at the back of the house, behind the audience. There is a point at which the man says, "He's your date, huh? Well, I'm gonna make him a fig." This is the worst play on words that you can imagine, and Sam turned and smiled as if to say, "Yeah, I got away with that." He gets great pleasure in language.

How will you direct the new play, Struck Dumb, *that Jean-Claude van Itallie and Chaikin have written together for Chaikin to perform?*

It's meant to be a companion piece to *War in Heaven*, the forty-minute play that Sam wrote and that Joe's performed around the world. It's going to be interesting, because since his stroke Joe's had no actor memory. He can't remember things like "Now I do this," or "The next thing I do is cross here." He has to read everything. So Jean-Claude created a piece in which Joe follows written directions. He has to follow them because his brain's not doing that job for him anymore. There's no connection from night to night. Every time Joe reads the words, he's reading them virtually for the first time. That becomes a real challenge and it becomes integral to creating that piece. How do you get these words to Joe? How does he know where to read them and where next to look? Things get thrown at him in life and he has to respond to stimuli that to him seem like a bombardment. That's why he's living in San Francisco now, because New York is a bit hectic for him. So I want the stimuli to be the text—whether it comes in the form of video monitors, slides, pieces of paper that are thrown at him or banners flying across the stage that he has to read.

That's quite different from the way you collaborated with the Flying Kara-mazov Brothers and the other new vaudevillians in **The Comedy of Errors.** *How did you develop that production?*

Basically, it was whoever had the best idea at any given moment. A lot of the time it was just sitting around the table with twenty-one people and saying, "Okay, we have to have a sword fight. What are we going to use for weapons?" Somebody yells out, "Swordfish!" After a certain point I would move from referee to aesthetic arbitrator and then to dictator.

How did you structure the action?

We tried to incorporate the rhythm of the different performing skills—jug-gling, tap dancing, baton twirling, etc.—into the rhythm of each scene, bom-barding the stage with a cacophony of skills and then paring down the action to focus on a single idea, a single skill, one action.

Did you really do Shakespeare's **The Comedy of Errors** *or did you simply use the play as a point of departure?*

I felt we did the play. We tried to find the spirit in which the piece was originally created—a late-night vaudeville. It appeared that we manipulated the text because there were so many sight gags that are not in there, but it was ninety-five percent Shakespeare. We cut maybe one hundred lines, prin-cipally in the first scene. For the first six minutes of each act, as well as the last three minutes of each, there was no dialogue. These were musical inter-ludes that created the tone for the ensuing action or extended the mood of the acts into finales.

Everyone in the production was expected to have a range of performance skills.

We had a saxophone player, Mark Sackett, who could walk a slack rope and eat fire—very hard to understudy. The production in New York was a little grittier than the one in Chicago. We added Ethyl Eichelberger, Karla Burns, Derique McGee, Raz and Rosalinda Rojas and the improvisational nature of the piece grew. That drove the television people crazy when it was televised live.

After the *Comedy of Errors* production in Chicago, we did *The Three Moscowteers*, in which [Karamazov] Paul Magid decided he wanted to take the Dumas story and set it in Russia after the revolution. We transposed the triangle of Richelieu, the King and de Treville to Stalin, Lenin and Trotsky, who had a similar power relationship. At that time, in the Russian army there was a troupe of soldiers who did agit-prop theatre in support of the revolution. Extending this idea allowed the musketeers to be performers. So we created this vaudevillian approach to the Russian revolution. Paul principally wanted to show how this moment in history was a glorious wellspring of possibilities, both for artists—Meyerhold, Mayakovsky, Mandelstam, Rodchenko—and for the society as a whole.

It was also Paul's idea to do Stravinsky's *L'Histoire du Soldat* with the Karamazovs. We wanted music and images. He had written the outline and I brought in Len Jenkin and they evolved the piece together. Len took the idea of myth and folktale very seriously and Paul's view was more the fractured fairy tale approach. We did a workshop in May of 1986 and then opened at BAM in December. We had this wonderful Stravinsky score, thirty-five minutes of music, and they had to evolve a juggling score for each of the four jugglers, musically aligned with a different instrument. Each had to have a juggling move that corresponded exactly with a given quarter note, half note, rest or whatever. Even the notation seemed mystical to me. They had done musical juggling in their own work, but Stravinsky was far more complex and the score kept changing tempi, which created a greater degree of difficulty. Also, with the band playing, they often couldn't hear one another's catches, and they rely on hearing that sound.

Is the Karamazovs' sense of silliness, of craziness, becoming a part of what you do now? This is a big change from what we saw in **Buried Child.**

But *Buried Child* was silly. A character who brings in corn that doesn't exist is pretty silly. It's always interesting when things appear in places where they're not supposed to be. In Bangkok, I saw a monk smoking Camel straights and talking on a pay phone. And I thought, "Well, of course, this is what's interesting." When he's sitting in prayer in a Buddhist temple, that's not interesting. Things happening out of context make you take notice in life. That's also what's arresting in the theatre.

You travel quite a bit. How does it connect with your work?

Travel makes it all right to feel lost. It validates wandering around, relieved of obligation so the mind can just entertain itself. Outside of our culture all the rules change, the familiar and unfamiliar change places. The comfort zone becomes minuscule. You come into contact with a whole other sense of time and history in ways you can both feel and touch. There is a sense in some cultures of history as something that is alive, to be respected, to be lived with and built upon.

In this country, we elect a different government every four years that neither creates the "new dynamic" it claims it will nor builds upon the work and lessons of a history. We seem to be constructing a society on a junk heap of "new beginnings" without any real regard for anything before the last second and past the next minute. And plays like *Figaro Gets a Divorce, A Man's a Man* and *The Tempest* incorporate the idea of history as a way of doing things.

You incorporated a lot of the images you collected from Southeast Asia in your production of A Man's a Man at La Jolla.

Des McAnuff wanted me to do a comedy. Brecht seemed like a good investment for the summer, and I had always thought it was a funny play. It was my first collaboration with Doug Stein. I had just come back from Southeast Asia (we had done *In the Belly of the Beast* in Australia and I just kept going) and our work was fast and very intense and taken from postcards and notes that I had about images I had seen. I don't take photographs. We just tried to get all of the strong images on the stage. The show was literally up three months after I came back, so those images were all fresh in my mind. It was just wonderful chaos. And the whole thing seemed to work.

That production seems to have been a turning point in your work.

Well, it was working with Doug. We wanted to get Brecht out of the "poor theatre" category. We still wanted to "present" it but we didn't say, "Let's see how *raw* we can make Brecht." We wanted size to the images. The production was all about attempting to join some group or idea that was bigger than yourself. And you had to watch out because you might join the wrong group—it involved that whole idea of cults.

Is it sound or visual images that stimulate your imagination most?

Sometimes the idea for a visual statement comes to me based on something I've seen in the street or something I've read, which I then try to translate into a visual picture. Sometimes ideas come when I'm on an airplane with a Walkman in my ears. I'm not sure now that the aural is wed to the visual, except that music and sound inspire ideas about movement and, therefore, space.

A Man's a Man at La Jolla was followed in subsequent seasons by Figaro and then The Tempest. What was your concept for The Tempest?

I think the play takes on the history of islands from Manhattan to Bikini to the Caribbean. There's a certain element of rape about islands in general, enslavement and rape. Those are the two dominant words. The same thing that the people in the play do to one another, they do to the physical space. We played with a few physical ideas and then wound up with two separate settings: a motel and a kind of amphitheatre. The amphitheatre was filled with every kind of natural resource and at the end of the play, Prospero takes them all. So he may be going back without the magic, but he's no dummy.

I wanted to assault the viewer in order to create a kind of upheaval— a tempest (which means violation, interruption)—which required changing periods, putting music where perhaps it didn't belong. I also wanted to manipulate the audience because, ultimately, every scene is about the idea of manipulation and conquest. So I wanted to do that to the audience. The road block I ran into was only having access to the stage for five days prior to opening: I found I couldn't do it in five days. I needed to look at things much longer than that. So I wound up softening things, pulling back when things didn't work the first or second time. I cut the head off to save the beast. The operation was a success, but the patient died. Some of the ideas were never going to work the first few times we did them and might not have worked until we'd done them for three weeks.

How could there be some action that could work after three weeks that couldn't work right away?

Every idea is a part of something else, so while you're building a piece, maybe you have a dozen things that don't work. They can't be judged as not working by themselves. They can only be judged when everything is on its way to finding its rhythm. The piece ultimately creates itself, it responds to itself. The elements respond to each other. The audience responds to the elements. I need to be able to see it and respond to it, and it's very difficult to do that fast. An actor has three days to deal with the fact that while he's speaking, some signs are flashing in the audience's face reading "laugh" or "cry" or "applaud." And he has to deal with that, or the fact that a piece of music under his dialogue becomes louder than his dialogue. Those are difficult things for an actor. So what happened was that we changed direction and tried to make the play work as a linear story. The narrative became more dominant than the values I was trying to create in the beginning. And I think we got caught in the middle.

I'd always wanted to underscore an entire Shakespeare play, but everyone said that you couldn't do it. And then I saw Ariane Mnouchkine's *Richard II*, which was fully underscored very successfully. So I felt bad that I hadn't done it before I saw her do it. I thought that Paul Dresher, as a minimalist composer, could create music that would make a cradle for the language without detracting from it. I wound up cutting back when I probably should have had Paul write more and have gone even further with it. That would have taken another three or four weeks.

What does The Tempest *mean to you at this point in your life?*

One of the problems with the play for me is that I don't understand surrender, or why anybody gives something up. I think one surrenders only to accomplish something else. And also, I don't value anything to a degree that would prevent me from giving it up. When Prospero went off to retire, I didn't understand that. I thought he was going back to be a political person and a part of the real world. I don't know if that is any more noble than staying on the island. I still think that escape is underrated.

Do you specifically include period references in your work, through costuming *for instance?*

I don't understand "period pieces" per se, because one has to understand how people's *minds* worked in the periods in which they lived and how they related to ideas. It's an enormous leap in sensibility, and I don't think it's possible to know how a person's mind made connections in a certain period. Any text is really about stream of consciousness, and their brains created different images from ours. You can't understand what those images might have been from looking at a photograph. How can an actor go about using an idea unless it resonates out of his present-day experience?

I prefer the phrase, "period references." We did a high-tech production of *Julius Caesar* at the Alliance Theatre in Atlanta, and Mark William Morton designed a three-tiered factory set out of corrugated metal for the first act. Behind one sliding door there was a single Roman column, a vestige and a decided period reference. Susan Hilferty's costumes for *Figaro* started in Mozart's period and incorporated elements of the contemporary Central American military. The clothes enforced the idea of the unchanging nature of these power relationships.

What is the primary skill a director needs?

Having a specific idea about wanting to contribute something, following that idea and making it his own. It has to be his own. I don't care if the director is doing the one hundred eighty-third production of a Thornton Wilder or a Sam Shepard play, there's got to be something about it that he feels is his own and worthwhile. That's the only thing that defines a director: somebody who's doing his own work.

What is the next step in the evolution of Robert Woodruff's work?

I'm being pulled by various ideas and I'm trying to satisfy them all. My work has an edge to it, but I'm not sure where that came from. I can't force it. I've gone without forcing since I began. When I'm not working, I'm fed mostly by "metaphysical angst and existential nausea," which provide an enormous amount of fuel. The nice part about working in the theatre is that it makes you aware of everything going on around you. And when I'm not involved in something, there is no reason to look and so I turn inside.

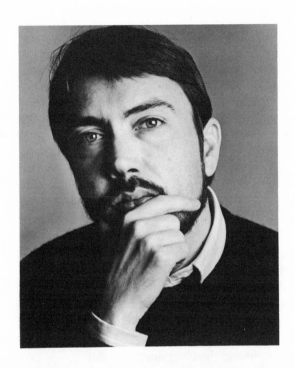

GARLAND WRIGHT

G arland Wright is the youngest of five artistic directors who have led Minneapolis's Guthrie Theater since its founding in 1963. At age thirty-nine, he was tapped by the Guthrie board to follow in the footsteps of Tyrone Guthrie, Michael Langham, Alvin Epstein and Liviu Ciulei.

In his formative years, Wright might have seemed an unlikely candidate to take over the direction of the Guthrie. By his own admission, he was more interested in new plays than the classics when he was an undergraduate in the theatre program at Southern Methodist University; and Wright's initial commercial success came as director of former SMU schoolmate Jack Heifner's *Vanities* in 1976. This play about the evolution of three cheerleaders from Texas became the longest-running play in Off-Broadway history. It was a cleverly conceptualized and staged production, but hardly gave an indication of Wright's full abilities—abilities that exactly ten years later, after directing at most of the country's major resident professional theatres, would make him ready for the rigors of running a major classical repertory theatre.

Three of those ten years spent directing around the country were, in fact, spent at the Guthrie. In 1980, Wright became the Guthrie's associate artistic director just as Romanian Liviu Ciulei was brought in to lead the organization. Because Ciulei was not native to the English language nor entirely familiar with American tradition, the Guthrie board thought it would be prudent to have an American director on staff. Wright had just completed his first guest production at the Guthrie and the board had been so impressed that they maneuvered him into the associate position. He was to remain there for three years and then resign, expecting never to return except as a guest director.

The range of works he has directed at the Guthrie during his tenures as associate and artistic director is rather remarkable: *Camille, Mary Stuart, Eli, Summer Vacation Madness, Candide, Guys and Dolls, The Importance of Being Earnest, Anything Goes, The Misanthrope, Richard III* and *The Piggy Bank*.

Meanwhile, his work at other theatres ranged from *The Imaginary Invalid, Happy End, Good Person of Setzuan* and *Undiscovered Country* at Washington's Arena Stage (where he was artistic associate 1985-86) to Sigourney Weaver and Christopher Durang's *Das Lusitania Songspiel* Off-Broadway, and James McLure's *Lone Star/Pvt. Wars* on Broadway.

Wright's earliest ambition was to be a painter, and his eye for composition, quality of light and the combination of elements is evident in his work. His productions characteristically show the dark underbelly of a play, compensated by an equally dark humor. He thinks that "odd take" humor may be a result of his growing up in Texas, where "everything just is funny. All of your aunts' names are funny, what you eat for dinner is funny, what you're driving is funny. Even funerals are funny."

At the Guthrie, Wright has undertaken two tasks that could provide a future guide for other American theatres: building a major acting ensemble dedicated to the classics, and providing the opportunity for young directors to test themselves by working in a laboratory environment that also serves to stretch and nourish the actors.

■　　■　　■

Your life in the theatre has taken its zigzag turns. When you joined American Shakespeare Theatre at Stratford, Connecticut, in 1970, was that your first job after graduating from Southern Methodist University?

Yes. A friend recommended me to Michael Kahn, who was artistic director. Michael thought I was good enough to be a journeyman actor. The first year, I carried Eva Le Gallienne's hat in *All's Well That Ends Well*, I was the Player Queen in *Hamlet* and the second blond wig from the right in *Othello*, which became my Broadway debut, carrying flags behind Moses Gunn.

But there was a little room in back of the Stratford stage called the TV room, presumably because it had housed a TV at some time or another. Michael had turned it into a place the company could use for whatever work we chose. And because we rehearsed most of the mainstage plays in the late winter and early spring and opened them in June, we had our days free for most of the summer. When creative people get together they tend to create projects spontaneously, and so it was at Stratford. Some of the actors wrote plays, others like myself wanted to direct, most just wanted to participate in some way. So we did these little original productions at midnight, virtually every week as I recall. And it began to grow into something.

Luckily, Michael got a grant from somewhere to hire two assistant directors the following year. He had noticed my directing in the TV room and apparently saw some hope for me, so I was lucky enough to get one of the positions. I stayed for another three years and had a great education as an assistant. In my final year there, I got to direct the student production of *Julius Caesar*.

Was Stratford your first serious encounter with the classics, or had your education at SMU prepared you for them?

I blush to say that my education *tried* to prepare me, but I wasn't very interested in the classics during my training. I was a bit of a renegade in school and more interested in new work or *odd* takes on established works. So Stratford was really my education in classical literature. Ironically, after that time everyone assumed I was a classical director. For three or four years after Stratford I couldn't get a job doing anything but Shakespeare. And then one day I did a play about some girls in Texas and for years I couldn't get a job doing anything except Texas plays. People want so desperately to categorize all of us.

Did the success of that Texas play, Vanities, *ultimately help you to get hired to direct the other things you wanted?*

Absolutely.

But before Vanities, *and after your stint at American Shakespeare Theatre, you co-founded Lion Theater Company in New York.*

Lion Theater Company was founded by a group of young actors from Stratford and their friends. Most of the original Lion company had been spear carriers there or friends of said spear carriers. It was a company, not unlike most young companies, based on a *need to work* more than upon an aesthetic.

Was your time with Lion the beginning of your working toward ensemble?

I had felt it at Stratford, but only in the TV room, where there was a real sensation of participation, creating together, celebrating our collaboration—and that magic feeling that *everyone's* work had consequence. Lion was very like that in the first year.

What was the work like at Lion?

Our first production was *The Tempest*, done in Levi's with twelve actors and nothing else. And it was a phenomenal thing. It was the *thing* itself. We were working out of a space on Nineteenth Street that's now Dance Theatre Workshop. We also did Len Jenkin's play *Kitty Hawk* and, believe it or not, a wildly successful *Gammer Gurton's Needle*.

The second year we moved up to Playwrights Horizons, their first space on Forty-second Street, which is now the Judith Anderson Theatre. But this was before the Anderson renovation. It had been a porno theatre and was a wreck. But that created a great sense of communal living—making the space, cleaning the bathrooms, running the box office, ushering and all of those romantic and boring things people talk about. In fact, those things do cement some central portion of the artist's soul to the work. Therefore, you can get a stronger *rush* from the work. In our case, I'm not sure that it made the work better, but it made the work *feel* better. It made it feel as if we were actually doing theatre. We weren't feeling that when we were going out and doing those free-lance things.

Later, when Playwrights Horizons moved next door to their present location, Lion leased the space, and while it was being renovated we used the vacant airlines terminal building on Forty-second Street and Tenth Avenue, which is now a video studio. The renovation took a year, and we had a long period with no performance plans, so we invested time in making a piece. It was called *K*, based on Kafka's *The Trial*. And that was the period when I located what ensemble really is and discovered that it's not only about the communal feeling but it's also about the work itself. In my memory, we rehearsed for about twelve weeks and found out how real ensemble collaboration truly affects the work.

What was the day-to-day regimen?

We did what I called "unison" exercises every day. The company would stand in front of mirrors for hours until each of them exactly duplicated a pose one of the actors had assumed. Each actor portrayed Joseph K at one point or other in the piece and they tried to learn each other's physicality. Then we'd read a chapter in the book, discuss it, talk about images that struck individuals in the company; and we talked about dreams and fears and the framework of paranoia. And over a period of time we began to actually deal with the text. By the time we had finished that piece, we had discovered what ensemble really meant and what the possibilities of it were. Unfortunately, we also discovered how much exploitation that required of the actors' time and energies without compensation. And let's remember, those were the old days when we were all working for free. We encountered how daunting it is to accomplish the mechanisms of starting an institution. None of us had the foggiest notion of what a board of directors was. We had no organizational structure, no real funding to make all these things possible.

We did Len Jenkin's *Life and Death of Jesse James* that year with Gene Nye directing. I followed it, after another long rehearsal period, with a piece based on some of Colette's writings, which I would have to say was merely beautiful—but without the same resonance of content that *K* had.

That is a theme of yours, that you go back to literary sources. You've done that four or five times with K, Candide, the Colette piece, Len Jenkin's New Jerusalem. What is it about exploring novels?

There are two answers to that. First, one wants to encounter work with vast ambition. A lot of new plays aren't being written with a large theatrical palette in mind. They are more likely to be "anthropological kinship studies" as Eric Overmyer puts it. It has to do with the depth of the material, and the luxury of exploring it. The writer of a novel can indulge in that exploration while a playwright sometimes doesn't give himself or herself the freedom to do that.

Second, I'm fascinated by the relationship of the reader to the book, by the release that happens when a reader encounters the novel. It's a very private one-on-one relationship—a relationship of the imagination. The reader is not absorbing anyone else's response to the work, as you do when you sit in a row of people in the theatre. It's like being in a private viewing room. There's this incredible intimacy in reading that fascinates me, that draws me to the novel. I'd like to find that relationship in the theatre. One of the ways to do that is to take all that detail away (the opposite of what the novelist does), so that an audience member singly has the option of having his or her own totally different perception of what's going on.

Isn't it dangerous to take away the detail and, therefore, the frame of reference for the audience?

I don't mean to imply that one wants to *obfuscate* to get a private experience with an individual audience member. Anytime you're ignoring the audience, it's my opinion that you're not only being pretentious but maybe slightly ignorant of what the theatre really is. On the other hand, if we are continually making an assumption that the audience has a dwindling ability to understand what we're about, then we're digging our own graves as well as theirs.

This is rather like Peter Sellars's comment that we've been trying to do theatre in this country for people who basically hate it in order to get more theatre-goers, while, at the same time, driving away those who really love good theatre.

I think that's true. If we're not willing to go through a period of losing a certain audience in order to generate another group of people who might be able to actually share this event with us, and who might be able to inhabit it in a way that nurtures it and, not only that, makes it *explosive*—as is true anytime there's a great audience in the face of a great event—then I think there's no real reason for making theatre. On the other hand, if you deny that you want people to like it, you're probably lying. My fears in that regard still play heavily in my work. And if that fear ever gets so great that I begin to accommodate it . . .

Or so great that you begin to consciously play against it, so that you deliberately disregard the audience.

Yes, either way, you can be your own worst enemy.

With the Lion company you did your exploration of Kafka, but it seems that you had really been thinking about that piece for a very long time prior to that.

Ah, Kafka and me. I've traced my interest back to when I was a junior in college. Dr. Bernard Hobgood, my teacher at SMU, gave me a copy of *The Trial*. He said, "I think you'll like this." I read it, totally illiterate about Kafka, and was astonished. You know, every once in a while, one has an epiphany where someone else is thinking your thoughts or vice versa. I had a deep response to the book. *The Trial* became a sort of obsession and was always in my head. It was about eight years later that one day I said at a Lion company meeting, just whimsically, "Listen, if twelve of you can sign up and have time to work, let's do it."

And in a way, my interest in Kafka also has to do with Texas. I suppose because of where I grew up, I'm fascinated by the surrealists. I tend to see that way. And Kafka, to me, captures the interior puzzlement, paranoia and absurdity of the terrain one can perhaps see inside one's own head but can't verbalize or doesn't want to admit.

I grew up in Midland, a desert town that you could see for a hundred miles before you got to it. There were few trees, little grass. It was totally fabricated by some companies who discovered a lot of oil there and built a little town for all of their executives. And it seemed totally wrong for its terrain. Because it couldn't be green, people painted their grass. And in the middle of this desert would be a forty-story building of marble; and a house that had a painted-green caliche gravel lawn along with a 1957 Chevy parked in front. This was reality to me. So Kafka's world wasn't bizarre to me—it was like my world. There's a great line in a Len Jenkin play where one of the characters says something like: "The trouble with this is, it's actually my life." A lot of people from Texas talk about the barrenness of the terrain, the lack of intellectual stimulation or whatever—which tends to make one retreat to the imagination. Yes, I think Texas prepared me well to embrace Kafka, even though most people assume his is a more urban kind of writing.

The setting for K *consisted of simple materials used in complex ways—lots of taut line with cloth panels moving across the line and then folding.*

The production was actually based on photographs from two books—one was Kafka's *Prague*, and another book was called *The Jewish Family Album*. And every single moment in the play was a literalization of a photograph. We spent hours in rehearsal in front of mirrors. It was deeply frustrating at the beginning, but after a while it became fascinating to the actors to try to inhabit some frozen moment that had actually been life, to get inside the photograph. We simply blacked—painted out—the background, and we left what was properly needed in the foreground. This is like my dreams, actually. Many of them have no backgrounds, only objects and people with no surround.

Similarly, just as the panels moved across lines on the stage in K, *your and John Arnone's design for* On the Verge, *produced for The Acting Company, had lines that were actually dots lighted from inside narrow columns, which moved across the stage horizontally and vertically and constantly redefined the playing areas.*

Our thinking for *On the Verge* started with blank maps, which are really just graph paper. I think the original set was going to be a white Plexiglas box that had black lines of longitude and latitude on the walls, ceiling and floor, and the squares would open up and do things. But then we began to get into the idea of maps and what those lines are. Of course they're charts, but if you get inside the abstraction of that, they're the lines we cross when we're traveling. And it began to be sort of interesting to think of them as that, instead of just as a blank map with no country on it yet. So we came up with these lines on the floor that the actors would have to go across each time they were making some emotional or geographical leap. Also, we began to realize that when the terrain is not defined, when the terrain isn't actually geograph-ical, the lines exist in three dimensions and they also move. They don't stay in the same place; you can't trust them. And I think that's when the lines began to take on a life of their own.

The fact of the lines being dotted was also visually interesting.

Well, I'm obsessed with dotted lines. They were also the major image in my production of *Candide*. I think they're the central image of the twentieth century—tear on the dotted line, sign on the dotted line. The dotted line has become to me the perfect visual metaphor for everything that's detachable and for everything that's *not* detachable. Dotted lines have been in many of my productions.

What is On the Verge *about?*

Somehow, I find *On the Verge* to be the equivalent of what we do in making theatre—you know, imagining and dreaming, and trying to discover, trying to understand a new reality without any equipment with which to do that. It's positive in its outlook, and that pleases me in this era of doom and gloom plays. Eric invested in the characters the spirit of exploring and discovering and testing and faith. I also admire Eric's stern test of the breakdown of language and the fact that someone is keeping tabs on that and recording it. *On the Verge* actually examines that as a metaphor for all kinds of other breakdowns: culture, ethics, courage.

Frequently, the most mystical vocabulary is that established between a director and a lighting designer. James Ingalls was your lighting designer for On the Verge. *What made you choose him for that project?*

It was Jim who actually suggested *me* to Eric as a director for the play. But as to choosing him as the lighting designer, I chose him first because he has a marvelously faceted way of seeing, and he's not afraid of the nonlogical light cue, which is really required in that play. Also, his ability to embrace that play's aesthetic was important—he's a great spirit and a lover of the play. It made a difference. And he's a great team player. It's important to match designers to make a true collaborative ensemble. He, John, and Ann Hould-Ward, the costume designer, along with Mac McKinney [music], made a great combination team and cheering section.

John Arnone has designed many productions with you. Why has this ongoing professional relationship lasted?

I have strong relationships with several designers, but I've worked with John for the longest time. We went to school together, worked together at Stratford and Lion, and for many years we have been developing a language. Now we actually speak the language, and when we talk we can know what the other one is seeing. I mean the words we share actually make pictures in our heads.

So the design process gives us pleasure. Also, he thinks ideas instead of sets. To me, that's the definition of a great designer.

When you use this language, do the images have texture?

Yeah. Plays are tangible. They're velvet or they're horsehair, noisy or quiet. When I was growing up, for example, certain words were colors to me. When I heard them, I'd think, "That's a yellow word," or "That's a purple one." Likewise, for me plays take on personalities, pictures, textures.

Do those personalities ever change?

Yes. Plays' personalities change as *we* change, as the world changes. Over the years, I've done *The Tempest* three times. Those productions barely relate to one another. My first production of *The Tempest* was my first professional job. The play was for me (I seem to recall) about making magic. My third production, at Arena Stage in 1984, was about how magic doesn't really solve the problem for the magician. I encountered the same sort of change in Molière's *The Misanthrope* between my first production at Seattle Rep in 1984 and the second at the Guthrie in 1987.

Why did you decide to do Misanthrope *again? Had your thinking significantly changed between the first and second productions?*

It became a very new and even more pungent play later—in a world experiencing an epidemic and a world where quackery of all kinds had become commonplace. The thinking had not changed violently in terms of its political base, its intellectual base. The manifestation of the production had changed. In reviewing the Seattle production I was a little puzzled by some of the choices I had made in that I found them a little lurid.

Lurid?

Well, for example: I did one scene in the bathtub that, when we were reviewing the text in the promptbook, I just couldn't remember why I had ever done that. It seemed so utterly wrong, and as I continued studying the scene I remembered that I thought putting Célimène in a bathtub was a literal, possibly puerile way to show vulnerability or sexuality. So I rethought the physical manifestation of those moments. I was intrigued to come back to it three years later and to encounter what these ideas mean in a new context. Do these ideas last? Do ideas transmogrify in a way that reveals growth? Is the world getting better so that these ideas do not have to be screamed so loudly anymore? Those things interest me.

The great classics always have their modern equivalents. What about the characters of the three Marquesses in Misanthrope *who seem to be nothing other than foppish? Where do we find them in today's society?*

There was a cover story in *New York* magazine about those people—the club people, who are only important because they are important. They're popular because they're popular. They're invited because they're invited. In both productions of *The Misanthrope*, but more extremely in the Guthrie production, I made them real party people whose power was totally social in a world that was really about power that is social. I felt that had to be put into a context that would show it to be a trivial activity in the world. That's why we moved the period of the play forward to the French Revolution to give it a context that heightened the sort of vapid activity and self-obsession of those people.

It has been commented that Célimène *was the real misanthrope in your production.*

It certainly wasn't by intention. Alceste contains the meaning of the play but Célimène is central. I truly think that she is the source of the play's problem, and she is the center of the play in that Alceste has to make his decisions based on this neurotic obsession he has with her. When I first read the play, I found it quite eerie that Alceste's last words to Célimène as he walks out of the room at the end of the play are the last time her name appears on the page. It doesn't say that Célimène exits or that the other characters exit and Célimène remains onstage. She literally vaporizes on the page. That was for me an incredibly powerful sensation I had from reading the play for evidence of vengeance. So clearly she was the source for a lot of Molière's anger.

You've announced that you're going to direct Hamlet *for the Guthrie's twenty-fifth season. Will that be your first* Hamlet?

Yeah. The production has not visualized itself for me yet. Some plays one ends up doing because of the visualization. For others, there's something in the play that nibbles at you. I'm finding more and more that the latter is true of my work—that I choose to do a play for reasons beyond what I think the production will be in the theatre, and then I go about trying to locate what the production will be. Earlier in my work it was very different. I'd get a strong visual sense or a fantastic casting idea. I'd be working from a far more concrete impulse. Now I think I choose plays because they nag me. They won't leave me alone so I finally give in. Then while I work on the play I discover what that nagging was, what it meant. Then I can usually locate the visual life.

Hamlet is a play I've always said I don't want to do. It has come up any number of times because it was the play that opened the Guthrie. And I kept saying, "No, I don't want to do it." Then someone asked, "Then should somebody else do it?" I said, "If anyone does *Hamlet* here it's going to be me, but I'm not going to do *Hamlet*." Then one day I woke up and said, "Oh, I get it. *Hamlet* is a play about me not wanting to direct *Hamlet*." The day I decided to do *Hamlet* was the day I began to locate what the interior of the play was from a personal place. It's a play about all those questions that every human being asks himself. So it started becoming personally important, which had never happened before. *Hamlet* had always been that sort of play you were supposed to do because it's the most difficult ever written (though I suspect *Lear* is the most difficult). And that never seemed reason enough for me to direct it. But now that I can feel a way in which my own thoughts and feelings can reverberate, I'm fascinated with it.

What was the fascinating aspect that made you want to direct Richard III at the Guthrie in 1988?

Many reasons emerged. One is that I believe it's a play about the art of acting, and most people know that's something that interests me. It's a play in which whoever "acts" best—gives the best performance—gets to be king, or to be close to the king. This play is also a virtual casebook on how people "adjust" their morality to a given circumstance and negotiate away their own ethics. It's also a play about deformity. Richard is definitely a metaphor for a type of moral or spiritual deformity that pervades power-hungry societies. Lives get misshapen when values are misplaced. Richard is not the only deformed character in the play. So there is a value to that as a symbol, as well as being a very real and valuable source for the actor who plays Richard to locate a lot of the psychological underpinnings of the character. His handicap and the fact that his mother hated him from birth give the actor a lot to work from. The historical research, as we all know by now, leads us to believe that Richard was not grotesquely deformed. I think, however, there is some signal in how violently everyone else in the play describes him—the amphibian imagery —a toad. So, clearly in Shakespeare's time he was seen as very deformed. That may have something to do with the fact that Shakespeare was writing for the Tudor queen, Elizabeth, whose grandfather Henry of Richmond was responsible for Richard's death.

In approaching the play, was there some example of a previous production that informed your approach?

I'd never seen a production of *Richard* other than the Olivier film. Olivier's film wasn't really the text, although there were two moments that were so indelible that one knows that at those points something important has to happen—the moment he turns on the young prince when he makes a bad joke about Richard's back and when he turns on Buckingham and makes him kneel down.

Did you make any obvious modern references in the production?

Yes. But they were not pointed up in any way. That's just information we used in our rehearsal period so that all my choices ended up being informed by those realities which we acknowledged. The production itself was sort of a travesty of a period production. We made several design choices that were incredibly strong and seemingly contradictory of one another. But when they were put together, they made a wonderfully theatrical message. The clothes were period but were exaggerated and were represented in "acid" colors, not earth tones and black. It had an air of cheap pageantry about it, which the play also contains. We largely used Bartok music, which was a contradiction to the period approach, and 1930s impressionist film lighting based on Eisenstein's *Ivan the Terrible*. The set was actually a bare stage. We ripped out everything to the back wall and painted it all gray, used about four pieces of furniture, one cloth drop and one sort of metal drop. There was a big nonperiod concrete column on one side of the stage that weeped blood throughout. If you take all of those elements separately, they don't make a lot of sense, but together they did. So the production had a feeling of modernism about it, but it didn't make any modern transposition.

Two of the Guthrie's greatest successes were your productions of the musicals Guys and Dolls *and* Anything Goes. *How do you direct musicals avoiding stock-version re-creations?*

I wouldn't describe it as a separate process. I touch musicals as I would nonmusical plays. To be honest though, I think music attached to words does narrow one's range of possibilities. That may inform why musicals are less violently reinterpreted than other works. I also know that most American musicals have at their center a desire to please. Few of them aspire to be profound, so perhaps directors don't feel they merit as much examination as, say, *Hamlet* would. I like to approach musicals with a sense of freedom. When I did *Anything Goes* I saw that it clearly was a victim of its own time with songs coming out of nowhere for no particular reason. I found that wonderfully cubist and freeing with no particular logic at all.

Generally, do you utilize improvisation in your rehearsals?

In my earlier work, improvisation was more common. I use it less and less recently, because I work with fewer and fewer actors who *will* improvise.

Now I tend to find ways of improvising that are "through the back door." Like what we did in rehearsing Labiche's *The Piggy Bank* at Arena Stage. We'd been working and working, and progress was slow. Finally I said, "For the next week you must do it in a French accent. I don't care how bad your accent is." Suddenly, we found out that arms came up off the bodies and that gestures were there. Bodies were in motion, actors found a new sort of "Gallic shrug" in the performances, when before they'd been pounding the text with American overemphasis.

When you directed The Good Person of Setzuan *at Arena Stage in Washington, you built a great sense of ensemble among the actors as well as giving a considerable amount of choice, even down to allowing them to choose their own costumes off the rack.*

The actors actually chose the set as well. And John Arnone was in rehearsals the whole time. It's the only time in my life when I began a rehearsal period (intentionally) by not *telling* a cast what the play would be about but asking *them* what it would be about.

But visually there was a sense of unity to the production. How was that achieved with so many different people coming at it?

That's the definition of rehearsing a play—arriving at a point where everyone understands the same idea and is trying to share that idea with the audience. If the ensemble isn't operating the play, then the play is operating them— and then you have a piece that will fall apart over time. So, for me, the process of rehearsing is getting everyone to understand what the production means at any given moment. In the case of *Good Person*, the actors themselves were defining the ideas and, therefore, they simply had a little more ownership of them. I became, in that case, largely a critic, a grain of sand in the oyster— a sort of irritant to them. And if there was ever a moment when their ideas crossed a boundary that I could not politically or aesthetically stand behind, we would have to talk this through at great length. Usually we could come to an agreement. In most rehearsal periods you're starting off with the idea and you spend four weeks, six weeks, nine weeks trying to convince everyone else to buy it. We simply changed the rules in that case, and I believe we arrived at a real place of consensus. We talked, we argued, we made decisions, compromises. We engaged in the very activity of politics, which seemed relevant given the play. We started with questions rather than the answers. Anytime one is doing a collaborative work and has *time to rethink*, then one doesn't have to enter with—to use the actor's word—"fascistic" directorial insistence.

337

All right. You started experimenting with this process of defining ensemble early in your directing. And this experimentation with some career zigzagging led you in 1980 to become the associate artistic director of The Guthrie Theater under the leadership of Liviu Ciulei. What was the lesson of that experience?

My experience at the Guthrie was incredibly valuable to me, and I have to say Liviu Ciulei is the person who made me choose whether to be a *director* or an *artist*. And I will treasure Liviu forever for having clearly laid that out for me. That was the choice I had to make—that everyone makes, I suppose, consciously or unconsciously. I had simply never before encountered it in such real terms. "Artist" is a word that floats in your head, but there's a point where you've got to come out of the closet and say, "That's what I intend to be," and saying that rules out a lot of things you might have done in your life. I suppose for me it meant defining the difference between "putting on plays" and participating in the world through theatre. When you make a choice like that, you have to make a commitment to treasure the work—the work above all else, the importance of the work, the seriousness of the work, hopefully the value of the work.

How did Liviu extract that decision from you?

By example, totally by example. It's in his very bones. The soul of an artist is there. He changed my life. And, paradoxically, being on the staff, I also discovered everything that can be rotten about running a theatre.

Does that have to do with an institution's bureaucratic structure?

It's so easy for a theatre to be about something that's totally off the subject. A theatre has to be about making theatre, and that's all it can be about. Hopefully, it also assumes that making theatre is an important, active way to share in the world's growth.

Is that the struggle you're going through at the Guthrie now?

The first task is to sort of rip the theatre all apart and readjust it so that it can see itself again. It's not only the Guthrie. I think this is true virtually everywhere. To remain vital, theatre must continually examine itself and reinvest itself. When I decided I was going to take the job, Zelda Fichandler said to me, "The only accurate thing I can say is that it will be relentlessly ongoing." And that's true. The wheels want to keep rolling in the preexisting ruts. You have to be able to smell when it's drifting back into old habits, or when it's getting too tired to start over again. If an institution can't be creative itself, can't be a work of art, then it can't really make works of art. So one has to keep it loosened as opposed to letting it turn into cement. This is hard work.

Nevertheless, in your first year as artistic director you directed three plays, a fairly busy schedule.

There were artistic objectives in that decision. I wanted to present the theme—to give a context for the variation. After that's clear to my audience, I'll probably only direct one or two plays a season.

What effect on your plans for developing the Guthrie resulted from your receiving the Winston Churchill Fellowship early in your career to observe at the Royal Shakespeare Company and Britain's National Theatre?

As it turns out, it was very valuable for me to watch two major classical repertory theatres at work. I'm not conscious that the experience has influenced me, but when my history is written, we'll probably see that it did have an effect.

I was there during what was called the box-set period when everything seemed to be done within three-wall settings. The RSC had a program where young directors moved from repertory theatres all over the country into associate positions there. That directors program, I believe, led to what we think of as the RSC style where they began to explore language and clarity and a sort of nondecorative approach to Shakespeare. Also, the theatre of cruelty workshop they conducted at that time probably resulted, by fall-out, in giving a sort of Brechtian approach to the work. What showed up most clearly was a very deep, probing intelligence. Many people called it cold as well. It usually had a strong political center, a strong social background and a pared-down visual style.

Ultimately, I think it was important for me to have been there at a time when so many great actors were collected in one place. It was very moving and something that I will always be envious of until I can say the same thing is true of my own company.

What is the long-range plan for your work at the Guthrie?

It's based on a very simple idea, that we'd like to have the finest company in the country. We don't see why one can't set that as a goal and actually put down some guidelines that will make it happen, as opposed to dreaming about the day when it might be possible. We're going into the first year of the plan. We just had the groundbreaking on the laboratory space, and we are going to be able to make good on our promise to raise the actors' salaries. On the planning side and on the side of our ability to make these things possible, we're making astonishing progress. And now I will learn if the acting community will respond. Certainly, in real terms, that has to do with money and with creating opportunities for actors that perhaps they can't encounter other places. That's what I want to invest my energies in, and I think that's what the Guthrie was founded upon—that there would be a classical repertory of plays and a company of actors doing them. If a company is what we want, then let's support that idea.

What's the logical first step toward achieving a company?

I think one just has to set unison goals. If the actors ever feel that the director has one set of goals, and they have another set, and that the theatre has yet a third set—I don't know how anything gets done under those circumstances. I don't mean creating a democracy. As a matter of fact, I think most actors who work with me would say I'm not democratic as a director. I will listen and I like their input, but I think most of them would agree that I tend to be fairly firm about where we are going. I simply feel that when we work, everyone has to know why we're doing it. When everyone knows, a lot of other problems fall away. But when the work has no ethical center—you know, you get together at a first rehearsal and you're sitting there and everyone says, "Well, this is going to be hilarious!" If that's the sum total of why you're doing something, then can't you guess that disappointment and disillusion are inevitable? But if you sit down and talk with people about the world and how art somehow has a need to manifest specific parts of larger arcs of human experience, and you can get everyone connected to that and then give them responsibility for that, then the work is going to be better for everyone. Again, no amount of everyone having a great time is going to make great theatre.

What are the central characteristics you look for in actors?

I look for actors who have a simple, centered place from which they work, a place that doesn't come burdened with a lot of cosmetic layers. And paradoxically, I look for actors who want to transform, actors who don't have to say, "Hamlet's a guy just like me," but who want to *find out* who Hamlet is and become/transform into that character. I like actors who have a skill with language, actors who understand that language is a complicated issue; who understand how imprecise one can be or how *precise* one can be; who appreciate words and who are interested in words. And I'm also interested in actors who have danger, a personal fire, in themselves. I like actors who are a little quirky, I think. And I prefer actors who are very smart. There is a cynical point of view, no doubt put forth by a director, that great actors should not be intellectual, that they should be children. I am appalled by such a point of view, both by its false assumption that thinking is noncreative and by its ludicrous presumption about a child's mind.

The world is different now than when you began as a director. The profession has changed. How should the young director prepare for that today?

Well, this is the sixty-four-thousand-dollar question, isn't it? When I entered the theatre, one went to New York because that's where the theatre was. The fact is, at that moment theatre was growing all over the country, but you still went to New York. That was the place to go if you wanted to take master classes in the life of the theatre. That's changed. That's not where a director will learn at the moment. But we never changed the rules, and so young directors are still going to New York. And they're wondering what the hell they're supposed to do there.

Given that, what should the young director try to do at first?

What he or she should probably do is assist for a long time to learn the good things to do and, just as important, what *not* to do, and to take or make every opportunity to work in the theatre—directing in dives, on the streets, whatever. This is sound advice, but it makes me sad. There should be a more effective system in place to receive these young talents.

Many of the new generation of directors are coming through conservatory training programs that didn't even exist until the advent of the resident theatre movement.

Through the training programs we're turning out a smarter group, intellectually grounded and better versed in theatre history and performance trends. I sense that. But the difference is that they graduate into a world where they're ready to work but they lack the practical "hands on" experience or the observational experience. They have too few opportunities to really direct in funky circumstances or otherwise. They haven't had the chance or are too impatient to sit there next to George Abbott or Moss Hart and watch them put together one of those big mothers, which is precisely the same activity as putting together a Shakespeare play in terms of the nuts and bolts. I learned everything I know about the theatre by watching. I don't mean my talent (it turns out that everything I had to give the theatre I already had before I watched), I mean the *how to* part of directing. You need to watch/assist to learn from good examples and from bad examples.

What ultimately led you to accept the job of artistic leader of the Guthrie?

I can chart maybe four or five arcs in my professional career where I instinctively made life choices as to what I would do in my work. In most artists'

341

lives, those are just instinctive moments and you smell them coming by knowing you're at sea. Never in a million years would I have known that I would say yes to the Guthrie.

What happened to change that?

I sensed a crack in the earth's crust through which I could see space and light, and possibility, and a moment in time that I knew wasn't ever going to come again. And I fell through it. And the moment after I said yes, I said, "Oops."

You were "on the verge." Maybe that's one of the reasons why you like that play.

That dotted line. Sometimes you step over it. Sometimes you tear off the other side or leave the coupon in the magazine.

What will occupy you for the next arc of your life?

It would be impossible to define what the next phase will be. But I know I really want to flex my muscles against the great plays. There are great classics I want to explore that I've avoided because of fear or hesitation and I'm entering the time in my life when I will undertake them. Because ultimately, what we do is confront our limitations at any given moment—when we can locate them, then we know what to work on.

I'm also entering a period where the health of the theatre itself concerns me. I know that concern will occupy some focus in my life. Let's not forget, I and my friends are part of the first generation whose life has wholly been in the nonprofit theatre. I've been trained by this movement.

DIRECTING
HISTORIES

The following are year-by-year listings through June 1988 of works staged by the directors interviewed in this book. Listings are as accurate as possible; the directors in some cases have not been able to fully reconstruct their production histories.

*Premier production   (A) American premiere   **Directed and acted

JoANNE AKALAITIS

1988

Green Card, JoAnne Akalaitis – Mark Taper Forum at the Joyce Theatre, New York

American Notes*, Len Jenkin – Public Theater, New York Shakespeare Festival, New York

1987

Leon and Lena (& Lenz), Georg Büchner – The Guthrie Theater, Minneapolis, MN

Help Wanted, Franz Xaver Kroetz – Mabou Mines/Theater for the New City, New York

1986

Green Card* – Mark Taper Forum, Los Angeles

The Balcony, Jean Genet – American Repertory Theatre, Cambridge, MA

1984

Endgame, Samuel Beckett – American Repertory Theatre

Through the Leaves, Franz Xaver
   Kroetz – Mabou Mines/Mark
   Taper Forum, Los Angeles

1983

Through the Leaves(A) – Interart
   Theatre/Mabou Mines, New York
Dead End Kids, JoAnne Akalaitis –
   Mabou Mines, New York
*The Photographer/Far from the
   Truth**, Philip Glass, Malasch,
   Richard Coe – Brooklyn Academy
   of Music

1982

Dead End Kids – Mabou Mines
Red and Blue*, Michael Hurson –
   New York Shakespeare Festival

1981

Request Concert(A), Franz Xaver
   Kroetz – Interart Theatre, New
   York

1980

Dead End Kids* – Mabou Mines
Dressed Like an Egg, adapted by
   JoAnne Akalaitis from Colette –
   Mabou Mines

1978

Southern Exposure*, JoAnne
   Akalaitis – Mabou Mines
Dressed Like an Egg* ** – Mabou
   Mines

1976

Cascando, adapted by JoAnne
   Akalaitis from Samuel Beckett –
   Mabou Mines

1975

Cascando – Mabou Mines

Born: Chicago, Illinois – 1937

ARVIN BROWN

*(productions at Long Wharf
Theatre, New Haven, Connecticut,
unless otherwise noted)*

1988

Ah, Wilderness!, Eugene O'Neill –
   O'Neill Theater Center, Waterford,
   CT; Yale Repertory Theatre, New
   Haven, CT; Neil Simon Theatre,
   New York
Regina, Marc Blitzstein
Don Giovanni, Mozart – Virginia
   Opera, Norfolk

1987

Our Town, Thornton Wilder
National Anthems, Dennis McIntyre
The Tender Land, Aaron Copland,
   Horace Everett
Self Defense*, Joe Cacaci – Long
   Wharf; Joyce Theatre, New York

1986

Turandot, Ferruccio Benvenuto
   Busoni – Connecticut Opera,
   Hartford
All My Sons, Arthur Miller – Long
   Wharf; Ford's Theatre,
   Washington, DC; John Golden
   Theatre, New York
Lost in the Stars, Kurt Weill, Maxwell
   Anderson
The Normal Heart, Larry Kramer

1985

The Normal Heart – Las Palmes
   Theatre, Los Angeles
Albert Herring, Benjamin Britten,
   Eric Crozier

Long Day's Journey into Night,
  Eugene O'Neill
Requiem for a Heavyweight, Rod
  Serling – Martin Beck Theatre,
  New York
A Day in the Death of Joe Egg, Peter
  Nichols – Longacre Theatre, New
  York

1984

Tobacco Road, adapted by Jack
  Kirkland from Erskine Caldwell
*Requiem for a Heavyweight**
American Buffalo, David Mamet –
  London

1983

American Buffalo – Booth Theatre,
  New York
The Cherry Orchard, Anton Chekhov
*Free and Clear**, Robert Anderson
A View from the Bridge, Arthur
  Miller – Ambassador Theatre,
  New York

1982

*Open Admissions** (full-length
  version), Shirley Lauro
Close Ties, Elizabeth Diggs – L. A.
  Public Theatre; The Entertainment
  Television Channel

1981

American Buffalo – Circle in the
  Square Downtown, New York
A View from the Bridge
A Day in the Death of Joe Egg
Close Ties
The Lion in Winter, James Goldman

1980

*Mary Barnes**, David Edgar
Watch on the Rhine, Lillian

Hellman – Long Wharf; John
  Golden Theatre, New York
American Buffalo
Who's Afraid of Virginia Woolf?,
  Edward Albee

1979

Privates on Parade(A), Peter Nichols,
  Dennis King
Strangers, Sherman Yellen – John
  Golden Theatre

1978

*I Sent a Letter to My Love**, Bernice
  Rubens
The Philadelphia Story, Philip Barry
*Two Brothers**, Conrad Bromberg
Amahl and the Night Visitors, Gian
  Carlo Menotti – NBC Television

1977

*The Lunch Girls**, Leigh Curran
Hobson's Choice, Harold Brighouse
*The Archbishop's Ceiling**, Arthur
  Miller – John F. Kennedy Center
  for the Performing Arts,
  Washington, DC

1976

The Autumn Garden, Lillian Hellman
Daarlin' Juno, Richard Maltby, Jr.,
  Marc Blitzstein, Geraldine
  Fitzerald – Long Wharf;
  Williamstown Theatre Festival
On the Inside(A), Thomas Murphy
On the Outside(A), Thomas Murphy,
  Noel O'Donaghue
A Memory of Two Mondays, Arthur
  Miller – Phoenix Theatre at the
  Playhouse Theatre, New York
27 Wagons Full of Cotton, Tennessee
  Williams – Phoenix Theatre at the
  Playhouse Theatre

Ah, Wilderness! – PBS *Theater in America*

1975

Artichoke*, Joanna Glass
You're Too Tall, But Come Back in Two Weeks*, Richard Venture
Ah, Wilderness! – Long Wharf; Circle in the Square Theatre, New York
Forget-Me-Not Lane, Peter Nichols – PBS *Theater in America*

1974

The National Health, Peter Nichols – Long Wharf; Circle in the Square Theatre
The Seagull, Anton Chekhov
The Widowing of Mrs. Holroyd, D.H. Lawrence – PBS *Theater in America*

1973

The Widowing Of Mrs. Holroyd(A)
Forget-Me-Not Lane(A) – Long Wharf; Mark Taper Forum, Los Angeles
Juno and the Paycock, Sean O'Casey
What Price Glory?, Lawrence Stallings, Maxwell Anderson
Cold Sweat*, I.C. Rappaport – Film
Saint Joan, George Bernard Shaw – Ahmanson Theatre, Los Angeles

1972

The Iceman Cometh, Eugene O'Neill
A Swan Song, Anton Chekhov

1971

You Can't Take It with You, Moss Hart, George S. Kaufman – Long Wharf; Edinburgh International Festival
Solitaire/Double Solitaire*, Robert Anderson – Long Wharf; John

Golden Theatre; Edinburgh International Festival
Long Day's Journey into Night – Promenade Theatre, New York

1970

Country People(A), Maxim Gorky
Hay Fever, Noel Coward – Helen Hayes Theatre, New York
Spoon River Anthology, Edgar Lee Masters
Yegor Bulichov(A), Maxim Gorky

Circa 1970s

Blessings, Murray Mednick – PBS *Visions*, Los Angeles
Wonderful Town, Betty Comden, Adolph Green, Leonard Bernstein – national tour

1969

A Whistle in the Dark, Thomas Murphy – Mercury Theatre, New York
Tango, Slawomir Mrozek
Ghosts, Henrik Ibsen
The Duchess of Malfi, John Webster
The Indian Wants the Bronx and *It's Called the Sugar Plum*, Israel Horovitz

1968

A Whistle in the Dark(A)
Don Juan in Hell, George Bernard Shaw
The Three Sisters, Anton Chekhov – Long Island Festival Repertory, Mineola, NY
The Indian Wants the Bronx – Wofford Palace, London

1967

The Rehearsal, Jean Anouilh

The Glass Menagerie, Tennessee
Williams
Misalliance, George Bernard Shaw

1966

The Three Sisters
Long Day's Journey into Night

Born: Los Angeles, California – 1940

RENÉ BUCH
*(productions at Repertorio
Español, Gramercy Arts Theatre,
New York, unless otherwise noted)*

1988

La Celestina, Fernando de Rojas
La Generala, A. Vires, Perrín &
Palacios

1987

El Burlador de Sevilla, Tirso de
Molina
La Zarzuela, Spanish music anthology
*Revoltillo**, Eduardo Machado
Don Juan Tenorio, José Zorrilla
La Dama Duende, Calderón – La
Compania de Alburquerque, NM

1986

*Habana: Antología Musical**, Cuban
music anthology, René Buch, Pablo
Zinger
*Las Damas Modernas de
Guanabacoa**, Eduardo Machado

1985

Acto Cultural, José Ignacio Cabrujas
Luisa Fernanda (Zarzuela), Federico
Moreno Torroba
Fuente Ovejuna, Calderón

1984

La Valija, Julio Mauricio

Café con Leche, Gloria González
*Habana**, René Buch, Pablo Zinger
Puerto Rico: Encanto y Canción, René
Buch, Pablo Zinger
Bodas de Sangre, Federico García
Lorca

1983

A Secreto Agravio, Secreta Venganza,
Calderón
Bailes de Cuenta y Cascabel, Pilar
Rioja dance concert

1982

Secret Injury, Secret Revenge,
Calderón – Milwaukee Repertory
Theater
Doña Rosita, La Soltera, Federico
García Lorca
El Día Que Me Quieras, José Ignacio
Cabrujas
Teoría y Juego del Duende, Pilar Rioja
dance concert
*Habana: Antología Musical**
The Cherry Orchard, Anton
Chekhov – CSC Repertory, New
York

1981

La Vida es Sueño, Calderón
Toda Desnudez Será Castigada,
Nelson Rodríguez
La Corte del Faraón (Zarzuela),
Vicente Lleo

1980

Los Fantastikos, Harvey Schmidt,
Tom Jones
The Glass Menagerie, Tennessee
Williams
La Celestina

1979

Un Hombre Sincero: José Martí

DIRECTING HISTORIES

Romeo y Julieta, William Shakespeare
La Moza de Ayacucho, Francisco
  Cuevas Cancino
La Casa de Bernarda Alba, Federico
  García Lorca

1978

Bodas de Sangre
Los Japoneses No Esperan, Ricardo
  Talesnik
La Revolución, Isaac Chocrón

1977

La Dama Duende
La Decente, Miguel Mihura
El Censo, Emilio Carballido
Te Juro Juana Que Tengo Ganas,
  Emilio Carballido

1976

Dona Rosita, La Soltera
La Fiaca, Ricardo Talesnik
La Celestina – CSC Repertory

1975

La Malquerida, Jacinto Benavente
Los Soles Truncos, René Márquez

1974

La Celestina
O Casi El Alma, Luis Rafael Sánchez
O.K., Isaac Chocrón
Teoria y Juego del Duende

1973

Un Hombre Sincero: José Martí
Bodas de Sangre
Esta Noche Juntos, Amándonos Tanto,
  Maruxa Villalta
La Valija, Julio Mauricio

1972

Don Juan Tenorio

Quien Le Teme a Virginia Woolf?,
  Edward Albee

1971

Yerma, Federico García Lorca –
  Greenwich Mews Theatre, New
  York
La Vida es Sueño, Calderón –
  Greenwich Mews Theatre

1970

Doña Rosita, La Soltera – Village
  South Theatre, New York
A Media Luz, Los Tres, Miguel
  Mihura – Lucretia Bori Theatre,
  New York

1969

Antigona, Jean Anouilh
Las Pericas, Nicholas Dorr – Theatre
  East, New York

1968

La Dama Duende – Greenwich Mews
  Theatre

1958

Private Lives, Noel Coward – Cape
  May Playhouse, NJ
A Design for Shadows, René Buch –
  The Heights Players, Brooklyn

1957

Cheri, Colette – Cape May Playhouse
Peg o' My Heart, J. Hartley
  Manners – Cape May Playhouse
27 Wagons Full of Cotton, Tennessee
  Williams – Cape May Playhouse
Suddenly Last Summer, Tennessee
  Williams – Cape May Playhouse
*Six Characters in Search of an
  Author*, Luigi Pirandello – The
  Heights Players

1956

Antigone, Jean Anouilh – The Heights
Players

1955

Euridice, Jean Anouilh – The Heights
Players

1954

Tonight We Improvise, Luigi
Pirandello – The Heights Players
*An Evening in Spain's Golden Age
Theatre* – Lope de Vega, Rojas,
Calderón, Tirso de Molina, etc. –
The Heights Players
As You Like It, William Shakespeare –
The Heights Players
Doña Rosita, the Spinster – The
Heights Players

1954

The Human Voice, Jean Cocteau –
The Heights Players

1950

Los Intereses Creados, Benavente –
Pro Arte, Cuba

**Born: Santiago de Cuba, Cuba –
1925**

MARTHA CLARKE

1988

*Miracolo d'Amore**, Martha Clarke,
Richard Peaslee – Spoleto
Festival, Charleston, SC; New
York Shakespeare Festival, New
York
Vienna: Lusthaus, Martha Clarke,
Richard Peaslee, Charles L. Mee,
Jr. – European Tour

The Garden of Earthly Delights,
Martha Clarke, Richard Peaslee,
Eugene Friesen, Bill Ruyle,
Steven Silverstein – Warner
Theatre, Washington, DC

1987

*The Hunger Artist**, Martha Clarke,
Richard Peaslee, Richard
Greenberg – Music-Theatre
Group, St. Clements Church, New
York
The Garden of Earthly Delights –
Israel Festival, Jerusalem; Minetta
Lane Theatre, New York; World
Theatre, St. Paul, MN; Seattle
Repertory Theatre

1986

*Vienna: Lusthaus**, – Music-Theatre
Group, St. Clements Church; New
York Shakespeare Festival; John F.
Kennedy Center for the
Performing Arts, Washington, DC
The Garden of Earthly Delights –
International Theatre Festival,
Baltimore

1985

*Fromage Dangeruese**, (precursor to
Vienna: Lusthaus) – Music-
Theatre Group/Lenox Arts Center,
Stockbridge, MA
The Garden of Earthly Delights –
Madrid, Vailladolid and Vigo,
Spain; American Dance Festival,
Durham, NC; American Repertory
Theatre, Cambridge, MA; James
A. Doolittle Theater, Los Angeles

1984

*The Garden of Earthly Delights** –
Music-Theatre Group, St.
Clements Church

1982

Metamorphosis in Miniature*, Martha Clarke, Jeff Wanshel – Music-Theatre Group, Cubiculo Theatre, New York

1980

Elizabeth Dead*, George W.S. Trow, Robert Dennis – Music-Theatre Group, Cubiculo Theatre

1979

Cabbages* and *Dr. Kheal*, Maria Irene Fornes – Music-Theatre Group/Lenox Arts Center, Stockbridge, MA

Born: Baltimore, Maryland – 1944

GORDON DAVIDSON
(productions at Mark Taper Forum, Los Angeles, unless otherwise noted)

1988

A Midsummer Night's Dream, Benjamin Britten – Los Angeles Music Center Opera Theatre

1986

Ghetto(A), Joshua Sobol
The Real Thing, Tom Stoppard
Terra Nova, Ted Tally – Darts Festival, Japan

1985

Harriet: The Woman Called Moses* – Virginia Opera, Norfolk

1984

Traveler in the Dark, Marsha Norman
The Hands of Its Enemy*, Mark Medoff

The Lady and the Clarinet, Michael Cristofer – Lucille Lortel Theatre, New York

1983

The Lady and the Clarinet – Long Wharf Theatre, New Haven

1982

Tales from Hollywood*, Christopher Hampton
Black Angel, Michael Cristofer – Circle Repertory Company, New York
Children of a Lesser God, Mark Medoff – Westport Country Playhouse, CT

1980

The Lady and the Clarinet*

1979

Children of a Lesser God* – Mark Taper Forum; Longacre Theatre, New York
Terra Nova
Who's Happy Now?, Oliver Hailey – PBS *Theater in America*
It's the Willingness, Marsha Norman – PBS *Visions*

1978

Black Angel*
Getting Out, Marsha Norman

1977

Savages, Christopher Hampton – Hudson Guild Theatre, New York
The Shadow Box, Michael Cristofer – Long Wharf Theatre; Morosco Theatre, New York

1976

And Where She Stops Nobody Knows,
  Oliver Hailey
Otello, Verdi – Israel Philharmonic

1975

The Shadow Box*

1974

Savages(A)
Hamlet, William Shakespeare

1973

Mass, Leonard Bernstein

1972

Mass – Metropolitan Opera House,
  New York
Henry IV, Part 1, William
  Shakespeare

1971

Murderous Angels, Conor Cruise
  O'Brien – Playhouse Theatre,
  New York
The Trial of the Catonsville Nine,
  Daniel Berrigan – The Pheonix
  Theatre, Good Shepherd-Faith
  Church, New York; Lyceum
  Theatre, New York; Mark Taper
  Forum; feature film
Mass* – John F. Kennedy Center for
  the Performing Arts, Washington,
  DC

1970

The Trial of the Catonsville Nine*
Beatrice and Benedict, Berlioz – Los
  Angeles Philharmonic
Rosebloom*, Harvey Perr
Murderous Angels*

1969

*In the Matter of J. Robert
  Oppenheimer*, – Heinar
  Kipphardt – Repertory Theater of
  Lincoln Center, New York; Mark
  Taper Forum

1968

*In the Matter of J. Robert
  Oppenheimer**

1967

Who's Happy Now?
The Devils, John Whiting

1966

Candide, Leonard Bernstein, Lillian
  Hellman, Richard Wilbur, John
  Latouche, Dorothy Parker – The
  Theatre Group, Schoenberg Hall,
  University of California, Los
  Angeles
La Boheme, Puccini – Corpus Christi
  Symphony
Così fan tutte, Mozart – Corpus
  Christi Symphony

1965

The Deputy, Rolf Hochhuth – The
  Theatre Group, Schoenberg Hall,
  University of California, Los
  Angeles, National tour

1963

Carmen, Bizet – Corpus Christi
  Symphony

1959

The Barrier, Langston Hughes, Jan
  Meyerowitz – Columbia
  University, New York

Born: Brooklyn, New York – 1933

ROBERT FALLS
(productions at Wisdom Bridge Theatre, Chicago, unless otherwise noted)

1988

Pal Joey, Richard Rodgers, Lorenz Hart, John O'Hara – Goodman Theatre, Chicago

Landscape of the Body, John Guare – Goodman Theatre

1987

Road(A), Jim Cartwright – Remains Theatre, Chicago

The Tempest, William Shakespeare – Goodman Theatre

Galileo, Bertolt Brecht – Goodman Theatre

1986

Orchards*, seven stories adapted from Chekhov by Maria Irene Fornes, Spalding Gray, John Guare, David Mamet, Wendy Wasserstein, Michael Weller, Samm-Art Williams – The Acting Company, national tour; Lucille Lortel Theatre, New York

1985

In the Belly of the Beast, adapted by Adrian Hall from Jack Henry Abbott – Tron Theatre, Glasgow, Scotland; Lyric Hammersmith Studio, London; Ivanhoe Theatre, Chicago

Hamlet, William Shakespeare

1984

Terra Nova, Ted Tally

Careless Love, John Olive

Life and Limb*, Keith Reddin

1983

Losing It, Jon Klein

1982

We Won't Pay! We Won't Pay!, Dario Fo

Sister Mary Ignatius Explains It All for You and *The Actor's Nightmare*, Christopher Durang

A Streetcar Named Desire, Tennessee Williams

1981

Standing on My Knees*, John Olive

Mother Courage and Her Children, Bertolt Brecht

A Sorrow Beyond Dreams, Peter Handke – St. Nicholas Theatre, Chicago

Bent, Martin Sherman

1980 and 1981

Midwest Playwrights' Lab, Minneapolis, MN: *Cassandra*, Kate Franks; *Clothes Conscious*, Nancy Beckett; *Basement*, Zan Skolnick; *Cisterns*, Julie Jensen; *The Bozo File*, David Levy; *The Last Prostitute*, William Borden; *Phillip and Felicity*, Paul D'Andrea; *Standing on My Knees*, John Olive

1980

Yentl, Isaac Bashevis Singer, Leah Napolin

Getting Out, Marsha Norman

The Importance of Being Earnest, Oscar Wilde

1979

Wings, Arthur Kopit

*Bagtime**, Alan Rosen, Louis Rosen, Thom Bishop (based on newspaper columns of Bob Greene, Paul Galloway) – Wisdom Bridge/Drury Lane Water Tower Theatre, Chicago

Curse of the Starving Class, Sam Shepard – Goodman Theatre, Stage 2, Chicago

Tartuffe, Molière (co-directed with Michael Maggio)

1978

The Runner Stumbles, Milan Stitt

Happy End, Bertolt Brecht, Kurt Weill – Athenaeum Theatre, Chicago

Othello, William Shakespeare – Oak Park Shakespeare Festival, IL

*Fits and Starts**, Grace McKeaney – Evanston Theatre Company (Northlight Theatre), Evanston, IL

The Idiots Karamazov, Albert Innaurato, Chistopher Durang

1977

Ladyhouse Blues, Kevin O'Morrison

The Tempest, William Shakespeare – Court Theatre, University of Chicago

Of Mice and Men, John Steinbeck

1976

The Wax Museum, John Hawkes – Direct Theatre, New York

Moonchildren, Michael Weller – St. Nicholas Theatre, Chicago

Born: Springfield, Illinois – 1954

ZELDA FICHANDLER
(nee Diamond)
(productions at Arena Stage, Washington, DC, unless otherwise noted)

1988

Enrico IV, Luigi Pirandello (co-directed with Mel Shapiro)

1987

The Crucible, Arthur Miller – Arena Stage; Israel Festival, Jerusalem

1984

The Three Sisters, Anton Chekhov

1983

Screenplay, Istvan Orkeny

1982

A Delicate Balance, Edward Albee

1980

After the Fall, Arthur Miller – Hong Kong Arts Festival

1979

After the Fall

1978

Duck Hunting, Alexander Vampilov

1976

Death of a Salesman, Arthur Miller

1975

An Enemy of the People, Henrik Ibsen

The Ascent of Mount Fuji, Chingiz Aitmatov, Kaltai Mukhamedzhanov

DIRECTING HISTORIES

1974

Death of a Salesman

1973

Inherit the Wind, Jerome Lawrence, Robert E. Lee – Hartke Theatre, Washington, DC; Pushkin Theatre, Leningrad; Arena Stage

1973

A Public Prosecutor Is Sick of It All, Max Frisch

1969

Edith Stein, Arthur Giron

1968

Six Characters in Search of an Author, Luigi Pirandello

1966

The Three Sisters

1965

The Skin of Our Teeth, Thornton Wilder

1964

Enrico IV

1963

The Devils, John Whiting
Twelve Angry Men, Reginald Rose

1962

Once in a Lifetime, Moss Hart, George S. Kaufman

1961

Silent Night, Lonely Night, Robert Anderson
Six Characters in Search of an Author

1959

The Lady's Not for Burning, Christopher Fry

1958

The Hollow, Agatha Christie
Romeo and Juliet, William Shakespeare
The Browning Version, Terence Rattigan

1957

Answered the Flute, Sam Robins
Witness for the Prosecution, Agatha Christie

1956

Dream Girl, Elmer Rice

1955

The Mousetrap, Agatha Christie
The World of Sholom Aleichem—A Tale of Chelm, Bontche Schweig, the High School, Arnold Perl

1954

Golden Boy, Clifford Odets
Room Service, John Murray, Allen Boretz
Blithe Spirit, Noel Coward

1953

A Phoenix Too Frequent, Christopher Fry
Boy Meets Girl, Bella and Sam Spewack

1952

The Country Wife, William Wycherley
Tonight at 8:30—Fumed Oak, Ways and Means, Still Life, Noel Coward
The Importance of Being Earnest, Oscar Wilde
Twelfth Night, William Shakespeare

1951

Ladder to the Moon, Holmes
    Alexander
The Importance of Being Earnest
Twelfth Night, William Shakespeare
The Inspector General, Nikolai Gogol
The Adding Machine, Elmer Rice

1950

The Playboy of the Western World,
    John Millington Synge
Pygmalion, George Bernard Shaw
The Firebrand, Edwin Justus Mayer

Born: Boston, Massachusetts – 1924

RICHARD FOREMAN
*(productions by Ontological-
Hysteric Theater, New York,
unless otherwise noted)*

1988

*The Fall of the House of Usher**,
    adapted by Arthur Yorinks, Philip
    Glass from Edgar Allan Poe –
    American Repertory Theatre,
    Cambridge, MA

1987

*Symphony of Rats**, Richard
    Foreman – Ontological-Hysteric
    Theater/The Wooster Group, The
    Performing Garage, New York
*End of the World (with Symposium to
    Follow)*, Arthur Kopit – American
    Repertory Theatre
*Film Is Evil, Radio Is Good**, Richard
    Foreman – Ontological-Hysteric
    Theater/New York University, New
    York

1986

*The Cure**, Richard Foreman –

Ontological-Hysteric Theater, The
    Performing Garage, New York
Largo Desolato, Vaclav Havel –
    Public Theater, New York
    Shakespeare Festival, New York
*Africanis Instructus**, Richard
    Foreman – Music-Theatre Group,
    St. Clements Church, New York

1985

*The Birth of the Poet**, Kathy Acker,
    Peter Gordon – Brooklyn
    Academy of Music
*Miss Universal Happiness**, Richard
    Foreman – Ontological-Hysteric
    Theater/The Wooster Group, The
    Performing Garage
*Ma Mort, Ma Vie, De Pier Paolo
    Pasolini**, Kathy Acker – Théâtre
    de la Bastille, Paris, following
    European tour

1984

The Golem, H. Leivick – Delacorte
    Theater, New York Shakespeare
    Festival
Dr. Selavy's Magic Theater, Richard
    Foreman, Stanley Silverman –
    Music-Theatre Group, St.
    Clements Church, New York

1983

*La Robe de Chambre de Georges
    Bataille**, Richard Foreman –
    Théâtre de Gennevilliers, Paris
*Egyptology (My Head Was a
    Sledgehammer)**, Richard
    Foreman – Public Theater, New
    York Shakespeare Festival
Die Fledermaus, Johann Strauss –
    Paris Opera

1982

Dr. Faustus Lights the Lights,

Gertrude Stein – Festival d'Automne, Paris

Don Juan, Molière – Delacorte Theater, New York Shakespeare Festival

Three Acts of Recognition, Botho Strauss – Public Theater, New York Shakespeare Festival

1981

Cafe Amerique*, Richard Foreman – European tour

Don Juan, Molière – The Guthrie Theater, Minneapolis, MN

Penguin Touquet*, Richard Foreman – Public Theater, New York Shakespeare Festival/ Ontological-Hysteric Theater

1980

Madame Adare*, Richard Foreman, Stanley Silverman – New York City Opera

Luogo & Bersaglio*, Richard Foreman – Teatro Piramide, Rome; CRT, Milan; Cabaret Voltaire, Torino

1979

Madness and Tranquility (My Head Was a Sledgehammer)*, Richard Foreman – workshop, New York

1978

Stages*, Stuart Ostrow – Belasco Theatre, New York

Strong Medicine*, Richard Foreman – film

1977

Blvd. de Paris: (I've Got the Shakes)*, Richard Foreman

Book of Splendors: Part II (Book of Levers) Action at a Distance*, Richard Foreman

City Archives*, Richard Foreman – video/Walker Art Center, Minneapolis

1976

The Threepenny Opera, Bertolt Brecht, Kurt Weill – Vivian Beaumont Theater/ Delacorte Theater, New York Shakespeare Festival

Livres des Splendeurs, Richard Foreman

Rhoda in Potatoland (Her Fall-Starts)*, Richard Foreman

1975

Pandering to the Masses: A Misrepresentation*, Richard Foreman

Out of the Body Travel*, Richard Foreman – video/American Dance Festival, Storrs, CT

1974

Pain(T) and Vertical Mobility (Sophia = [Wisdom]: Part 4)*, Richard Foreman

Hotel for Criminals*, Richard Foreman, Stanley Silverman – Music-Theatre Group/Lenox Arts Center, Stockbridge, MA

1973

Classical Therapy or a Week Under the Influence . . .*, Richard Foreman

Particle Theory*, Richard Foreman

Honor*, Richard Foreman

Sophia=(Wisdom) Part 3: The Cliffs*, Richard Foreman

1972

Evidence*, Richard Foreman
Dr. Selavy's Magic Theater* – Music-
Theatre Laboratory/Lenox Arts
Center; Sheridan Square
Playhouse, New York
*HcOhTiEnLa (or) Hotel China: Parts 1
& 2**, Richard Foreman

1971

*Total Recall (Sophia = [Wisdom]:
Part 2)**, Richard Foreman
*Dream Tantras for Western
Massachusetts**, Richard Foreman,
Stanley Silverman – Lenox Arts
Center, Stockbridge, MA

1970

Real Magic in New York*, Richard
Foreman

1969

Ida-Eyed*, Richard Foreman

1968

Elephant Steps*, Richard Foreman,
Stanley Silverman – Berkshire
Music Festival
Angelface*, Richard Foreman

Born: New York, New York – 1937

ADRIAN HALL
*(productions at Trinity Repertory
Company, Providence, RI, unless
otherwise noted)*

1988

Mensch Meier, Franz Xaver Kroetz

1987

A Lie of the Mind, Sam Shepard –
Dallas Theater Center
The Tempest, William Shakespeare –
Dallas Theater Center
All the King's Men, Robert Penn
Warren

1986

Kith and Kin, Oliver Hailey
All the King's Men* – Dallas Theater
Center
The Visit, Friedrich Dürrenmatt
The Country Girl, Clifford Odets
The Marriage of Bette and Boo,
Christopher Durang – Dallas
Theater Center

1985

The Marriage of Bette and Boo
Good, C. P. Taylor – Dallas Theater
Center
Passion Play, Peter Nichols – Dallas
Theater Center

1984

Passion Play
A Christmas Carol, adapted by Adrian
Hall, Richard Cumming from
Charles Dickens – Dallas Theater
Center
Jonestown Express*, James Reston, Jr.

1983

The Wild Duck, Henrik Ibsen –
Dallas Theater Center
Galileo, Bertolt Brecht – Dallas
Theater Center
In the Belly of the Beast*, adapted by
Adrian Hall from Jack Henry
Abbott
The Tempest

DIRECTING HISTORIES

1982

*The Web**, Martha Boesing
The Hothouse(A), Harold Pinter –
Trinity; Playhouse Theatre, New
York
Dead Souls, Nikolai Gogol

1981

A Christmas Carol
Of Mice and Men, John Steinbeck
*The Whales of August**, David A.
Berry
The Journey of the Fifth Horse,
Ronald Ribman – American
Repertory Theatre, Cambridge,
MA

1980

Inherit the Wind, Jerome Lawrence,
Robert E. Lee
Buried Child, Sam Shepard
Edith Wharton Biography –
Television

1979

The Night of the Iguana, Tennessee
Williams
Buried Child – Yale Repertory
Theatre
House of Mirth, adapted by Adrian
Hall, Richard Cumming from
Edith Wharton – PBS Television

1978

*Uncle Tom's Cabin: A History**,
Adrian Hall, Richard Cumming
*Seduced**, Sam Shepard

1977

A Christmas Carol, Charles Dickens
An Enemy of the People, Henrik
Ibsen – The Guthrie Theater,
Minneapolis, MN
Rosmersholm, Henrik Ibsen

Ethan Frome, adapted by Owen &
Donald Davis from Edith Wharton
King Lear, William Shakespeare

1976

Of Mice and Men
Seven Keys to Baldpate, George M.
Cohan
*Eustace Chisholm and the Works**,
adapted Adrian Hall, Richard
Cumming from James Purdy
The Little Foxes, Lillian Hellman
Life Among the Lowly, Adrian Hall,
Richard Cumming – PBS *Visions*
Television

1975

Another Part of the Forest, Lillian
Hellman
*Cathedral of Ice**, James Schevill
Seven Keys to Baldpate, George M.
Cohan
Peer Gynt, Henrik Ibsen – Missouri
Repertory Theatre, Kansas City

1974

Peer Gynt
Well Hung(A), Robert Lord
A Man for all Seasons, Robert Bolt
*Aimee**, William Goyen, Worth
Gardner
Feasting with Panthers, Adrian Hall,
Richard Cumming – PBS *Theater
in America*

1973

Brother to Dragons, Robert Penn
Warren
*Feasting with Panthers**, Adrian Hall,
Richard Cumming
School for Wives, Molière

1972

The Royal Hunt of the Sun, Peter
	Shaffer
School for Wives
*Down by the River Where Waterlilies
	Are Disfigured Every Day**, Julie
	Bovasso

1971

Troilus and Cressida, William
	Shakespeare
Child's Play, Robert Marasco
The Threepenny Opera, Bertolt
	Brecht, Kurt Weill
*The Good and Bad Times of Cady
	Francis McCullum and Friends**,
	Portia Bohn

1970

The Taming of the Shrew, William
	Shakespeare
Son of Man and the Family*, Timothy
	Taylor, Adrian Hall
Lovecraft's Follies*, James Schevill
The Skin of Our Teeth, Thornton
	Wilder
Wilson in the Promised Land, Roland
	Van Zandt – Trinity; ANTA
	Theatre, New York

1969

House of Breath and *Black/White**,
	William Goyen
The Old Glory, Robert Lowell
Exiles, James Joyce
Billy Budd*, Herman Melville
The Homecoming, Harold Pinter

1968

Macbeth, William Shakespeare
Brother to Dragons* – Trinity; the
	Edinburgh International Festival
Red Roses for Me, Sean O'Casey
Phaedra, Jean-Baptiste Racine

An Enemy of the People
Year of the Locust*, Norman Holland

1967

Julius Caesar, William Shakespeare
The Threepenny Opera
The Three Sisters, Anton Chekhov
The Birthday Party, Harold Pinter
Dutchman, Leroi Jones, and *The
	Questions*, John Hawkes

1966

The Grass Harp*, Kenward Elmslie,
	Claibe Richardson
A Streetcar Named Desire, Tennessee
	Williams
Saint Joan, George Bernard Shaw
American Dream and *The Zoo Story*,
	Edward Albee
Mother Courage and Her Children,
	Bertolt Brecht – Milwaukee
	Repertory Theater
Long Day's Journey into Night,
	Eugene O'Neill
The Playboy of the Western World,
	John Millington Synge
The Eternal Husband*, Feodor
	Dostoevsky

1965

Twelfth Night, William Shakespeare
The Balcony, Jean Genet
Tartuffe, Molière
The Crucible, Arthur Miller
The Zoo Story
All to Hell Laughing*, Trevanian
Don Juan in Hell, George Bernard
	Shaw
Desire Under the Elms, Eugene
	O'Neill

1964

The Caretaker, Harold Pinter
The Rehearsal, Jean Anouilh

Dark of the Moon, Howard
Richardson, William Berney
The Death of Bessie Smith and
American Dream, Edward Albee
The Hostage, Brendan Behan – Fred
Miller Theatre, Milwaukee

1963

Orpheus Descending, Tennessee
Williams
*The Milk Train Doesn't Stop Here
Anymore*, Tennessee Williams –
Barter Theatre, Abingdon, VA
Productions for the Repertory Players,
Omaha

1962

Riverwind, John Jennings – Actors
Playhouse, New York

1961

Toys in the Attic, Lillian Hellman –
national touring company
Donogoo, Jules Romains – Greenwich
Mews Theatre, New York
Red Roses for Me – Greenwich Mews
Theatre
Summer productions at the Civic
Auditorium, Charlotte, North
Carolina

1960

The Mousetrap, Agatha Christie –
Maidman Playhouse, New York

1959

Orpheus Descending – Gramercy Arts
Theatre, New York
The Ballad of Jazz Street, Norton
Cooper – Greenwich Mews
Theatre
The Trip to Bountiful, Horton Foote –
Equity Library Theatre, Theatre
East, New York

1957

The Time of Your Life, William
Saroyan – Equity Library Theatre,
Lenox Hill Playhouse, New York

1957-60

Summer productions at the Pheonicia
Playhouse, NY

1956

Another Part of the Forest, Lillian
Hellman – Equity Library Theatre

1953-54

Productions at the Playhouse Theatre
and the Alley Theatre, Houston,
TX

Born: Van, Texas – 1927

JOHN HIRSCH

1988

Coriolanus, William Shakespeare –
Old Globe Theatre, San Diego, CA

1987

American Dreams: Lost and Found,
adapted by John Hirsch from Studs
Terkel – Alliance Theatre
Company, Atlanta, GA
Three Men on a Horse, John Cecil
Holm, George Abbott – Royal
Alexandra Theatre, Toronto

1985

The Glass Menagerie, Tennessee
Williams – Stratford Festival,
Canada
King Lear, William Shakespeare –
Stratford Festival

1984

A *Streetcar Named Desire*, Tennessee
    Williams – Stratford Festival
Tartuffe, Molière – Stratford Festival
A *Midsummer Night's Dream*, William
    Shakespeare – Stratford Festival

1983

Tartuffe – Stratford Festival
As You Like It, William Shakespeare –
    Stratford Festival

1982

Mary Stuart, Friedrich von Schiller –
    Stratford Festival
The Tempest, William Shakespeare –
    Stratford Festival

1981

*Number Our Days**, Suzanne
    Grossmann – Mark Taper Forum,
    Los Angeles

1980

The Grand Hunt, Gyula Hernady –
    Seattle Repertory Theatre
Pal Joey, Richard Rodgers, Lorenz
    Hart, John O'Hara – Seattle
    Repertory Theatre
*American Dreams: Lost and Found** –
    Seattle Repertory Theatre
Strider: The Story of a Horse, Mark
    Rozovsky, Uri Riashentsev, Steve
    Brown, Robert Kalfin, S. Vetkin,
    Norman L. Berman – Seattle
    Repertory Theatre

1979

*The Grand Hunt** – Shaw Festival,
    Niagra-on-the-Lake, Ontario
Saint Joan, George Bernard Shaw –
    Seattle Repertory Theatre
The Tempest – Mark Taper Forum,
    Los Angeles

1976

The Three Sisters, Anton Chekhov –
    Stratford Festival

1975

The Dybbuk, adapted by John
    Hirsch – Mark Taper Forum

1974

*The Dybbuk** – Manitoba Theatre
    Center, Winnipeg

1973

Guys and Dolls, Frank Loesser, Abe
    Burrows, Jo Swerling – Manitoba
    Theatre Center

1972

A *Midsummer Night's Dream*, William
    Shakespeare – The Guthrie
    Theater, Minneapolis, MN

1971

Antigone, Sophocles – Repertory
    Theater of Lincoln Center, New
    York
Playboy of the Western World, John
    Millington Synge – Repertory
    Theater of Lincoln Center
What the Butler Saw, Joe Orton –
    Manitoba Theatre Center

1970

Beggar on Horseback, Marc Connelly,
    George S. Kaufman, Stanley
    Silverman, John Lahr – Repertory
    Theater of Lincoln Center
AC/DC, Heathcote Williams –
    Chelsea Theater Center, Brooklyn
A *Masked Ball*, Verdi – New York
    City Opera
The Seagull, Anton Chekhov –
    Habimah Theatre, Tel Aviv, Israel
A *Man's a Man*, Bertolt Brecht –

Manitoba Theatre Center; The Guthrie Theater

1969

Satyricon, Tom Hendry, John Lahr, Stanley Silverman – Stratford Festival

The Time of Your Life, William Saroyan – Repertory Theater of Lincoln Center

Hamlet, William Shakespeare – Stratford Festival; University of Michigan, Ann Arbor; Blackstone Theatre, Chicago

Tyger! Tyger! and Other Burnings, John Hirsch – National Theatre of the Deaf, Longacre Theatre, New York City and on tour

1968

A Midsummer Night's Dream – Stratford Festival

The Three Musketeers, Alexandre Dumas – Stratford Festival

Saint Joan, George Bernard Shaw – Repertory Theater of Lincoln Center

We Bombed in New Haven*, Joseph Heller – Ambassador Theatre, New York

1967

Richard III, William Shakespeare – Stratford Festival

Colours in the Dark*, James Reaney – Stratford Festival

Galileo, Bertolt Brecht – Repertory Theater of Lincoln Center

1966

Henry VI, William Shakespeare – Stratford Festival

Yerma, Federico Garcia Lorca –

Repertory Theater of Lincoln Center

1965

The Cherry Orchard, Anton Chekhov – Stratford Festival

1964

Mere Courage, Bertolt Brecht – Théâtre du Nouveau Monde, Montreal

Circa early 1960s

Cat on a Hot Tin Roof, Tennessee Williams – The Crest Theatre, Toronto

Circa 1959-1965

The Manitoba Theatre Centre, Winnipeg
Death of a Salesman, Arthur Miller
Andorra, Max Frisch
Mother Courage and Her Children, Bertolt Brecht
Who's Afraid of Virginia Woolf?, Edward Albee
The Taming of the Shrew, William Shakespeare
All About Us, Len Peterson
Volpone, Ben Jonson

Circa 1957-1959

Rainbow Stage, Winnipeg
Carousel, Richard Rodgers, Oscar Hammerstein
Pajama Game, Richard Adler, Jerry Ross
Brigadoon, Alan Jay Lerner, Frederick Loewe
The King and I, Richard Rodgers, Oscar Hammerstein
Do You Remember?, Tom Hendry, John Hirsch
Bonfires, John Hirsch, Tom Hendry

1951

The Time of Your Life – Little
Theatre, Winnipeg

Early 1950s

Childrens' Theatre of Winnipeg
Names and Nicknames, James
Reaney
Sour Kringle, John Hirsch
Destination Planet D, John Hirsch
Rupert the Great, John Hirsch
Passport for Mr. Brown, John
Hirsch

1949

Muddy Water Puppets, Winnipeg

1946

Peter and the Snowman, puppet play
by John Hirsch – UNRA camp,
Aschau, Germany

Born: Siofok, Hungary – 1930

MARK LAMOS
*(productions at Hartford Stage
Company, Connecticut, unless
otherwise noted)*

1988

Desire Under the Elms, Eugene
O'Neill – Pushkin Theatre,
Leningrad
The School for Wives, Molière

1987

Hamlet, William Shakespeare
The School for Wives – La Jolla
Playhouse, CA
Morocco, Allan Havis
Hedda Gabler, Henrik Ibsen
Pericles, William Shakespeare

1986

The Gilded Age*, adapted by
Constance Congdon from Mark
Twain and Charles Dudley Warner
The Voyage of Edgar Allan Poe*,
Dominick Argento – Storan
Teatern, Göteborg, Sweden
*On the Verge or The Geography of
Yearning*, Eric Overmyer
Distant Fires*, Kevin Heelan

1985

Twelfth Night, William Shakespeare
The Tempest, William Shakespeare
Passion Play, Peter Nichols

1984

Anatol**, Arthur Schnitzler
The Merchant of Venice, William
Shakespeare – Stratford Festival,
Canada
The Three Sisters, Anton Chekhov

1983

As You Like It, William Shakespeare
Arabella, Strauss – Santa Fe Opera,
NM
The Misanthrope, Molière
Don Giovanni, Mozart – St. Louis
Opera
*The Portage to San Christobal of
A.H.*(A), adapted by Christopher
Hampton from George Steiner

1982

The Great Magoo, Ben Hecht, Gene
Fowler
Greater Tuna, Jaston Williams, Joe
Sears, Ed Howard; (co-directed
with Ed Howard)
The Greeks, John Barton, Kenneth
Cavander; (co-directed with Mary
B. Robinson)

1981

Kean, Jean-Paul Sartre
Antony and Cleopatra, William
    Shakespeare
Undiscovered Country(A), adapted by
    Tom Stoppard from Arthur
    Schnitzler
Cymbeline, William Shakespeare

1980

The Beaux Stratagem, George
    Farquhar
A Midsummer Night's Dream, William
    Shakespeare – California
    Shakespearean Festival, Visalia
Hamlet – California Shakespearean
    Festival
Twelfth Night – Arizona Theatre
    Company, Tucson
The Seagull, Anton Chekhov –
    Arizona Theatre Company

1979

A Flea in Her Ear, Georges
    Feydeau – Arizona Theatre
    Company
Romeo and Juliet, William
    Shakespeare – California
    Shakespearean Festival
The Taming of the Shrew, William
    Shakespeare – California
    Shakespearean Festival
The Show-Off, George Kelly –
    Arizona Theatre Company

1978

Winter's Tale*, opera by John
    Harbison – San Francisco Opera
Equus, Peter Shaffer – Arizona
    Theatre Company
Mackeral*, Israel Horovitz –
    Hartford Stage, Old Place Theatre

1977

Too True to Be Good, George Bernard
    Shaw – Old Globe Theatre, San
    Diego

1976

Hello and Goodbye, Athol Fugard –
    The Guthrie II, Minneapolis, MN
Dear Liar, Jerome Kilty – The
    Guthrie II

Born: Chicago, Illinois – 1946

MARSHALL W. MASON
*(productions at Circle Repertory
Company, New York, unless
otherwise noted)*

1988

V & V Only*, Jim Leonard, Jr. –
    South Coast Repertory, Costa
    Mesa, CA
Summer and Smoke, Tennessee
    Williams – Ahmanson Theatre,
    Los Angeles
Sleuth, Anthony Shaffer – national
    tour

1987

Burn This*, Lanford Wilson – Mark
    Taper Forum, Los Angeles; Circle
    Rep; Steppenwolf Theatre
    Company, Chicago; Plymouth
    Theatre, New York

1986

Picnic, William Inge – Denver
    Theatre Center Company;
    Ahmanson Theatre, Los Angeles;
    WNET/Showtime Television
In This Fallen City*, Bryan
    Williams – White Barn Theater,
    Westport, CT; Circle Rep
Caligula, Albert Camus
The Mound Builders, Lanford Wilson

1985

Talley & Son (A Tale Told), Lanford Wilson – Saratoga Performing Arts Center, Saratoga Springs, NY; Circle Rep

Who's Afraid of Virginia Woolf?, Edward Albee – National Theater of Japan, Tokyo

Angelo's Wedding*, Julie Bovasso

As Is*, William M. Hoffman – Circle Rep; Lyceum Theatre, New York

1984

Showcase – scenes from Shepard, Wilson, Mamet, Rabe, et al. – American College Theater Festival, Kennedy Center, Washington, DC

Who's Afraid of Virginia Woolf? – Saratoga Performing Arts Center

Last Summer at Bluefish Cove, Jane Chambers – Theater on the Square, San Francisco

1983

Full Hookup, Conrad Bishop, Elizabeth Fuller

Faded Glory*, Timothy Burns

Passion, Peter Nichols – Longacre Theatre, New York

Angel's Fall, Lanford Wilson – Longacre Theatre

1982

Angel's Fall* – New World Festival, Miami; Whitebarn Theater, Westport, CT; Saratoga Performing Arts Center; Circle Rep

Fifth of July, Lanford Wilson – WNET/Showtime Television

Talley's Folly, Lanford Wilson – Lyric Theatre, Hammersmith, London

The Rennings Children, Kenneth Lonergan – Young Playwrights' Festival, Circle Rep

1981

The Great Grandson of Jedidiah Kohler*, John Bishop (co-directed with John Manulis) – Entermedia Theater, New York

Richard II, William Shakespeare – Entermedia Theater

Kennedy's Children, Robert Patrick – CBS Cable Television

A Tale Told*, Lanford Wilson – Circle Rep; Mark Taper Forum

Foxfire, Susan Cooper, Hume Cronyn – The Guthrie Theater, Minneapolis, MN

In Connecticut*, Roy London (co-directed with Daniel Irvine) – GeVa Theatre, Rochester, NY; Circle Rep

Childe Byron, Romulus Linney

1980

Fifth of July – New Apollo Theater, New York

Talley's Folly – Goodman Theatre, Studebaker Theater, Chicago; Brooks Atkinson Theatre, New York

1979

Mary Stuart, Friedrich Schiller

Hamlet, William Shakespeare

One Hundred Percent Alive, Shelby Buford, Jr. – Westwood Playhouse, Los Angeles

Talley's Folley* – Circle Rep; Mark Taper Forum

Fifth of July, Lanford Wilson – Mark Taper Forum

Murder at Howard Johnsons, Ron Clark, Sam Bobrick – Golden Theatre, New York

Winter Signs*, John Bishop

Slugger, Shelby Buford, Jr. – P.A.F. Playhouse, Huntington, NY

DIRECTING HISTORIES

1978

*In the Recovery Lounge**, James
    Farrell
Serenading Louie, Lanford Wilson –
    Academy Festival Theatre, Lake
    Forest, IL
*After the Season**, Corinne Jacker –
    Academy Festival Theatre; Boston
*Fifth of July**
A Streetcar Named Desire, Tennessee
    Williams – Arena Stage,
    Washington, DC
*Ulysses in Traction**, Albert Innaurato

1977

Old Times, Harold Pinter – Academy
    Festival Theatre
Tobacco Road, adapted by Jack
    Kirkland from Erskine Caldwell –
    Academy Festival Theatre
Gemini, Albert Innaurato (co-directed
    with Peter Mark Schifter) – The
    Little Theater, New York
*My Life**, Corinne Jacker

1976

A Tribute to Lili Lamont, Arthur
    Whitney
The Farm, David Storey
Mrs. Murray's Farm, Roy London (co-
    directed with Neil Flanagan)
Summer and Smoke, Tennessee
    Williams – Eastern Michigan
    University
Serenading Louie
*Knock Knock**, Jules Feiffer – Circle
    Rep; Biltmore Theatre, New York

1975

The Elephant in the House, Berrilla
    Kerr
*The Mound Builders**, Lanford
    Wilson – Circle Rep; WNET TV

The Farm, David Storey – Academy
    Festival Theatre
*Harry Outside**, Corinne Jacker

1974

Battle of Angels, Tennessee Williams
Come Back, Little Sheba, William
    Inge – Queens Playhouse, New
    York
One Person, Robert Patrick
*The Sea Horse**, Edward J. Moore

1973

Prodigal, Richard Lortz
*The Hot l Baltimore**, Lanford
    Wilson – Circle Rep; Mark Taper
    Forum

1972

*A Road Where the Wolves Run**,
    Claris Nelson
*The Family Continues**, Ikke, Ikke,
    Nye Nye Nye*, and *The Great
    Nebula in Orion*, Lanford Wilson
*The Elephant in the House**, Berrilla
    Kerr
The Three Sisters, Anton Chekhov

1971

The Doctor in Spite of Himself,
    Molière
Sextet (Yes), Lanford Wilson

1970

*The Doctor and the Devils**, Dylan
    Thomas
The Three Sisters (traditional &
    experimental productions)

1969

*In Praise of Folly**, Donald Julian –
    La Mama E.T.C., New York

366

1968

Spring Play, William M. Hoffman –
The New Theatre, New York

Good Night, I Love You, William M.
Hoffman – The Old Reliable
Tavern Theater, New York

The Madness of Lady Bright, Lanford
Wilson – Mercury Theatre,
London

Home Free, Lanford Wilson –
Mercury Theatre

The Gingham Dog*, Lanford Wilson –
The New Dramatists Theater, New
York

Untitled Play*, Lanford Wilson –
Judson Poet's Theatre, New York

1967

*A Coffee Ground Among the Tea
Leaves**, Donald Julian – La
Mama E.T.C.

The Sandcastle, Lanford Wilson – La
Mama E.T.C.; Caffe Cino, New
York

The Clown, Claris Nelson – Caffe
Cino

The Exhaustion of Our Son's Love,
Jerome Max – Temple Emanu-El,
New York

One Room with Bath*, Donald
Kvares – 13th Street Theatre,
New York

1966

Wandering*, Lanford Wilson – Caffe
Cino

The Mutilated, Tennessee Williams –
Actors Studio, New York

The Love Pickle*, David
Starkweather – Caffe Cino

1965

Krapp's Last Tape, Samuel Beckett –
Actor's Studio

The Sandcastle* – La Mama E.T.C.

The Girl on the B.B.C.*, Claris
Nelson – La Mama E.T.C.

The Bottled Room*, Michael
Matthias – 41st Street Theatre,
New York

Lethma*, Michael Matthias – 41st
Street Theatre

Blind Guy*, Michael Matthias – 41st
Street Theatre

Home Free – Cherry Lane Theatre,
New York

Balm in Gilead*, Lanford Wilson –
La Mama E.T.C.

1964

The Haunted Host*, Robert Patrick –
Caffe Cino

Neon in the Night*, Claris Nelson –
Caffe Cino

Little Eyolf, Henrik Ibsen – Actor's
Playhouse, New York

1963

Romance d'Amour, Rostand, Musset,
Shakespeare – Caffe Cino

1962

Medea*, Claris Nelson – Caffe Cino

The Clown*, Claris Nelson – Caffe
Cino

The Rue Garden*, Claris Nelson –
Caffe Cino

1961

Cyrano de Bergerac, Edmond
Rostand – Eagles Mere Playhouse,
Eagles Mere, PA

The Doctor's Dilemma, George

Bernard Shaw – Eagles Mere
Playhouse
The Wild Duck, Henrik Ibsen –
Northwestern University,
Evanston, IL

1960

The Bridge at Rio Campana, Carlos
Gorostiza – Northwestern
University
Mary Stuart – Eagles Mere
Playhouse
The Trojan Women, Euripides –
Northwestern University
Cat on a Hot Tin Roof, Tennessee
Williams – Northwestern
University

Born: Amarillo, Texas – 1940

DES (DESMOND) McANUFF
*(productions at La Jolla Playhouse,
California, unless otherwise noted)*

1988

*80 Days**, Ray Davies, Snoo Wilson
*Two Rooms**, Lee Blessing
A Walk in the Woods, Lee Blessing –
Booth Theatre, New York

1987

The Matchmaker, Thornton Wilder
*A Walk in the Woods**, Lee Blessing –
Yale Repertory Theatre, New
Haven, CT; La Jolla Playhouse

1986

Gillette, William Hauptman
*Shout Up a Morning**, Paul Avila
Mayer, George W. George, Julian
Adderly, Nathaniel Adderly, Diane
Charlotte Lambert
*Big River: The Adventures of
Huckleberry Finn*, adapted by

William Hauptman, Roger Miller
from Mark Twain – national tour

1985

*Big River: The Adventures of
Huckleberry Finn*, – Eugene
O'Neill Theatre, New York
The Seagull, Anton Chekhov
A Mad World, My Masters, Barrie
Keeffe

1984

*Big River: The Adventures of
Huckleberry Finn*
As You Like It, William Shakespeare

1983

Macbeth, William Shakespeare –
Stratford Festival, Canada
Romeo and Juliet, William
Shakespeare
*Big River: The Adventures of
Huckleberry Finn** – American
Repertory Theatre, Cambridge,
MA

1982

*The Death of Von Richthofen As
Witnessed from Earth*, Des
McAnuff – Public Theater, New
York Shakespeare Festival, New
York

1981

Henry VI, Part 1, William
Shakespeare – Delacorte Theater,
New York Shakespeare Festival
How It All Began, John Palmer –
Dodger Theater in residence at
New York Shakespeare Festival
Mary Stuart, Wolfgang
Hildescheimer – Dodger Theater
in residence at New York
Shakespeare Festival

1979

Leave It to Beaver Is Dead, Des
McAnuff, Larry David – Dodger
Theater at New York Shakespeare
Festival
Holeville, Jeff Wanshel, Des
McAnuff – Dodger Theater at
Brooklyn Academy of Music

1978

Gimme Shelter, Barrie Keefe –
Dodger Theater at Brooklyn
Academy of Music

1977

The Crazy Locomotive, Stanislaw
Ignacy Witkiewicz – Chelsea
Theater Center, Brooklyn

1976

The Bacchae, Euripides – Green
Theatre, Toronto
Doctor Faustus, Marlowe – Theatre
Passe Muraille, Toronto
On the Job, score for CBC television

1975

The Choke Sisters*, Des McAnuff,
Larry Davis – Annex Theatre;
Harbourfront Theatre, Toronto

Born: Princeton, Illinois – 1952

GREGORY MOSHER
*(productions at the Goodman
Theatre, Chicago, unless otherwise
noted)*

1988

Speed-the-Plow*, David Mamet –
Royale Theatre, New York

1987

Danger: Memory! – Clara and *I Can't
Remember Anything**, Arthur
Miller – Mitzi E. Newhouse
Theater, Lincoln Center, New
York

1985

Prairie du Chien* and *The Shawl*,
David Mamet – Mitzi E.
Newhouse Theater, Lincoln Center
The Spanish Prisoner* and *The
Shawl**, David Mamet – New
Theatre Company, Chicago

1984

A Christmas Carol, Charles Dickens
The Cherry Orchard, Anton
Chekhov – New Theatre
Company, Chicago
Glengarry Glen Ross(A), David
Mamet – Goodman Stage 2
Theatre, Chicago; John Golden
Theatre, New York

1983

The Disappearance of the Jews*,
David Mamet
Gardenia, John Guare

1982

Edmond*, David Mamet – Goodman
Stage 2; Provincetown Playhouse,
New York
Lakeboat, David Mamet

1981

Panto*, Derek Walcott

1980

Plenty, David Hare
The Suicide, Nikolai Erdman
A Life in the Theatre, David Mamet

1979

*Bal****, Richard Nelson
An Enemy of the People, Henrik Ibsen
The Island, Athol Fugard, John Kani,
    Winston Ntshona
Emigres, Slawomir Mrozek
*Lone Canoe or the Explorer****, David
    Mamet

1978

Native Son, Richard Wright
Battering Ram(A), David Freeman
The Seagull, Anton Chekhov

1977

*A Life in the Theatre****

1976

Sizwe Bansi Is Dead, Athol Fugard,
    John Kani, Winston Ntshona
Streamers, David Rabe
Statues and *The Bridge at Belharbour*,
    Janet L. Neipris
*American Buffalo****, David Mamet

1975

The Son(A), Gert Hofman

Born: New York, New York – 1949

HAROLD S. PRINCE

1988

The Phantom of the Opera, Richard
    Stilgoe, Andrew Lloyd Webber,
    Charles Hart – Majestic Theatre,
    New York

1987

Rosa, adapted by Julian More from
    Romain Gary, Gilbert Becaud –
    Mark Taper Forum, Los Angeles;
    Royale Theatre, New York

Cabaret, Joe Masteroff, John Kander,
    Fred Ebb – national touring
    company at the Minskoff Theatre,
    New York

1986

*Rosa**** – Center Stage, Baltimore
Cabaret – national touring company
*The Phantom of the Opera**** – London

1985

*Grind****, Larry Grossman, Ellen
    Fitzhugh, Fay Kanin – Mark
    Hellinger Theatre, New York

1984

*Diamonds****, revue – Circle in the
    Square Downtown, New York
Play Memory, Joanna M. Glass –
    Longacre Theatre, New York
End of the World (with Symposium to
    follow)****, Arthur Kopit –
    John F. Kennedy Center for the
    Performing Arts, Washington, DC;
    The Music Box Theatre, New York

1983

Madame Butterfly, Puccini – Chicago
    Lyric Opera
Turandot, Puccini – Vienna State
    Opera
*Play Memory****, Joanna M. Glass –
    McCarter Theatre, Princeton, NJ

1982

Candide, Hugh Wheeler, Leonard
    Bernstein, Richard Wilbur,
    Stephen Sondheim, John
    LaTouche – New York City Opera
*A Doll's Life****, Betty Comden, Adolph
    Green, Larry Grossman – Mark
    Hellinger, New York

1981

Merrily We Roll Along*, Stephen
  Sondheim, Hugh Wheeler – Alvin
  Theatre, New York
Willie Stark, adapted by Carlisle
  Floyd from Robert Penn Warren –
  Houston Grand Opera; John F.
  Kennedy Center for the
  Performing Arts, Washington, DC

1980

Silverlake, Kurt Weill – New York
  City Opera
*Sweeney Todd, The Demon Barber of
  Fleet Street*, Stephen Sondheim,
  Hugh Wheeler – London
Evita, Tim Rice, Andrew Lloyd
  Webber – Vienna

1979

Evita – Broadway Theatre, New York
The Girl of the Golden West,
  Puccini – San Francisco Opera
*Sweeney Todd, The Demon Barber of
  Fleet Street** – Uris Theatre, New
  York

1978

On the Twentieth Century*, Betty
  Comden, Adolph Green, Cy
  Coleman – St. James Theatre,
  New York
Evita* – London
The Girl of the Golden West,
  Puccini – Chicago Lyric Opera

1977

Some of My Best Friends*, Stanley
  Hart – Longacre Theatre, New
  York

1976

Pacific Overtures*, John Weidman,
  Stephen Sondheim – Winter
  Garden Theatre, New York
Ashmedai, Josef Tal – New York City
  Opera

1974

Candide – The Chelsea Theater
  Center, Brooklyn; Broadway
  Theatre, New York
Love for Love, William Congreve –
  New Phoenix Repertory Company,
  Helen Hayes Theatre, New York

1973

The Visit, Friedrich Dürrenmatt –
  New Phoenix Repertory Company,
  Ethel Barrymore Theatre, New
  York
A Little Night Music*, Hugh Wheeler,
  Stephen Sondheim – Sam S.
  Shubert Theatre, New York

1972

The Great God Brown, Eugene
  O'Neill – New Phoenix Repertory
  Company, Lyceum Theatre, New
  York
Follies, James Goldman, Stephen
  Sondheim – London

1971

Follies*, (co-directed with Michael
  Bennett) – Winter Garden
  Theatre, New York

1970

Company*, George Furth, Stephen
  Sondheim – Alvin Theatre, New
  York

1968

*Zorba**, Joseph Stein, John Kander, Fred Ebb – Imperial Theatre, New York

Cabaret – London

Beggar's Opera, John Gay – London

1967

*Cabaret** – Broadhurst Theatre, New York

1966

*It's a Bird . . . It's a Plane . . . It's Superman**, David Newman, Robert Benton, Charles Strouse, Lee Adams – Alvin Theatre, New York

1965

*Baker Street**, Jerome Coopersmith, Marian Adams – Broadway Theatre, New York

1964

She Loves Me, Joe Masteroff, Jerry Bock, Sheldon Harnick – London

1963

*She Loves Me** – Eugene O'Neill Theatre, New York

1962

*A Family Affair**, James Goldman, John Kander, William Goldman – Billy Rose Theatre, New York

Born: New York, New York – 1928

LLOYD RICHARDS
(productions at Yale Repertory Theatre, New Haven, Connecticut, unless otherwise noted)

1988

Joe Turner's Come and Gone, August Wilson – Barrymore Theatre, New York

1987

Joe Turner's Come and Gone – Seattle Repertory Theatre

Fences, August Wilson – 46th Street Theatre, New York

*The Piano Lesson**, August Wilson

1986

Fences – Goodman Theatre, Chicago; Seattle Repertory Theatre

*Joe Turner's Come and Gone**, Yale Rep; Huntington Theatre Company, Boston

1985

*Fences**

1984

*Ma Rainey's Black Bottom**, August Wilson – Yale Rep; Cort Theatre, New York

1983

A Touch of the Poet, Eugene O'Neill

Major Barbara, George Bernard Shaw

1982

Medal of Honor Rag, Tom Cole – PBS, *American Playhouse*

A Doll House, Henrik Ibsen

Johnny Bull, Kathleen Betsko

1981

Uncle Vanya, Anton Chekhov

Hedda Gabler, Henrik Ibsen

1980

Timon of Athens, William Shakespeare

1979

Paul Robeson, Phillip Hayes Dean –
PBS
Roots: The Next Generation, Segment
#6 –
Bill Moyers Journal, "No Easy Walk
to Freedom" – WNET

1978

Night Must Fall, Emlyn Williams –
Hunter College
The Antique Bearers, Ray Aranha –
National Public Radio, *Earplay*

1977

Paul Robeson*, Phillip Hayes Dean –
Lunt-Fontanne Theatre, New York
Freeman, Phillip Hayes Dean –
Visions, KCET TV
The Lion and the Jewel, Wole
Soyinka, Billy Taylor – Richard
Allen Center, New York

1976

Gold Watch, Momoko Iko – *Visions*,
KCET TV
*The Sign in Sidney Brustein's
Window*, Lorraine Hansberry –
Hunter College

1973

The Past Is the Past* and *Goin' Thru
Changes*, Richard Wesley – Billie
Holiday Theatre, Brooklyn
Eight Ball, Richard Wesley – WNET
TV
The Last Chapter, Ron Cowen – ABC
Television
Eight Ball – University of North
Carolina
Richard III, William Shakespeare –
Boston University

1972

Freeman* – American Place Theatre,
New York

1971

You Are There – "Harriet Tubman"
and "Galileo" – CBS Television

1969

Miss Black America – television
*The Hide and Seek Odyssey of
Madeleine Gimple*, Frank
Gagliano – Project Create,
Connecticut School System

1966-68: O'Neill Theater Center,
Waterford, CT

Summertree, Ron Cowen
Valentine's Day, Ron Cowen
Just Before Morning, Tom Oliver
A Man Around the House, Joe Julian
Bedford Forest, Joel Olianski
Rainless Sky, Neil Yarema
*Don't End My Song Before I Sing
Redemption Center*

1966

The Yearling*, Lore Noto, Herbert E.
Martin, Michael Leonard – Alvin
Theatre, New York
The Ox Cart, Rene Marques –
Greenwich Mews Theatre, New
York; Puerto Rican Traveling
Theatre, New York
Who's Got His Own*, Ron Milner –
American Place Theatre, New York

1965

Lower Than the Angels*, John
Killins – American Place Theatre
Ghosts, Henrik Ibsen – Cincinnati
Playhouse in the Park

The Amen Corner, James Baldwin – European tour

1964

I Had a Ball*, Jerome Chorodov, Jack Lawrence, Stan Freeman – Martin Beck Theatre, New York

1962

The Moon Besieged*, Seyril Sehochen – Lyceum Theatre, New York

The Crucible, Arthur Miller – Boston University

The Desperate Hours – Mineola Playhouse, NY; Westport County Playhouse, CT

1960

The Long Dream*, Ketti Frings – Ambassador Theatre, New York

1959

A Raisin in the Sun*, Lorraine Hansberry – Ethel Barrymore Theatre, New York; Adelphi Theatre, London

1955-57

Resident Director – Northland Playhouse, Detroit, MI

1954

Resident Director – Great Lakes Drama Festival

Born: – Toronto, Canada

PETER SELLARS

1988

Le Nozze de Figaro, Mozart – PepsiCo Summerfare, Purchase, NY

The Nose, Dmitri Shostakovich, Nikolai Gogol – The Netherlands Opera

Nixon in China, John Adams, Alice Goodman – John F. Kennedy Center for the Performing Arts, Washington, DC; The Royal Netherlands Opera

1987

Nixon in China* – Wortham Theater, Houston Grand Opera; Brooklyn Academy of Music

Zangezi, Velimir Khlebnikov – Brooklyn Academy of Music

The Last Summer, Nigel Osborne – Glyndebourne Festival, England

Don Giovanni, Mozart – PepsiCo Summerfare

Così fan tutte, Mozart – PepsiCo Summerfare

Ajax, Sophocles – Theatre Royale de la Monnaie, Brussels; the Holland Festival, Amsterdam; the Vienna Festival; World Theatre Festival, Stuttgart

Apprentice to Jean-Luc Godard for film of *King Lear*

1986

Zangezi* – Ahmanson Auditorium, American Museum of Contemporary Art, Los Angeles

Così fan tutte – Castle Hill Festival, Ipswich, MA

Ajax – American National Theatre, John F. Kennedy Center for the Performing Arts, Washington, DC

Idiot's Delight, Robert E. Sherwood – American National Theatre, Washington, DC

1985

A Seagull, Anton Chekhov –
American National Theatre
Guilio Cesare in Egitto, George
Frederich Handel – PepsiCo
Summerfare
Little Mahagonny, Bertolt Brecht,
Kurt Weill – PepsiCo Summerfare
The Count of Monte Cristo, Alexandre
Dumas – American National
Theatre

1984

Hang on to Me, adaptation of Maxim
Gorky's *Summerfolk*, George and
Ira Gershwin – The Guthrie
Theater, Minneapolis, MN
Hard Rock, music video for Herbie
Hancock
*Monkey Eats Peach, Rat Steals
Pumpkin or The Phoenix Among
the Peonies*, traditional 14th
century Chinese village play –
Harvard University

1983

The Lighthouse*, Peter Maxwell
Davies – Boston Shakespeare
Company
Pericles, William Shakespeare –
Boston Shakespeare Company
The Visions of Simone Marchard,
Bertolt Brecht – La Jolla
Playhouse, CA
Mikado, Gilbert and Sullivan –
Chicago Lyric Opera

1982

Play/Macbeth – Boston Shakespeare
Company
Ping – Boston Shakespeare Company
My One and Only, George and Ira
Gershwin (pre-Broadway) – Boston

1981

Armida(A) and *Saul*(A), Handel –
Emmanuel Church, Boston
Orlando(A), Handel – American
Repertory Theatre, Cambridge,
MA
Kabuki Western – National Theater of
the Deaf, national tour and Japan
Plays by Frank O'Hara & V. R.
Lang – La Mama E.T.C., New
York

1980

Santur Opera, Ivan Tcherepnin –
Festival d'Automne, Paris
Don Giovanni, Mozart – New
Hampshire
The Inspector General, Nikolai
Gogol – American Repertory
Theatre

1976-80

Harvard University: *When We Dead
Awaken*, Ibsen; *The Ring Cycle*,
Wagner (four-hour production with
puppets); *Facade*, Walton, Sitwell;
Play and *Come and Go*, Beckett;
Striptease, Mrozek; *What
Happened*, Gertrude Stein; *Bastien
and Bastienne*, Mozart; *Revue
Sketches, The Dumbwaiter*, Pinter;
Egmont, Goethe; *Orpheus and
Eurydice*, Gluck; *Tarelkin's Death*,
Sukhovo-Kobylin; *The Masque of
Cupid and Death*, Locke;
Genevieve, Piege de Meduse, Satie;
*Ballo delle Ingrate, Combattimento
di Tancredi e Clorinda*,
Monteverdi; *Medea*, Euripides;
*Salzburg Dance of Death, Happy
Days*, Brecht; *Prometheus Bound*,
Aeschylus; *Così fan tutte*, Mozart;
Lysistrata, Aristophanes; *King*

Lear, Much Ado About Nothing, Coriolanus, Anthony and Cleopatra, Macbeth, Shakespeare; *Chang Boils the Sea* (renamed *Schwartz Boils the Sea*); *Death Knocks,* Woody Allen; *Boris Godunov,* Pushkin; *The Three Sisters,* Chekhov; *Bedbug, Vladimir Mayakovsky, A Tragedy,* Mayakovsky; *Lulu,* Wedekind; *Calling for Help,* Handke; *Trumpets and Drums,* Brecht/ Farquhar.

1971-75

Phillips Academy: *The Gas Heart,* Tzara; *The Tempest,* Shakespeare; *Danse Macabre, The Bald Soprano, The Lesson,* Ionesco; *The Nightingale,* Stravinsky/Andersen; *Revue Sketches,* Pinter; *Everyman; Dr. Faustus,* Marlowe; *Carnival of the Animals,* Saint-Saens/Nash; *The Bear, Smoking Is Bad for You, The Wedding,* Chekhov; *Picnic on the Battlefield,* Arrabal; *The Firebugs,* Frisch; *Humulus the Mute,* Anouilh; *The Party,* Harold Robbins; *Calm Reigns in the Country,* John Stephen; *Lord Byron's Love Letter, Portrait of a Madonna,* Tennessee Williams; 7 episodes from WPA radio theatre; *L'Histoire du Soldat,* Stravinsky; *En G-g-garrde,* Daumal; *Architruc,* Pinget.

Born: Pittsburgh, Pennsylvania – 1957

ANDREI SERBAN

1988

Don Carlo, Verdi – Bologna Opera

Flaming Angel, Prokofiev – Geneva Opera

1987

Fragments of a Trilogy – La Mama E. T. C., New York
I Puritani, Bellini – Paris Opera
The Good Woman of Setzuan, Bertolt Brecht – American Repertory Theatre, Cambridge, MA
Turandot, Puccini (film for BBC)
Flaming Angel – Los Angeles Opera

1986

Fidelio, Beethoven – Covent Garden, London
The Juniper Tree, Philip Glass, Arthur Yorinks, Robert Moran – American Repertory Theatre
Sweet Table at the Richelieu*, Ronald Ribman – American Repertory Theatre
Elektra, Richard Strauss – Geneva Opera

1985

The Marriage of Figaro, Beaumarchais – Circle in the Square Theatre, New York
The King Stag, Carlo Gozzi – American Repertory Theatre
Norma, Bellini – New York City Opera

1984

Turandot, Puccini – Olympic International Festival, Los Angeles; Covent Garden, London
The Love of Three Oranges, Prokofiev – Geneva Opera

1983

Uncle Vanya, Anton Chekhov – La Mama E.T.C.

The Master and Marguerita, Mikhail
Bulgakov, Jean-Claude Carriere,
Jean-Claude van Itallie, Andrei
Serban – Théâtre de la Ville, Paris
Alcina, Handel – New York City
Opera
I Puritani – Welsh National Opera
The Magic Flute, Mozart – Théâtre
Chatelet, Paris

1982

The Three Sisters, Anton Chekhov –
American Repertory Theatre
Zastrozzi, George Walker – Public
Theater, New York Shakespeare
Festival, New York
Sgnarelle (four Molière farces
including: *The Flying Sailor*,
*Sgnarelle, A Dumb Show, The
Forced Marriage*) – The Goodman
Theatre, Chicago
The Marriage of Figaro – The
Guthrie Theater, Minneapolis, MN

1981

Sgnarelle – American Repertory
Theatre
La Traviata, Verdi – American Opera
Center, Juilliard School, New York
Rodelinda, Handel – Welsh National
Opera

1980

The Seagull, Anton Chekhov – Shiki
Theatre, Tokyo; Public Theater,
New York Shakespeare Festival
The Magic Flute – Nancy, France
As You Like It, William Shakespeare –
La Mama E.T.C., New York
Directs ten-minute section within a
film on Jane Austin

1979

The Umbrellas of Cherbourg*, Jacques

Demy, Sheldon Harnick, Charles
Burr, Michel Legrand – Public
Theater, New York Shakespeare
Festival
Eugene Onegin, Tchaikovsky – Welsh
National Opera
The Cherry Orchard, Anton
Chekhov – Tokyo
Happy Days, Samuel Beckett – New
York Shakespeare Festival

1978

The Master and Marguerita, – New
York Shakespeare Festival; Paris
Sgnarelle – Yale Repertory Theatre,
New Haven, CT
Mad Dog Blues – Yale Repertory
Theatre

1977

The Ghost Sonata, August
Strindberg – Yale Repertory
Theatre
Agamemnon, Aeschylus – New York
Shakespeare Festival at the Vivian
Beaumont Theater/Delacorte
Theater
The Cherry Orchard – New York
Shakespeare Festival at the Vivian
Beaumont Theater, Lincoln Center

1976

Good Woman of Setzuan, Bertolt
Brecht – La Mama company,
European tour
As You Like It – Perigny and Saintes,
France
The Trojan Women, Electra and
Medea, Euripides – La Rochelle,
France

1975

The Good Woman of Setzuan – La

Mama E.T.C.; Berlin International
Festival

The Threepenny Opera, Bertolt
Brecht, Kurt Weill – American
Conservatory Theatre, San
Francisco

*Fragments of a Trilogy** – La Mama
E.T.C.

1974

*The Trojan Women** – La Mama
E.T.C.

1973

*Electra** – Bordeaux, France; La
Mama E.T.C.

1972

*Medea** – La Mama E.T.C.

1971

Assists Peter Brook with *Orghast at
Persepolis* – France; Iran

1970

Arden of Faversham, Thomas Kyd and
Ubu Roi, Alfred Jarry – La Mama
E.T.C.

1969

*Jonah**, Marin Rsoreseu – Zagreb
Theatre Festival, Yugoslavia

1966

*I'm Not the Eiffel Tower**, Catarina
Oproiu – Zagreb Theatre Festival

1965

Arden of Faversham – Academy of
Theatre and Film, Bucharest

Julius Caesar, William Shakesepare –
Academy of Theatre and Film

Circa 1980-85

The Merry Widow, Franz Lehar –
Royal Opera North

Il Trovatore, Verdi – Royal Opera
North

Aida, Verdi – Welsh National Opera

I Puritani, Bellini – Opera of Holland

Born: Bucharest, Romania – 1943

DOUGLAS TURNER WARD

*(productions at Negro Ensemble
Company, St. Marks Playhouse,
New York, unless otherwise noted)*

1986

The War Party, Leslie Lee – Theatre
Four, New York

*Jonah and the Wonder Dog** **, Judi
Ann Mason – Theatre Four

*Louie and Ophelia***, Gus Edwards –
Theatre Four

1985

*Ceremonies in Dark Old Men***,
Lonne Elder, III – Theatre Four

1984

*District Line**, Joseph A. Walker –
Theatre Four

*Ceremonies in Dark Old Men*** –
Ford's Theatre, Washington, DC

A Soldier's Play, Charles Fuller – The
Guthrie Theater, Minneapolis, MN

1983

*About Heaven and Earth: The
Reedeemer**, Douglas Turner
Ward; *Nightline*, Julie Jensen;
*Tigus***, Ali Wadud – Theatre
Four

A Soldier's Play – Coconut Grove
Playhouse, Miami; Cincinnati
Playhouse in the Park

1982

A Soldier's Play – Mark Taper Forum, Los Angeles; Goodman Theatre, Chicago

1981

A Soldier's Play* – Theatre Four
Home, Samm-Art Williams – Theatre Four
Weep Not for Me*, Gus Edwards – Theatre Four
Zooman and the Sign, Charles Fuller – Theatre Four

1980

Home – Cort Theatre, New York

1978

Twilight Dinner*, Lennox Brown
Black Body Blues* **, Gus Edwards

1977

The Offering* **, Gus Edwards
The Great MacDaddy, Paul Carter Harrison

1976

Livin' Fat*, Judi Ann Mason

1975

Waiting for Mongo*, Silas Jones
The First Breeze of Summer* **, Leslie Lee – St. Marks Playhouse/ Palace Theatre

1974

The Great MacDaddy*

1972

The River Niger* **, Joseph A. Walker – St. Marks Playhouse; Brooks Atkinson Theatre, New York; New Locust Theatre,

Philadelphia; Shubert Theatre, Philadelphia
A Ballet Behind the Bridge*, Lennox Brown

1971

Perry's Mission*, Clarence Young, III
Ride a Black Horse*, John Scott

1970

Brotherhood*, Douglas Turner Ward
Day of Absence*, Douglas Turner Ward

1969

Contribution*, Ted Shine
Man Better Man*, Errol Hill

1968

Daddy Goodness* **, Richard Wright

Born: Burnside, Louisiana – 1930

ROBERT WOODRUFF

1988

Struck Dumb*, Jean-Claude van Itallie, and *War in Heaven*, Sam Shepard – Mark Taper Forum, Los Angeles
A Lie of the Mind, Sam Shepard – Mark Taper Forum

1987

The Tempest, William Shakespeare – La Jolla Playhouse, CA
The Comedy of Errors, William Shakespeare – Lincoln Center Theater, New York

1986

L'Histoire du Soldat, Stravinsky, Len Jenkin, Paul Magid – Brooklyn Academy of Music

Figaro Gets a Divorce(A), Odön von Horváth – La Jolla Playhouse

Looking in the Dark For, Paul Bernstein – Bay Area Playwrights Festival, Mill Valley, CA

1985

Madrigal Opera, Philip Glass, Len Jenkin – Mark Taper Forum

A Man's a Man, Bertolt Brecht – La Jolla Playhouse

In the Belly of the Beast, adapted by Adrian Hall from Jack Henry Abbott – Mark Taper Forum; Sydney Theatre Festival; Joyce Theatre, New York

1984

The Comedy of Errors – Olympic Arts Festival, Los Angeles

The Three Moscowteers, Flying Karamazov Brothers – Goodman Theatre, Chicago

In the Belly of the Beast – Mark Taper Forum Laboratory

Julius Caesar, William Shakespeare – Alliance Theatre Company, Atlanta

1983

Red River(A), Pierre Laville – Goodman Theatre

The Comedy of Errors – Goodman Theatre

1982

*The Return of Pinocchio**, Richard Nelson – Bay Area Playwrights Festival

Filthy Rich(A), George F. Walker – Northlight Theatre, Evanston, IL

1981

Film Noir(A), George F. Walker – Bay Area Playwrights Festival

True West, Sam Shepard – Marines Memorial Theatre, San Francisco

1980

*True West** – Magic Theatre, San Francisco; New York Shakespeare Festival

*The Death of Von Richthofen As Witnessed from Earth**, Des McAnuff – Bay Area Playwrights Festival

Tongues and *Savage/Love**, Sam Shepard, Joseph Chaikin – Paris; Rome; Milan; New York Shakespeare Festival; Mark Taper Forum Lab

1979

Ice, Michael Cristofer – Manhattan Theatre Club, New York

Suicide in B Flat, Sam Shepard – Magic Theatre

Shout Across the River, Stephen Poliakoff – Phoenix Theatre, New York

1978

*Buried Child**, Sam Shepard – Magic Theatre; Theater for the New City, New York; Circle Repertory Company, New York; Philadelphia Playhouse in the Park

Great Solo Town, Thomas Babe – Bay Area Playwrights Festival

Curse of the Starving Class(A), Sam Shepard – New York Shakespeare Festival

1977

*Wolves**, John Robinson – Magic Theatre

Sizwe Bansi Is Dead, Athol Fugard, Winston Ntshona, John Kani – Eureka Theatre, San Francisco

When You Comin' Back Red Ryder?,
Mark Medoff – Eureka Theatre;
Little Fox Theatre, San Francisco
The Exception and the Rule, Bertolt
Brecht – Eureka Theatre

1976

The Sad Lament of Pecos Bill*, Sam
Shepard – Bay Area Playwrights
Festival
Ralph Who Must Run*, Ed
Weingold – Julian Theatre, San
Francisco
Are You Lookin', Murray Mednick –
Magic Theatre

1975

The Birthday Party, Harold Pinter –
Eureka Theatre
Night Must Fall, Emlyn Williams –
Eureka Theatre

1974

The Threepenny Opera, Bertolt
Brecht – Eureka Theatre

Born: Brooklyn, New York – 1947

GARLAND WRIGHT

1988

Richard III, William Shakespeare –
The Guthrie Theater, Minneapolis,
MN

1987

The Piggy Bank, Eugene LaBiche, A.
Delacour – The Guthrie Theater
The Misanthrope, Molière – The
Guthrie Theater
*On the Verge or The Geography of
Yearning*, Eric Overmyer – The
Acting Company, John Houseman
Theater, New York

1986

Old Times, Harold Pinter – Arena
Stage, Washington, DC
The Cherry Orchard, Anton
Chekhov – Denver Center
Theater Company

1985

Anteroom, Harry Kondoleon –
Playwrights Horizons, New York
The Good Person of Setzuan, Bertolt
Brecht – Arena Stage
Don Juan, Molière – Denver Center
Theater Company
Anything Goes, Cole Porter, Howard
Lindsay, Russel Crouse, Guy
Bolton, P. G. Wodehouse – The
Guthrie Theater

1984

The Misanthrope, Molière – Seattle
Repertory Theatre
The Tempest, William Shakespeare –
Arena Stage
The Importance of Being Earnest,
Oscar Wilde – The Guthrie
Theater; national tour
Happy End, Kurt Weill, Bertolt
Brecht – Arena Stage

1983

A New Approach to Human Sacrifice*,
Paul Getty – Young Playwrights
Festival, Dramatists Guild at
Circle Repertory Company, New
York
Guys and Dolls, Jo Swerling, Abe
Burrows, Frank Loesser – The
Guthrie Theater
Imaginary Invalid, Molière – Arena
Stage

DIRECTING HISTORIES

1982

Summer Vacation Madness, Goldoni –
The Guthrie Theater
Candide, adapted Len Jenkin from
Voltaire – The Guthrie Theater
The Country Wife, William
Wycherly – The Acting Company,
American Place Theatre; national
tour

1981

*Eli: A Mystery Play of the Sufferings
of Israel*, Nellie Sachs – The
Guthrie Theater

1980

Camille, Alexandre Dumas – The
Guthrie Theater
Mary Stuart, Friedrich Schiller – The
Guthrie Theater
*Star Treatment**, Jack Heifner – Lion
Theater Company, New York
The Duenna, Richard Brinsley
Sheridan – Center Stage,
Baltimore
*Das Lusitania Songspiel**, (supervised)
Sigourney Weaver, Christopher
Durang – Chelsea Theater
Center, New York

1979

*New Jerusalem**, Len Jenkin – Public
Theater, New York Shakespeare
Festival
Lone Star and *Private Wars*, James
McLure – Century Theatre, New
York
The Road to Babylon, Peter Link –
Milwaukee Repertory Theater

1978

*Patio/Porch**, Jack Heifner – Century
Theatre, New York

1977

*Music Hall Sidelights**, Colette –
Lion Theater Company
Cat on a Hot Tin Roof, Tennessee
Williams – Seattle Repertory
Theatre
*K-Impressions of the Trial**, Franz
Kafka – Lion Theater Company

1976

*Marathon '33**, June Havoc – Lion
Theater Company
*Vanities**, Jack Heifner – Playwrights
Horizons; Westside Theater, New
York

1975

Twelfth Night, William Shakespeare –
Lion Theater Company;
Playwrights Horizons
Kingdom of Earth, Tennessee
Williams – McCarter Theatre,
Princeton, NJ
The Tempest – Lion Theater
Company

1974

*Kitty Hawk**, Len Jenkin – Lion
Theater Company
*The Grand American Exhibition**, Len
Jenkin – Westside YMCA Clark
Center, New York

1973

The Tempest – Cincinnati Playhouse
in the Park
Julius Caesar, William Shakespeare –
American Shakespeare Theater,
Stratford, CT

Born: Midland, Texas – 1946

382